W. Walsh

W9-AWJ-332

Baedeker's ISRAEL

A SPECTRUM BOOK

PRENTICE-HALL, Inc., Englewood Cliffs, New Jersey 07632

Cover picture: Dome of the Rock

221 colour photographs
90 maps, plans and sketches
1 large road map

Text:
Dr Otto Gärtner (Introduction to Israel, except for the section on Climate, Israel from A to Z, Practical Information)
Prof. Dr Wolfgang Hassenpflug, Kiel (Climate)

Editorial work:
Baedeker Stuttgart
English Language: Alec Court

Cartography:
Ingenieurburo für Kartographie
Huber & Oberlander, Munich (maps, plans, sketches etc. in the text)
Hallwag AG, Bern (road map)

Design and layout:
HF Ottmann, Atelier für Buchgestaltung und Grafik-Design, Leonberg

Conception and general direction:
Dr Peter Baumgarten
Baedeker Stuttgart

English translation:
Babel Translations Norwich

© Baedeker Stuttgart
Original German edition

© The Automobile Association
United Kingdom and Ireland

© Jarrold and Sons Ltd
English Language edition Worldwide

Published in the U.S. and Canada by
Prentice-Hall Inc., Englewood Cliffs, N.J. 07632

Licensed user:
Mairs Geographischer Verlag GmbH & Co.,
Ostfildern-Kemnat bei Stuttgart

Reproductions:
Gölz Repro-Service GmbH
Ludwigsburg

The name *Baedeker* is a registered trademark

Source of illustrations:

Most of the colour photographs were provided by *Dr Otto Gärtner*, Giessen.

Others:
L. Ander, Munich: (pp. 10, 27, 50, 126/127, 167, 203, 217)
Bildagenture, Stuttgart (Eichler; pp. 7, 53, 89, 104, 146, 175, 232, 237, 249, 273, top)
Hetzel-Reisen GmbH, Stuttgart (p. 97, foot)
W. Rogge, Lünen (pp. 75; 78, foot; 134, foot; 139, foot left and middle; 141, top and foot; 143, top; 170, all 3; 171, all 3 at foot)
A. Sperber, Hamburg (cover picture; pp. 8; 23, all 8; 26, 30, 38; 42, top; 80; 132, both; 133, both; 134, top right; 138; 139, top and right foot; 140; 144, top; 145, left foot; 149, foot; 150, left and right; 152; 154, both; 155, all 4; 158, foot left and right; 159; 160, top; 161, top; 162, top; 163, 166, 168; 171, top; 173, 254, 257, 259, 268, 271)
Zentrale Farbbild Agentur GmbH (ZEFA), Düsseldorf (Schranner; p. 224)

How to Use this Guide

The principal towns and areas of tourist interest are described in alphabetical order. The names of other places referred to under these general headings can be found in the Index.

Following the tradition established by Karl Baedeker in 1844, sights of particular interest and hotels and restaurants of particular quality are distinguished by either one or two asterisks.

In the lists of hotels and other accommodation r.=rooms; b.=beds; SP=swimming pool; k=kosher. Hotels are classified in the categories shown on p. 268.

The symbol ⓘ at the beginning of an entry or on a town plan indicates the local tourist office or other organisation from which further information can be obtained. The post-horn symbol on a town plan indicates a post office.

Only a selection of hotels and restaurants can be given: no reflection is implied, therefore, on establishments not included.

In a time of rapid change it is difficult to ensure that all the information given is entirely accurate and up to date and the possibility of error can never be entirely eliminated. Although the publishers can accept no responsibility for inaccuracies and omissions they are always grateful for corrections and suggestions for improvement.

Printed in Great Britain by Jarrold & Sons Ltd, Norwich ★★

0-13-056176-2

This guidebook forms part of a completely new series of the world-famous Baedeker Guides.

Each volume is the result of long and careful preparation and, true to the traditions of Baedeker, is designed in every respect to meet the needs and expectations of the modern traveller.

The name of Baedeker has long been identified in the field of guidebooks with reliable, comprehensive and up-to-date information, prepared by expert writers who work from detailed, first-hand knowledge of the country concerned. Following a tradition that goes back over 150 years to the date when Karl Baedeker published the first of his handbooks for travellers, these guides have been planned to give the tourist all the essential information about the country and its inhabitants: where to go, how to get there and what to see. Baedeker's account of a country was always based on his personal observation and experience during his travels in that country. This tradition of writing a guidebook in the field rather than at an office desk has been maintained by Baedeker ever since.

Lavishly illustrated with superb colour photographs and numerous specially drawn maps and street plans of the major towns, the new Baedeker Guides concentrate on making available to the modern traveller all the information he needs in a format that is both attractive and easy to follow. For every place that appears in the gazetteer, the principal features of architectural, artistic and historic interest are described, as are its main areas of scenic beauty. Selected hotels and restaurants are also included. Features of exceptional merit are indicated by either one or two asterisks.

A special section at the end of each book contains practical information, details of leisure activities and useful addresses. The separate road map will prove an invaluable aid to planning your route and your travel within the country.

Contents

Abu Gosh · Afula · Akko · Allone Abba · Arad · Ashdod · Ashqelon · Atlit · Avdat · Banyas · Beersheba · Belvoir · Benot Ya'akov · Bet Alfa · Bet Guvrin · Bethlehem · Bet Oren · Bet Shean · Bet Shearim · Bet Shemesh · Caesarea · Cana · Capernaum · Carmel · Chorazin · Dan · Dead Sea · Dor · Eilat · El-Azariye (Bethany) · En Avdat · En Boqeq · En Gedi · En Gev · Galilee · Golan · Hadera · Haifa · Hamat Gader · Hazor · Hebron · Hefer Plain · Herodeion (Herodion) · Herzliya · Horns of Hittim · Hula Plain · Jenin · Jericho · Jerusalem · Jezreel Plain · Jordan · Judea · Lakhish · Latrun · Lod (Lydda) · Maktesh Hagadol · Maktesh Ramon · Mamshit (Mampsis) · Maresha · Mar Saba (Monastery of St Sabas) · Massada · Megiddo · Meron · Modiim · Montfort · Mount of the Beatitudes · Mount Gilboa · Mount Tabor · Nablus · Nahariyya · Nazareth · Nebi Musa · Nebi Samvil · Negev · Netanya · Paran · Qumran · Ramallah · Ramla · Rehovot · Rosh Ha'ayin · Rosh Pinna · Safed (Zefat) · Samaria · Sea of Galilee · Sede Boqer ·

Sharon Plain · Shivta (Subeita) · Sinai · Tabgha · Tel Aviv-Jaffa · Tiberias · Timna · Wadi Qilt · Yavne · Yodefat · Zikhron Ya'akov · Zippori (Sepphoris)

Introduction to Israel

Special Note

The **writing of Hebrew** names creates a problem in that there is no standard way in which modern Hebrew (Ivrit) is spelled in English. In this guide, names have been taken from the English Bible, historical and classical writers, while other words have been written in accordance with modern Hebrew usage. At the present time there is no final arbiter on spellings, as even reliable Israeli sources occasionally give different versions.

The Mediterranean coast at Netanya ▶

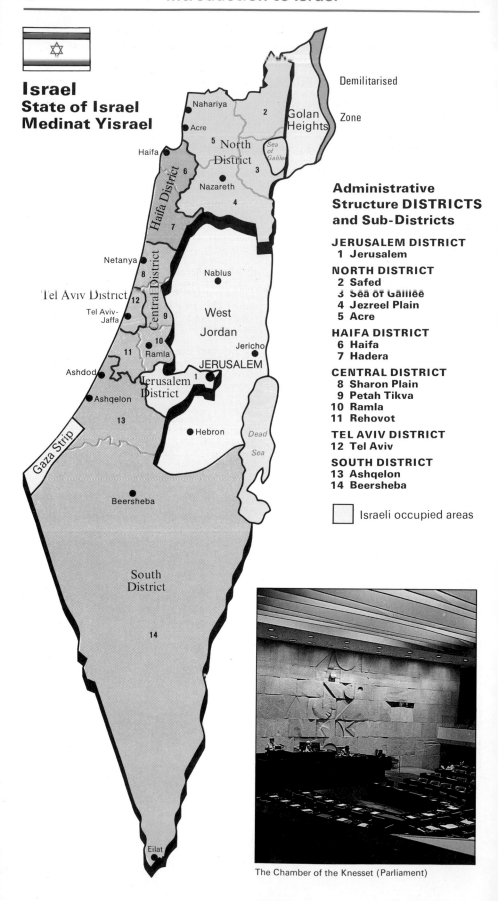

Israel
State of Israel
Medinat Yisrael

Nahariya

Acre

2

Golan Heights

Demilitarised

Zone

5 North District

Sea of Galilee

Haifa

6

Nazareth

3

Haifa District

4

7

Netanya

Central District

8

Nablus

Tel Aviv District 12

Tel Aviv-Jaffa

9

West Jordan

10

11 Ramla

Jericho

Ashdod

Jerusalem District

1

JERUSALEM

Ashqelon

13

Hebron

Dead Sea

Gaza Strip

Beersheba

South District

14

Eilat

Administrative Structure DISTRICTS and Sub-Districts

JERUSALEM DISTRICT
1 Jerusalem

NORTH DISTRICT
2 Safed
3 Sea of Galilee
4 Jezreel Plain
5 Acre

HAIFA DISTRICT
6 Haifa
7 Hadera

CENTRAL DISTRICT
8 Sharon Plain
9 Petah Tikva
10 Ramla
11 Rehovot

TEL AVIV DISTRICT
12 Tel Aviv

SOUTH DISTRICT
13 Ashqelon
14 Beersheba

☐ Israeli occupied areas

The Chamber of the Knesset (Parliament)

The **State of Israel (Medinat Yisrael)**, founded in 1948, is a PARLIAMENTARY DEMOCRACY. There is, so far, no written Constitution. A number of Acts of Parliament, passed in 1958, form the basis of State legislature and at a date yet to be decided these Acts will become the foundation for the Constitution.

The Head of State is the *President* who is elected every five years by Parliament and may stand once for re-election; he largely carries out representative and formal official duties. The President nominates ambassadors, judges and also the Paymaster General. He also recommends a *State Comptroller* to the Parliament who, once elected by the Parliament, is answerable to it. The Comptroller oversees all the bodies of State.

The Israeli *Parliament*, the **Knesset**, consists of 120 members, who are elected on the basis of proportional representation to serve for a period of four years. The Knesset is the supreme authority in the country and acts as the Legislature. Laws are usually drafted by the Cabinet, but can also be tabled by individual members of political parties. All Parliamentary debates are conducted in modern Hebrew (Ivrit) but Arab Members may submit their motions in their mother tongue.

The Government is formed by a Member of the Knesset at the request of the President. The Government is composed of the Prime Minister and his Ministers and acts as the Executive. All members of the Government are answerable to Parliament and rely on its confidence to govern. David Ben Gurion became Israel's first Prime Minister in 1948 (currently Yitzhak Shamir).

Israel's democracy is based on a *multi-party system* which reflects the ethnic, cultural and ideological multiplicity in Israeli society. As no one party has ever commanded an overall majority, every Government so far has had to depend on forming a coalition. Since the State of Israel was founded the smaller religious parties have often held the balance of power; two of Israel's religious parties, the Agudas Israel and the Poalei Agudas Israel, are opposed to a written Constitution and call for a theocracy, with legislation solely in the hands of the Rabbis. The two largest party groupings are the nationalist Likud block and the Socialist block (including Mapai and Mapam). To the left of the socialist grouping one finds the Israeli Communist Party, which espouses the cause of the Palestinian refugees, and the New Communist Party, which is influenced by Moscow. The Government consisted of left-wing coalitions up until 1977 when the right-wing Likud block came to power.

The Israeli courts are independent. The highest body in the *Judiciary* is the Supreme Court in Jerusalem. Each religious group has its own jurisdiction in matters of personal litigation (e.g. divorce).

The Law of Return, passed in 1950, gives all Jews the right to return to Israel and become Israeli citizens. However, the Minister of the Interior is authorised to withhold this right from persons with a criminal past or whose presence could endanger public health or security.

Israel is a Member of the United Nations (UN) and the General Agreement on Tariffs and Trade (GATT); since July 1, 1975 it has had a free trade agreement with the European Economic Community (EEC).

For administrative purposes the country is divided into **six Districts** which are further divided into *Subdistricts*. West Jordan and the Gaza Strip, which have been occupied by Israel since 1967, are under military administration. The Golan Heights, which were also captured in 1967, were annexed by Israel in 1981.

The whole of the Sinai Peninsula was returned to Egypt at the end of April 1982 in accordance with the 1979 Agreement; in many places the evacuation of the area was much against the will of those Israelis that had settled there.

District	Area in sq. miles/ sq. km.	Population (1982)	Seat of Administration	Resident population per sq. mile/ per sq. km
Jerusalem District	242/627[1]	468,000	Jerusalem	747/1,935
North District	1,738/4,501[2]	661,000[2]	Nazareth	381/147[2]
Haifa District	330/854	576,000	Haifa	1,748/675
Central District	479/1,242	830,000	Ramla	1,722/665
Tel Aviv District	66/170	1,009,000	Tel Aviv-Jaffa	15,369/5,934
South District	5,445/14,107	497,600	Beersheba	91/35
Israel	8,302/21,501[3]	4,063,600[4]	Jerusalem	487/188[5]

1 Including East Jerusalem, 27 sq. miles/70 sq. km
2 Including the Golan Heights
3 Excluding inland waters
4 Including Israelis on the West Bank and in the Gaza Strip
5 Including the Golan Heights (without the West Bank and the Gaza Strip)

Mediterranean surf pounds the walls of Acre

The Middle-Eastern State of Israel lies in an area that is holy ground for the three great monotheistic religions – Christianity, Islam and Judaism. Judaism and Christianity were born here, and Jerusalem, where Mohammed is said to have ascended to heaven, is for Islam the most important place after Mecca and Medina. The Holy Land is therefore of supreme and unequivocal significance for the followers of these three religions.

Although never a great power and for a long while not a state in its own right, Israel, as a crucial site in Middle-Eastern history, is richly endowed with evidence of its eventful past extending as far back into prehistory as the 8th millennium when one of the world's earliest urban settlements existed in Jericho, and even earlier when Early Stone Age Man began laboriously evolving his primitive culture. Here in this confined space, all have left their traces: the people of Jericho, the Canaanites, the Israelites of the Old Testament, Greeks, Romans, Byzantines, Arabs, European Crusaders, Mamelukes, Turks and, last but not least, the European and Russian Christians who in later centuries built their many churches and monasteries here.

However, the country not only derives life from its past but also lives on in the present. Although surrounded by enemies, in the few decades since it was founded (leaving out the preliminary stages in the 19th c.) Israel has undergone an astonishing revival. The extent and quality of its reconstruction is a testament to an elemental will to survive and achieve self-determination, fired by despair in the 19th and above all the 20th c. and by the forces of its ancient religions which have enabled the Jewish people to overcome the long years of persecution and dispersion (the Diaspora).

All this exists within the confines of a small country, a microcosm of entire regions of the globe, where the most disparate of climatic zones and types of landscape go hand in hand: flower-filled Galilee and the arid Negev, mountains and coastal plains and deserts.

Whether you come as pilgrim, art-lover or historian, whether or not the problems and achievements of the present day are your concern, a fascinating world awaits you. Even if you only come to spend a holiday on the beaches of the Red Sea or the Mediterranean you cannot help but be moved by the special qualities of this unique country.

Topography

The country of Israel (Eretz Yisrael) lies on the coast of the Eastern Mediterranean in the Levant. It extends from latitude 29°30'N to 33°20'N and from longitude 34°20'E to 35°40'E. It is 260 miles/420 km from N to S, and from E to W varies between only 12 miles/20 km and 72 miles/116 km. In the N Israel shares its borders with Lebanon, in the E with Syria and Jordan, and in the W with Egypt. Its southernmost point reaches to the Gulf of Aqaba (Gulf of Eilat; Red Sea). The State of Israel, which was declared the homeland of the Jewish people by a United Nations Resolution in 1948, covers an area of 8,020 sq. miles/20,770 sq. km which includes East Jerusalem. Jerusalem has been declared the country's capital.

The occupied territories of West Jordan (2,151 sq. miles/5,572 sq. km), the Golan Heights (444 sq. miles/1,150 sq. km) and the Gaza Strip (78 sq. miles/202 sq. km) have been under Israeli administration since 1967 bringing an added land area of 2,673 sq. miles/6,924 sq. km. Although under the terms of the 1979 Agreement between Israel and Egypt the Sinai was evacuated by 1982, Israel's borders are constantly the scene of unrest, disturbance and military conflict.

The country's landscape is marked by abrupt changes from mountains to plains. The S is taken up by the Negev Desert while the N can be divided into three regions – the coastal plain, the western mountains and the Jordan Valley.

Interrupted only by rocky Rosh Haniqra on the northern border and Cape Carmel at Haifa, an extensive **coastal plain** stretches along the Mediterranean. It covers some 169 miles/270 km from Lebanon in the N to the Sinai Desert in the S. The Bay of Haifa, on which lies the country's principal port, provides the only indentation in the gently curving coastline. The coastal plain, which is on average 10 miles/16 km wide, broadens out to about 25 miles/40 km towards the S. It is built up from fine sand and more recent marine sediments and the landscape varies from soft rolling ridges covered with sand dunes to steep cliffs.

The plain, which is traversed by several rivers, such as the Kishon near Haifa and the Yarkon near Tel Aviv, can be divided into several sections. The coastal strip between Rosh Haniqra and Acre, which barely reaches a width of 4½ miles/7 km, adjoins the *Sebulon Plain* further S. The narrow coastal plain of Carmel, S of Haifa, is a favourite vacation area with many resorts. Continuing S again the *Sharon Plain*, running for 35 miles/55 km to Tel Aviv-Jaffa, bordered by the Yarkon, forms the central coastal area. This region, formerly covered in forest and later a swamp which was drained, is now of great importance for Israel because it is so fertile. There are many towns and rural settlements here, with industry as well as

The Judean Desert from the Mar Saba Monastery

agriculture. Hadera, Netanya, Kefar Sava and Herzliya are the main urban areas in this region, whose development has also been helped by its good communications. To the S of Tel Aviv, the *Shefela Plain*, which terminates at the Gaza Strip, covers a distance of some 56 miles/90 km from N to S and between 16 and 19 miles/25 and 30 km from E to W. The road network in these coastal areas is extremely well developed.

Inland from the coastal plains the landscape becomes mountainous, the **mountains** being largely composed of limestone or dolomite: in the N there are the *mountains of Upper Galilee*, rising to 3,963 ft/1,208 m at Mount Meron, and to the S, the *mountains of Samaria*, reaching 3,333 ft/1,016 m, and the *mountains of Judea*, 3,346 ft/1,020 m. The Judean range reaches to the Negev Desert in the S. The average height of the mountains is 2,789 ft/850 m.

These mountains, part of the Syrian Plateau, appear from their geological structure and petrographic composition to be a continuation of the Lebanon range. The hills of Galilee and Samaria are dissected by faults; the diagonal cut of the *Jezreel rift valley* (Emeq Yizrael) is the result of a particularly severe disruption.

The Qilt Wadi

This valley is some 12 miles/20 km long and forms a border between Galilee and Samaria. To the N the Galilean range reaches up to Mount Meron, with its wide basalt outcrops; towards southern Galilee the country becomes flatter and at Mount Tabor attains a height of only 1,844 ft/562 m. The Samarian hills include Mount Carmel in the NW at 1,791 ft/546 m and Mount Gilboa in the NE, 1,700 ft/518 m. The mountains of Samaria and Judea are separated by the rivers Yarkon and Shilo.

The country's most massive range, the Judean mountains, extends for 50 miles/80 km from N to S and between 9½ miles/15 km and 12½ miles/20 km from E to W. This chain of mountains, which largely follows the watershed, is notable for its terrace-shaped slopes. To the S lies the Hebron range. Joining these from the N are the mountains of Jerusalem, on a ridge of which lie the Mount of Olives and Mount Scopus. The northernmost part of the chain is completed by the Bet El Mountains. Fewer towns are found on these thinly wooded slopes than on the coastal plain and most of the settlements in this area are Arab villages.

To the E, the mountains drop down to the **Jordan Valley**. This starts in the N of the country, S of Mount Hermon, the summit of which is 9,186 ft/2,800 m high, with the *Hula Valley* (Emeq Hula). What is now a fertile plain was once a lake surrounded by swamps. This land was drained in the 1950s and is now one of the most intensively cultivated areas of Israel.

The Jordan Valley follows the course of the Upper Jordan and at the *Sea of Galilee* (also known as Lake Tiberias – Yam Kinneret) is 690 ft/210 m below sea level. The Sea of Galilee is over 12½ miles/20 km long, and covers an area of some 66 sq. miles/170 sq. km. It reaches a depth of 197 ft/60 m and abounds in fish.

From the Sea of Galilee, the Jordan Valley, the southern part of which is called the "Ghor" (meaning "hollowed-out"), follows the river to the *Dead Sea*, the lowest point on earth (1,300 ft/396 m below sea level; 2,720 ft/829 m below sea level to the sea bed). The fault continues through the rift of the *Wadi Ha'Arava* and at Eilat reaches the Red Sea. The Jordan Valley is a part of the Afro-Syrian Rift; the valley has been built up to a shallow trough by deposits from early lava flows.

The Zin Desert in the Negev

unique Nubian sandstone, often worn into pillars or fantastic shapes. Characteristic of some regions of the Negev are the sand and stone wildernesses of "Serir" and "Hamada". In the E the Negev falls away to the Arava rift and thence to the Jordan Valley.

The Jordan flowing out of the Sea of Galilee

The **Jordan** (*Yarden*), Israel and Jordan's longest and most abundant river, has three sources – the rivers *Banyas, Dan* and *Hazbani* in the N of the Hula Valley – and flows into the Dead Sea. Several tributaries feed the Jordan, the largest of which, the *Yarmuk*, joins it from the E below the Sea of Galilee. The Jordan Valley is 158 miles/252 km long. The river has an overall length of 207 miles/330 km because of its meandering. Its flow varies with the time of year and its many bends make it unnavigable. The River Jordan currently forms the border between Israel and Jordan which also continues on through the Dead Sea.

Beyond the Jordan rift the land rises to the East Jordanian Mountains, which have Biblical connotations – Gilead and Ammon (in the N), Moab (in the middle) and Edom (in the S), reaching a height of 5,696 ft/1,736 m.

At the southern end of Israel, the **Negev** Desert reaches the Mediterranean by way of a small spur and stretches in a wedge from Beersheba to the Red Sea. The northern section, built up of layers of chalk covered with loess soils, receives an annual precipitation of 8 in./200 mm. Irrigation schemes are making large areas of it fertile. To the S the land becomes hilly, interspersed with folds of upper chalk, reaching a height of 6,350 ft/ 1,935 m at Har Ramon. Through erosion, large corries (mountainside hollows), called "Makhtesh", have been formed in the chalk. The southernmost tip of the Negev is a part of the Archaic Massif which eventually becomes the mountains of Sinai. Here and there can be found the

Between the mountains of Samaria, the Dead Sea and the Jordan Valley, stretches the *Judean Desert*. The annual rainfall is greater here, however, than in the Negev. Its dryness is caused by its location on the lee side of a mountain range. Sparsely covered canyons and valleys are a feature of this landscape. On its eastern border can be found the famous town of Massada and the caves of Qumran.

The **Dead Sea** (*Yam Hamelach*), a sea without a source, covers an area of 378 sq. miles/980 sq. km and extends for

The Dead Sea

Timna – colourful rock formations in the S of the country

49 miles/78 km from the River Jordan to the Wadi Ha'Arava in the S. It is up to 11 miles/18 km wide. To the W it is bordered by the Judean Mountains and to the E by the East Jordanian Mountains. A small peninsula, the "Tongue" (Ha Lashon), divides the sea into a northern part (up to 1,312 ft/400 m deep) and a shallower southern section (13–20 ft/4–6 m deep). Because of high evaporation the sea has a salt content of up to 25%. Minerals such as potash and bromine salt are obtained from the Dead Sea. On its shores hot springs, sulphurous and radio-active, well out of the ground; Neveh Zohar and En Boqeq on the south-eastern shore of the Dead Sea have therefore developed into health resorts.

For administrative purposes Israel is today divided into six Districts and further divided into Subdistricts. For the visitor, however, the historical countryside areas of *Galilee, Samaria* and *Judea*, the scene of so many events recorded in the Bible, are of special interest. Galilee is bordered in the E by the Upper Jordan Valley, in the W by the Mediterranean, in the N by the Litani River and in the S by the Jezreel Valley. Nazareth and the Sea of Galilee are famous sites in this region. Samaria adjoins the Sharon Plain in the W and the Jordan Valley in the E and Jesus cited its people as a good example to the Jews in the parable of the Good Samaritan. Judea, the southernmost of the three regions, extends from the Mediterranean coast, between the Yarkon in the N and the Gaza Strip in the S, to the Jordan Valley and the Dead Sea. It contains Bethlehem, the birthplace of Jesus, and Jerusalem with the Mount of Olives.

Climate

Israel lies in a zone of climatic transition between the Mediterranean and the desert. Its climate is also affected by its southerly situation (lat. 29°30'N to 33°20'N) and the strong vertical pattern of the landscape. The prevailing winds are influenced by the Trade Winds and above them by the Westerlies.

A **Mediterranean climate** is distinguished by its dry hot summer and its mild humid winter, brought about to some extent by storage of heat in the Mediterranean itself. Thus, in the summer the weather is determined by subtropical zones of high pressure and in the winter by the Westerlies and their attendant depressions. The winter lasts from about November to April and the summer from May to October. During the winter, snow may fall in the mountains. In early summer the desert wind, known as *Sharav* (or in Arabic *Hamsin*), can bring heatwaves up to 122°F/50°C.

To the S the influence of the subtropical high-pressure zone becomes stronger and in consequence precipitation decreases and temperatures increase. The climate changes gradually over the area between the Gaza Strip and the Dead Sea and S of this it becomes a hot desert climate (with great temperature fluctuations in the course of a day) which is at its most extreme in the Jordan Valley and the Negev.

The change of climate from N to S is accompanied by a change from W to E. At the coast the Mediterranean has a moderating effect; inland, to the E, the temperature variations become greater. The following table clearly shows the changes in climate.

Average Annual Precipitation and Temperatures

	Coast	Mountains	Jordan Valley
NORTH	Haifa	Tabor	Tiberia
	24·9 in./	19 in./	18 in./
	640 mm	494 mm	463 mm
	71°F/	69°F/	73°F/
	21·6°C	20·5°C	22·9°C
	Tel Aviv	Jerusalem	Jericho
	20·7 in./	20·7 in./	6·3 in./
	532 mm	533 mm	162 mm
	66°F/	64°F/	77°F/
	19·1°C	17·6°C	25·0°C
SOUTH	Gaza	Beersheba	En Gedi
	15·4 in./	8·9 in./	2·7 in./
	390 mm	227 mm	70 mm
	68°F/	67°F/	77°F/
	20·1°C	19·5°C	25·0°C

In the mountainous areas temperatures are below the national average, and the climatic changes are less affected by maritime influences. Here a reverse phenomenon, peculiar to mountainous areas, is experienced: it is warmer on the heights than in the valleys. Winter precipitation comes later than in the coastal plains and is at its greatest during January and February.

Generally speaking the **coastal plain** is warmer. There is seldom any frost and the Sharav (Hamsin) blows frequently. Despite this it can become very hot in the highrise areas of the cities owing to lack of air movement and the fact that the tall buildings act as storage heaters, radiating heat again after sunset. The maximum winter precipitation is reached in December and January; during this period nearly two-thirds of the total annual rainfall occurs.

In the Jordan Valley the subtropical climate becomes even more noticeable than in the mountains. The Hula Plain, on the lee side of the mountain range, is consequently protected from wind and rain. The summer is hot, but in winter cold winds blow down from Mount Hermon. Here the reverse temperature syndrome brings night frosts to low areas, so that tropical plants cannot survive, but apple trees, for example, thrive.

Around the Sea of Galilee there is a varying microclimate, principally because the water radiates heat, leading to winter temperatures of some 57°F/14°C. Thus plants which require warmth, such as date palms and bananas, can be found here. Rainfall is low, increasing gradually towards the Lower Jordan Valley.

The Dead Sea and its surroundings also enjoy a special climate, mainly because the high salt concentration increases heat retention to an unusually high level. This is particularly noticeable in the deeper northern part of the sea where temperatures change less markedly during the course of the year. The shallower southern part has been cut off by salt deposits since the heatwave of 1979.

The **Negev**, the desert in the S of Israel, consists of a semi-arid zone around Beersheba and an arid zone. Summer temperatures can reach 86°F/30°C and at Eilat they can be over 113°F/45°C. The climate is clearly subtropical and is variable in summer with temperatures which occasionally only reach 61°F/16°C. The annual precipitation is very low, only 8–12 in./200–300 mm at Beersheba and 2 in./50 mm on the Arava Plain.

Because of the long dry summers and the high temperatures, the rate of evaporation means that most of Israel's rivers only flow intermittently; these are known as wadis. The Jordan, however, has a constant flow because it is fed by springs in the Hermon range of mountains.

Despite its high summer temperatures, the Mediterranean climate is generally quite tolerable for Europeans because the humidity stays low. Nonetheless, visitors should be careful to acclimatise themselves gradually and not undertake any strenuous tours at the beginning of their stay. It is essential to have proper protection from the sun.

In planning your day it is often important, particularly where photography is concerned, to know how many hours you have of daylight. The following local times serve as a guide and apply to the center of the country. Sunrise ranges from 5 a.m. in June to 7 a.m. in December and sunset from 7 p.m. in June to 5 p.m. in December. Dusk barely lasts half an hour, which means, for example, that a North European or an American, visiting Israel in the summer, should be prepared for darkness to draw in about two hours earlier than at home.

Regional climatic variations are shown on page 18 in **climatic graphs** giving the changes in rainfall and temperature throughout the year (from left to right, January to December). The blue columns, showing rainfall per month, are graduated in inches on the blue scale of figures at the side.

Climatic Zones of Israel

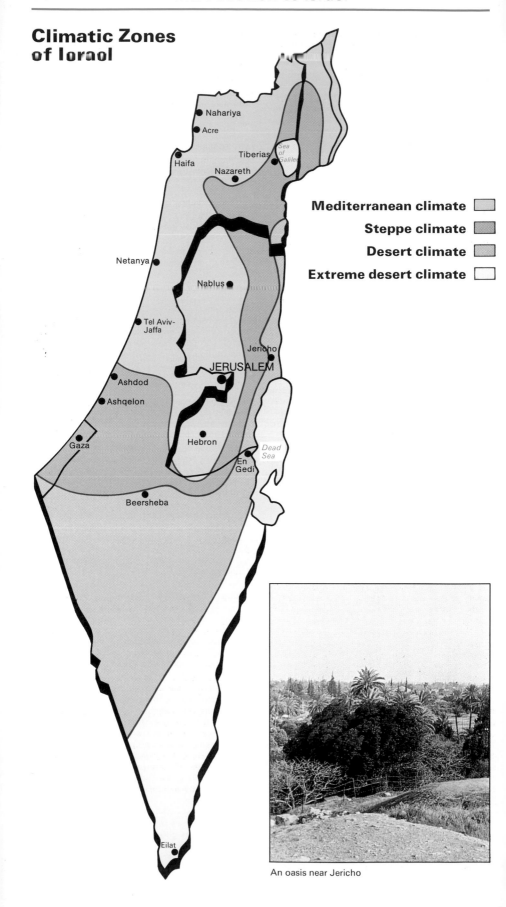

Nahariya

Acre

Haifa

Tiberias

Sea of Galilee

Nazareth

Mediterranean climate

Steppe climate

Desert climate

Extreme desert climate

Netanya

Nablus

Tel Aviv-Jaffa

Jericho

JERUSALEM

Ashdod

Ashqelon

Gaza

Hebron

Dead Sea

En Gedi

Beersheba

Eilat

An oasis near Jericho

The temperatures are shown by an orange band. The upper profile shows the average highest daily midday temperature, and the lower profile the average lowest night temperature. The red scale at the side shows the figures in degrees Fahrenheit.

The figures given for the three typical weather stations also apply to the surrounding regions. Variations can be calculated for areas between the sites shown in the tables. However, in doing so, care must be taken to ensure that the effect of differences in altitude are also taken in account, even over relatively short distances.

Central Mountains
(*Jerusalem Weather Station*)

The town lies at an altitude of 2,460 ft/750 m in a hollow on a plateau in this mountain range which to the N and S reaches heights of just over 3,280 ft/1,000 m. The table clearly shows the disparity between the damp cool winter and the dry hot summer. The greatest rainfall occurs from November to March; in this period there will be between seven and eleven rainy days each month. In spring and autumn there will still be some three days a month, while from June to September it will be less than one day a month. Even on rainy days it may not rain all day: a short shower with rainfall only just exceeding 0·04 in./1 mm counts as a rainy day.

Because of the altitude, the temperatures are lower than on the coastal plain. The daily and yearly variations are also greater, because the moderating effect of the sea is not so great. Even so, daily changes of temperature are two to three times as great as in most parts of the United States or Central Europe, and this should be taken into account when deciding what to wear. The nightly winter temperatures are only a little over freezing point, whereas at midday it can be nearly as warm as the Central European or Eastern United States summer. Cold winter winds from southern Russia may even bring frost and snow.

Coastal Plain
(*Haifa Weather Station*)

The graph for the Haifa Weather Station shows the climate of the central coastal area of Israel (south-wards rainfall decreases). It is typical of a Mediterranean climate, with mild, damp winters and dry, hot summers. In the course of the year the temperature change is less evident than inland, rainfall is higher than in Jerusalem, largely the effect of the Carmel mountain range, which has some of the heaviest rainfall in Israel. The relative humidity is around 60–70% (while in Jerusalem in summer it is between 40% and 50%). Cold winds coming in during the winter can bring occasional frost, but even so the average temperature is considerably above freezing point.

In winter the sea temperature can sink to 61°F/16°C and in summer it can reach 82°F/28°C. Northerly winds blow frequently in summer and help to keep temperatures down.

Desert
(*Eilat Weather Station*)

The graph for Eilat, at the southernmost tip of Israel, shows the hot, subtropical climate of the desert, typical of the S of the country (Negev and Jordan Valley). High temperatures, enormous variations in temperature and minimal rainfall are the principal characteristics.

The annual rainfall of between 1 and 1·6 in./25 and 40 mm is concentrated in a few heavy showers in the winter months. Most of the time the sky is cloudless and a day without sunshine is very rare.

The "winter" temperatures from November to March, with cool nights and warm days, are in fact very pleasant. Even the lowest night temperatures are well above freezing point. For the rest of the year it is extremely hot; the highest temperatures can exceed 113°F/45°C. In contrast to the coasts of the Red Sea further S, the relative humidity in Eilat is low: in summer, daytime 20%, nights 40% and in winter, daytime 45%, nights 60%. This is caused by winds constantly blowing from a northerly direction through the Jordan Valley. Without this wind, life here in summer would be considerably less agreeable: the wind reduces the humidity so that the heat becomes bearable, and it encourages calm seas, making water sports possible. When the wind turns, as it does on some days in May and June, it then becomes unbearably close and the swell at sea increases.

The Jordan Valley to the N of the Dead Sea also has a desert-like hot climate. This is particularly true of the Dead Sea itself. Its low position (1,300 ft/396 m below sea level) together with its situation in the lee of the mountains reduces rainfall and causes sharp increases in temperatures. The annual rainfall, between 2 and 4 in./50 and 100 mm, concentrated in the winter months, has little effect because of the high temperatures. The highest summer temperatures exceed 104°F/40°C and even in winter the lowest temperatures are rarely less than 53°F/12°C, the midday temperature often reaching 68°F/20°C. So anyone wishing to avoid a rainy day in Jerusalem or other places in the mountains needs only to travel up to the Dead Sea to exchange the rain for the sun, the cold for warmth.

Continuous evaporation is the reason for the high concentration of salt (25%) in the Dead Sea. The constant influx of fresh water from the Jordan (averaging 48 cu. yd/37 cu. m a second) does not alter the situation: the evaporation more than equals the incoming water and at times even exceeds it. To the N the climate of the Jordan Valley becomes moister; the Sea of Galilee is still 690 ft/210 m below sea level, but it is a freshwater lake with the Jordan as its source.

The climate here is mild in winter, hot in summer (in the middle of January 57°F/14°C, April 68°F/20°C, July 86°F/30°C, October 47°F/25°C). It is so pleasant that since ancient times this has been the most densely settled area of Palestine; this is where the winter health resorts can be found, where fruit and vegetables can be cultivated very early in the year and where even tropical fruits such as bananas can ripen.

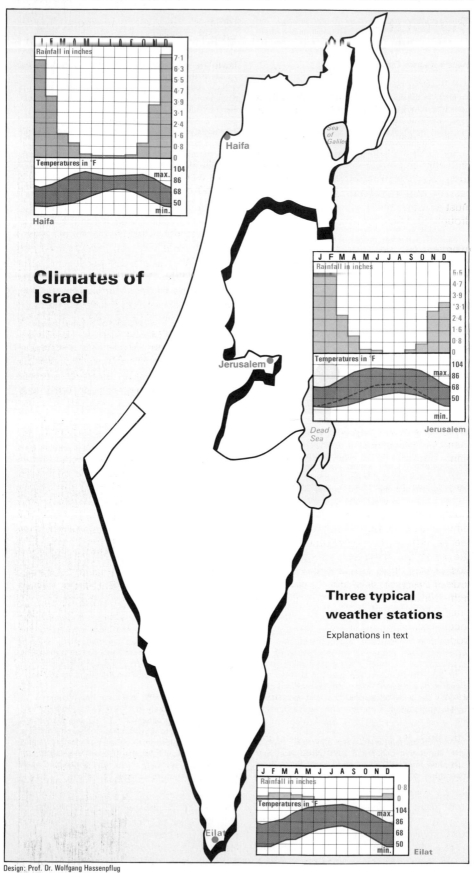

Climates of Israel

Three typical weather stations

Explanations in text

Design: Prof. Dr. Wolfgang Hassenpflug

Plant Life

Two factors have a bearing on the **plant life** of Israel:
1. The location of the country where three continents meet (Europe, Asia and Africa) and its situation on the shores of the Mediterranean.
2. The Mediterranean climate together with the beginning of the arid climatic zone running through the southern and eastern countryside means that plants must adapt themselves to long periods of drought and little moisture.

In order to survive in the semi-arid and arid climates, plants have developed different methods of reducing water loss and adapting themselves to take in water in any way possible. Thus some plants (succulents) have a fine layer of wax on their leaves which inhibits evaporation; others have a multi-branched root system, so that they can search for moisture at considerable depths. Some plants form bulbs or corms to store water during the dry summer in order to bloom in the rainy winter, for example the Persian cyclamen (*Cyclamen persicum*) and the common anemone (*Anemone coronaria*). Other plants such as quill or sea onion (*Urginea maritima*) grow long wide leaves early in the year and blossom only in the autumn.

Most plants adapt their life cycle to the rainy period, when no protection is needed against excessive moisture loss. The drier the climate, the shorter the blossoming time. In the Negev and Judean Desert seeds of various plants rest in the ground for several years, waiting for a rainy winter. Then they shoot up all at once, bloom and in a very few weeks produce new seeds. A particularly unusual group of plants is the halophytes (salt plants) whose sap is enriched with salt. These plants can be found in the Arava Valley, around the Dead Sea and in the Lower Jordan.

In the pre-Christian era many areas of the country were heavily wooded. These woods were eroded by war and neglect and also were cleared for agriculture which meant that the soil, no longer held together by the roots of trees, was washed away by heavy rainfall, leaving the bare rocks exposed. These areas became wasteland, and with further erosion and grazing by goats the woods came to be replaced by scrub and thorny undergrowth, maquis and garigue.

Israel can be divided into four large zones of vegetation:
1. The Mediterranean zone
2. The Irano-Turanian zone
3. The Saharo-Sindian zone
4. The Sudano-Oasis zone

The **Mediterranean** zone covers those areas which have an annual rainfall of 14 in./350 mm or more, and includes large parts of the coast and mountains.

A characteristic feature of the central and northern parts of the Coastal Plain, as well as the SW of Lower Galilee, is the Tabor oak (*Quercus ithaburensis*), a tall tree with a broad crown. However, the oak forests have been almost totally destroyed and in their place the ground is covered by scrub. But large numbers of evergreen, narrow and long-leaved shrubs, tulips, anemones and annual grasses can be found, together wth oleanders, myrrh bushes, pines, olives and sycamore (*Ficus sycomorus*).

On the hills above 985 ft/300 m and in the mountains considerable reforestation has taken place, with Aleppo pines (*Pinus halepensis*). Gall oaks, the evergreen Palestine oak, laurels, cyprus, arbutus, the Judas tree (*Cercis siliquastrum*) and carob trees (*Ceratonia siliqua*); there are also garigue-covered areas where the cistus rose predominates.

The **Irano-Turanian** zone confines itself to the region around Beersheba, where the annual rainfall averages 6–12 in./150–300 mm and the soil is largely loess or chalk. Low bushes and dwarf shrubs grow in this area, one of the main plants being wormwood. To the E the zone reaches into the Judean Desert and the Jordan Valley.

The **Saharo-Sindian** zone stretches into the S of Israel. It includes the greater part of the Negev, the Judean Desert, the Arava Rift and the region of the Dead Sea. These areas which have an annual rainfall between 2 and 6 in./50 and 150 mm have true desert vegetation. Here one mainly finds bushes with small thick leaves or thorns. Often there is on average only one plant to the square yard. The regions of the Hamada (stony wilderness) are mostly without any vegetation at all, while thorny

Vegetation Zones in Israel

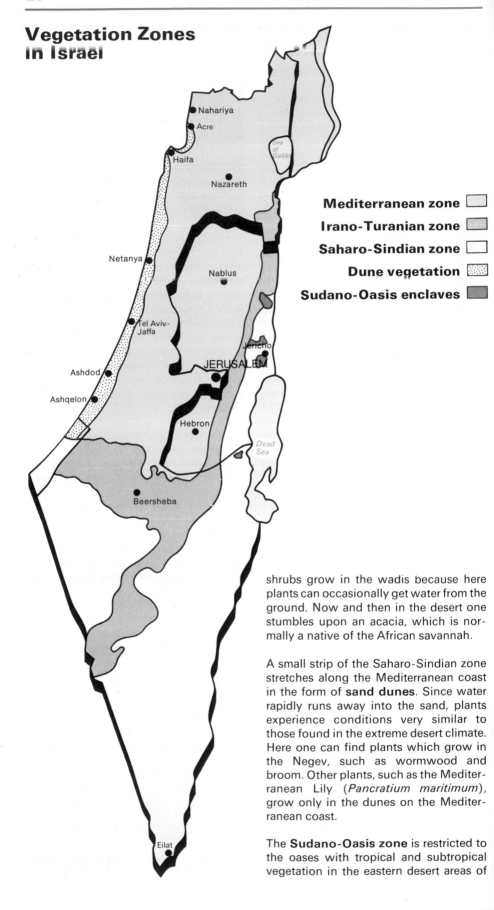

Mediterranean zone

Irano-Turanian zone

Saharo-Sindian zone

Dune vegetation

Sudano-Oasis enclaves

shrubs grow in the wadis because here plants can occasionally get water from the ground. Now and then in the desert one stumbles upon an acacia, which is normally a native of the African savannah.

A small strip of the Saharo-Sindian zone stretches along the Mediterranean coast in the form of **sand dunes**. Since water rapidly runs away into the sand, plants experience conditions very similar to those found in the extreme desert climate. Here one can find plants which grow in the Negev, such as wormwood and broom. Other plants, such as the Mediterranean Lily (*Pancratium maritimum*), grow only in the dunes on the Mediterranean coast.

The **Sudano-Oasis zone** is restricted to the oases with tropical and subtropical vegetation in the eastern desert areas of the country. These oases are to be found, for example, at En Gedi on the Dead Sea and at Jericho. Forty different species thrive here, all needing high temperatures as well as a good deal of water. The most famous of these is Christ's Thorn (*Zizyphus spina Christi*) which is said to have been used for the crown of thorns.

Tropical and subtropical plants can also be found in the swamps and shallow lakes. Before the Hula Plain was drained, the Hula Valley was the place where most plants of this kind were to be found. The drainage was completed in 1958 and now they only exist in the Hula Nature Reserve and alongside the canals which cross the Plain: particularly noteworthy among these is the Papyrus (*Cyperus papyrus*) because nowadays it only grows in Egypt, Israel and near Syracuse.

When settlers established themselves in Israel in the early 20th c. as part of the Zionist Movement, they soon realised that the stock of trees needed to be increased by forestation. Eucalyptus trees were planted and it was quickly discovered that these also grew in dry areas. The most common species in Israel is *Eucalpytus rostrata*. *Eucalyptus gomphocephala* also thrives in the mountains.

After the First World War, forestation projects were stepped up, particularly on

Mediterranean coast near Rosh Haniqra

rocky mountain slopes, where the soil was too poor to grow fruit trees or cereals. In the areas where conifers were planted, pines (particularly the Aleppo pine) are predominant, since they do not need good soil and require little moisture. Other trees planted included acacia, cyprus and poplars.

Eucalyptus and tamarisk have been planted among the sand dunes and around fields extremely exposed to the wind or erosion to prevent the soil from drifting or being blown away.

Useful plants: see Agriculture, p. 48.

Wildlife

Israel's coastal waters and its various regions support many different forms of *wildlife* (reptiles, fish, birds, mammals, etc.). However, as in other parts of the world, many species have become extinct in the course of the centuries. This may have been caused by a sudden change in climate or an alteration in man's land-use. Thus the Bible mentions many animals which are no longer to be found in the country: lions, tigers, bears, antelopes and even ostriches and crocodiles. Fish and other sea creatures are to be found in the coastal waters of the Mediterranean and in the Red Sea, but because of its high salt content (up to 4%) the Mediterranean cannot support all the species usually found in the open sea. Directly on the coast the salt content of the water is only about 3.1% since an ocean current from

the SW carries water here from the Nile. the water temperature is between 61 and 84°F/16 and 29°C.

Because of its high temperatures and intense sunlight, Israel boasts a large number of reptiles. Hence, there are seven kinds of tortoises, four of them amphibious, and three living on dry land. The gecko, a kind of lizard, is widespread and often makes its way into houses. The chameleon, which can change its colour to match its surroundings, moves slowly but catches insects by suddenly shooting out its tongue. Of the non-poisonous snakes the Sand Boa and the Black Snake, which can grow to a length of over 6 ft, are the most common, while the Palestinian Viper (*Vipera palaestinensa*) is the most dangerous of the poisonous snakes.

There are 300 different species of birds in Israel. Some live here the whole year round, others only in summer. With the spread of human habitation, various species such as the goshawk and the vulture, have retreated to distant regions, while others, such as the blackbird, make their homes in the newly planted gardens and woods or, like the swallows and crested larks, take to the cornfields.

In the immediate vicinity of the coast one can find sponges, sea anemones, bristle-worms, shrimps, crabs, starfish and sea urchins. Further offshore there are various corals as well as lobsters, crayfish and moray eels; also many kinds of shellfish, often buried in the sea bed. In the open waters, directly opposite the beach, one sometimes finds squid, rays, mackerel, perch and bream. Weever fish bury themselves in the sand in the shallows and, since they can inject poison from spines in their fins, they can prove dangerous. Out at sea there are tuna and even some of the larger sharks, which may also approach closer to land in the wake of ships. Occasionally one encounters turtles, dolphins and even a toothed whale.

The Red Sea is particularly popular with scuba-divers because of its wealth of creatures. Along the coast stretch coral reefs which are the homes of magnificently coloured fish including various kinds of butterfly fish (Chaetodontidae), surgeon fish (Acanthuridae) and cow fish (Ostraciontidae). In addition to the many sharks here one can also find saw-fish, which are a type of ray.

The largest freshwater lake is the Sea of Galilee, with carp, catfish and perch-like Galilee cichlids or St Peter's Fish, which broods its young in its mouth.

Gulls and other sea birds live along the Mediterranean coast. Of the few species of bird which survive in the desert, the best known are the Fantailed Raven (*Corvus rhipidurus*) and the Cream-coloured Courser (*Cursorius cursor*). Bare rocks are the chosen habitat of the Trumpeter Finch (*Rhodopechys githaginea*), whose colouring so cleverly matches the desert floor that its presence can often only be detected from its call. Other species are strictly local, such as the Dead Sea Sparrow (*Passer moabiticus*) and the Mourning Wheatear (*Oenanthe lugens*).

In spring the flight path of the migrating birds is generally from the S to the N of the country and in autumn they travel in the opposite direction. Most of the larger birds fly over in the daytime, while the smaller ones travel at night. An interesting phenomenon, which is also reported in the Bible, is the autumn arrival of enormous flocks of quail on the coasts of the Negev and the Sinai Peninsula. The birds fall exhausted to the ground and are trapped in their thousands by the local Bedouin and Fellahin.

There are some sixty species of mammals, which is quite a large number for this relatively small country, but there were many more in the past. Most of the mammals that live in Israel can be found in other parts of the world but there are a few unique species such as the Lesser Jerboa (*Jaculus jaculus*) and various gazelles.

Most of Israel's animals have largely adapted themselves to its semi-arid and arid climatic conditions. The mammals are mainly nocturnal and, since they rest during the day, they can survive on very little water. Some species, however, need a good deal of water and live in the swamps or near the lakes. This also applies to the wild boar (*Sus scrofa*), which often inflicts considerable damage on the orchards, fields and vegetable plots in the Hula Valley and around the Sea of Galilee.

Leopards are among the big cats that used to inhabit the Holy Land. They can weigh as much as 80 lb/35 kg and have spotted coats. While many leopards could still be seen towards the end of the last century, by 1948, when the State of Israel was founded, only a few animals remained. In 1964 the Knesset passed a Nature Conservation Act with an added clause covering wild animals. A zoologist combing the countryside in an attempt to list all its beasts of prey, came upon what looked like the spoor of a leopard in the Judean Desert. He staked out an animal as bait one night and in the morning it had been eaten. He eventually managed to photograph a leopardess with her young. Recent observations indicate that there are about 20 mature leopards with their offspring in an area of some 386 sq. miles/1,000 sq. km W of the Dead Sea. They mostly hunt hares and, because of the intense heat in the Judean Desert, catch their prey at night.

With the constant growth of settlement in Israel the number of mammals surviving in the wild is steadily declining. Consequently, the howling of the jackal, which is a night sound in most country areas, can no longer be heard around the towns.

People of Israel

Population

After the Romans had destroyed the Temple in A.D. 70 and put down the Bar-Kochba uprising in the 2nd c., the Jewish population in what was then Palestine shrank at an increasing rate over the following centuries. By the start of the 19th c. the total population only numbered about 250,000; the Jews living "in the Diaspora" often became a persecuted minority in the countries in which they had settled. After 1870 the Jews started to return to abandoned areas of Palestine, away from the towns. From 1882 until the State was founded in 1948 several waves of immigrants (Aliyah) brought a sharp increase in the Jewish share of Israel's population.

The country's **population** increased from 878,000 in 1948 (1949 – 1,174,000; 1958 – 2,032,000) to a total of 3,780,000 in 1979 when, according to official figures, there were 3,135,000 Jews and about 595,000 Arabs; to this should be added other small groups such as the Druse. In 1982 the total population, including those living in East Jerusalem and the Israeli administered zones, was over 4 million. About another million people live in the occupied zones but do not have Israeli citizenship.

The Circassians are one ethnic minority. Emigrating from Russia in 1880, they were settled in parts of the Ottoman Empire, around Amman (today in Jordan) as well as in the Galilean villages of Kefar Kama and Rihaniye (Israel), where about 1,200 members of this group of the population live today.

The majority of Israel's Jews have been born in Israel ("Sabras"). At least a quarter of Israeli Jews stem from Europe and from North and South America while another quarter were born in Asia and Africa (mainly in the Arab countries in these continents). In 1977 48% of Israeli Jews had been born in the country, 27% in Europe (including the U.S.S.R.) and America and 25% in North Africa. Of these, 346,000 came from Poland, 75,000 from the U.S.A. and Australia and 428,000 from Morocco. Others came from the Yemen, Iraq, Iran, Afghanistan and southern India.

Immigrants from Europe fall into two larger groups, the Ashkenazim and the Sephardim. The **Ashkenazim** (Ashkenaz=Germany) stem from either Central or Eastern Europe or from America where they had emigrated. They spoke (and to some extent still speak) Yiddish, a language which traces its origins back to Middle High German and which also has a grammatical structure that broadly corresponds to German. Elements of the vocabulary also come from the Slav languages as well as from Hebrew, and Yiddish is written in Hebrew script.

Spain (Sepharad) is the homeland of the **Sephardim**. One famous Sephard was the Rabbi Yehuda Halevi, who made his way to Palestine in 1140 and was a considerable poet; another was the founder, in 1266, of the Jewish community in Jerusalem, Rabbi Ben Nachmanides, the interpreter of the Torah. When the Jews were driven from Spain in 1492, the Sephardim moved to the Netherlands, Greece and Palestine, where in the 19th c. they constituted the greater part of the Jewish population.

The factors that have contributed to the integration of people from so many different cultural backgrounds have included the introduction of Modern Hebrew (Ivrit) in the schools and military service. Another factor has been the settlements where Jews from every country of origin live together.

The Jewish Agency

In 1933 the **Jewish Agency for Palestine** was established as the agency of the World Zionist Organisation in Palestine by a Treaty of Mandate between Great Britain and the League of Nations. The Agency acted as advisor to the British Mandate Administration and the Jewish National Committee.

Since 1948, the final year of the British Mandate and the year of the foundation of the State of Israel, this body has been known as the **Jewish Agency for Israel**; it particularly concerns itself with questions of immigration and settlement. It receives financial support from the United Jewish Appeal and the Jewish National Fund for Land Development.

Israel has **settlements** of many different kinds. The population of the country is largely concentrated in the towns, with about 50% living in Jerusalem, Tel Aviv-Jaffa and Haifa alone. About 86% of the inhabitants live in towns and urban settlements. Twenty-eight towns are Jewish, two are Arabic and six are a mixture of the two.

The population density ranges from 15,172 per sq. mile/5,000 per sq. km in Tel Aviv to less than 80 per sq. mile/30 per sq. km in the Negev. By planning the settlement of new immigrants an attempt is being made to spread the population as evenly as possible.

Apart from towns (singular Ir; plural Arim) and the traditional villages (singular Moshava; plural Moshavot), there are three characteristic forms of settlement which have developed since the turn of the century and about 8% of the Jewish Israelis now live in them.

Kibbutz (plural *Kibbutzim*) is the name given to a form of village which is communally administered by all the residents and where everything is in common ownership. Its members provide their labour and receive their board and lodging and some pocket money in return. The Kibbutz also looks after the education of the children.

The first Kibbutz, Deganya (on the southern shore of the Sea of Galilee), was founded in 1909. Many Kibbutzim now have their second, third and even fourth generation living there. The number living in a Kibbutz varies between 60 and 2,000 members but the average Kibbutz has between 200 and 400 people. In Israel today there are around 230 Kibbutzim. Whereas in 1948 the Kibbutzniks represented 7·6% of the population, this figure has now fallen to 2·8%. The Kibbutz is completely democratic; once a week there is a general meeting in which all members take part and at which important decisions are made, and a committee is responsible for each economic sector in which the Kibbutz is involved.

The Kibbutz movement played a leading role in the building and re-establishment of the State of Israel. For most Jews the return home to Israel from the Diaspora meant more than the resurrection of national independence: they wanted to form a society that was close to the land. Consequently a relatively large number of public figures were, or still are, members of Kibbutzim.

Kibbutz

Moshav

Moshav-Shitufi

Today many Kibbutzim are facing the problem of industrialisation. In order to keep up in commercial terms, many settlements have already added industrial manufacture and catering (Kibbutz Guest Houses) to their farming activities.

The **Moshav** (plural *Moshavim*) is a community-oriented settlement. Each family runs its own household (ownership of house and garden) and works its own land. Machinery and large items of equipment, however, are acquired collectively and the products are marketed by the community.

Nahalal (in the Jezreel Valley), the first Moshav, was founded in 1921. The average Moshav has between 100 and 1,000 inhabitants. Today there are 250 Moshavim in Israel, accounting for 4% of the total population.

The **Moshav-Shitufi**, like the Kibbutz, is based on collective ownership and communal cultivation of the land but here each family runs its own household. Work and pay are geared to individual requirements. The first settlement of this kind, Kefar Hittim, was founded in 1936. Today Israel has 45 Moshavim-Shitufi with a total of 7,000 inhabitants.

Many countries in Asia, Africa and Latin America have sent students to Israel to experience the communal lifestyle as well as inviting Israeli instructors to help them with the organisation of similar arrangements.

Education in Israeli is held in high esteem. **Schooling** is compulsory up to the age of 15 and is free of charge – 57% of pupils attend the State schools, 21% Jewish denominational schools and 22% schools where the teaching is in Arabic.

Since part of Israel's population hails from underdeveloped countries such as the Yemen and Morocco and part from the U.S.A. and Western Europe, the level of learning can differ substantially. The number of pupils originating from Asian and African countries shrinks considerably in percentage terms as they progress from the primary and secondary schools to university.

The elimination of educational differences is a major preoccupation of the Israeli educational establishment. Thus, for example, children from less well-off families get grants every year towards buying schoolbooks.

There are **universities** in Jerusalem, Tel Aviv, Ramat Gan, Haifa and Beersheba. In addition there is the "Technion" polytechnic in Haifa, the Weizmann Institute for Science in Rohovot and the Academy for Art and Drama ("Bezalel") in Jerusalem. The total number of students receiving further education in Israel is close to 60,000. About 20,000 students attend **Talmud Schools** (plural Yeschivot; singular Yeschiva).

An important part of the educational process is undertaken by the **Israeli Defence Army** (Zahal), both inside and outside the military field. Measures include further education and university studies for soldiers from underprivileged backgrounds. No soldier leaves the army without having completed his basic education.

The Israeli Defence Army, as the Israeli armed forces are called in Hebrew, evolved from the Haganah, the self-protection organisation at the time of the Mandate. The foremost duty of the army is to assure the independence of the State.

The standing army consists of a small nucleus of career officers, non-commissioned officers and soldiers. Military service is compulsory for Jews, Druse and Circassians (36 months for men, 24 months for women). Moslems and Christians can volunteer.

The army is largely composed of reservists. Men can be called back into reserve service until the age of 55 and women without children until 34. In this way the Israeli forces can be transformed in a short time from a small standing army to a very large strike force. The army, airforce and navy are under a joint command with a Major General (Rav-Aluf) at its head.

The fighting Pioneer Youth Corps (Nahal) is recruited from volunteers. They are subject to military discipline but also receive practical agricultural training. These young people are placed in border areas which are intended for settlement or which, because of local living conditions, are considered unsuitable for the civilian population.

Histadrut

Histadrut was the name given in 1922 to the general workers' union which is Israel's largest labour organisation (headquarters in Tel Aviv). It is open to members of all professions, who can join as individuals. Adult membership stands at over 1 million and includes Arabs and Druse. The wage-rates, which are index-linked to the cost of living, are fixed jointly with the employers' associations.

The Histradrut operates a health insurance scheme (Kupat Cholim) and a welfare fund (Misch'an) which advances loans to needy members and runs homes for children and old people.

Vocational training and adult evening classes are similarly provided by the Histadrut, which also promotes cultural and sporting activities for its members.

Religions

The State of Israel guarantees freedom of religious practice for members of all faiths. In this small country Jews, Moslems, Druse, Christians, etc. all live together.

The **Jews**, with 85·2% of the population, are by far the largest religious group. The *Chief Rabbinate* is the supreme Jewish religious authority and consists of the Ashkenazi and Sephardi Chief Rabbis as well as members of the Supreme Rabbinical Courts (the membership of the Chief Rabbinate reflects the fact that most Jews have their origins in Ashkenazi and Sephardi Judaism). The Chief Rabbinate is responsible for questions of Jewish Law and the ritual purity laws.

The Rabbinical Courts are subject to its rulings. Israel has both civil and religious courts. The Supreme Court, the highest in the country, has its seat in Jerusalem. In matters of marriage and divorce, Jewish inhabitants of the State of Israel are subject to Rabbinical jurisdiction – similar provisions also apply to the courts of other religious communities.

The two sacred books of the Jews are the **Torah** (Five Books of Moses, Pentateuch) and the **Talmud**, consisting of the *Mishna* and the *Gemara*. The weekly day of rest is the **Sabbath**, which lasts from Friday evening to Saturday evening. Jewish festivals include: *Purim*, a carnival and a fast commemorating the deliverance from persecution by the Persians in the 6th c. B.C. (14th day of Adar; February/March); *Pesach* (Passover), commemorating the exodus from Egypt (14th/15th day of Nissan; March/April); *Shaboth* (Pentecost), commemorating the gift of the Ten Commandments (6th/7th day of Sivan; May/June); *Rosh Hashanah*, New Year (1st/2nd day of Tishri; September/October); *Yom Kippur*, Day of Atonement (10th day of Tishri; September/October) and *Sukkoth*, Feast of the Tabernacles (15th–21st days of Tishri; September/October), both commemorating the Israelites' sojourn in the desert; *Hanuka*, dedicated to the memory of the purification of the Temple by Judas Maccabaeus (25th day of Kislev to 2nd day of Tevet; December).

The most important *place of prayer* is the **West Wall** (Wailing Wall) in Jerusalem marking the boundary of the Temple at the time of Herod which, since 1967, has again become accessible to the Jews. From the time when the Temple of Jerusalem was still standing, the *Jewish people* were traditionally divided into *three groups*, which was particularly significant for their religious life: the *Cohanim* (singular, Cohen), who trace their line to the sons of Aaron, have certain privileges in the synagogue, but also have to perform certain duties of temple service; the **Levites** (singular, Levi), descendants of Levi, the son of Jacob and Leah, are at a lower level in the religious hierarchy and assist in the temple service; **Israel**, the ordinary people, have no part in the temple service. The family names Cohen (Kogan, Kahn, etc.) and Levi are derived from the ancient tribal designations.

The Chief Rabbinate represents orthodox Jewry. In addition there are conservative and liberal, or reform, Jews and an ultra-orthodox group who live in Mea Shearim,

Jew praying at the Wailing Wall in Jerusalem

The Dome of the Rock in Jerusalem

a suburb of Jerusalem. There are also a-religious and anti-religious Jewish groups.

The *Karaites* (Karaim), a group founded in the 8th c. B.C. by Anan Ben David in Persia, recognises only the law of Moses and not the Rabbinate. They now have a membership of about 11,000, half of whom live in Israel, with about 3,000 in and around Ramla alone. The *Samaritans* are a small group whose holy ground is Mount Gerizim near Nablus (Sechem), and who broke away from the rest of Jewry after the Babylonian captivity. Their sacred writings are the Five Books of Moses and the Book of Joshua from the Old Testament.

Most of the Arabs living in Israel are Sunni **Moslems** *(Muslime)*. Their principal holy places in Israel are the Dome of the Rock and the El Aqsa Mosque in Jerusalem which, after Mecca and Medina, is the most important holy site for Islam.

The canonical book of the Moslems is the **Koran** ("reading"); divided into 114 *Suren*, it is venerated as a Revelation of God to the Prophet Mohammed (571–632). It is accompanied by two other works, the *Hadith* ("Delivery") and the *Sunna* ("Custom"). Islam ("the surrender of the will to God") also recognises Christian and Jewish holy books as preparatory to the final revelation, as well as the prophets of the other two monotheistic religions (Jesus is considered the greatest prophet after Mohammed).

The five duties of Islam are: to believe in Allah as the only God; to pray five times daily; to give alms; to observe the Fast of Ramadam; and to make a pilgrimage to Mecca. The weekly day of rest is Friday. The leaders of the Moslems in Israel are the Kadis (judges of the religious jurisdiction).

The **Druse**, named after Ismail ad Darazi (b. 1019), split from Islam under the

Caliph El Hakim (992–1021); they live in Syria and parts of Israel. Their secret teachings hint at mystical knowledge; fundamental to their belief is the oneness of God, who reveals himself in human incarnations, finally culminating in the person of El Hakim. The majority of members belong to the Juhal ("uninitiated") while the select few to whom the teachings are revealed, the Uhal ("initiated"), are able to lead the services which take place in the "Chalweh" on Thursdays. In Israel the Druse are not considered as Arabs.

The **Christians** in Israel belong to innumerable religious communities. The followers of several creeds have been established here since early Christian or Byzantine times. From these others branched off in different directions at a later date (mostly in 451, following the Edict of Monophysitism at the Fourth Ecumenical Council in Chalkedon). In addition there are Roman Catholic and allied churches, as well as the Protestants, who have only lived here since the 19th c.

The **Greek Orthodox** Church has had a Patriarchate in Jerusalem since 451, consisting of about 80,000 believers. – *Greek Catholics* are those of the Orthodox persuasion that has been united with Rome since 1709, i.e. while observing Orthodox rites they recognise the Pope as head of the Church (Melchites).

The **Copts**, i.e. Egyptian Christians, have also had their own Church since 451 – the branch of this Church which is united with Rome is called *Copto-Catholic* (not represented in Jerusalem).

The **Syrian Orthodox** or **Eastern** Church *(Jacobites)*, whose liturgy is conducted in Syriac, has also existed since 451; their Patriarch resides in Damascus. Since 1662 there is also the *United Syrian Catholic Church* (Patriarch in Antioch and seat in Beirut).

The **Armenian Orthodox** Church which can also be traced back to 451 is the national Church of the Armenians. The *United Armenian Catholic Church* was founded in 1740.

The **Roman Catholic** (*Latin*) Church has a Patriarchate in Jerusalem. Franciscan monks maintain the Holy Places belonging to the Church.

The **Abyssinians**, also represented in Jerusalem, belong to the monophysitic Church of Ethiopia. There are two Church leaders: the Abunda of Gondar (for secular clergy) and the Etshege (for monastic clergy), who until the end of the monarchy was also father confessor to the Emperor.

The **Protestant** and **Anglican** Churches have been represented in Jerusalem since the 19th c. From 1841 to 1881 there was an Anglo-German bishopric, but since that time the Anglicans have had their own hierarchy.

The **Bahai**, adherents of a religion stemming from Persia, live mainly in Haifa, their spritual headquarters. The **Ahmadiva**, members of a movement originating in India, live in the village of Kababir on Mount Carmel.

Kashrut

The concept of "kosher" is related to rules regarding food and other areas of daily life. The whole body of ordinances on cleanliness is known as **Kashrut**. They hark back to Moses who, in compiling them, was governed by considerations of hygiene and aesthetics, but was specially intent on setting the Israelites apart from other peoples.

The 12th Chapter of the Third Book of Moses gives directions for the cleanliness of expectant mothers and for the circumcision of the newborn. The 18th Chapter gives rules for marriage and chastity, the 19th the law on the consecration of daily life and observation of the Sabbath. In the 17th Chapter of the 5th Book of Moses, praying to heathen gods is forbidden, and in the 24th is found advice on husbandry. The laws on clean and unclean animals and food can be found in the 3rd Book of Moses, Chapters 11 and 17, and the 5th Book of Moses, Chapter 14. – The prohibition on eating pork and the recommendation not to mix milk and meat were reactions to the sacrificial customs of the Canaanites, which are known to us through the archives at Ugarit. The rules on the preparation of food are today adhered to by all Government institutions, public bodies and the armed forces, as well as in most hotels and restaurants. In accordance with the ordinances for the veneration of the Sabbath, there is no public transport (trains, buses and some air transport) on that day.

Pilgrimage to the Holy Land

The most prominent father of the Latin church, St Augustine (354–430), dismissed pilgrimages to the original sites of Christianity as having no relevance to one's belief. However, his contemporary, the ecclesiastical scholar **Hieronymus** (347–420), considered that prayer at a place where Christ had been was an act of faith and it was the opinion of this patriarch from Dalmatia, who founded a monastery in Bethlehem and translated the Bible into Latin (the Vulgate), which prevailed.

As early as the 3rd c. devout Christians went to Bethlehem and Jerusalem to pray at the sites of Christ's birth, passion and resurrection. When, through Constantine the Great, Christianity came to be the established religion of the Roman Empire, St **Helena**, the mother of the Emperor, made a pilgrimage to Palestine and there became the first successful archaeologist. During her journey through the Holy Land (326) she made them demolish Hadrian's Temple to Venus on the site of Golgotha, and uncovered the site of the crucifixion and the tomb, thus finding the cross which has henceforth been worshipped as the cross of Christ – one of the most important relics. Her son then built the Church of the Holy Sepulchre on the site of the Temple, and although subsequently altered it still exists today. He also had the Church of the Nativity built at Bethlehem.

In the years that followed, more and more people made pilgrimages to the Holy Land. The faithful refused to be put off by *Gregor of Nyssa* (394), who complained that Jerusalem was a den of adulterers, thieves, heathens and murderers. About 400 the French nun, Atheria, travelled to the Holy Land, where she succeeded in getting as far as Sinai and – as her diary found at Arezzo in 1884 proves – tracked down the location of many of the holy places with the help of the Bible.

In 438/439, the Empress **Eudoxia**, daughter of a heathen Athenian philosopher and the wife of Theodosius II, undertook, with her magnificent entourage, a pilgrimage to Jerusalem where Bishop Juvenalis presented her with several relics, including two chains that were supposed to have been St Peter's fetters in prison. She gave one of them to the Church of the Apostles in Constantinople and the other was brought by her daughter Eudoxia to Rome, where it can still be seen in a Renaissance tabernacle under the High Altar of the 5th c. Church of San Pietro in Vincoli (i.e., St Peter in Chains). When Theodosius II died in 450, Eudoxia returned to Jerusalem, where there were already many monasteries and hospices for pilgrims, and lived there until her death in 460.

The cult of relics, started by Helena, was given a boost by the Empress Eudoxia and heightened the interest in the Middle East of those in the West. Runciman wrote, "If a lady from Maurienne brought back the thumb of John the Baptist from her travels, all her friends would immediately be fired with the urge to make the long journey to behold his trunk in Samaria and his head in Damascus." Many pilgrims voyaged to Palestine on trading vessels until sea journeys became very dangerous during the Arabian wars of conquest in the 7th c. Even then the stream of pilgrims was not at an end. Among the pilgrims was Charlemagne, who came to an arrangement with the Caliph, Haroun al-Raschid, and had pilgrim hostelries built.

When, in the 10th c., the Byzantines were successful in their struggle with the Arabs, the number of pilgrims went up again. They either took the land route through the Byzantine Empire, via Constantinople, or embarked on board ship at Venice or Bari.

Pilgrimages had come to be recognised as a form of penance by the Catholic Church, a view particularly counselled by the Cluniac order, who were also instrumental in enabling many of the faithful to make the journey. The pilgrims included French, German and English and a growing number of Scandinavians.

In the 11th c. when the Seljuks from Turkey advanced against Byzantium and their conquests stretched across Asia Minor as far as Palestine, the pilgrims fell upon very hard times. This was resolved in 1096 by the First Crusade. The end of the era of the Crusades in 1291 still did not see the last of the pilgrimages. In the 16th c. the motive for travel changed. Travel of a secular nature, prompted by the discovery of new lands such as America and India, and for commercial or scientific reasons, sprang to the fore.

Christian pilgrims from the various denominations are still part of the scene in the holy places. But even those who do not have a religious motive for visiting Israel will still find in this country special insights into spiritual experience.

Languages

Ivrit (*Iwrith*, *Ivrit*: Modern Hebrew) is the first official language of Israel. *Arabic* is the second official language. Both Hebrew and Arabic belong to the semitic group of languages; both are written from right to left – but the characters take very different forms.

As a west-semitic language, **Hebrew** is also related to Assyrian and Aramaic. Following the Babylonian exile (587–538 B.C.) the influence of Aramaic became more pronounced. This was the administrative language of the Persian Empire and from the 6th c. B.C. to the 6th c. A.D. it was the language in general use throughout the Middle East. *Aramaic* (and in Hellenic times, Greek) became the common language of the Jewish people and took the place of Hebrew, which, however, continued to be used in religious services and by scholars and writers. The "Mishna", which was compiled around A.D. 200, is largely written in an Aramaic form of Hebrew, enriched with words from Greek and Latin.

Hebrew flourished between the 11th and 16th c. in Moorish Spain. Its revival began in Germany in the late 18th c. in connection with the Haskala ("Enlightenment") and from there it spread to Italy, Poland and Russia.

With the beginning of the Zionist movement in the 19th c. an attempt was made to heal the ancient breach between the sacred and profane languages; Hebrew was no longer to be restricted to religious matters but to be made the vernacular, a unique step that has largely been accomplished in Israel.

Eliezer Ben Yehuda, who came to Palestine in 1881, played a large part in transforming Hebrew into a colloquial language. He also helped to coin the new concepts that were indispensable for a modern society.

An Israeli is usually able to read the Bible in Hebrew with ease, but anyone proficient in biblical Hebrew will have some difffficulty in reading an Israeli newspaper. Many Israelis also speak other languages, such as English, French, German, Russian, Polish, Spanish, Arabic, Hungarian or Yiddish.

Arabic is the south-western branch of the semitic languages. With the spread of Islam, Northern Arabic came to the fore and is commonly spoken today, in numerous dialects, throughout North Africa and the Near East. The most important of these dialects, and the one spoken by the Arab population of Israel, is Egyptian Arabic.

Glossary of Jewish Terms

Aliyah
Waves of Jews returning to Palestine. The first Aliyah (Jews from Russia and Poland) started in 1882; the second Aliyah (1904–14) signalled the start of the Zionist Labour Movement.

Aron Hakodesh (Ark of the Covenant)
According to the 2nd Book of Moses, Chapter 37, on Moses' instructions, Bezalel made the Ark of the Covenant, the portable shrine in acacia wood and covered inside and out with gold which the Jews took with them in their wanderings. It was the symbol of the presence of God and was borne on a throne flanked with golden cherubim. Later the Ark contained the tablets of the Ten Commandments which Moses was given in Sinai. At the time of Judges the Ark was in Silo and it was subsequently stolen by the Philistines. Recaptured by David, the Ark was taken to Jerusalem where David's son, Solomon, built the Temple for it. When Jerusalem was destroyed by Titus in A.D. 70 the Ark, together with other religious objects, was taken to Rome.

Ashkenazim (Ashkenaz=Germany)
Term for Jews originating from central and eastern Europe, who came to Palestine via the Balkans.

Bet ha Midrash
School for the Talmud and prayer house.

Bracha
Blessing, prayer.

Cabbala (tradition)
In Talmudic times this was the term for the oral tradition which existed alongside the written laws; in the Middle Ages the term stood for the ancient Jewish mystical tradition based on an esoteric interpretation of the Old Testament. Interest in the Cabbala reached its peak in the 13th c. in Spain, the source of the mystical work the Zohar.

Chassidim (the pious)
1. A Jewish sect of the 2nd c. B.C. formed to combat Hellenistic influences.
2. A sect of Jewish mystics founded in Poland about A.D. 1750, characterised by religious zeal and a spirit of prayer, joy and charity.

Chatan Hatora
Prayer leader in the Synagogue.

Gabbai
The governing body of the Synagogue.

Gemara
The later part of the Talmud dating from A.D. 500 and a commentary on the Mishna.

Hagada (a story)
The now legal part of the Talmudic literature and associated with Jewish tradition.

Halacha (guiding principles)
That part of traditional Jewish literature concerned with the law and the basis of religious practice.

Karaim (Karaites)
A Jewish sect originating in Persia in the 8th c. A.D. which rejects the Talmud and the Rabbanical tradition and favours strict adherence to, and a literal interpretation of, the Old Testament. In 850 a group moved to Ramla in what is now Israel where they have stayed ever since.

Kehilla
Jewish religious community.

Kibbutz
Self-governing settlement in communal ownership.

Menorah
The seven-branched candelabrum which, according to the 2nd Book of Moses, was fashioned by Bezalel. A large bronze Menorah sculpted by Benno Elkan and given by the British to the Israeli Parliament stands in front of the Knesset in Jerusalem (see cover picture).

Midrash (interpretation)
Rabbinical commentaries on the Bible dating from between 30 B.C. and A.D. 900 incorporating interpretations of legal (Halacha) and non-legal (Hagada) texts.

Mikva
Ritual bath.

Minian
Prayer meeting of at least ten men.

Mishna (repetition)
A compilation of precepts passed down as oral tradition and collected in the late 2nd c. A.D., forming the earlier part of the Talmud. It is divided into six parts (Sedarim).

Mizva
Religious commandment.

Moshav
A communally organised settlement.

Rabbis
Jewish religious teachers chosen by the congregation (not ordained). Their duties include certain acts in the services in conjunction with the prayer leader (the Chatan Hatora), directing and supervising religious instruction and religious ceremonies such as weddings. The term *Rabbi* (my teacher) comes from an Aramaic and Hebrew word "rab" meaning "learned" and is an honorary name for Jewish teachers.

Sanhedrin (from the Greek, "Sunedrion")
The supreme judicial, ecclesiastical and administrative council of the Jews in New Testament times, having 71 members. After the destruction of Jerusalem and the Temple in A.D. 70, Rabbi Jochanaan ben Zakkai received permission to transfer the seat of the Sanhedrin to Jamnia. It subsequently moved (A.D. 140) to Usah (Galilee) and later to Tiberia.

Sephardim (Sepharad=Spain)
Term for Jews who had settled in Spain and, following their expulsion in 1492, made their homes in Holland, Greece and Palestine.

Shofar
A ram's horn which is sounded on the Day of Atonement and the celebration of the New Year.

Shulchan Aruch
A relatively modern compilation of the religious laws.

Synagogue
Greek term for the assembled congregation, later also for the assembly building. Probably first used during the Babylonian Exile (587–538), it became of increasing importance in the following years. The oldest synagogues can be traced to about 250 B.C. in Egypt. In Hellenic times synagogues were the centre of Jewish life throughout the Mediterranean. Most synagogues found in Palestine and Syria date from between the 3rd and 7th c. The prayer room faced Jerusalem and the scrolls were kept in a wooden shrine in a recess or in a neighbouring room.

Tabernacle
According to the 2nd Book of Moses, Chapters 25–31 and 35–40, during the Israelites' sojourn in Sinai following the Exodus a tent was fashioned of linen, as a form of portable temple, in which were kept the Ark of the Covenant, the table for the twelve loaves and a seven-branched candlestick (Menorah).

Talit
A large pale-coloured prayer shawl, with dark borders.

Talmud (teaching)
The main authoritative compilation of ancient Jewish law and tradition, comprising the *Mishna* and the *Gemara*. It was begun in the 6th c. B.C. and completed in the 5th c. A.D. There are two recensions of this compilation, the *Palestinian Talmud* of about A.D. 375 and the longer and more important *Babylonian Talmud*, written in Aramaic about A.D. 500.

Tefila
A prayer belt made of dark leather, with a box containing texts from the Torah. The Tefila is worn on weekdays at morning prayer.

Torah (doctrine)
The Five Books of Moses (Pentateuch).

Yeshiva
Talmud School.

The words of the Torah

History

Stone Age (*prehistory:* 1000000–3000 B.C.). – The materials used for making tools serve as the basis for chronology in the very early history of mankind. Thus in the *Palaeolithic* era man has only rough stone tools. In the *Mesolithic* era weapons and implements made from flint or tipped with flint make hunting and cultivation possible. In the next epoch, the *Neolithic* era, man has already begun to make clay pots, and finally in the *Chalcolithic* era has learned to work with a metal (copper).

1000000–14000 **Old Stone Age** *(Palaeolithic)* – divided into three epochs.

1000000–300000 Primitive hunters and gatherers use sea or river pebbles as tools. Remains of this culture have been found at Ubeidiye, S of the Sea of Galilee.

300000–70000 Hand-axe period, marked by hand-axes with chamfered edges such as those found in caves on Mount Carmel – the damp climate encourages tropical plant and animal life.

70000–14000 A change in climate brings about the disappearance of the tropical forests and their creatures. In the Carmel caves, near Nazareth, and in the Wadi Amud on the Sea of Galilee remains have been found of *Palaeoanthropus palaestinensis*, who used spears and daggers with flint heads. The arrangement of the bodies, inside a ring of stones together with items of everyday use, indicates the dawn of spiritual development.

14000–7500 **Middle Stone Age** *(Mesolithic).* – The use of bow and sling make hunting more effective (it appears that dogs were used as well). Flint sickles proclaim the beginning of agriculture. The start of the "Stone Age Revolution" in which man progresses from gathering plants to planned cultivation. He settles in one place (beginnings of house building), thus creating the conditions for more advanced cultural development.

7500–4000 **New Stone Age** *(Neolithic).* – Continuation of the development begun at the end of the Mesolithic era. *Homo sapiens* works the land according to the seasons (upper Jordan Plain, Yarmuk Valley, Oasis of Jericho). Because yields differ, social strata emerge, communities become larger. Discovery of potter's craft indicates progress in cultural development; formation of agrarian fertility cult (figurines of Shaar ha Golan on the Yarmuk). Temple at Jericho for Divine Trinity (man, woman, child); skulls with modelled additions are an indication of belief in life after death.

4000–3000 **Copper Stone Age** *(Chacolithic).* – The art of metal extraction joins the ability to make stone tools and pottery. Finds from this era have been made in the Jordan Valley, around Beersheba, at En Gedi on the Dead Sea and on the coastal plain. A temple was discovered at En Gedi and a temple treasure in the "treasure cave" in the Judean Desert.

Bronze Age *(Canaanite Period;* 3000–1200 B.C.). – Emergence in Canaan of the Semite City States, at times under Egyptian rule. Abraham, the first of the patriarchs and father-founder of the Israelites, journeys from Mesopotamia to what was later Judah. About 1700 B.C. the *Israelites go into Egypt*; over 500 years later they return to Canaan.

3000–2000 **Early Bronze Age.** – Emergence of early advanced cultures in Mesopotamia which influence lands to the S and E. The land lived in by the west Semitic **Amorites** (Amurru="people of west",

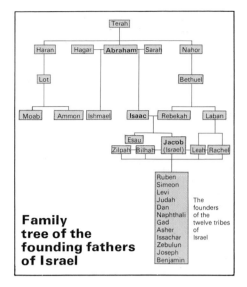

Family tree of the founding fathers of Israel

originating from Acre) on the Mediterranean coast and in the upper Jordan Valley (Canaan) is divided up into city states. The towns are fortified: Hazor in the N, Megiddo and Bet Shean in the Jezreel Plain, Sichem, Geser, Jerusalem and Hebron in the highlands. Each town has its Baal or resident god, represented by the town's king or priest. From the 3rd millennium onwards, Egypt exerts growing influence over the Canaanite towns.

2000–1600 **Middle Bronze Age.** – Around the 18th c. B.C. **Abraham**, who, according to the Old Testament, came from Ur in Chaldaea, journeys through the fertile crescent of the Euphrates, crossing Sichem on his journey southwards to Hebron and Beersheba. From reports of the Pharaoh Amenhotep II (1438–1412 B.C.) we know that at that time, besides the resident tribes, there was a nomadic population, the Apiru or Habiru, which probably included the early Hebrews. The *Exodus of the Israelites to Egypt*, which the Bible connects with Abraham's grandson Jacob and his son Joseph, possibly coincides with the campaign of the Hyksos (Asiatic conquerors who, after the heyday of Egypt's Middle Kingdom, conquered the country around 1650 B.C.).

1600–1200 **Late Bronze Age.** – In the 2nd millennium the Pharaohs of the New Kingdom such as Tutmosis I (1528–1510 B.C.) and Tutmosis II (1468–1436 B.C.) control the most important roads and cities; some of these cities have Egyptian garrisons. Canaanite kings take advantage of Egypt's decline under the heretical Pharaoh Ahkenhaton (1364–1347 B.C.) to extend their power.

1285 At Kadesh (near Homs in modern Syria) there is a battle between the Egyptians under Ramses II (1290–1224 B.C.) and the **Hittites** who have already been living in north Canaan and Syria for several hundred years, resulting in both sides demarcating their spheres of influence.

About 1250 Different dates (15th or 13th c. B.C.) have been advanced for the *Israelites' return to Canaan* with the latter date now assumed to be correct. This being the case, the Israelites leave the Nile Delta in the time of Ramses II and, led by **Moses** as recorded in the Bible, cross Sinai and East Jordan, where the kingdoms of Ammon, Moab and Edom had been established in the 14th c. They press on, led now by *Joshua*, into Cannan. "The seizure of the westland by the Israelites in Jordan was a lengthy process, during which different tribe (one of Leah in the N and S, sons of Rachel in the center) settled one after the other." (Avi Yonah.) Jericho and Hazor are conquered; the Canaanites hold Jerusalem as well as parts of the coastal plain.

Early Iron Age (*Israelite Period*; 1200–600 B.C.). – Under the Judges and later the Kings, the Israelites are at war with the **Philistines**. The kingdom reaches its zenith under David and then Solomon, who orders the building of the Temple in Jerusalem. After his death the country is divided into two kingdoms. The Israelites are defeated in battle first by the Assyrians and then the Babylonians, with the **Babylonian Captivity** commencing in 587 B.C.

1200–1025 **The Judges.** – The start of the Israelite Period sees incursions by the **Philistines**, Indo-Germanic seafarers who also threaten Egypt. They take the coast and establish strongholds at Gaza, Askalon, Asdod, Ekron, Gath and Jaffa, subsequently extending their dominion up to the southern shore of the Sea of Galilee.
In the 12th c. the ill-organised tribes of Israel, under their leaders the "Judges" (Deborah, Gideon, Samuel, etc.), fight the Philistines who, with their iron weapons, are at a distinct advantage. At the end of the 11th c. the Philistines defeat the Israelites at Eben Ezer, capture the Ark of the Covenant and destroy the sacred shrine in Silo.

1025–587 **The Kings.** – The last Judge, Samuel, anoints **Saul** King at Gilgal near Jericho. Thus begins the age of the Kings, which lasts until Nebuchad-nezzar captures Jerusalem in 587 B.C.

1025 Saul becomes King of the Israelites and together with his son *Jonathan* conquers the Philistines.

1006 Saul falls in battle against the Philistines. The tribe of Judah elects **David**, born in Bethlehem, as Saul's successor and he is crowned King in Hebron. With the assassination of Saul's son, Ishbosheth, David becomes King of all Israel.

1000 David conquers Jerusalem and makes it his seat. When the Ark of the Covenant is subsequently housed on Temple Mount, Jerusalem also becomes the religious center for the Jewish people. David captures the Jezreel Plain from the Philistines; he defeats the Moabites at Madaba and captures the capital of the Ammonites, Rabath Ammon, and Damascus, the capital of the Aramaeans. Through his victory at Edom he extends his kingdom to the Red Sea.

965 **Solomon**, David's son, becomes King of the great kingdom. The country enjoys an economic boom; Solomon makes the country secure with fortresses such as Hazor and Megiddo, brings in a firm system of administration and from Elat trades with Ophir (in East Africa?), conquers Geser, but loses Damascus.

953 Building of Temple of Solomon.

928 Death of Solomon and the Kingdom breaks into two, with the **Kingdom of Judah** (capital – Jerusalem) in the S ruled by Solomon's son, Rehoboam, with the tribes of **Judah** and **Benjamin**, and the **Kingdom of Israel** in the N formed by the ten northern tribes under Jeroboam I (982–907 B.C.).

924 Palestinian campaign of King Shishak of Egypt. The sacking of Jerusalem.

910 Death of Rehoboam, the King of Judah. His immediate successors are a number of relatively undistinguished rulers.

878 *Omri* becomes King of Israel. He consolidates the State and founds the capital of Samaria. The marriage of his son, Ahab, to Jezebel, daughter of the King of Sidon, sees the introduction of Phoenician influences, including the cult of Baal, which brings dire warnings from Prophets such as *Elijah*.

871 *Ahab* becomes King of Israel. He withstands three onslaughts by the Aramaic city state of Damascus (Aram), but falls in 852 B.C.

842 *Jehu* overthrows the Omri Dynasty and becomes King of Israel (842–814 B.C.). He fights against Damascus which, in 806 B.C., is neutralised by the Assyrians under Adad Mirari III. In Judah, *Athaliah*, the mother of King *Ahaziah*, introduces the cult of Baal which leads to unrest.

836 *Joash* comes to power in Judah as a result of a coup.

801 *Amaziah* succeeds *Joash* on the throne and vanquishes the Edomites.

769–733 *Uzziah* is King in Judah. Attempt to develop the Negev.

733 *Ahaz*, Uzziah's son, becomes King of Judah; he submits to the growing might of the Assyrians and also gets Judah to adopt their religious practices.

732 Israel, ruled by King *Pekah*, loses in battle against the Assyrians under Talgath-pilneser III; large parts of the country are annexed by the Assyrians.

727 *Hezekiah* becomes King of Judah. He purges the Temple of alien cults and brings in economic reforms.

721 Samaria, the capital of the Northern Kingdom, is conquered by Sargon II of Assyria. Many local people are carried off and replaced by settlers from Babylon. The **Samaritans** result from intermarriage between the remaining Jews and Babylonians.

712 The Assyrians create a province (Philistia) around Ashdod. Hezekiah secures Jerusalem's water supply by building a tunnel. He joins with Egypt, Babylon and Ashkelon in a coalition against Assyrians.

701 Unsuccessful *siege of Jerusalem* by Sennacherib of Assyria.

696–642 *Menasseh*, son of Hezekiah, is a vassal of the Assyrians.

641–640 *Amon*, King of Judah, is murdered for his policy of friendship with Assyria.

639 *Josiah* is the new ruler of Judah. Following defeat of the Assyrians by the Babylonians, he annexes Samaria and Galilee. He purifies the Temple and purges the Jewish sites of worship outside Jerusalem as part of a centralist religious reform, chiefly under the influence of the Prophet Jeremiah.

609 Death of Josiah; his son, *Joachim*, comes to power. He is at first dependent upon the Egyptian Pharaoh Necho, then on the Babylonian ruler Nebuchadnezzar.

598 *Zedekiah* becomes King of Judah.

597 After an attempted uprising by Joachim, Nebuchadnezzar II takes Jerusalem. Joachim's rule is at an end. His son *Johoiachin*, together with the nation's ruling class, is deported by Nebuchadnezzar to Babylon (the first Exile).

589 Zedekiah rises up against the Babylonians.

Palestine 6th–1st c. B.C.

SYRIA
• Damascus
Tyros
GALILEE
Caesarea
SAMARIA
Mediterranean
JUDAH
• Jerusalem
Gaza • IDUMEA
NABATAEA
Sinai
EGYPT
Red Sea

587 After laying siege to Jerusalem Nebuchadnezzar II recaptures it and destroys the Temple. This marks the end of the Kingdom of Judah and the start of the **Babylonian Captivity** (second Exile). Judah becomes a Babylonian province. The Edomites settle in the area around Hebron and Beersheba, which is now called Idumea.

Persian Rule/Hellenistic Influence (538–332 B.C.). – After the end of the Babylonian Captivity Judah becomes a Persian province.

539 King Cyrus II of Persia conquers the Babylonian Empire.

538 Cyrus II frees the Jews from bondage and allows them to return to their homeland; rebuilding of the Temple. – Acre and Gaza become royal citadels, the coastal area is divided up between the Phoenician cities of Tyre and Sidon, and the rest of the country is made into provinces.

520 Building of the second Temple in Jerusalem.

519 *Shesh-bazzar*, a descendant of Joachim, is installed as Governor of Judah. He and his successors are aided by the high priests and the council of elders. Dedication of the second Temple under the governorship of *Nehemiah*.

445 Jerusalem gets new city walls.

5th and 4th c. Increasing Greek influence, long before the country is conquered by Alexander the Great. In the 4th c. B.C. there are Greeks living in Acre; mercenaries settle in Attlit.

Hellenistic Era (332–166 B.C.). – Alexander the Great brings Judea under Macedonian rule. With progressively greater Hellenisation there is conflict between the Greek Seleucids and the law-abiding Jews. Antiochus IV orders the Jews to worship Greek gods and Jewish services in the Temple are suspended.

336 **Alexander the Great** becomes King of Macedonia.

333 Alexander defeats the Persians under Darius II at Issos.

332 Alexander conquers Tyre, Syria and Egypt; Judea comes under Macedonian rule.

323 Death of Alexander. Judea becomes a battleground under his successors, the Diadochi. *Antigonos Monophthalmos* fights the **Nabataeans**, Arab people living around Petra (today Jordan).

312 *Ptolemy I*, the ruler of Egypt, captures Jerusalem and Judea becomes part of his Empire. Many Jews, either by force or of their own free will, go into the *Diaspora* in Egypt. Judea is administered by high priests from the House of Oniades; there is a Macedonian colony in Samaria. Galilee's seat of government is at Mount Tabor. The Phoenician cities on the coast become autonomous. The Tobiades, a powerful family in East Jordan, become influential throughout the Near East, advancing the process of Hellenisation, as indicated by the renaming of cities such as Acre (Ptolemais) and Rabath Ammon (Philadelphia). The Jewish colony in Egypt also becomes Hellenised and the books of the Bible that make up the Old Testament are translated into Greek in the 3rd c. B.C. (Septuagint).

198 In the *battle at Paneion* (today Banias) the Ptolomaeans, under Ptolemy V, are defeated by the Greek Seleucids, already ruling in Syria under *Antiochus III* (223–187 B.C.). Antiochus combines Syria and Phoenicia into a new satrapy (provincial governorship) and in Palestine creates four eparchys (dioceses): Samaria, Idumea, Gilead (East Jordan) and Paralia (the coast). Antiochus III grants the Jews the right to live according to "the Laws of their Fathers", the Temple receives funds. – When Syria loses a war with Rome and has to pay out considerable reparations, one of the Ministers of Seleukos IV (187–175 B.C.) tries to take charge of the Temple treasury, thus engendering tension between the Seleucid rulers and the Jews. The next Seleucid ruler, *Antiochus IV* (175–163 B.C.), through consistently implementing greater Hellenisation of the country, is constantly coming into sharper conflict with the Jewish faithful. He replaces the High Priest *Onias III* with his brother *Jason* who, in furthering Hellenisation, builds a gymnasium on the lower reaches of Temple Mount. This also meets with the priests' disapproval and Jason's term of office is short.

172–171 *Menelaus*, brother of Simeon, the head of the Temple, succeeds in getting the office of High Priest transferred to himself even though he is not of the house of Onias. Menelaus misappropriates treasures from the Temple in order to pay his tributes to the King and has Onias III, the former High Priest, murdered.

169 Antiochus IV appropriates the remainder of the Temple treasury. Conflict between Menelaus and the Tobias dynasty forces Antiochus to take military action. Menelaus is ordered to suppress the practice of the Jewish religion and therefore erects an altar to Dionysos Sabazios in the Temple at Jerusalem and plans to build a temple to Zeus.

167 Jewish services in the Temple at Jerusalem are suspended.

Maccabean Uprising and Hashmonean Rule (166–37 B.C.). – Under the Hashmoneans, Mattathias, and Judas Maccabeus, there is an uprising against Antiochus IV who repeals the anti-Jewish laws and permits the Jews to practise their religion. After the Hashmoneans have held the office of governor and High Priest for over a hundred years, friction arises between them and the Jewish population. Some years later the capital, Jerusalem, is captured by Pompey, the Roman General.

166 The religious persecution leads to a revolt by the Jews against the foreign ruler. In the city of Modiim (near Lydda, now Lod) the Hashmonean priest *Mattathias* kills a royal official and one of the sacrificial priests during a heathen service and then flees to the mountains with fellow revolutionaries. Following his death in the same year, his son **Judas Maccabeus** places himself at the head of the rebels. The group grows in strength and goes to war with Antiochus IV.

165 Antiochus IV repeals the anti-Jewish laws.

164 Judas Maccabeus purifies the Temple. To this day this event is commemorated by the Jewish Feast of Dedication and Light (Hannukkah).

160 After long years of fighting Antiochus IV and Demetrius I, Judas Maccabeus falls at Eleasa. His brother *Jonathan* takes up the struggle.

152 Jonathan is appointed Governor by Demtrius I.

150 The Seleucid King, Alexandros Balas, makes Jonathan High Priest. "Thus as Governor and High Priest the Hashmoneans wielded power, de facto and de jure, in Judea, and the object of the revolution had largely been attained." (Avi Yonah.)
Jonathan exploits tensions among the Seleucid rulers and between the Syrian Seleucids and the Egyptian Ptolemaics to extend his territory and his powers.

147 At the *battle of Jamnia* the troops of the Seleucids are defeated by the Hashmonean army under Jonathan.

142 Jonathan is taken prisoner and killed. His brother, *Simeon*, becomes High Priest in his stead. He achieves recognition of the *independence of Judea*. (The Judean dynasty of the Hashmoneans combines temporal and spiritual power.)

135 End of Simeon's rule. *Hyrcanus I* comes to power. He wishes to re-establish the Kingdom of David (forcing Judaism on the Idumeans, conquering the Samaritans).

104 End of Hyrcanus I's rule.

103 *Alexandros Jannaios*, who has the support of the Hellenised citizens, comes to power. He conquers the coastal towns, Galilee and parts of East Jordan – the largest expansion of the Hashmonean kingdom. The Jewish opposition to the Hashmonean dynasty, which had already been voiced when Jonathan seized the office of High Priest, grows as Jannaios declares himself King.

76 End of the rule of Alexandros Jannaois – unrest grows during the reigns of his sons *Hyrkanus II* and *Aristobulos II.*

63 The Roman General *Pompey*, under orders to end the 3rd Mithraditic War in Asia, exploits the conflicts with the Hashmonean dynasty to capture Jerusalem. The Hashmonean State becomes a vassal state to Rome.

37 Execution of the last Hashmonean King, Mattathias Antigonos, by the Romans.

The Roman Occupation (63 B.C.–A.D. 324). – The **birth of Jesus** occurs during the reign of King Herod who is half Jewish. After Herod's death, Judea is administered by Roman Procurators. Tensions between the Jews and the Romans lead to armed conflicts (destruction of the Temple in Jerusalem). Following the Bar-Kochba uprising, the *Jews are driven out of Jerusalem*; Tiberias in Galilee subsequently becomes the center of Jewry and its patriarchates. Establishment of the first Christian communities.

37 **Herod**, son of an Idumean father and a Nabataean mother, becomes, with the help of the Romans, ruler of the country (Herod the Great). To secure his unpopular rule, Herod builds many citadels and fortresses, including Machaerus in East Jordan, Massada, Herodion and Kypros. The Temple is rebuilt on the enlarged site in Jerusalem. The king has a palace built in Jerusalem, as well as the Antonia fortress, a theatre and a hippodrome, on Graeco-Roman lines.

30 **Augustus** (until 27 B.C. *Octavius*) becomes Roman Emperor. He confirms Herod I as King of Judea; in his honour, Herod builds the harbour at Caesarea, has Samaria rebuilt and renames it Sebastia, which is Greek for Augustus, and erects a temple there to Augustus.

7/6 B.C. **Jesus** is born in Bethlehem (the year of his birth was wrongly calculated in the earth 6th c.)

4 B.C. Death of King Herod. The kingdom is divided between his three surviving sons: *Archelaus* becomes Ethnarch of Idumea and Samaria; *Phillipos* becomes Tetrarch of the north and Transjordan and founds Caesarea Philippi near Parneas (now Banias). *Herodes Antipas* rules as Tetrarch over Galilee and Peraea; he founds the town of Tiberias. Herodes Antipas is the sovereign of John the Baptist whom he causes to be killed at the instigation of his wife, Herodias.

Year 1 The start of the Christian time-scale.

A.D. **6** Augustus deposes Archelaus.

14 End of the reign of Augustus.

26 The Roman *Pontius Pilate* becomes Procurator and Prefect of Judea.

29 First appearance of **John the Baptist.**

About **33** **Crucifixion of Jesus** in Jerusalem.

34 *Phillipus*, son of King Herod, dies.

36 Pontius Pilate loses his post as Procurator and Prefect of Judea.

37 *Agrippa I*, a grandson of Herod the Great, becomes King of Judea. He orders the persecution of the original community of Christians in Jerusalem.

**Roman Provinces
1st–7th c. A.D.**

SYRIA
● Damascus
Tyros
PALAESTINA
SECUNDA
Caesarea
Mediterranean
PALAESTINA
PRIMA
Aelia Capitolina ●
(Jerusalem)
PALAESTINA
TERTIA
Sinai
● Aela
ARABY
EGYPT
Red Sea

Introduction to Israel   35

The Roman Emperor Caligula banishes Herodes Antipas.

44   After Agrippa's death Palestine becomes the *Roman Province of Judea.*

66   The Roman Procurators, cruel and corrupt low-ranking officials, have little understanding for the way the life of the Jews is ruled by their religion and especially misunderstand their belief in the coming of a Messiah. Growing tensions lead to the *Jewish uprising against the Romans.*
Leaders of the resistance are the fanatical Zealots. The Romans garrisoning the royal palace at Jerusalem are massacred after surrendering.

69   Vespasian becomes Roman Emperor.

70   Titus, the son of Vespasian, captures Jerusalem; **destruction of the Temple**, religious and political focal point of the Jews.

74   *Massada,* the last Jewish stronghold, is captured by the Romans after a long siege. Its Jewish defenders commit mass suicide.
Following the destruction of Jerusalem and the Temple, leadership passes from the Priests to the Pharisees. Under *Rabbi Jochanaan,* the Sanhedrin chooses the town of Yamnia (Yavne) as its head-quarters where the study of the laws ensures the continued existence of the Jewish faith.
Rome strengthens the position of the governors in Judea, giving them command over the legions stationed in Jerusalem. Caesarea becomes a Roman colony. Near Samaria-Sabastia Vespasian founds the soldiers' colony of Flavia Neapolis (now Nablus).

79   End of the rule of Vespasian.

79–81   Titus is Emperor of Rome.

81–96   Domitian reigns as Emperor in Rome – during this time the Jewish King *Agrippa II* dies and his kingdom is divided between Judea and Syria.

98   Trajan becomes Roman Emperor.

106   Incorporation of the Nabataean kingdom into the Roman Empire.

115   Jewish uprisings in Cyrene, Egypt and Cyprus spill over into Judea, where several Rabbis are executed.

117   End of Trajan's reign. Hadrian becomes Roman Emperor.

130   Hadrian forbids the Jewish rite of circumcision.

132   The ban on circumcision leads to a Jewish uprising led by *Bar Kochba* (Simeon ben Kosbah).

135   The Romans put down the *Bar Kochba Revolt* (caves west of the Dead Sea served as hiding places for some of the rebels; and Bar Kochba's letters have subsequently been found here). Jerusalem becomes the Roman military colony of Aelia Capitolina. The Romans erect an equestrian statue of Hadrian in front of the Temple and bar the Jews from Aelia Capitolina. Usah in Galilee now becomes the centre of Jewry.

138   End of the rule of the Emperor Hadrian. Antonius Pius becomes Roman Emperor. He allows the return of Jewish religious practices, which had been banned after the Bar Kochba uprising.

About 140   The Sanhedrin meet in Usah and elect *Simeon II* as Patriarch. The Jews receive legal autonomy and urban self-government. Roman urban culture spreads to distant parts of the country.

2nd and 3rd c.   Under *Judah I* the Patriarchate becomes of an almost monarchic character. Judah's grave in Bet Shearim becomes the center of a large Jewish cemetery. The seat of the Patriarch and the Sanhedrin moves from Usah to Tiberias. During this period the Christians have a community in Jerusalem, where Bishop Alexander (212–251) founds a library. Other communities have, since the 1st c., been in existence in Caesarea, Ptolemais (Acre), Joppe (Jaffa), Lydda (Lod) and Pella; since the 2nd c. in Flavia Neapolis, since the 3rd c. in Caesarea Philippi, Bostra, Sabastia, Philadelphia (Amman), Bethlehem, Gaza, Jericho, etc. The leading community is at Caesarea, where the religious teachers Origenes (*c.* 185–254) and Eusebius (*c.* 260–339) are to be found.

Palestine under Eastern Roman/Byzantine Rule (324–638). – Under Constantine the Great, who makes *Christianity the established religion of the Roman Empire,* many Jews become Christians. Palestine wins prestige as "The Holy Land". A constant source of tension among the great powers, after 600 it comes within the Arab sphere of influence.

324   *Constantine the Great* re-unites the Roman Empire which had been divided into four kingdoms and wins power as the supreme ruler.
The rule of Constantine the Great marks a decisive turning point for Palestine: "Not only was Christianity now a 'religio licita', but the hitherto unimportant province had become the Holy Land of the dominant religion." (Avi-Yonah.) In Jerusalem and its surroundings churches are built on all the sites of significance for Christianity (Church of the Nativity in Bethlehem, Church of the Holy Sepulchre on Golgotha in Jerusalem). The Jews continue to be allowed into the city only once a year, on the anniversary of the destruction of the Temple.

379–385   Under the rule of Emperor Theodosius I Christianity is considerably extended. Theodosius divides the Empire into the Eastern Empire and the Western Empire.

408–450   By the end of the reign of Theodosius II most of the people of Palestine are Christians.

Before 429   With the death of Gamaliel IV, the office of Jewish Patriarch lapses.

451   The Bishop of Jerusalem is esteemed a Christian Patriarch. At the Council of Chalkedon the differences between the orthodox State Church and the Monophysites, who do not accept the teaching of the dual nature of Christ, come very much to the fore. Most of the people of Palestine are Monophysites and are at odds with the Byzantine State and its Church.

484   Uprising of Samaritans and Jews, which is suppressed by the Byzantine State.

526–565   Under the Byzantine Emperor *Justinian* there is renewed conflict with rebellious Samaritans and Jews. Justinian initiates settlements in the Negev and cultivation of the desert areas using Nabataean irrigation techniques.

614   The Persians, the second largest power in the eastern Mediterranean after Byzantium, led by *Chosroes II* conquer Palestine. The Patriarch *Zacharius* and 37,000 other Christians are deported to Persia (together with the Holy Cross from the Church of the Holy Sepulchre). Jerusalem is ruled by the Jews, who offer the remaining Christians (some 4,500) the choice of renouncing their faith or death.

628   Emperor *Heracleus* (601–640) defeats the Persians, releases the captives and has the Holy Cross returned to the Church of the Holy Sepulchre.

634   Two years after the death of the Prophet Mohammed (571–632) the Byzantine governor falls in the battle against the advancing **Arabs**.

639 At Yarmouk the Byzantine army is defeated by the Arabs.

...th Rule (666 1099). The Arab Caliphs conquer Jerusalem and govern Palestine first from Ramla, later from Damascus and finally from Baghdad. Most of the Caliphs tolerate non-believers such as Jews and Christians. In the 11th c. the Seljuks, from Turkey, seek to invade Palestine. Their brutality towards Christian pilgrims brings about the *Crusades*.

638 Patriarch *Sophronius* surrenders Jerusalem to the Caliph *Omar*.

About 640 The administrative headquarters of the Arabs is Emmaus (Latrun), then the newly founded Ramla. Jews and Christians, as "People of the Book", are tolerated, having only to pay a poll tax.

661–750 Ruled from Damascus by the Omayyad Caliphs, the country undergoes a considerable revival (apart from the Negev towns which partly fall into decay).

About 700 Caliph *Abd el Malik* builds the Dome of the Rock on the site of the Temple. Because of the Dome of the Rock and the El-Aqsa Mosque Jerusalem is considered the most important city after Mecca and Medina for Mohammedan believers (the rocks of Temple Mount are revered as the place from which Mohammed ascended into heaven on his horse, Burak).

750 The Abbasides supersede the Ommayyads and make their seat in Baghdad.

807 Caliph *Haroun al-Raschid* recognises **Charlemagne** as the Lord Protector of the holy places.

878 The Turkish mercenary leader *Ahmed ibn Tulin* becomes the most powerful man in Palestine; even after his death Turkish mercenaries oppress the local people.

About 977 The Fatimids, Arab Caliphs who had conquered Egypt in 696, rule in Palestine.

1004 *Al-Hakim*, the new Caliph, who the Druse make supreme head of their religion, persecutes those living in Palestine who are not Moslems.

1009 Destruction of the Church of the Holy Sepulchre.

1021 End of Al-Hakim's rule.

1055 The Turkish Seljuks conquer Baghdad; they also threaten to advance on the Near East.

From 1078 The Seljuks attack Christian pilgrims from byzantium and Europe. – Their acts of brutality lead to the launching of the Crusades.

Palestine at the time of the Crusades (1099–1291). – In the 11th c., at the behest of Pope Urban II, Catholic *Christians* from Europe take part in a number of Crusades to *Palestine* to protect the Holy Places from "the infidel". Jerusalem becomes the center of a Crusader state which lasts until 1291.

1095 At the Council of Clermont Pope *Urban II* urges Christians to take up arms against Islam because "Dieu le vult" (God wishes it). There is an overwhelming response.

1096 Start of the *First Crusade*, composed mainly of French knights and south Italian Normans. – The Crusaders travel through the Byzantine Empire to reach the Mediterranean near Tripoli (now in Lebanon). They are defeated by the Turks at Nicaea.

1099 After 39 days of siege, the Crusaders take Jerusalem on July 15; they slaughter the Moslems and Jews of the city. – **Godfrey of Bouillon**, who

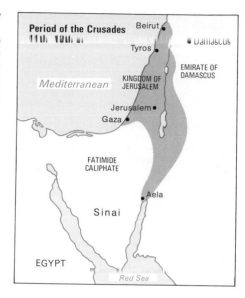

Period of the Crusades 11th-13th c.

had played a decisive part in the storming of Jerusalem, assumes the title of "Advocatus sancti sepulchri" (Guardian of the Holy Sepulchre).

1100 Death of Godfrey of Bouillon. His brother has himself crowned *Baldwin I*, King of Jerusalem. The *Christian Kingdom of Jerusalem* is constituted along French lines as a feudal state. – Baldwin I conquers the coastal towns from Askalon to Acre, West Jordan and, east of the Jordan, the area from Kerak to Aila (Eilat).

1119 *Founding of the Order of the Knights Templar* by *Hugo von Payen* to protect pilgrims to Jerusalem. The Grand Master has his headquarters in Jerusalem. The Templars wear a white cloak with a red Maltese cross.

1131–43 *Fulco*, Count of Anjou, as King of Jerusalem has many forts built to secure the country. – Central power is restricted, however, through the feudal system and the existence of many principalities (Tripoli, Edessa, Antioch and Galilee).

1147–49 *Second Crusade*, led by Louis VII of France and Emperor Conrad II (skirmishes with the Turks; quarrelling among the European participants).

1162–74 King *Alamrik I* tries to conquer Egypt.

1187 *Saladin*, the Seljuk Sultan of Egypt, defeats the Crusaders at the Horns of Hittim W of the Sea of Galilee and three months later occupies Jerusalem.

1189–92 *Third Crusade*, led by Barbarossa, the Holy Roman Emperor Frederick I.

1191 *Richard I* (Richard the Lion-Heart) and Philip Augustus of France assail Palestine by sea and recapture Acre, which becomes the capital of the Crusader States.

1202–04 *Fourth Crusade*.

1228–29 *Fifth Crusade* under Emperor Frederick II, who negotiates a treaty with the Sultan of Egypt giving him Jerusalem, where he crowns himself King, together with Bethlehem, Nazareth and a corridor from Jerusalem to the Mediterranean.

1240 The English Crusade led by Richard of Cornwall.

1244 Jerusalem is conquered on behalf of the Sultan of Egypt.

1248–54 *Sixth Crusade.*

1261–72 Sultan *Baybars*, a Mameluke, conquers virtually all the remaining Crusader States.

1270 *Seventh Crusade*, led by Louis IX of France and Edward I of England, succeeds in achieving only a ten-year truce.

1291 Sultan *El Aschraf Chalil* occupies Acre. – *Dissolution of the Crusader States.*

The Rule of the Mamelukes (1291–1517). – The Mamelukes, freed slaves of Turkish or Circassian origin, come to power in Egypt in 1250 and extend their rule to other territories. The Egyptian "dynasty" of the Mamelukes can be divided up into the *Bahrites* (1252–1390) and the *Burdchites* (1382–1517). The era of the Mamelukes, who rule Palestine after the dissolution of the Crusader States, is marked by internal unrest and sees the building of roads, bridges, caravanserais and mosques.

1492 Jews driven out of Spain come to Palestine.

Palestine in the Ottoman Empire (1517–1917). – With the capture of Jerusalem by Sultan Selim I, Palestine becomes part of the Ottoman Empire. After the death of Suleiman II, decline of the Ottoman Empire; and the European great powers wield increasing influence in the Eastern Mediterranean. With the end of the First World War, Palestine becomes a British Mandate. At the turn of the century the Zionist movement gains in importance.

1516 The Ottoman Sultan *Selim I* defeats the Mamelukes at Aleppo.

1517 Selim I captures Jerusalem and goes on to conquer Egypt.

1520–66 Under Selim's son, *Suleiman II* (the Magnificent), Palestine experiences a period of growth and internal consolidation. The Jerusalem Wall is gradually rebuilt, the Dome of the Rock is clad with faience and the water supply improved. In Safed begins the era of the famous Cabbalists (Cabbala is a medieval Jewish mystical tradition based on an esoteric interpretation of the Old Testament). With the death of Suleiman the Ottoman Empire starts to decline.

About 1660 The Druse Emir *Fakhr-al-Din* rebuilds Acre which had been destroyed in 1291.

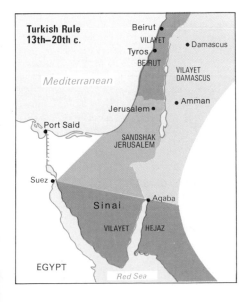

Turkish Rule
13th–20th c.

Mediterranean

Beirut
VILAYET
Tyros
BEIRUT
VILAYET
DAMASCUS
• Damascus

Jerusalem •
• Amman

Port Said

SANDSHAK
JERUSALEM

Suez •

Aqaba

Sinai

VILAYET   HEJAZ

EGYPT

Red Sea

1730–70 *Daher el-Omar* rules all of Galilee from Acre.

1775–1804 *Ahmed el-Jazzar* ("the Butcher") defeats Daher el-Omar and makes Acre his seat.

1805 *Mohammed (Mehmed) Ali*, an Albanian officer from Macedonia, declares himself Pasha of Egypt in the place of the expelled Turkish governor.

1833 *Ibrahim Pasha*, the son (or possibly adopted son) of Mohammed Ali rules Palestine and Syria after a successful military campaign.

1840 Under pressure from a quadruple alliance (Great Britain, Russia, Prussia and Austria) Ibrahim Pasha surrenders the administration of these countries. Turkey resumes power with the help of the Europeans. France sees itself as the protector of the Catholics in Palestine, while Russia views itself as protector of the Orthodox Church.

1841 Great Britain and Prussia, as patrons of the Protestants, jointly found a *Bishopric of Jerusalem*.

1848 An Ashkenazi community (i.e. of Jews from central and eastern Europe) comes into being in Jerusalem.

1878 At Petah Tekva, east of Jaffa, Jews from Jerusalem found the first Jewish agricultural settlement.

1882 First great *wave of Jewish immigrants* (First Aliyah), mostly from Russia and Poland, supported by Baron *Edmond de Rothschild*. Egypt is occupied by the British.

1896 **Theodor Herzl** publishes his book "The Jewish State" with, as its theme, the creation of a Jewish State in Palestine (Zionism).

1897 *First Zionist Congress* in Basle; it declares that "the aim of Zionism is to create for the Jewish people a home in Palestine secured by public law".

1904–14 *Second wave of Jewish immigrants* (Second Aliyah). – In 1914 there are 600,000 Arabs living in Palestine compared with 100,000 Jews.

1909 Founding of Tel Aviv as a purely Jewish city.

About 1910 Emergence of the first Kibbutzim (voluntary collective settlements).

1914 The murder of the Austrian heir to the throne in Sarajevo (June 28) precipitates the **First World War**. On November 1 Turkey allies itself with the Central Powers (Germany, Austria and Hungary). – Declaration of the British Protectorate of Egypt on December 18.

1915 The British High Commissioner in Egypt assures Hussein of Mecca that an Arab Kingdom will be established in the event of a victory over the Turks.

1916 The Sykes-Pico Agreement (May 16) sets out the "spheres of influence and territorial acquisitions" of the Allies (Britain and France) in Turkey, implying a division of the territory in question with Palestine subject to an international administration.

1917 In his letter to Baron *Rothschild* (November 2) the British Foreign Minister, Arthur Balfour, states his Government's decision to establish "a national home for the Jewish people" in Palestine, provided that this does not detract from the rights of the non-Jewish communities (Balfour Declaration).

1917/18 *Palestine* is captured by the British and comes under *British military administration*.

1918 End of the First World War; the Ottoman Empire capitulates in the ceasefire agreement of October 30, 1918.

The Austrian-Jewish writer and politician **Theodor Herzl** (born May 2, 1860 in Budapest, died July 2, 1904 in Edlach, Austria) is considered the founder of ZIONISM.

After studying law in Vienna (1878–84) and a stay in Paris (1891–95), he published his manifesto "The Jewish State" in Vienna in 1896, organised the first Zionist Congress in Basle in 1897 and tried to get the Turkish Sultan and the European powers to establish a Jewish State in Palestine (as envisioned in his book "Old-New Land", published 1902). Herzl's tomb was moved from Vienna to Jerusalem in 1949.

The tomb of Theodor Herzl on Mount Herzl in Jerusalem

Palestine under British Mandate (1920–48). – After the First World War Palestine becomes a British Mandate Territory. Tension builds up between Arabs and Jews, especially as *Jewish immigration* is stepped up after 1933. In 1947 the UN General Assembly approves the partition of Palestine into two States, which is rejected by Arabs. The British Mandate expires a year later.

1920 In the *Treaty of San Remo* Great Britain receives the League of Nations *Mandate over Palestine* (April 25). – Growing tension between Jews and Arabs leads to violent clashes. – Founding of the "Haganah", a military organisation for the protection of Jewish settlements (incorporated into the Israel army when the State of Israel is established in 1948).

1922 Emergence of the Jewish Agency for Palestine, which acts on behalf of the Jews in their dealings with the British.

1933 Beginning of a substantial *surge of Jewish immigration* sparked off by the persecution of Jews in Germany by the Third Reich.

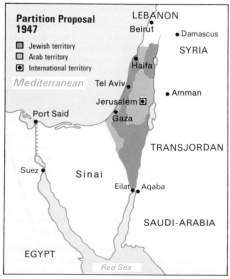

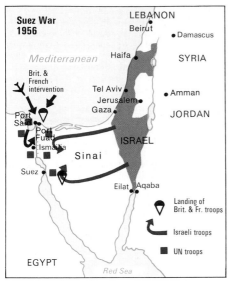

1936   An Arab uprising against the sudden increase in the Jewish population is put down by British troops.

1937   The Peel Report recommends that Palestine be partitioned between Jews and Arabs but the Arabs still demand independent status for Palestine under the prevailing Arab majority.

1939   White paper issued by the British Government agrees to the limitation of Jewish immigration into Palestine.

1945   At the end of the *Second World War* there are 600,000 Jews living in Palestine. – U.S.A. speaks out in favour of Jewish immigration.

1947   The General Assembly of the United Nations adopts the plan for the **division of Palestine** into a Jewish State (in the areas of Palestine predominantly settled by Jews) and an Arab State (with the areas of mostly Arab settlement accruing to the Kingdom of Jordan); Jerusalem is to be under international administration. The Arabs reject this solution.

1948   The British Mandate over Palestine expires (May 15)

The State of Israel (1948 to the present day). – After the *proclamation of the State of Israel* in May 1948 there are four wars in the following 25 years between Israel and its Arab neighbours. In the Six Day War of 1967 Israel occupies large areas of neighbouring Arab States, the Palestinians step up their activities. The Yom Kippur War (1973) ends in a ceasefire through the mediation of the United Nations. Many years of Peace Conferences on the Middle East plus intervention by the U.S.A. finally lead, in 1979, to a Peace Treaty between Egypt and Israel. In 1980 the proclamation of Jerusalem as the capital of Israel calls forth vigorous protests. In the middle of 1982 Israeli troops enter Lebanon to crush the power of the Palestinians on their country's northern border.

1948   On May 14, one day before the end of the British Mandate, *David Ben Gurion* proclaims the sovereign **STATE OF ISRAEL** (Medinat Yisrael). – Jordan, Egypt, Iraq, Syria and Lebanon immediately declare **war** to prevent the State of Israel coming into existence. East Jerusalem and the Arab areas in West Jordan fall to the Hashemite Kingdom of Jordan.

January 15, 1949   *Ceasefire Agreement* between Israel and Egypt, Lebanon, Jordan and Syria. Jordan

retains the territory it has conquered, the Gaza Strip remains under Egyptian control. Almost all of Galilee goes to Israel as well as West Jerusalem. The borders of the young State of Israel are drawn along the battle lines at the time of the 1949 ceasefire but are not recognised by the Arabs. – Many Arabs had left the country at the start of the fighting.

February 4, 1949   The *Knesset* (parliament; elected by a system of equal, direct and secret proportional representation) meets for the first time. – The country's largest party is the social-democratic Mapai; *Chaim Weizmann* becomes Israel's first President.

May 11, 1949   Israel becomes a member of the United Nations.

June 26, 1956   President Nasser of Egypt nationalises the Suez Canal which leads to military action by France and Great Britain.

October 29, 1956   **Suez War:** Israel attacks Egypt and occupies the Gaza Strip and Sinai Peninsula.

March 1957   Ending of the war through the United Nations. Israel withdraws from the occupied territories in exchange for guaranteed freedom for its shipping in the Gulf of Aqaba.

1958   The parliamentary republic of Israel which as yet has no written Constitution passes its *first basic (constitutional) law*. (The supreme authority of the State is vested in the Knesset, to which the Government is responsible.)
In the years that follow the Arab States come under increasing pressure from the Palestinians, i.e. the Arabs who had formerly lived in Palestine.

June 5–11, 1967   **Six Day War:** preventive war by Israel on her Egyptian border following mobilisation of troops in Egypt and Syria. Israeli troops, commanded by General *Moshe Dayan*, occupy the Gaza Strip, the Sinai Peninsula, up to the Suez Canal, the Golan Heights, West Jordan and East Jerusalem.

1967   A UN Resolution empowers the Arabs to make recognition of Israel's Statehood dependent upon her withdrawal from the occupied territories and recognition of the rights of the **Palestinians.**

1968   The Palestinians launch commando raids from Syria, Jordan and the Lebanon against Israel, which counters with military action.

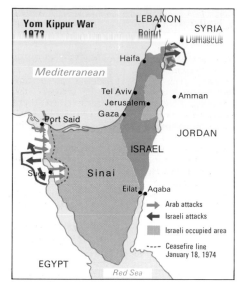

1977   Following the elections on May 17, when the right wing Likud block wins a majority, *Menachem Begin becomes Prime Minister. He represents the* concept of Israel as an expansionist State. Moshe Dayan takes over as Foreign Minister (until 1979). – In November the Egyptian President, *Anwar Sadat*, visits Jerusalem and delivers a highly regarded speech in the Knesset (peace initiative).

1978   After protracted talks on a solution for the Middle East Conflict at Camp David, Maryland, between Begin, Sadat and Carter, the U.S. President, they sign a draft agreement for peace in the Middle East and a draft agreement for the conclusion of a Peace Treaty between Egypt and Israel. Sadat and Begin receive the Nobel Peace Prize.

1979   On March 26 a **Peace Treaty between Israel and Egypt** is signed in Washington. Its terms are that Israel will leave the Sinai Military Withdrawal Zones A and B by the end of 1979 amd withdraw from Zone C by April 1982. The Treaty is boycotted by most Arab States and by the Palestinians.

January 25, 1980   The Israeli Army withdraws from the Sinai as far as El-Arish-Kap Ras Mohammed.

February 26, 1980   Israel and Egypt exchange ambassadors.

May 25, 1980   Minister of Defence *Ezer Weizman* resigns because of fundamental differences of opinion with Prime Minister Begin.

May 26, 1980   The time limit set in the 1978 draft agreement for the solving of the question of Palestinian autonomy elapses without agreement having been reached.

July 30, 1980   Jerusalem – including the old Arab quarter – is declared *"Capital of Israel for all time"* by the Knesset. The Arabs, and other countries, too, frown upon this move since it makes a solution of the Middle East conflict more difficult.

August 18, 1980   At its session in Casablanca the "Jerusalem Committee" calls on the Islamic world to boycott, economically and politically, all countries sanctioning Israel's annexation of Jerusalem.

August 24, 1980   The building of a canal from the Mediterranean to the Dead Sea (prevention of water loss from the inland sea; construction of a hydro-electric power station) is agreed by the Israeli Government; this meets with protest from the Arab countries since the canal will cross the Gaza Strip.

December 22, 1980   The Israeli Government re-futes the allegation that it wishes formally to annex the occupied Golan Heights.

1970   The U.S. Secretary of State for Foreign Affairs, William Pierce Rogers, puts forward the "Rogers Plan" to solve the Middle East conflict, in which he calls for a limited ceasefire along the Israeli-Arab demarcation lines as a first step towards negotiations.

October 6, 1973   **Yom Kippur War:** On the Jewish Day of Atonement, Yom Kippur, Egypt and Syria attack Israel. The Egyptian troops penetrate deep into the Sinai Peninsula, while the Syrians concentrate on the Israeli positions along the Golan Heights.

October 22–26, 1973   After heavy fighting and severe losses on both sides the great powers intervene; with the help of the United Nations it is possible to achieve a *ceasefire*.

December 21–22, 1973   Beginning of the first round of the *Middle East Peace Talks* in Geneva, between Egypt, Israel and Jordan. U.S. Secretary of State for Foreign Affairs, *Henry Kissinger*, considers an agreed military withdrawal to be a precondition for the negotiations.

January 18, 1974   *Signature of Agreement on Egyptian-Israeli Military Withdrawal.*

January 24, 1974   Agreement comes into force. Israel withdraws from the West Bank of the Suez Canal (UN troops subsequently occupy the buffer zone and there is an exchange of prisoners).

May 29, 1974   *Agreement on Syrian-Israeli Military Withdrawal.*

May 31, 1974   Signing of the Syrian-Israeli Agreement in Geneva. Return of the territories occupied in the Yom Kippur War as well as Kuneitra and Rafid; exchange of prisoners. UN troops police the neutral buffer zone.

1975   Following the breakdown of Kissinger's fresh mediation talks with Egypt and Israel in March, the *second military withdrawal Agreement* between them is reached in September; Israel withdraws from the Sinai Passes of Gidi and Mitla and the Abu Rodeis oilfields. Both States express the wish to settle their disputes peaceably. Egypt guarantees Israel freedom of passage for non-military goods to and from Israel through the Suez Canal.

1981   Resignation of the Finance Minister, *Yigael Hurwitz*, because of mounting economic difficulties (very high rate of inflation). Begin calls for an early election. Murder of Abu Rabia, the member of the Knesset for the Bedouin. Egyptian Parliamentarians visit Israel. The Islam World Conference (ICO), in the "Mecca Declaration", calls for a Holy War to free Jerusalem and an economic boycott of Israel (January).
The United Nations Commission on Human Rights condemns the Israeli annexation of East Jerusalem (February). – President Begin meets the U.S. Secretary of State for Foreign Affairs, *Alexander Haig*, who is seeking to reduce Soviet influence in the Middle East. At the elections to the Israeli Trade Union Association (Histadrut) the Workers' Party and allied groups win 64% of the votes. – Israel makes air strikes on Palestinian positions in South Lebanon, where Syrian rockets are stationed. *Philip Habib*, the

U.S. Special Envoy, tries to mediate between the Middle Eastern States (April/May).

Early in May Begin attacks the West German Chancellor, Helmuth Schmidt, accusing him of antisemitism during the Second World War, thus clouding the relationship between the two countries. In the Sinai Peninsula Begin meets with Sadat who urges Israel to hold back over the crisis in the Lebanon. Israeli Airforce destroys an Iraqi atomic reactor; the U.S.A. votes in favour of the condemnation of Israel in the UN.

Parliamentary elections (June): the Likud block, under Prime Minister Begin, win by a narrow margin. Further Israeli air strikes on Palestinian positions in Lebanon heighten the danger of war. The U.S.A. postpones the delivery of fighter planes to Israel. Habib, the American mediator, persuades Begin to order a ceasefire between Israel and the Palestinians (July).

Formation of a Coalition Government with Begin as Prime Minister, consisting of the Likud group and members of the three religious parties (General Zionists, Agudah Israel, Tami) and which, with 61 of the 120 seats in the Knesset, has a majority of only one vote. Begin makes considerable concessions to the religious parties. *Ariel Sharon*, the new Defence Minister, is an advocate of a "Great Israel". – Saudi Arabia puts forward a comprehensive eight point peace plan for the Middle East which includes a call for the formation of an independent Palestinian State with the Arab section of Jerusalem as its capital. The Israeli Government rejects the plan.

U.S. President Reagan lifts the ban on delivery of fighter planes to Israel. – At a meeting in Alexandria Begin and Sadat agree to a resumption of talks on autonomy for the areas occupied by Israel. – When archaeologists uncover an ancient tunnel in the neighbourhood of Temple Mount (Mount Moriah) in Jerusalem, there are protests from extreme Orthodox Jews (August).

Building starts on the canal between the Mediterranean and the Dead Sea. – Begin visits the U.S.A. and, during talks with Reagan in Washington on securing peace in the Middle East, agreement is reached on closer cooperation in strategic military matters.

The strained economic situation forces the Israeli Government to make drastic cuts. – In Cairo representatives of Egypt, Israel and the U.S.A. hold talks on the autonomy of the Palestinians in West Jordan and the Gaza Strip.

In September Israel is condemned by the International Atomic Energy Organisation (IAEO) for its bombing of Osirak, the Iraqi Reactor Center, in June. The assassination of President Sadat in Cairo (October 6) comes as a severe blow to the Middle East peace moves and is met with varying reactions in Israel. Begin takes part in Sadat's funeral in Cairo and meets the President Designate Mubarek. – Moshe Dayan dies in Tel Aviv (October 16).

The Knesset approves (December 14) the annexation of the Golan Heights, occupied by Israel since 1967.

1982 Three Arab mayors on the West Bank are removed from office; their place is taken by an Israeli civilian administration that assumes various functions of the military government (March).

The part of the Sinai occupied since 1967 is handed back to Egypt (April 25).

Israeli troops march into Lebanon aiming to destroy the PLO as a political and military power in the Middle East (June 6). – Fighting between Syrian and Israeli forces in the vicinity of Beirut. – The Israeli Government calls for all PLO members to leave the Lebanon (end of June).

In Israel reaction is mixed to the intervention in Lebanon; in early July about 70,000 people demonstrate in Tel Aviv for "Peace with the Palestinians".

The PLO leader, Yasser Arafat, encircled by Israeli troops in West Beirut, signs a declaration which includes acknowledgment of Israel's right to exist (July 24).

Through the mediation of Philip Habib, U.S. Special Envoy to the Middle East, the Palestinian evacuation of Beirut gets under way on August 21.

After Israeli troops have marched to West Beirut, on September 16–18 many civilians are massacred in the Palestinian camps of Sabra and Chatila; the outcry against the massacres is worldwide.

In Tel Aviv 400,000 demonstrators demand an explanation for the massacres and call on Prime Minister Begin and Defence Minister Sharon to resign (September 24).

1983 Israel's domestic political situation is dominated by economic recession and a high inflation rate.

Resignation of Defence Minister Sharon (February 2); *Moshe Arens* replaces him on February 13.

Reagan calls on Begin to vacate the Golan Heights. On May 17 Israel and Lebanon sign an agreement to end the state of war.

Prime Minister Begin resigns from office (September 9). *Yitzhak Shamir* becomes Israel's Prime Minister (October 10). – The devaluation of the shekel by 23% is followed shortly afterwards by the resignation of Finance Minister Aridor. *Yigal Cohen-Orgad* is subsequently appointed in his place.

1984 At the end of January Helmut Kohl, the German Chancellor, meets Prime Minister Shamir during his State Visit to Israel; subjects discussed include economic relations between the two countries and Federal Germany's planned arms shipments to Saudi Arabia.

During a demonstration in Jerusalem about 50,000 Israelis call for the withdrawal of Israeli forces from Lebanon and for a policy of Jewish settlement in the occupied territories (early February) – A few days later the Israeli Government announces that it wishes to prevent future encroachment of Jewish settlers in the occupied territories. – The Israeli Cabinet discusses partial withdrawal of Israeli troops from Lebanon.

Prime Minister Shamir holds talks with European Community representatives in Brussels on the consequences for Israel's agriculture of Spain and Portugal's entry into the EC.

Lebanon revokes the troop withdrawal agreement reached with Israel in May 1983 (March 5).

Art

Prehistory and Canaanite period. –
The earliest structures, the beginnings of
settled culture, are in Jericho, where in the
8th millennium there were already circular
dwellings and a round tower 28 ft/8·5 m
high, with an internal flight of stairs,
adjoining what may have been a city wall
that was 14 ft/4 m high and 10 ft/3 m wide
at the base. Dwellings were built here in
the 7th millennium on a rectangular
ground plan. These contained skulls
modelled in human likenesses as an early
form of portraiture. After a considerable
interim, during which Jericho and other
settlements were abandoned, this area
was resettled by nomads in the 5th
millennium. In the Negev near Beersheba
semi-nomads lived in oval caves with roof
entrances (Beersheba culture).

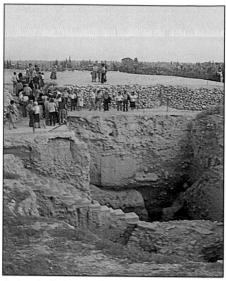
Archaeological excavation in Jericho

A Canaanite settlement with a shrine
existed in the neighbourhood of Megiddo
on the Jezreel Plain in the 4th millennium.
There were other Canaanite towns further
S at Gezer (ruins at Tel Gezer) and Arad. –
In the N of the country in the 2nd
millennium the Canaanites founded a
sizeable township at Hazor and built Bet
Shean with its impressive temples.

The Canaanites were a settled people.
They had a polytheistic religion and built
temples for their gods, of which there
were over 30, with Baal at their head.
There was, therefore, a deep religious
divide between the original populations of
Canaan and the incoming tribes of the
Israelites pushing into their lands, who
knew only one god, Jahveh (Jehovah).
Jahveh dwelt in the portable tent which

housed the Ark of the Covenant. – The
remains of the Canaanite temples which
have been excavated at Lachish indicate
the existence of a principal chamber
narrowing towards an altar at one end.

**The age of the Judges and the
Israelite Kings.** – When the Hebrews
settled in Canaan in the 13th c. B.C. they
had no architecture or pictorial art form of
their own. In the 2nd Book of Moses there
is a report of skilled craftsmanship – its
37th Chapter contains a description of the
making of the Ark of the Covenant and its
golden ornament. The Biblical ban on
graven images (2 Moses 20, 4; 5 Moses 5,
8) served, in accordance with the Mishna,
to restrict the worship of idols. "The
entrenched dogma of the Israelites and
the incessant strife with neighbouring

Arad: view of the Canaanite town from the citadel

peoples and foreign rulers militated against the development of art" (Carel J. du Rhy). The religious component in the intellectual life of the people led to a fixation on scripts (Old Testament and later theological books).

Solomon and his heirs were responsible for much building, including, as frequently mentioned in the Bible, the rebuilding and fortification of the town of Megiddo by King Solomon. The most important building of this time was the Temple in Jerusalem (953 B.C.) in which the Ark of the Covenant was henceforth to be preserved. For the building of this first temple Solomon imported Phoenician craftsmen from Tyre. After the division of the kingdom on the death of Solomon, several towns followed one another as the capital of the northern kingdom of Israel. In 878 King Omri established Samaria as the future capital and built the city on a hill. The site of the palace and the administrative buildings was surrounded by a wall. Excavations of the remaining sections of this ashlar masonry wall were the first to establish the influence of Phoenician stone-masons in Palestine. Carved ivory which may have been used to decorate furniture was also discovered in Samaria.

A Nabataean government building at Mamshit

Hellenistic Period. – After Alexander the Great had brought Judea under his control at the end of the 4th c., the 3rd c. saw Greek cultural elements making their appearance in the country. Theaters, hippodromes, temples and aqueducts were built on lines familiar throughout the classical world but partly displaying the influence of local building methods. Thus in Bet Shean one finds large marble columns that belonged to a Greek temple of the 3rd c. The most impressive remains at Bet Shean, however, are the ruins of the Roman theater, which are the most extensive and best preserved in Israel.

Nabataean house in Avdat

The period before Palestine became part of the Roman Empire was the heyday of the Kingdom of Nabataea which stretched from Petra to the Negev. The Nabataeans, who were gifted architects and craftsmen, built towns such as Avdat, Shivta and Mamshit along their trade routes.

Roman Period. – The start of the Roman rule in the 1st c. B.C. saw Palestine increasingly influenced by the late classical style of architecture. Herod the Great covered the land with monumental structures (Hebron, Herodian, Massada, Caesarea, Samaria-Sebastia, Ashqelon). In Jerusalem he was responsible for the Antonia Fortress and the rebuilding of the Temple. The law proscribing graven images continued to exist so the images of animals in the palace of Herodes Antipas at Tiberias were condemned as unlawful and removed at the earliest possible opportunity.

After the destruction of the Temple, worship formed the bond that united all Jews. Many synagogues – meeting places for the community to hold services – were built. These are mostly rectangular, with an apse or a niche facing E and divided off by a curtain, behind which was kept the Ark of the Torah containing the scrolls of the law. The scrolls of the Torah were rolled on staves ending in crowns or finials (Rimonim). – The oldest synagogue is believed to be the one at Capernaum dating from the 2nd or 3rd c. The synagogue of Chorazin, of which the ruins are still standing, was built of black basalt about the same period. Both structures have three naves. the remains of an old synagogue can also be found at Gush-Halav.

The 3rd c. saw completion by the Jews of the move away from the basically aniconic standpoint. Galilean synagogues had

Caesarea – Herodian Aqueduct

depictions of angels, people and animals, including even the Greek God Helios in the center of the Zodiac; the 3rd c. synagogue at Dura Europos on the Euphrates (now Es-Salahije in Syria) is completely decorated with Biblical paintings.

Tombs were also subject to Graeco-Roman or even Palmyran influences. Sarcophagi with mythological representations were permitted, as is evident from examples at Bet Shearim.

Early Christian/Byzantine Period. – The Christian influence began to show in the 4th c. After Constantine the Great had built the Church of the Nativity in Bethlehem and the Church of the Holy Sepulchre in Jerusalem, a host of churches and monasteries sprang up. This movement reached its peak in the 6th c. under Justinian with the building of more churches, etc., as well as extensive urban development in the Negev, where this was tied in with the settlement and irrigation techniques of the Nabataeans.

At Tabgha, where the "feeding of the five thousand" is said to have taken place, a 5th c. basilica with three naves was erected on the foundations of an older church. Its floor mosaics still depict, among other things, a basket with loaves and fishes. Floor mosaics of Christian churches (5th/6th c.) have also been uncovered in Bet Guvrin with representations of animals and the seasons.

Jewish synagogues of this period were also decorated with mosaics. Floor mosaics from a synagogue (5th/6th c.) have been found in Jericho and in 1928 the floor mosaics from a 6th c. synagogue were uncovered at Bet Alfa.

Arabic Period. – From the 7th to the 11th c. Arabic-Islamic culture left its mark on the country; the Omayyad Caliphs put in hand the building of mosques, palaces and fortresses. – The ban on images,

North wall of the Synagogue at Capernaum

Early Christian mosaics at Shave Zion

Buttressed wall – Crusader fort in Caesarea

which Islam shares with Judaism, still held good in the Omayyad era until the middle of the 8th c. Besides the Dome of the Rock and the El-Aqsa mosque in Jerusalem and the Hisham Palace, the winter residence for the Omayyad Caliphs in Jericho, caravanserais (Kahns) were also being built.

Age of the Crusades. – During the Crusades (12th/13th c.) the Crusaders, many of them French knights, erected fortresses in the Holy Land and there are Crusader castles at such places as Acre, Atlit, Belvoir, Caesarea and Montfort. They also built churches, particularly in Jerusalem (Church of St Anne, Church of the Dormition, Church of the Holy Sepulchre). The Crusader church at Abu Gosh is one of the best preserved in the country and one can still see traces of painted frescoes on the walls of its triple-naved basilica. – The buildings of the Crusader era combine elements of the styles of the W with those which the Knights found in the E. The architecture of the churches and castles represents a transition from the solid structures of the 12th c. to the more delicate Gothic of the 13th c.

Ottoman Period. – A host of monuments remain from the period of Turkish rule (1517–1917), such as the mosque

built in Acre in 1781 and the Mahmoudiya Mosque in Jaffa. – During the Ottoman era the Christian influence began to revive, so that many churches went up alongside the Islamic buildings, including in 1898, the Protestant Church of the Redeemer in Jerusalem.

After the 16th c. elaborate furnishings were being produced for the synagogues in metal (Torah finials and candlesticks),

Chapel of the Ascension on the Mount of Olives

Window from the Omayyad Palace in Jericho

Details of the Dome of the Rock in Jerusalem

Protestant Church of the Redeemer in Jerusalem

Israel (opened in 1965), as well as the Bezalel Museum (Jewish folk-art, religious objects and archaeological finds), the Bronfmann Biblical and Archaeological Museum, the Billy Rose Art Garden (sculpture) and the "Shrine of the Book", which houses the world-famous Dead Sea Scrolls from Qumran. The roof of the Shrine is shaped like the lid of one of the jars in which the Scrolls were found. There is also a considerable amount of modern architecture in Tel Aviv, such as the Shalom Tower (430 ft/130 m).

The 20th c. has also seen new religious buildings. The new Church of the Annunciation in Nazareth was finished in 1969 and is one of the greatest holy places for the Christian world in the Middle East.

PAINTING and SCULPTURE also show the influence of modern western movements. The Israeli landscape, whether a hill with trees or the desert, whether figurative or abstract, is the theme of painters such as *Anna Ticho* (1894–1980), *Raffi Kaiser* (b. 1931) and *Tamara Rikman* (b. 1934). From purely representational pictures of the landscape, artists moved on, in their different ways, to projects based on one particular area. Thus in October 1970 several artists carried out the "Jerusalem River Project" whereby, in a valley in the dry hills around Jerusalem, using a recording of the sound of falling water relayed through loudspeakers they sought to re-create the feeling of a river in full spate. – The works of other artists show a preoccupation with the problems of city life; a picture by *Yossef Asher* (b. 1946), for instance, shows the monotony of a block of apartments ("Apartment Building", 1971).

ceramics (Purim plates), fabrics (Torah curtains) and wood (Torah caskets).

British Mandate. – During the British Mandate (1920–48) the Church of the Beatitudes was built in 1937 on the site of the Sermon on the Mount. The floor covering around the altar depicts the seven virtues.

From 1948 to the present. – Following the foundation of the State of Israel in 1948, the modern ARCHITECTURE alongside the historical monuments reflects European and American styles. New secular buildings went up, particularly in the cities. These included the Knesset (dedicated in 1966), the Israeli Parliament building in Jerusalem, and the Museum of

Jerusalem – the Shrine of the Book and the Knesset

In the seventies abstract painting came increasingly to the fore. A leading figure in this respect is *Moshe Kupferman* (b. 1926), whose works have great strength of expression. *Alima* (b. Haifa) uses geometric abstraction, while contrasting fields of colour dominate the compositions of *Reuven Berman* (b. 1929).

Wood and metal are the materials used for sculptures reminiscent of Naum Gabo (*Nahum Tevet*, b. 1946) or grouped sculpture that is interrelated, thus projecting a strong spatial effect (*Michael Gitlin*, b. 1943).

The seventies also saw the arrival of large-scale works which were frequently located in squares or in front of public buildings. The creators of these mostly abstract sculptures include *Yehiel Shemi* (b. 1922), *Israel Hadani* (b. 1941), *Michael Gross* (b. 1920), *Yigael Tumarkin* (b. 1933) and *Ezra Orion* (b. 1934), whose 60 ft/18 m high stepped sculpture "Ma'alot" (1979–80) stands in a street in Jerusalem. On Mount Scopus the steel

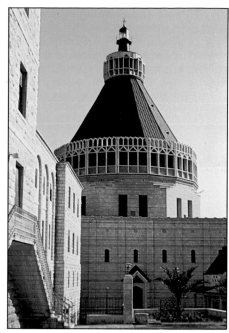

Catholic Church of the Annunciation in Nazareth

sculpture "Ma'agalim" by the well-known Israeli artist *Menashe Kadishman*

Archaeology

Israel has a very large number of ancient monuments spanning the history of many centuries, even though a vast number have been destroyed with the passage of years. Many buildings remained intact, while others were uncovered by archaeologists in the 19th and 20th c.

After earlier scientific research by *U. Seetzen* and *C. Burckhardt*, *E. Robinson*, an American, began in 1824/5 to explore the topography of Palestine. The first accurate cartographic study of the country between Dan and Beersheba was undertaken in 1871–77 by the British Palestine Exploration Society led by *Condor* and *Kitchener*. Digs in Jerusalem were carried out by *F. de Saulcy* (1864), *Ch. Warren* (1867–70) and *H. Guthe* (1882), as well as *F. Bliss* and *R. S. A. Macalister* (1891–94) who in 1899–1900 were also active on the Sebulon Plain; Macalister then went on to further excavation in Gezer from 1902 to 1909.

Early in the 20th c., when Palestine was still under Ottoman rule, *E. Sellin* worked at Taanach (1902–04), Jericho (1907–08) and Sichem (1913–14). The synagogues in Galilee were investigated by *H. Kohl* and *C. Watzinger* (1905). Mention should also be made of the excavations by *G. A. Reisner* and *C. S. Fisher* in Samaria and by *G. Weill* in Jerusalem (1914, 1923–24).

During the British Mandate, excavation was largely carried out by British and American archaeologists: *G. M. Fitzgerald* and *A. Rower* in

Bet Shean (1921–23), *P. L. O. Guy* and *G. Loud* in Megiddo (1925–29) and *J. W. Crowfoot* in Jerusalem and Samaria (1923–27 and 1931–35). *Flinders Petrie* who, in 1891, during his work at Tell el-Hesi in the S of the country, had developed a method of dating the history of settlements from ceramic finds, worked in several parts of the SW between 1926 and 1936. According to Avi Yonah, *W. F. Albright* carried out a "model excavation" in southern Judea (Tel Beit Mirsim, 1926–32), which established the strata for almost the entire Bronze and Iron Age period.

Exploratory work was suspended during the Second World War and the immediate post-war period. *Kathleen M. Kenyon* made momentous discoveries in Jericho (1955–58) and in Jerusalem (1961–67). *L. Harding* and *de Vaux* studied the Essene settlement at Qumran between 1951 and 1958. In Bet Shearim *N. Avigad* (1953–59) continued the work of *B. Mazar* (1936–40). Hazor (1955–58, 1968–69) and Massada (1963–65) were the sites chosen for his work by *Yigael Yadin*. Since 1967 B. Mazar and N. Avigad have been excavating in Jerusalem, working mainly on the exterior of the Temple site. New exploration is currently under way on the hill site at Acre, in Ashdod, Ramat Rahel, Beersheba and Lachish, in the framework of the intensive scientific research planned by the Israel Survey.

All these projects, which in recent decades have been particularly enlightening, thanks to the refinements of modern methods, have helped to give us in the present an almost complete picture of Israel in the past.

(b. 1932) is in the form of a ring, with one segment displaced and another missing. Israeli painting of the seventies is also marked by its political and social themes: countless pictures express the artist's reaction to current events. Distinguished figures in this prolific movement include *Zvi Goldstein* (b. 1947), *Pinchas Cohen Gan* (b. 1942), *Tamar Getter* (b. 1953) and *Misha Ullmann* (b. 1940). The works of *Moshe Gershuni* (b. 1936) tend to harp on war, sorrow and death, but also contain elements of solace ("Shalom Soldier", 1981).

Economy

Since its foundation in 1948, the economy of the State of Israel has had to contend with many difficult factors: the country was underdeveloped, many of its people had neither training nor possessions, conflicts with Arabs and Palestinians kept its defence costs high and it lacked substantial resources. Despite all this it enjoyed an economic boom. This can be attributed to a rapid increase in the labour force and its productivity, a high influx of capital (including reparations from West Germany and loans from the U.S.A. and the World Bank) and high personal taxation.

Israel has private, State and trade union enterprise. The Histadrut, Israel's largest labour union, is the second biggest owner of businesses in the country after the State. About 63% of the work force are in the services sector, 12% in trade, 6% in agriculture and the remainder are in industry. In 1983 unemployment was barely 5%.

A crucial factor in **agriculture** is that, because of unfavourable climatic conditions, particularly in the S, only 20% of the surface area can be cultivated and much of that is only possible through artificial irrigation. To bring water to the dry areas, the Israelis have laid pipelines which carry water from the Sea of Galilee and the Yarkon (Kinneret–Negev pipeline and Yarkon–Negev pipeline) to the southern coastal plain and the Negev. When

there is occasional rainfall on the edges of the desert, this is channelled from the highlands into lower lying fields which are surrounded by dams allowing controlled flooding. To reduce evaporation, the plants are also partly grown under plastic sheeting. Bananas and citrus fruits grow in the fertile soil of the coastal plain. These plantations, which are very intensively cultivated and largely artificially irrigated, produce high yields. Lemons introduced from California flourish alongside the native Jaffa orange and grapefruit. The coastal plantations cover an area of 193 sq. miles/500 sq. km and provide Israel's most important agricultural products which are exported as canned fruit, particularly to Great Britain and Germany.

The agricultural produce of the uplands, apart from tobacco, goes for domestic consumption. The winter rains allow farmers, mostly Arabs, to grow cereal crops, particularly wheat, in their terraced fields. Grapes, olives, figs, almonds and peaches are also cultivated in the uplands.

The Jordan Valley area has three important agricultural regions: the Hula Plain; the area around the Sea of Galilee; and the valley of the Ha'Arava Wadi. – Cotton, cereals and peanuts grow in the drained marshes of the Hula Plain and there are peach, apple and pear orchards on the valley slopes. Dates and bananas, as well as avocados, vines and citrus fruits, flourish in the good soil around the Sea of Galilee. In the Ha'Arava Wadi tomatoes and vegetables are grown as well as flowers in the winter.

There is cereal cultivation in the Negev on the border of the agronomic dry zone which, with artificial irrigation, can also produce fruit. As in the southern Jordan Valley, fields here are protected from the wind by planting hedges of tamarisk, eucalyptus and acacia. For some time now, sisal, for making ropes, etc., has been a crop in this area.

Farm on the Nabataean model near Avdat

The Jezreel Plain, S of Haifa, with cotton, cereals and sugar-beet, is one of Israel's most highly productive agricultural areas. There is forestry on the chalky slopes.

The farming of many crops – citrus fruits, sugar-cane, peanuts and cotton – is planned and on a large scale so as to increase agricultural production. Although less than 10% of the workforce is engaged in agriculture, which is highly mechanised, Israel is largely self-sufficient and needs only to import grain, oil and fats.

Israel's agricultural exports

Apart from its traditional agricultural produce such as fruit (especially citrus fruits), vegetables and poultry, Israel is stepping up its exports of *specialties* such as dates, Japanese persimmons, pomegranates, medlars and pecans, as well as improved strains, such as seedless grapes and melons. Organically grown products are also increasingly being exported. – Another special feature utilising the Israeli sun is the *cultivation* of nursery plants which are then exported to Europe's market-gardens. Many plant-breeding experiments are under way, e.g. sweet potatoes, bananas, and many others.

Whereas Israeli livestock used to consist primarily of sheep and goats, nowadays the emphasis in *livestock farming* is on eggs and dairy products. Beef production is limited because of the lack of feedstuffs. The religious parties have insisted that pig-farming should be disallowed in principle and only the Christian Arabs are permitted to keep pigs. In order to increase the supply of meat, farmers have in recent years gone over to turkeys. Fish-farming has also been stepped up as an alternative source of animal protein for the domestic consumer, and the carp ponds in the northern coastal plain, the Hula Plain and the Sea of Galilee produce high yields. Fisheries in the Mediterranean, on the other hand, have so far proved less productive but are to be increased nevertheless.

Since its foundation Israel has intensified its search for **mineral resources**. Minerals are taken in large quantities from the Dead Sea. Because of the high rate of evaporation (*c*. 200–300 million cu. ft/ 6–8 million cu. of water a day), its clear deep-blue waters have a very high salt content (*c*. 25%), making it difficult to dive and impossible to sink. The Dead Sea Works on the southern shore near Sodom is one of the largest producers of potassium salts and also manufacturers cooking salt. The brine is pumped from the sea into artificial salt-pans with a high rate of evaporation. The pans with the largest expanse produce the highest mineral yields so that in 1963, with the help of the World Bank, Israel made a start on establishing enormous new salt-pans in the southern basin of the Dead Sea. – The asphalt and bitumen, which is also to be found in and around the Dead Sea, goes partly for export.

The Negev is the region of Israel with the most mineral resources. Copper was mined at Timna, near Eilat, from 1955 but because of the fall in world prices the mines were closed 20 years later. At Maktesh Hagadol quartz-sand is quarried to supply glass factories, together with kaolin for the ceramics industry and phosphates for fertilisers, while the phosphate-bearing rocks also contain uranium. The Negev also has iron ore deposits, as does Galilee. New roads and railways, such as the one to Beersheba, are being built to transport all these minerals from the Negev to the industrial centers, while the port of Eilat is important for exports.

Israel is short of primary energy sources such as coal, oil and hydroelectric power. There has been a great deal of drilling for oil which has met with little success. Crude oil is therefore imported through the port of Eilat and piped 250 miles/400 km northwards to Haifa, where there is a large refinery. Another pipeline runs from Eilat to Ashqelon. SE of Ashqelon in the Shefela Plain drilling during the fifties did meet with some success. Since the return of the Sinai oilfields to Egypt, Israel is once more almost wholly dependent upon imported oil. – The petroleum-fired power stations at Haifa, Tel Aviv-Jaffa, Ashdod and Eilat generate over 90% of the country's electricity supply. In the south of Israel rooftop solar panels are used to harness the sun's rays to meet the energy needs of the private householder.

Although Israel has only a limited supply of raw materials and is largely lacking in energy sources, it has a high degree of industry compared with other countries in the Middle East. One of the major industries is building materials. Prefabricated sections, asbestos sheets and reinforced concrete rods are among the items turned out by innumerable specialist manufacturers. Cement production is also of considerable importance. The ports of Acre. and Ashqelon with their large steelworks are centers for heavy industry. Other coastal towns produce machinery and machine tools and there is shipbuilding in Haifa and an aircraft industry at Lod. Chemicals, precision engineering and the electrical industries have experienced a considerable boom.

After the end of the Second World War diamond cutters from Belgium were brought to Israel. Nowadays the diamond industry is concentrated at Netanya, although the Diamond Exchange is in Tel Aviv. Imported rough diamonds are processed in several hundred firms. A great many of the gemstone diamonds offered for sale on the world market have been cut in Israel; since the start of the eighties, however, the number of cut stones being exported has fallen and to counter this trend the industry has largely automated the production process. Large stones (one to ten carat) that were previously cut only in Belgium and the U.S.A. have for some time now also been cut in Israel.

Despite every economic endeavour, the balance of trade continues to show a deficit. The value of Israel's imports far exceeds its exports. Its major exports are cut diamonds, citrus fruits and canned fruit, chemical products, fertilisers, metal manufactures, aircraft, machinery and news media equipment. Its principal trading partners are the U.S.A., West Germany, Great Britain, the Netherlands, France, Belgium and Luxembourg, Switzerland, Italy and Japan. In 1975 Israel came to an agreement with the EEC for a progressive reduction of customs duty on Israeli goods imported into the Common Market.

The **communications network** has been expanded and improved by the newcomers to Israel. The country has been opened up by a network of over 2,500 miles/4,000 km of asphalt roads which are at their densest on the coastal plain. Most people travel by road as does much of the commercial traffic. Heavy goods tend to be carried by rail.

The ports are particularly important for the Israeli economy since the country has a considerable overseas trade. The busiest port is Haifa; fertilisers from the eastern hinterland and citrus fruit are exported through Ashdod. The port of Eilat trades by sea with Asia. – The country's international airport is at Lod.

Tourism has become one of Israel's major industries. Tourists and pilgrims come to enjoy the many sights that the country has to offer – the monuments of its ancient civilisations, its medieval Crusader fortresses and above all the Christian and Jewish holy places. The resorts on the Mediterranean and the Gulf of Eilat provide a further incentive. The number of tourists fell after the war in 1973, but has since picked up again. Israel has about 300 hotels, with a total of over 20,000 rooms. In 1983 the Holy Land had about 1.2 million foreign visitors.

Eventide on the Mediterranean at Caesarea

Israel
A to Z

The Dome of the Rock in Jerusalem

Abu Gosh

Jerusalem District.
Population: 2000.
(i) Government Tourist Office,
24 King George Street,
Jerusalem;
tel. (02) 24 12 81.

Abu Gosh is an Arab village lying 8 miles/13 km W of Jerusalem, just N of the highway to Tel Aviv. It is worth a visit on account of its *Crusader church.

Abu Gosh takes its name from a Bedouin sheikh from the Hedjaz district. He settled here about 1800 together with his four sons, receiving from the Osman government the right to protect the pilgrim route from the coast to Jerusalem. In return he took a toll, and this was the foundation of his fortune. The present inhabitants consider themselves the descendants of this man.

HISTORY. – The place was inhabited before the coming of the Bedouin. There was an abundant spring here, and in the 1st c. the Romans built a fort here for detachments of the Tenth ("Fretensis") Legion, which was probably the one employed when Jesus was crucified. Next, in the Islamic period, a caravanserai developed here. The Crusaders on the way to Jerusalem came to Abu Gosh; on account of its spring they thought it was the ancient village of Emmaus. They built the castle of Fontenoide here and also, in 1142, a church, which was abandoned by the Christians after the Battle of Hittim (see Horns of Hittim) in 1187.

SIGHTS. – The village is dominated by the *Crusader Church. Its architect adopted the pointed arch from the already existing caravanserai; this was an architectural feature which was to have great influence on the development of the Gothic style in the West. For a long time it served as stabling. In 1899 the French government purchased the building, originally entrusting it to the Benedictines. Since 1956 the church, on one side of which a mosque has been built, has belonged to the Lazarists.

A stone with the inscription "Vexillatio Leg(ionis) Fret(ensis)", set in the wall of the church near the entrance, serves as a reminder that the building occupies the site of a Roman fort at least 1,000 years older. The basilica with its central nave and aisles on either side has been restored in exemplary fashion. It is, along with the somewhat earlier church of Notre Dame in Tartus (Syria) and the church of St Anne in Jerusalem, which dates from the same period, a prime example of 12th c. monumental Crusader ecclesiastical architecture. The spring, which was of such importance to the development of the place from the outset, wells up in the crypt of the Crusader church (open 8.30–11 a.m. and 2.30–5.30 p.m.).

A second church stands on the heights over the village. It is easily identified from a distance on account of the statue of Mary which has been placed in a dominating position. The church was erected in 1924 over the remains of a 5th c. Byzantine church and belongs to the French Sorority of St Joseph. It is called **Notre Dame de l'Arche de l'Alliance** (*Our Lady of the Ark of the Covenant*). The name relates to the tradition that Qiryat Yearim once was here, the place where from time to time the Ark of the Covenant stood.

SURROUNDINGS. – **Qiryat Anavim** ("village of grapes") may be reached by taking the Jerusalem road and turning off into a side road shortly after leaving Abu Gosh. It was here that the first kibbutz in the Judean Highlands was founded, in 1920. It occupies a magnificent site far up a valley. The spacious guest house (category II), with a swimming pool in carefully tended gardens, is a quiet and pleasant place for a stay either before or after a visit to Jerusalem which lies only a short distance away.

The young people's village of **Qiryat Yeavim** ("village of the woods"), ⅔ mile/1 km W of Abu Gosh, was founded in 1952. The name of the place is mentioned in the Old Testament, in connection with the Israelites' Ark of the Covenant.

When campaigning against the Philistines in the 11th c. B.C. the Israelites carried with them the Ark which otherwise normally stood in Silo. It was captured by their enemies who took it first to Asdod (see Ashdod) and then to Gath and Ekron (1 Samuel 4 and 5). As the Philistines conceived that the Ark was bringing them misfortune, they handed it back to the Israelites who took it to Qiryat Yearim. There it stood for 20 years in the house of Abinadab (1 Samuel 6 and 7). When David had become king of all Israel and had captured Jerusalem, he brought the Ark to the city. At first, however, it was transported only so far as Perez-uzzah on Mount Qastel (2¼ miles/4 km E of Abu Gosh). Three months later it was brought to Jerusalem, where David greeted its arrival with "shouting and with the sound of the trumpet" (2 Samuel 6).

The young people's village has taken its name from Biblical Qiryat Yearim which must have stood on the Tell 2 miles/3 km NE. Many think, however, that Qiryat Yearim lay where Abu Gosh now is.

A pleasant excursion can be made to a spot a short distance SE of Abu Gosh. Going towards Jerusalem the highway is soon reached, then the route leads off to the right at the Hemed crossroads. Here lies the idyllic spot known as **Aqua Bella** (in Hebrew, En Hemed, meaning Well of Grace). The Arabs call it Deir el Benat (Women's Convent), after a nunnery of the

12th c. which was destroyed in 1187. The rooms of the four-square building have been restored. The gardens and a grove of pomegranates by a spring which gave the place its Latin name of "beautiful water" are now a National Park. It attracts many visitors, and there are facilities for picnics and camping.

Acre

see Akko

Afula

Northern District.
Population: 20,000.
Telephone code: 0 65.
ⓘ Government Tourist Office,
Casanova Street,
Nazareth;
tel. (065) 7 05 55.

The city of Afula was founded in 1925 W of Mount Hamore (Giv'at Hamore) which rises to a height of 1,690 ft/515 m. It occupies the site of the Arab village of Afule and lies at an important crossroads in the plain of Jezreel. The inhabitants practise agriculture, commerce and various crafts.

HISTORY. – The place is not mentioned in the Bible. To defend the roads meeting here the Crusaders built the fortress of La Fève which was destroyed by Sultan Baibars. In modern Turkish times the Arab village became a halt on the railway line from Haifa via Bet Shean and through the valley of the Yarmuk to Damascus. In the course of the First World War the Turks and Germans constructed the link line from Afula via Jenin towards the S.

SIGHTS. – Only insignificant remains of the old settlement that grew up around the chief market place for the Plain of Jezreel are to be seen nowadays. – About 1 mile/2 km E of the town, in the *Merhavya* kibbutz which was founded in 1911, are found the ruins of the Crusader castle of **La Fève.**

SURROUNDINGS. – The road to the E leads to the Arab village of **Sulam** (in Hebrew, *Shunem*). This is the Shunam of the Old Testament. In the 10th c. B.C. the comely young Abishag lived here before she was taken to the residence of the aged King David (1 Kings 1, 1–4). The village spring takes its name of "En Avishag" from her.

9 miles/14 km NE of Afula lies the **En Dor** kibbutz. This was founded in 1948, taking its name from the Biblical Endor whose Tell lies E of the kibbutz. In anguish when confronted by the Philistine host drawn up at Sunem, King Saul consulted the Witch of Endor, and the oracular response was a prediction of his

downfall (1 Samuel 18, 8–25). The prophecy was fulfilled the next day. In the battle by Mount Gilboa, SE of Afula, Saul and his sons were slain, and Saul's corpse was hung on the walls of Bet Shean.

Near En Dor a side road turns off to Mount Tabor. – 1¼ miles/2 km NE of En Dor there is a fork near *Kefar Tavor*. The main road goes N, joining, 6 miles/10 km further on near the Horns of Hittim (see entry), the Nazareth–Tiberias Road.

The right fork leads E towards the Sea of Galilee (12 miles/19 km). The village of **Kafr Kama** lies a short distance along this road. In 1880 Cherkesses came and settled here. At the time many of them were leaving Russia because they acknowledged the Islamic faith. They were given the opportunity of settling in the Near East by the Turks, some going to Amman and Djerash (Gerasa) in present-day Jordan. As well as this Cherkesses settlement at Kafr Kama there is another in Israel, at Rihanya in Upper Galilee, 8 miles/13 km N of Safed. The Cherkesses sided with the Israelis in 1948 and since then have served in the Israeli army.

Close by Kafr Kama lies *Yavne'el*, founded in 1901. ½ mile/1 km NE is a Tell under which the Bronze Age city of Yin'an is thought to lie. After climbing to a summit the road descends to the **Sea of Galilee**. There is a sign indicating altitude, and by it there is a parking spot from which a splendid view over the water may be enjoyed.

A National Park, *Ma'ayan Harod*, lies 6 miles/10 km SE of Afula, near the village of Gidona which was founded in 1949 (Camping, Youth Hostel), at the foot of Mount Gilboa. There is a man-made lake (swimming), surrounded by gum trees. It was at the spring of Harod that Gideon selected 300 warriors to do battle with the Midianites (Judges 7, 5–7).

Bet Shean, Sea of Galilee, Jenin, Plain of Jezreel, Megiddo, Nazareth and **Mount Tabor,** see relevant entries.

Akko/Acre

Northern District.
Altitude: 66 ft/20 m.
Population: 36,800.
Telephone code: 04.
ⓘ Government Tourist Office,
Town Hall,
Weizmann Street;
tel. 91 02 51.

HOTELS. – *Palm Beach* (k), Hatmarim Court, I, 136 r., SP, sauna, tennis; *Argaman Motel* (k), Argaman Beach, II, 75 r; *Nes Ammim Guesthouse*, II, 48 r., SP.

YOUTH HOSTEL. – *Old City*, NE of the lighthouse, 120 b.

RESTAURANTS. – *Arcad*, Khan Shwarda (Old City); *Hatmarim Court*, Tzomet Akko Naharia; *Oda Brothers* (Old City); *Zor*, 2 Hahaganah Street.

COMMUNICATIONS. – Railway and bus connections with Haifa and Nahariya. – Also Sherut taxis: "Kawej Hagalil", Rehov Trumpeldor (tel. 91 01 11). – Travel in the city: Akko Taxi, Rehov Ben Ami (tel. 91 01 11).

Akko – View from the Tower of the Khan el-Umdan (the Arcaded Market) across to the Ahmed Jezzar Mosque

From ancient times until the 19th c. *Akko was the most important sea port of Palestine. It is a city with an abundance of monuments dating from the Middle Ages and the early Modern Period. The densely populated Old City with its mosques, caravanserais, fortifications, buildings dating back to Crusader times, market alleys and old port installations offers the greatest imaginable contrast to Haifa, which lies just 14 miles/23 km away.

HISTORY. – Akko dates back to the Canaanite era. Originally it was sited on the Tell es Fukhar lying 1 mile/2 km E, which international groups of archaeologists have been investigating since 1973. It is hoped that, under layers of material from the Hellenistic and Persian periods, evidence will be found about the early history of the city which, on account of its strategic position, was captured by the pharaohs Thutmosis III and Ramses II. The *Phoenicians* who settled here were deported by Assurbanipal in 640 B.C. Akko was a Persian possession from 532 B.C. until the Greeks took it in 332 B.C. In 261, while under the sway of Ptolemy II who ruled in Egypt, it received the name of *Ptolemais*, but in 219 it fell to the Seleucids who were masters of Syria, retaining, however, its independent status as a city state. The Hashmoneans failed twice in their attempts to annex Akko. It was here that Herod the Great received the Roman emperor Augustus in 30 B.C., erecting a gymnasium at a later date. In A.D. 67 Vespasian used Akko, along with Caesarea (see entry) as a base for his campaigns in Palestine.

The city's economy also boomed in the Byzantine period, as it did, too, from the 7th c. onwards under the Ommayyad caliphs who used Akko as a supply port for Damascus where they resided.

It was not until 1104, five years after the conquest of Jerusalem, that the *Crusaders* succeeded in taking Akko. They gave it the name of *St Jean d'Acre*, building a palace there and the mighty vaults of the so-called crypt of the Knights of St John, Akko being its headquarters of the Order. The Italian cities of Genoa, Pisa and Venice established trading depots here, and Akko developed into a flourishing, busy port. In 1187 the Crusaders had to surrender to Sultan Saladin, but the English king Richard the Lion-Heart won the city back again in 1191

After the loss of Jerusalem in 1187 Akko became the capital of the diminished Crusader kingdom. The population at the time is estimated to have been 50,000. St Francis of Assisi visited the city in 1219, founding a nunnery. In 1228 the emperor Frederick II landed in the harbour of Akko when making his crusade, as did the French king Louis IX after his unsuccessful crusade to Damietta. Soon afterwards there followed disorders between the religious chivalric orders, the Knights of St John and the Templars, which almost took on the character of civil war. In 1290 the Crusaders slaughtered large numbers of Moslems. When the Mameluke Sultan al Ashraf Khalil took possession of Akko on May 18, 1291 he took his revenge; after barely 200 years of existence the Crusader state came to a bloody end.

For more than 300 years the sacked sea port remained unoccupied. It was only in the 17th c. that the Druse Emir Fakhr ed Din had it rebuilt. The work was continued on a yet larger scale first by Tahir al Umar around 1750 and then by his murderer and successor, Ahmed Jezzar ("The Butcher"). Ahmed Jezzar, who was of Bosnian extraction, ruled as pasha here from 1775 to 1805 with the support of his Jewish counsellor and treasurer Chaim Farchi. With help from the British he was able to hold out when the city was besieged by Napoleon in 1799. Between 1833 and 1840 Akko fell under the sway of Ibrahim Pasha who led Egyptian forces into Palestine and defeated the Turks. But the European powers obliged him to retreat. In the 19th c. Akko lost its importance as a port first to Beirut, then to Haifa. When the British captured Akko from the Turks in 1918 it had a population of 8,000, most of whom were Arabs. Jewish underground fighters were held captive by the British in the citadel in 1920 and also during the Second World War. On May 17, 1948 Israeli troops took possession of the city. Since then large Jewish residential areas have developed outside the Old City.

Akko has an iron and steel works; there is also plant for the chemical, ceramic and metalworking industries.

SIGHTS. – Weizmann Street leads from the central bus station past the cultural center and the *Town Hall* to a breach in the **City Wall** erected by Ahmed Jezzar in the 18th c. It is worth climbing the ramp and going along the wall as far as the land gate, passing on the way the NE corner of the massive *Burj el-Kummander* tower which defied all Napoleon's efforts in 1799. It rises on the foundations of the "Accursed Tower" on which in 1191 Richard the Lion-Heart ordered the Duke of Austria's banner to be lowered.

In the Courtyard of the Ahmed Jezzar Mosque

Until a breach was made for what is now called Weizmann Street in 1910, the **land gate** was the sole access from the land side. Salah-ed-Din Street leads to the *Ahmed Jezzar Mosque, the largest of the four mosques in Akko. Ahmed Jezzar built it in 1781 on the site of the Crusader cathedral in the style of the Osman domed mosques. The *fountain* at the entrance to the courtyard is especially interesting. There, under the palm trees and in green surroundings, stands the *sarcophagus of Ahmed* over which grow flowers.

Opposite the mosque is the entrance to the massive complex of buildings erected by the Knights of St John, the **Crusader city** which today is below ground level. It was buried in a great mound of earth after 1291, and Ahmed Jezzar sited his citadel (see below) on top. In recent years considerable portions of the medieval buildings have been uncovered by Zeev Goldmann. In the N section seven halls were discovered; presumably they correspond to the seven "Langues" (national divisions) of the Order. One of them is now a concert hall. These halls and a very large room (a dormitory?) have been only partially excavated so far, because there are problems with stability owing to the fact that the citadel stands above them. The **Refectory**, however, has been completely cleared; it is often incorrectly called the crypt because it was possible, before the excavations, to step into the room through a window which stands at the present-day street level. It is a vast

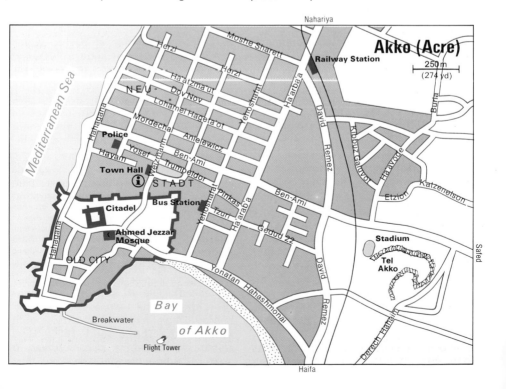

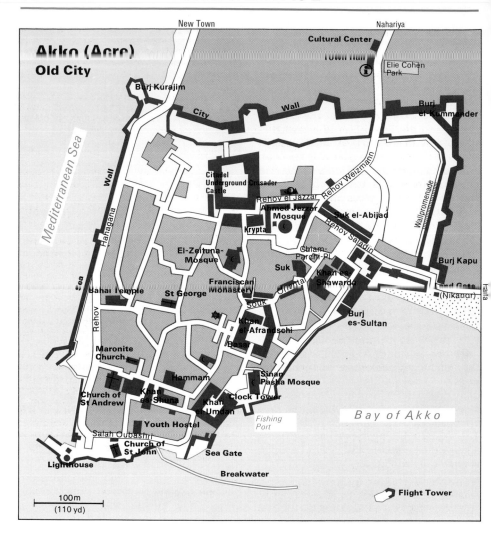

rectangular room the groined vaulting of which is supported by three massive round pillars. An indication of the date is provided by the coats of arms with the fleur-de-lis cut in the stone of two beam supports; these have a connection with the stay of the French king Louis VII in 1148. Such a detail makes, however, less of an impression than the extraordinary articulation of space in these monumental buildings put up by the Knights of St John.

From the refectory it is possible to go down into the bowels of the earth, along an illuminated subterranean passage about 1150 ft/350 m long. It dates back to the Persian era and was used even by the Crusaders as a secret link with the port. Near the exit is an Arab school, occupying what used to be the Pilgrims' Hospital.

Opposite is the entrance to the **City Museum**. It is housed in the Pasha's

bath-house (Ḥamman el Basha) which was erected for Ahmed Jezzar in 1780 and remained in use until 1947. In the numerous, but for the most part rather small rooms visitors can gain an impression of the history of the city and its surroundings from several permanent displays; there is an archaeological exhibition of finds from Akko and an Islamic art collection, and costumes, weapons and other relics of popular customs are on show, as well as photographs illustrating more recent history.

Outside the Museum a right turn towards the old port leads through busy market alleys into the S part of the Old City with two large caravanserais (or Khans, as they are called). The **Khan el-Afrandschi** (The Khan of the Franks, i.e. the Europeans) is the older of the two. It was built by Fakhr ed Din around 1600. Here stands, too, a small *Franciscan nunnery*. It serves as a reminder that it was here that stood the nunnery of the Poor Clares which Francis of Assisi founded in 1219. The nuns there mutilated their faces so as not to awaken the interest of the Arab conquerors in 1291. – S lies the *old harbour*, whose importance was eclipsed by Haifa; it is now a delightful and picturesque fishing port. A little further S is found the **Khan el-Umdan** (The Pillared Khan), which is so called because Ahmed Jezzar used granite and porphyry columns from Caesarea (see entry) when he laid out the premises on the site of the Crusaders' Dominican monastery. Over its N entrance is a lofty clock tower, erected to commemorate Sultan Abdulhamit's jubilee in 1906. From the top there is a splendid view of the city and the bay.

To reach the **lighthouse** and the **sea wall** it is necessary to continue in a westerly direction through a lane where the Youth Hostel and the *Church of St John* are situated. A great breach in the sea wall dates back to the earthquake of 1837.

The Maronite church may be reached by following the sea wall N and turning right by the Greek Catholic church of St Andrew. From the Khan es Shuna a street then leads N to the Greek Orthodox **church of St George**, which stands on medieval foundations. There is a memorial tablet to Major Oldfield, a British officer who was killed during Napoleon's siege of Akko. *Burj Kuraijim*, a Turkish bastion against sea-borne assaults which stands at the NE corner of the wall on foundations dating back to the Crusader period, can be reached by returning to the sea wall and going along it in a N direction.

From the wall which follows the sea wall, an alley leads to the entrance of Ahmed Jezzar's 18th c. **citadel** which became a prison during the period of the British Mandate. There is a memorial chamber with a collection of photographs and documents recalling the Jewish underground fighters who were held prisoner and, in some cases, executed here by the British.

E of the Old City lies a new district, dating from 1948.

SURROUNDINGS. – 8 miles/13 km SE of Akko lies the village of *Yodefat* (see entry), at the foot of Har Azmon. A narrow, but pretty country road then leads E past Mount Netofa (1726 ft/526 m) and 7 miles/ 11 km further on it bears left towards Meron (see entry; 13 miles/21 km). From here a pleasant excursion is to *Safed* (see entry), or else it is possible to return via *Sassa* (10 miles/16 km), *Mi'ilya* (near Montfort Castle, see entry) and *Nahariya* (see entry; 20 miles/33 km) back to Akko (6 miles/10 km).

On the road from Nahariya to Akko, S of Regba, lies the **Lohamei Hageta'ot** kibbutz. It was founded in 1949 by survivors from Nazi concentration camps and has a *museum with important collections.

A cultural center and a documentary collection which is named after Beit Katznelson, a poet who was murdered in Auschwitz in 1944, the multi-storey building also contains information about the various concentration camps and the Jews' resistance to National Socialism in Poland and Lithuania. Every year on April 19, the anniversary of the uprising in the Warsaw ghetto, there are special exhibitions and lectures here. – On the ground floor there are displays illustrating the history of the city of Wilna, the "Jerusalem of Lithuania", and its Jewish community during the period from 1551 to 1940. There are a range of wooden figurines and reminders of the beginning of the Socialist-Zionist movement at the end of the 19th c., and objects recalling Jewish life in Poland. – From the entrance hall, stairs lead down to two underground rooms. On the staircase plans and Nazi insignia recall the extermination camps in E Europe. In one of the rooms there is a large plan of Treblinka, in another a display commemorating Janusz Korczak (1879–1942), doctor and teacher, as well as some 2,000 drawings and paintings, including portraits of prisoners. – The rooms of the first floor contain displays of documents about antisemitism under Hitler, the ghettos and the deportation, a plan of Anne Frank's house In Amsterdam and pictures of the Theresienstadt camp. The Warsaw Uprising is commemorated in some 2,000 photographs.

Allone Abba

Northern District.
(i) **Government Tourist Office,**
18 Herzl Street,
Haifa;
tel. (04) 66 65 21.

Allone Abba lies 15 miles/25 km SE of Haifa. It is a commune which was originally founded by Germans. Access to Allone Abba is by a left turn 2½ miles/4 km S of Qiryat Tivon off the Haifa–Nazareth road.

In 1908 the settlement of *Waldheim* was founded here by German Templars. Its inhabitants practised agriculture, selling their produce in Haifa. In the Second World War the British evacuated the population. In 1948 the place was taken over by Israeli settlers. They gave Waldheim a new name in honour of Abba Bardishev, who in the Second World War was dropped as a saboteur behind the German lines in Europe; he was taken prisoner and executed. A few of Waldheim's buildings have been restored, and the church serves as the commune's cultural base.

SURROUNDINGS. – A mile/2 km NE of Allone Abba is the commune of **Bethlehem HaGalilit**. This, too, sprang up in 1948 on land forming part of the Bethlehem settlement which the German Templars had founded in 1906 and which had likewise been evacuated at the behest of the British in the Second World War.

Arad

Southern District.
Population: 13,000.
(i) **Government Tourist Office,**
Shopping Center;
tel (057) 981 44

0577 957 140

HOTELS. – *Masada* (k), I, 104 r., SP; *Margoa*, Moav Street, II, 97 r., SP; *Nof Arad* (k), Moav Street, II, 96r., SP; *Arad* (k), 6 Hapalmach Street, III, 51 r.

YOUTH HOSTEL. – *Blue-White Bet Hostel*, 200 b.

*Tell Arad, an important archaeological site, lies W of the Dead Sea on a hill N of the Beersheba–Arad road. The town of Arad was founded in 1961. 6 miles/10 km W of it an unmarked side road forks off towards this hill which is visible from a long way off. Excavations by Y. Aharoni and Ruth Amiran between 1962 and 1967 uncovered two major complexes, a city and a hill fort from successive epochs, from pre-Israelite Canaanite times and from

the Israelite period. Restoration has been carried out carefully and expertly.

HISTORY. – The site was occupied as far back as the Early Bronze Age (4th millennium B.C.). In the 2nd millennium B.C. an extensive Canaanite city grew up here. Their king drove the Israelites back when they tried to push forward from the S into the Promised Land (Numbers 21, 1). After Joshua had taken the city (Joshua 12, 14) it fell to the tribe of Judah and the "children of the Kenite", who were related to Moses (Judges 1, 16). Further developments and the fortification of the city are attributed to King Solomon who also had a new temple to Jehovah erected on the site of a Kenite hill-top shrine. Soon afterwards, in 920 B.C., Arad was captured by the Pharaoh Sheshonk (the Shishak of the Old Testament). But it was soon recovered by the kingdom of Judah to which it belonged until its downfall in 586 B.C. Arad remained important because of its favourable position on important trade routes until Roman times. It was abandoned only after the victorious Islamic campaign in the 7th c.

SIGHTS. – The excavated city belongs to the Canaanite period, 2 millennia B.C. The precincts of the royal palace and the temples are to the NW; to the SW lies the residential quarter which has not yet been fully excavated. For considerable stretches the trace of the *embrasured wall* which was further strengthened with round towers can be seen; it leads up to the citadel.

The buildings in the **hill fort** are post-Canaanite. They were built between the early Israelite era and the Roman period, that is in the course of some thousand years. There is a tower from Hellenistic times and a Roman military fort, but these

Arad –View from the Canaanite city across to the Citadel

Holy of Holies in the Temple at Arad

are of less importance than the Israelite buildings dating back to the 10th to 7th c. B.C. They were, like the even more ancient Canaanite city, surrounded by an embrasured wall (10th c. B.C.).

The most important building is the Israelite *temple. Quite small rooms are placed all around the courtyard in which there stands on the right-hand side a *sacrificial altar* made of rubble and clay tiles. Leading up to the Holy of Holies the bases for two cult pillars have been discovered; there is evidence that, under the names of Jachin and Boas, similar pillars were placed in Solomon's temple in Jerusalem. Two low horned altars flank the entrance into the small rectangular Holy of Holies (Hekal), in which two Aniconic culture stones still stand *in situ*. – In the precinct of the temple channels have been hewn in the rock for water supply and storage; there is, for instance, an open watercourse some 6 ft/2 m deep which comes through the city wall left of the Holy of Holies.

The temple is the only Jewish religious building of its type which has so far been excavated. Since excavations are not permitted in the grounds of the temple of Jerusalem, information about it can only be gained from written sources. The temple of Arad, which was destroyed and rebuilt on several occasions, is therefore of particular importance in archaeology and the history of religion. The remains provide evidence for the decentralisation of religion in the first century after the Jews came into possession of Canaan, as there were religious sites here in Arad as in Betel and Dan, in addition to the shrine at Silo. This all came to an end when King Josiah of Judah, in connection with a wide-ranging reform of religious life, concentrated the temple ceremonies in Jerusalem.

Ashdod

Southern District.
Altitude: 0–33 ft/0–10 m above sea level.
Population: 56,500.
Telephone code: 055.
ⓘ **Government Tourist Office,**
7 Mendele Street,
Tel Aviv;
tel. (03) 22 32 66–7.

HOTELS. – *Miami* (k), Nordau Street 12, II, 38 r; *Orly* (k), Nordau Street, III, 29 r.

RESTAURANT. – *Pagoda* (Chinese), 11 HaEschel Street.

The new Israeli Mediterranean harbour of Ashdod lies some 24 miles/ 40 km S of Tel Aviv-Jaffa (Yafo). It is a port of call visited by a steadily increasing number of cruise liners.

HISTORY. – Ancient **Asdod** S of the modern settlement was named, along with Gaza and Gath, in the 12th to 11th c. B.C. as a city of the Anachims (Joshua 11, 22). It figures together with Gaza, Askalon (Ashqelon), Gath and Ekron as one of the five

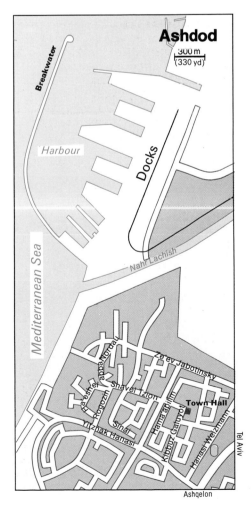

lordships of the *Philistines* (Joshua 13, 3). When they had seized the Ark of the Covenant from the Israelites they took it first to Askalon and then to the temple of Dagon in Asdod (1 Samuel 5, 1–5). Asdod was captured by the Assyrians in 732 B.C., becoming an autonomous city state. It became important as a port under the Persians in the 6th to 5th c. B.C. under Hellenistic suzerainty. Asdod took the name of Azulus in the 3rd c. B.C. This name was taken up in the 12th c. A.D. by the Crusaders, while the Arabs called the city *Minat el Qala* (castle harbour). In more recent times Asdod used to be a modest village. New developments began when the state of Israel decided in 1959 to lay out, 2 miles/3 km N of the ruins of the old city, the industrial settlement of **Ashdod** with a deep-water harbour. Within a short period of time the new settlement had developed into a city with numerous industrial and transport firms.

SIGHTS. – Ashdod is a modern city with an impressive network of streets. The best view of the city and the coast (fine beach) is from the hill in the city center (photography forbidden).

SURROUNDINGS. – The city is an important port of call for cruise ships and consequently the point of departure for visits to **Tel Aviv, Jaffa, Jerusalem** and **Beersheba** (see relevant entries).

Ashqelon

Southern District.
Altitude: 0–33 ft/0–10 m above sea level.
Population: 50,000.
Telephone code: 051.
(i) **Government Tourist Office,**
In Merkas Mis'hari (Commercial center), Afridar;
tel. 324 12.

HOTELS. – *Ganei Shulamit* (k), 11 Hatayasim Street, I, 108 r., SP, sauna, tennis; *Dagon* (k), Hatayasim Street, on the beach, I, 62 r., SP, //a/\fa/a/\h Shau/ (k), 28 Harakefet Street, II, 108 r., SP, sauna; *Ganei Shimshon* (k), 38 Hatamar Street, IV, 22r. – *Club Ashqelon*, holiday village, 192 r., SP, tennis, horse-back riding.

CAMPING. – In the National Park.

SPORT AND LEISURE. – Bathing on the beach, N from the National Park as far as the suburb of Barnea.

TOURS. – These are organised by *Egged Tours* (Bus Station – tel. 4 10 97).

COMMUNICATIONS. – Buses and Sherut taxis to Tel Aviv, Jerusalem, Ashdod, Rehovot and other places in the vicinity. – Central bus station near the stadium on Derekh Hanitzahon Street (tel. 2 29 11 and 2 23 34). Branches of the Sherut Taxi Co. Ga'el Daroma: 1 Migdal, Rehov Zahal (tel. 2 23 34); 2 Afridar, Merkas Mis'hari. – Town journeys: Shimshon Taxi Service, Rehov Keren Kajemet (tel. 2 22 66 and 2 22 67).

The city of *Ashqelon (Askalon) lies 35 miles/56 km S of Tel Aviv on the shores of the Mediterranean. Its history goes back to the days of the Canaanites and Philistines. It is interesting because of its ancient remains, and its extensive bathing beach makes it popular with visitors.

HISTORY. – The Canaanite trading town of **Askalon** is mentioned as early as the 18th and 15th c. B.C. in Egyptian texts. When the *Philistines* in the course of their sea-borne immigration arrived in the area about 1200 B.C., Askalon became the seat of one of their five principalities. Of these the situation of Gaza, Askalon and Asdod (see Ashdod) are known, whereas it has proved impossible to locate Ekron and Gath precisely.

Ashqelon – Ancient columns built into the Crusader's port defences

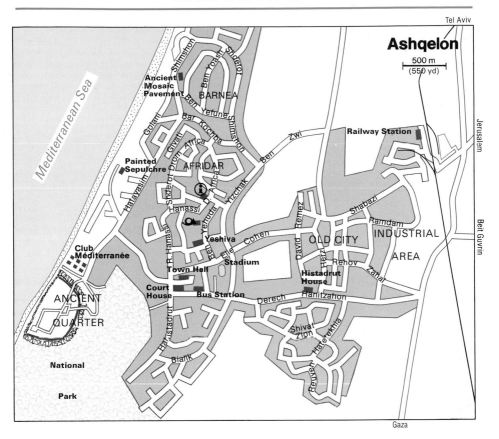

Askalon was probably the most important of the five principalities.

Until the time of the Jewish rebellion against Rome (1st c. A.D.) there was always enmity between Askalon and the Israelites. This is reflected in the Biblical story of Samson which is recorded in Judges 13–16. Concerning Samson, son of Manoah who lived in Zorah, it is written that he was "a Nazarite unto God from the womb" who should "deliver Israel out of the hand of the Philistines" (Judges 13, 5). After marrying a woman of the Philistines in Timnath, conflict broke out, and he slew thirty Philistines in Askalon. After the Philistines had burned his wife to death this man who was as strong as a bear killed a thousand men with the jaw bone of an ass (Judges 14 and 15). He then became acquainted with Delilah, a Philistine woman from Hebron, and he told her the riddle of his strength, that is to say, that his strength was insuperable so long as the hair of his head remained uncut. After seven locks of his hair had been shorn off, he was taken prisoner, shackled and blinded. But as his hair grew once more, his strength returned. When he was led out to a festival in honour of the god Dagon so that the people could make mock of him, he pulled down the temple of Dagon, causing the death of many Philistines and their leaders who were present in the building, "so the dead which he slew at his death were more than they which he slew in his life" (Judges 16, 30).

The Philistines adopted the Phoenician deities – the grim fertility god Dagon who was revered in Ugarit as the father of Baal and in Byblos as the brother of El (temple in Asdod), together with mighty Baal (Baal-Zebub, which the Israelites interpreted as meaning "God of the Flies") and his consort Astarte. About the middle of the first millennium B.C. the Philistines were absorbed in the Phoenician population which was becoming more and more predominant as a result of massive immigration from N coastal regions.

The Philistine principality of Askalon was captured by the Assyrian Tiglatpilesar in 732 B.C. and by Sanherib in 701. In the 6th c. the area was under Persian suzerainty and belonged to the Phoenican city of Tyre. It was Hellenised in 332 B.C. Under the Seleucid Antiochos IX Askalon was granted rights of self-government and its own calendar in 104 B.C. Evidence of intellectual life at this time is provided by the career of Antiochos of Askalon: he was born here about 120 B.C., became head of the Platonic academy in Athens, founded the "Fifth Academy" and was the tutor of Cicero.

About 73 B.C. it seems likely that Herod was born here. Though he was the son of an Idumean and a Nabataean woman, i.e. of non-Jewish parents, he later became the Jewish king Herod I. As Josephus records "he furnished the city with magnificent bath-houses and fountains as well as with an arcaded chamber of astonishing size and craftsmanship" (History of the Jewish Wars 1, 21, 11). Under the *Romans* Askalon developed into a prosperous trading city on account of its convenient position on the important N–S route (Via Maris – the coastal road). It was also famous for its play festivals.

Two basilicas from the Byzantine period are known. After the Islamic conquest the Omayyad caliph Abd el Malik, who built the dome of the rock in Jerusalem, had a mosque erected here in 685.

In 1099 Godfrey of Bouillon with the *Crusaders* defeated the army of the Egyptian Fatamides in the battle of Askalon, thus clearing the way to Jerusalem, but it was not until 1135 that King Baldwin II took the city itself. In 1187 it fell to Sultan Saladin. In 1192 Richard the Lion-Hearted rebuilt the city after winning it back in the course of the Third Crusade; the city walls, which still remain, date from this time. In 1290 the Mameluke sultan Baibars captured Askalon and its decline then set in.

At the end of the 18th c. Ahmed Jezzar took materials from the ruins of Askalon, as he did, too, from those of Caesarea, for his building works in Akko. The Arab village of *Migdal* ("Tower") sprang up on the site of the ancient port.

In 1952 Jews from South Africa founded the settlement of *Afridar* E of Migdal. Today it is the business center. From this developed the modern town of Ashqelon.

SIGHTS. – Turning towards the sea off the N–S Tel Aviv–Gaza road, Derekh Hanitzahon leads into the city. N of this street lies, just W of the railway, the industrial area where the pipeline from Eilat terminates and the village of MIGDAL, which was Arab until 1948 and was incorporated into the new town of Ashqelon in 1955. The center of the town with its bus station, hospital and court house, is reached by going on past the Histadrut building; Rehov Hanassi turns off to the right. This street where the town hall stands leads into the part of the town called AFRIDAR; founded in 1952, it was the nucleus from which the modern town developed and is now a busy business quarter (clock tower, Information Office). In 1972 during bull-dozing operations two magnificent Roman **sarcophagi** were discovered here; they can be seen under a shelter in the street. – The suburb of BARNEA, further to the N, adjoins the town.

About 1 mile/2 km S of the town center there lies in a **National Park** (camping permitted) the *ancient part of the historic city of Askalon; it is separated from the modern settlements by a broad park belt planted with orange trees.

A semicircular **city wall** dating back to the Crusader period, and which ter-minates at each end down at the coast, forms the boundary of the site. It has finds from all periods from the Philistines to the Middle Ages and is well worth a visit.

The city wall was laid out by the English king Richard the Lion-Heart in 1192. It had four gates: **Jaffa Gate** (N), **Jerusalem Gate** (E), **Gaza Gate** (S) and **Sea Gate** (W). From the Jaffa Gate a pathway leads to ruins of the Roman period. There are great Corinthian capitals, bases and other remains of the vast **Hundred Pillared Stoa** which was erected by Herod the Great. There is an absidal annex to the Stoa which was often rebuilt in later times, finally becoming a prayer niche

forming part of a mosque. In it there stands a massive *relief*; above a globe borne on the shoulders of a bearing figure of Atlas sit a god and goddess of victory. Another relief depicts the civic goddess of Askalon, a female figure wearing a castellated crown and with a child on her right. In the beautifully laid out gardens there is an abundance of other ancient remains, especially pillars and fountains.

The Tell marking the settlement where the Philistine city stood lies close by the old port and is reached by turning right from the central pathway. The wall leading down to the old port is not faced with stone and the Roman pillars that had been built into it as reinforcements can be seen protruding.

Another sight is the **"painted sepulchre"** from the Roman period (3rd c.). It is in Hatayasim Street near the Ganei Shulamit hotel. Four steps lead down to a barrel-vaulted room with frescoes. The fresco on the wall opposite the entrance portrays two naked nymphs sitting amid trees and animals beside a stream. On the ceiling there is a fresco of a female portrait (Demeter or Cora), and above it there is a dog chasing a gazelle and the head of a Gorgon. A boy with a basket and grapes, Pan with shepherd's pipe, gazelles and birds can be made out amidst a pattern of intertwined vine tendrils.

Nearby on a hill stands the former Dervish monastery of *Haram el Khidr* which is now closed. It used to be important on account of the relic kept there, the skull of Hussein, second son of the fourth caliph Ali. The status of Hussein as the last genuine successor of the prophet Mohammed became a bone of contention between Sunnites and Shiites. Hussein was killed at the battle of Kerbela in 680, 19 years after the assassination of Ali. The Shiites hold his tomb there in particular re-verence. He is called "el Khidr" (i.e. the Green One) and also bears the same nickname as the Christian St George who has connections with Lydda (see Lod).

A little further N the remains of a Byzantine basilica are to be found in the BARNEA district and also a *mosaic* which probably also originally formed part of the floor of a church (both 5th–6th c.).

Atlit

Haifa District.
ⓘ **Government Tourist Office,**
16 Herzl Street,
Haifa;
tel. (04) 66 65 21.

**The great Crusader castle of *Atlit
lies 9 miles/16 km S of Haifa on a
peninsula jutting out into the
Mediterranean. There was a settlement there as early as Phoenician
times. The Phoenicians constructed,
as was their custom, a harbour on
both sides of a headland so that they
could approach or leave it whatever
the direction of the wind.**

HISTORY. – The *Crusader* period in the history of Atlit
opened in 1187 when the knights lost Jerusalem to
Sultan Saladin. The Grand Master of the Templars had
his residence near Solomon's Temple (i.e. near the
Omayyadan Dome of the Rock on the Mount of the
Temple in Jerusalem), which gave the Order its name.
But this site now had to be abandoned by the
Templars. Therefore they built for themselves new
quarters, in Akko (see entry) and Atlit, as well as
elsewhere. To this castle which they constructed in
1218 the Templars gave the name of *Castrum
Peregrinorum* or Château des Pèlerins (Pilgrims'
Castle). The name of Atlit comes from a later period.

After the unfortunate Crusade against Damietta in the
delta of the Nile in 1249 the French king Louis IX
stayed for a while in Akko and Atlit. In 1265 Atlit was
attacked for the first time by the *Arabs*. They destroyed
the suburbs, and the Templars were obliged to
disburse tribute money to the Arabs, though they were
able to continue living there.

On May 18, 1291, however, Sultan Melik el-Aschraf
stormed Akko, the capital of the Christian kingdom.
This really marked the end of the Crusader state in
Palestine, even if for a short time longer individual
fortresses were able to hold out. Among them were
Tortosa in Syria and Atlit. After the fall of Tortosa on
August 3, 1291 the Templars resolved to return home
to France. They evacuated the great stronghold of
Pilgrims' Castle in mid-August 1291. It was only after
some little delay that the Arabs ventured to take
possession of it. – In France Philip IV laid charges
against the Order in 1307, accusing them of denying
Christ, of worshipping the secret symbols of Baphomet and immorality. He had Jacques de Molay, the
Grand Master, burnt to death together with many of
his knights, and confiscated the immense treasury of
the Order which was dissolved by Pope Clement V in
1312.

In the centuries that followed, the buildings of Atlit fell
into decay, though considerable remains were left
even after the earthquake of 1837. When the Emperor
William II interrupted his journey from Haifa to
Jerusalem and made a halt at Atlit, two families of
Arabs were the sole inhabitants of the former fortress.

The land around Atlit was by then already in the
possession of Baron Edmond de Rothschild, and his
initiatives are responsible for the modern developments in the area. In 1903 he founded the Jewish

village of Atlit ½ mile/1 km S of the castle. Aaronson
sited an experimental agricultural station amidst the
marshes, and in salt-pans valuable kitchen salt was
obtained by means of the evaporation of sea water.
Today most of the kitchen salt needed by Israelis is
produced here. Since 1948 the village of Atlit has
taken in large numbers of immigrants.

The British Mandate authorities used the ruins of Atlit
during the Second World War as a camp for German
and Italian prisoners of war. In the post-war period it
was used as a prison for illegal Jewish immigrants. In
1956 and 1967 Egyptian troops were held captive
here. – The citadel is used by the Israeli navy; it is not
open to visitors.

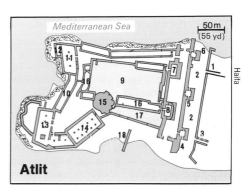

Atlit

1 N Portal	10 Vaulted Chambers
2 Moat	11 NW Pillared Hall
3 S Portal	12 NW Tower
4 S Gate-house	13 SW Pillared Hall
5 Middle Gate-house	14 S Pillared Hall
6 N Gate-house	15 Round Church
7 N Donjon	16 Crypts
8 S Donjon	17 S Outer Courtyard
9 Inner Courtyard	18 Breakwater

SIGHTS. – **The *Crusader castle** forms
a rectangle 656 ft by 1,477 ft/200 m by
450 m. It occupies the rocky peninsula
which juts out towards the W into the sea.
Entry is by the E short side of the rectangle.
In front of it there used to be a suburb
which was partially excavated before
1938. The castle itself is protected by a
moat – in the construction of which a
Phoenician burial ground was bisected –
and a strong double wall.

By the inner wall rises the main donjon, El-
Karnifeh. It is rectangular in plan and is
made of massive freestone blocks with
quoins of dressed stone. The chapter
chamber is adjacent to this tower. Of this
there remain the buttresses of the vaults
which are supported on brackets carved
with the heads of saints.

In the W part of the site a stairway leads
down to the landing stage. The octagonal
Templars' church used to stand there; its
foundations are still there. The building
was a copy, on a reduced scale, of the
Dome of the Rock in Jerusalem which

was lost in 1187. Similar chapels were erected wherever the Templars settled. The altar did not occupy its usual position in an apse, but in the middle of the church. "The complete rite of the Order was obviously celebrated only behind closed doors" (Th. F. Meysels). This strange rite was, together with the suspicion that the Templars revered Baphomet, the reason given for the charge of heresy in 1307.

Avdat

Southern District.
(i) **Government Tourist Office,**
Bet Tnuat Hamoschavim,
Nordau Street,
Beersheba;
tel. (0 57) 3 60 01.

The ruins of the city of *Avdat (Arabic Avda) lie 40 miles/64 km S of Beersheba, just to the left of the road to Eilat. Standing on a hill, they are visible from afar. They have been partially reconstructed and are among the most important monuments from the Nabataean, Roman and Byzantine periods in the Negev.

HISTORY. – The first excavations which were begun in 1870 have been followed since 1953 by systematic archaeological investigations under the direction of Michael Avi-Yonah and Abraham Negev. They have produced evidence that the city was not founded as late as the reign of the Nabataean king Obodas II (30–9 B.C.) but dates back rather to the 3rd c. B.C. That

was the period when the *Nabataeans,* who had immigrated from NW Arabia and who were, it has been established the first inhabitants in 312 B.C. made the transition from a nomadic to a settled life-style. They established their capital in Petra, E of the Arava Depression; the city has become famous on account of the many buildings hewn out of the sandstone cliffs. Preponderantly caravan drivers and traders, who owed their prosperity to the commerce along the old caravan routes, the Nabataeans protected the link between Petra and the Mediterranean harbour of Gaza by means of a chain of settlements – Nizzana, Subeita (see Shivta), Obodas and Mampsis (see entry). There were also guard posts along the road. These settlements are among the more than 2,000 Nabataean settlements whose existence has been established by Nelson Glueck in southern Jordan, the Negev and the area around Sinai. It was only possible to develop settlements in these parts thanks to advanced irrigation methods (so-called cascade irrigation). This permitted the Nabataeans to lay out fields in the arid zone and to provide the inhabitants with water and food.

Towards the end of the 1st c. B.C. the city took its name from the Nabataean king Obodas II; its present name of Avdat is derived from it. Obodas was buried in Avdat and revered as a deity. It was under him and his important successor Aretas IV (9 B.C.–A.D. 40) that the city knew its greatest prosperity.

The *Romans* conquered the Nabataean region in A.D. 106, incorporating it into the empire as the province of Arabia Petraea. They constructed a road from Eilat to Damascus which by-passed Avdat, and this led to the decline of the city. Later on, towards the end of the 3rd c., a military camp was laid out N of the city, and a temple in honour of Jupiter was built on the summit, where the temple to Obodas had stood; this reinvigorated the city. Under the emperor Theodosius I (379–399) the Nabataeans were converted to Christianity. The Byzantine emperor Justinian (527–564) settled monks in the Negev; they devoted themselves to the reconstruction of the irrigation system and to agriculture. New buildings were erected, among them

View of the fortified hill-top city of Avdat

Byzantine wine-presses

two churches and a monastery in the precincts of the old temple on the hill-top. It was at that time that the city knew its second great period of prosperity. The capture of Avdat by the Persians in 614 and by the Islamic Arabs in 634 led, however, to the decline of the city. After that Avdat was abandoned, and the irrigation system fell into disrepair.

After the foundation of the state of Israel in 1948 the botanist Michael Even-Ari studied and reconstructed the ancient Nabataean/Byzantine irrigation system, succeeding in creating an experimental farm along the old lines and growing the crops which were cultivated in Nabataean times. Encouraged by this success he founded similar farms near Beersheba and Shivta.

SIGHTS. – From the Beersheba–Eilat road a track leads to a car park, with kiosk and pavilion, W of the Avdat ruins. Cars may proceed to a larger car park just S of the ancient city. It is worth stopping half-way along to walk up a footpath which goes off to the right towards a **sepulchre**. Entry is through a vaulted antechamber built of freestone; straight ahead is a door on the jambs of which is portrayed, in relief, a horned altar flanked by the moon and star (left) and the sun (right), along with a pair of pillars. Entry to the sepulchre is gained by passing through. It is hewn in the rock, as was the Nabataean custom, and there are numerous narrow burial niches in the walls (five on the left, eight straight ahead, and nine on the right). From the square in front of the tomb there is a fine view over Even-Ari's "Nabataean" experimental farm.

From the upper car park through a *residential quarter* dating from the Roman period which stands to the N, a path leads to a wine-press which was used from Nabataean to Byzantine times. Its upper part is semicircular, its bottom rectangular. Close by stands a stone with a Nabataean inscription.

The path leads next through the S gateway into the rectangular **Byzantine castle**. The vantage point in the SE corner offers a view over the whole extent of the site with its partially restored walls and

towers, the great cistern in the middle of the courtyard and also the ruins of a late Byzantine chapel by the N wall. A gap in the N wall leads into the Roman *military camp* (295 ft by 295 ft/90 m by 90 m).

To the W a second courtyard lies next to the castle. It is the sacred precinct, dating from the Byzantine era, with two churches which were erected on the site of the Nabataean and Roman temples respectively. To the left is the *church of St Theodoros, dedicated to a Greek 4th c. martyr. It is an arcaded basilica with central nave and aisles on either side and triple apse. The central portal is decorated with two Nabataean horned capitals.

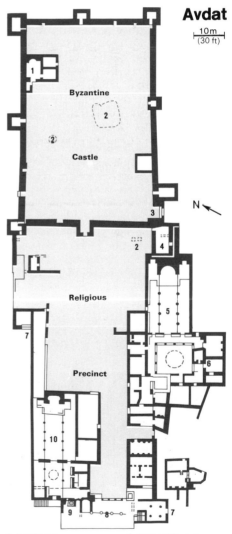

Avdat

10 m
(30 ft)

1	Late Byzantine Chapel	6	Rooms of Byzantine Monastery
2	Cistern	7	Nabataean Gate
3	Main Gate of Castle	8	Nabataean Peristyle
4	Late Roman Tower	9	Baptistry
5	Church of St Theodoros	10	N Church

The Church of St Theodoros on the hill-top at Avdat

Gravestones with Greek inscriptions have been let into the floor of the aisles. In the S aisle one tablet portrays the menora together with the cross; another records that here was buried one Zachariah, son of John, "in the martyr church of St Theodoros". – The sanctuary, in front of which, on the left, the round stem of the ambo (or lectern) still remains, is two steps higher. In it the old altar table may be seen. On the right-hand side of the central apse as well as in front of the side apses remnants of the templon – i.e. the partition between the sanctuary and the portion of the church reserved for the congregation – are visible. To the S, monastery buildings stand next to the church.

Terrace on the W side

The square where the church of St Theodoros stands is bordered on the W, where the ground falls away steeply, by a broad terrace; access is through the courtyard with its pillars. Entry is through a gateway which, like the central portal of the church of St Theodoros, has Naba-taean capitals. On the terrace there is a cruciform *baptismal font* which has been restored.

Nearby is the entrance to the atrium of the **N church** whose original name is not known. This, too, is an arcaded basilica with central nave and side aisles. On the S range of pillars remain the carved brackets on which the roof timbers of the aisle rested. In front of the sanctuary, to the left, the four-sided base of the ambo can be seen.

Two steps lead up into the sanctuary with its rectangular altar.

It is possible to return to the lower car park by leaving the terrace by way of a stairway near the font. On the way down two sepulchres are passed. There is also the *Saints' sepulchre*, so called on account of an icon with a Greek inscription. It stands near the remains of a Byzantine house. W of the car park there is a Byzantine bath.

SURROUNDINGS. – Not far N of the ruins of Avdat is the **En Avdat** spring (see entry). It is one of the most abundant in the area of the Zin Desert which stretches from Avdat down into the Arava Depression. – The road N from Avdat goes to the **Sede Boqer** kibbutz (see entry) with David Ben Gurion's grave in the grounds of the Negev High School.

Banyas/Baniyas

Golan Region.
Altitude: sea level.
Population: 5,000.

RESTAURANT with self-service.

Banyas (Baniyas) lies 8 miles/13 km E of Qiryat Shemona on a tributary of the Jordan, SW of Mount Hermon. It is set in a beautiful landscape. It has been occupied by Israel since 1967, and is a favourite resort for Israeli families and groups.

Cult niches near the spring where the Jordan rises

HISTORY. – The name of Banyas is derived from the Greek *Paneas*. By the spring there stood from Hellenistic time onwards an important shrine to the pastoral diety Pan whose cult had replaced a more ancient Baal religion. It was here that Antiochus III defeated the Ptolemaean forces in 200 B.C., thus winning Coelesyria and Palestine and adding them to the Seleucid empire. Augustus presented the region to Herod whose son Philip built the capital of his tetrarchy here, naming it Caesarea in honour of the Roman emperor. To distinguish it from other cities of the same name, it was also called *Caesarea Philippi*. It was in these parts that Jesus declared that Peter was the rock on which he would build his church and promised him the keys of the Kingdom of Heaven (Matthew 16, 13–20). In the 4th c. Caesarea became a bishopric. In the 7th c. it fell to the Arabs, then was taken by the Crusaders who held it until 1165. Subsequently it was an Arab village until 1967.

SIGHTS. – As excavations have so far not been carried out, there is nothing to be seen of ancient Caesarea Philippi. The *Banyas*, a strong E tributary of the Jordan (see entry), gushes out of reddish-grey stone cliffs. In these there are a few niches with Greek inscriptions, where statues of Pan used to stand. Nearby, to the left, is a large cave; the river used to emerge from it until an earthquake blocked the watercourse. Even further to the left, on a hillock, stands the gravestone (weli) of an Islamic saint, Sheikh el Khidr (the Green Man). About $\frac{1}{2}$ mile/1 km W of the spring is a waterfall with a drop of about 30 ft/10 m.

2 miles/3 km E, to the left of the road into the Hermon region, on a mountain ridge, stands mighty **Banyas Castle**. It was founded by the Moslems and given the name of *Qalat Subeiba*. Then the Crusaders took it. Today the Arabs call it *Qalat Nemrud* (Nimrod's Castle).

Weli above the spring where the Jordan rises

Beersheba/ Be'er Sheva

Southern District.
Altitude: 788 ft/240 m.
Population: 111,000.
Telephone code: 0 57.
ⓘ **Government Tourist Office,**
Bet Tnuat Hamoshavim,
Nordau Street;
tel. 3 60 11.

HOTELS. – *Desert Inn* (k), I, 164 r., SP, tennis; *Zohar* (k), 3 Shadar Street, II, 64 r.; *Arava* (k), 37 Histadrut Street, III, 27 r.; *Aviv* (k), 40 Mordei-Hagetaot Street, III, 22 r.; *Hanegev* (k), 26 Ha'azmaut Street, III, 13 r.

YOUTH HOSTEL. – *Bet Yatzif*, 400 b.

RESTAURANT. – *Aninat Hataam*, 95 Histadrut Street.

EVENTS. – Beersheba has a *theater* and a *chamber orchestra*. There are also visits by touring theater companies and the Israel Philharmonic Orchestra.

SPORTS and LEISURE. – Swimming (Shikun Gimmel swimming baths, near the Bet Ha'am, May to September; Omer swimming baths); tennis (Tennis Club, 70 Shikun Aleph; Country Club, tel. 3 34 44).

GUIDED TOURS. – *Ben Gurion University*, Rehov Hacharoshel (tel. 7 12 41); *Biological Institute and Arid Museum*, Rehov Ha aamout (tel. 3 83 44); *Arid Region Research Institute*, Rehov Hashalom (tel. 7 83 83; bus route No. 5).

MARKET. – The Bedouin *camel market* in Rehov Hebron starts trading at six in the morning every Thursday.

COMMUNICATIONS. – Rail links to Dimona and Tel Aviv, with connections to Haifa and Jerusalem in Lod: information from the railway station (tel. 3 72 45). – From the Central Bus Station (between the Town Hall and the Market Building) Egged Buses depart for all the country regions (tel. 7 43 41). Sherut Taxis belonging to the Yael Daroma Taxi Co., Rehov Keren Kayemet (tel. 3 91 44) ply on the routes to Eilat, Jerusalem and Tel Aviv. – Transport within the city is provided by twelve bus routes and two taxi firms (Sinai Taxi, 48 Rehov Sahistadrut, tel. 7 75 25; Mezada Taxi, 41 Rehov Ha'azmaut, tel. 7 55 55).

Beersheba (Be'er Sheva) is known as the city of the patriarchs on account of references to it in the Old Testament. Yet it looks like a young city, and in a few decades it has developed to become the "capital of the Negev". On the border between the arid grazing land to the S and the arable land in the N, it is important for its university and its industries.

HISTORY. – The earliest settlements in the Beersheba region lay on the E edge of the present city, on Tell Abu Mattar in Wadi Beersheva. An Early Bronze Age settlement dating from the 4th millennium B.C. was discovered during excavations here. In it there lived semi-nomads who constructed water tanks on the banks of the river and oval caves with entry from the top. In the dry season they left these quarters and went N with their herds. A few finds from their settlement are on show in the municipal museum, and there is a fertility idol carved in bone in the Israel Museum in Jerusalem. The caves were also inhabited by the Horiten (i.e. sons of the hollows) who are mentioned in Genesis and with whom the patriarch Abraham came into contact. As the Old Testament relates, it was at the "well of the oath" or the "seven springs" (both corresponding to Bir Seba) that the heads of two tribes, namely King Abimelech of Gerar and Abraham, made a treaty which guaranteed Abraham unimpeded use of the spring which he had dug out (Genesis 21, 32). This compact was renewed by Abraham's son Isaac (Genesis 26, 33).

Beersheba, part of the grazing ground of the Amalekites, formed in the time of the Judges the S border of the Israelites' territory which stretched from Dan to Beersheba (Judges, 20, 1). About 1100 B.C. an Israelite town sprang up on Tell Be'er Sheva, 4 miles/6 km E of the modern city. It was excavated in 1969 by Yohanan Aharoni; an Israelite fort was uncovered, and finds were made that date back to Aramaic, Edomite, Persian and Hellenistic times. Subsequently Beersheba became a garrison town: between the 2nd c. B.C. and the 7th c. A.D. Maccabean, Roman and Byzantine soldiers were stationed here in turn. For a long while, however, the place was uninhabited; just a few Bedouin congregated here at the spring with their herds.

A new era opened in the history of the town when the Turkish overlords set up an administrative center to control the Bedouin in the Negev. At their request the Germans drew up a city plan with straight streets – what is now called the Old City – and the Bedouin market place. In 1915 a railway was constructed to provide supplies for the Turkish and German troops, and a mosque was built (which is now the Municipal Museum). In 1917 Beersheba was the first Palestinian city to be taken by General Allenby. During the period of British rule which began at that time, a police barracks was erected in Beersheba, and the "Hunger Road" was constructed; it was a tarmac road to Gaza which was built in order to provide employment in the region.

Around 1900, Jews had settled in Beersheba, but they left the city during the Arab riots of 1929. After Israel was declared an independent state in 1948 Jews came back. At the time it had just 3,000 inhabitants. Today Beersheba is a completely Jewish city, its inhabitants coming from every imaginable country. In the N of the Old City an extensive residential quarter has sprung up. In the E industry has been developed to process produce from the Negev. Specialists in the Ben Gurion University and the Arid Region Research Institute investigate the special conditions of life in the Negev.

Abraham's Well

SIGHTS. – The main axis of the Old City which dates back to the Turkish period is Ha'azmaut Street. At the NW end lies the British First World War military cemetery and the **Biological Institute**. A little further N are the station buildings of the railway constructed by the Germans in 1915. Ha'azmaut Street leads S, with the Administrative Offices on the left and a mosque from the Turkish period. The mosque is the **Municipal Museum** nowadays, with finds dating back to the early settlement at Tell Abu Mattar (4th millennium). At the junction of Ha'azmaut Street and Hebron Street (Derekh Hevron) stands an ancient Bedouin well, called the *Well of Abraham*. On Derekh Hevron, just before it crosses Eilat Street (Derekh Elat), is held the Bedouin market. Sderot Ha'nessim turns off to the left from Derekh Elat and goes towards the city park past the *town hall*, close to which lie the *Bet Ha'am* community center and the **Arid Zone Research Institute**. Sderot Ha'nessim goes N towards the medical center and **Ben Gurion University**.

Beersheba
Be'er Sheva

500 m
(550 yd)

A little N of Beersheba along Derekh Hevron, just beyond the railway line, a track leads to the memorial to the Negev Brigade which distinguished itself in the struggle for independence.

SURROUNDINGS. – **From Beersheba via Maon to Nizzana** (124 miles/199 km). – The highway goes S, with a fork leading up to the *Bor Mashash Spring* (12 miles/20 km). The road then bears right and, 7 miles/11 km further on, comes to the junction near *Mash'abbe Sade* kibbutz. Further NW lies *Tell Haluza*, a city which was originally Nabataean before becoming Roman and Byzantine. It was abandoned in the 7th c. (to left: 9 miles/15 km; remains of city gates and other buildings). After anotheer 9 miles/14 km the Gaza–El Arish road is reached. From here another road goes E to *Tell Sharuhen* (2½ miles/4 km) where, beneath layers indicative of settlements here in the Persian, Israelite, Philistine and Canaanite period, a Hyksos fortress (18th c. B.C.) has been discovered. – The left turn 3 miles/5 km further along the road to Gaza leads to the *Nirim* kibbutz which was founded in 1946 and moved to its present position in 1949. SE of it, on the way to the *Nir Oz* kibbutz, are found the ruins of **Maon** (½ mile/1 km) which is mentioned in the time of King Hezekiah (8th c. B.C.; 1 Chronicles 4, 41). In 1957 when a road was being constructed the remains of a synagogue were found; it was either destroyed or abandoned when the Arabs took over in the 7th c. Its fine mosaic pavement has Greek and Hebrew inscriptions and portrays animals, including a pair of lions with a menora between them.

It is then possible to return to the Mash'abbe Sade kibbutz (37 miles/60 km). The motorway runs SW to a fork (14 miles/22 km) where a track branches off to the extensive ruins (not always accessible) of the Nabataean city of Subeita or **Shivta** (see entry; 3 miles/5 km). It has important buildings of the Byzantine period. – The road continues to **Nizzana** (17 miles/27 km), a city which was excavated in 1935. Like Shivta it was founded by the Nabataeans and had its period of greatest prosperity in the 5th–6th c. Nizzana lies only a few miles E of the demarcation line which since 1982 has again formed the border between Egypt and Israel.

From Beersheba to Eilat (144 miles/231 km). – The road from Beersheba runs SE towards Yeroham (20 miles/32 km). From there it goes SE, reaching (12 miles/19 km) the *Sede Boqer* kibbutz (see entry) which was founded in 1952. Israel's first prime minister, David Ben Gurion, used to live there. The "Negev School" (Midreshet Sede Boqer), which was created by Ben Gurion and in front of the library of which he lies buried, is seen on the left 2 miles/3 km further on. The complex lies above Wadi Zin into which a road leads off here. From the car park a short walk along a path leads to the En Avdat spring (see entry; 3 miles/5 km). It takes its name from the city of Avdat (see entry) which was originally Nabataean and became Byzantine later on. Its ruins, which have been partially reconstructed, are on a hill top 3 miles/5 km S, to the left of the road. Nearby lies a Bedouin encampment.

Beyond the settlement of *Mizpe Ramon* (14 miles/23 km) which was founded in 1953 and today has a population of 2,000, Maktesh Ramon (see entry) is found. It is the greatest depression in Israel. In the E part of It the Nabataeans sited the fort of Mezad Mishhor to protect the caravan route between their capital Petra and Avdat. The "Ma'ale Ha'azmaut" (Independence pass) leads 547 yd/500 m down into the depths of the "mortar". Next the road crosses the Plain of Meshar and Wadi *Paran* (see entry; 28 miles/ 45 km), into the Arava Depression near Gerofit (31 miles/50 km), and then continues to the harbour of **Eilat** (see entry; 30 miles/49 km).

From Beersheba via Ashqelon to Hebron and back (111 miles/178 km). – The route leaves Beersheba and goes NW to Netivot (19 miles/31 km), turning N here via the *Yad Mordekhay* kibbutz (with memorials recalling the Warsaw ghetto uprising and the defence against Egyptian attacks in 1948) towards **Ashqelon** (see entry; 21 miles/33 km), then E towards Qiryat Gat (16 miles/25 km). Passing, on the right, the ancient sites of *Tell Lakhish* (see Lakhish) and *Tell Maresha* (see Maresha), the route continues to *Bet Guvrin* (see entry). Crossing the Judaic highlands the route then comes to **Hebron** (see entry; 16 miles/25 km) with its Islamic mosque and the graves of the Jewish patriarchs over the Cave of Machpelah. – Turning towards the SW, the road leads back (31 miles/50 km) to its starting point, Beersheba.

From Beersheba via Massada to Mamshit and back (124 miles/200 km). – The route runs NE out of Beersheba towards Hebron. Then, after 8 miles/13 km, it bears left and, going along a by-road, comes to *Tell Arad* (see Arad) and then to the city of Arad (20 miles/32 km). The fortress of **Massada** (see entry) lies NE (13 miles/21 km). Returning to Arad (13 miles/21 km), the route then turns SE, continuing along a road through impressive scenery to the Dead Sea. Just beyond a sign indicating the altitude two viewpoints are found close together. From the first there is a view over the splendid mountain scenery and down towards the fortress of *Mezad Zohar*. It was first Nabataean, then Byzantine, and was built to protect the road along the valley from Judea to Edom. The second vantage point offers, particularly towards evening, a magnificent view over the Dead Sea and the Mountains of Moab. Near *Neve Zohar* (13 miles/21 km) the Dead Sea is reached. The route next goes S, past the Dead Sea Works, taking a right turn (14 miles/23 km), and, 7 miles/12 km further on, it passes on the left the remains of a Roman fort. This figures on the 6th c. Madaba map under the name of Thamara and is called *Mezed Tamar* (Palm Fort) in Hebrew. 9 miles/14 km beyond this, a left fork leads up to the *Maktesh Hagadol* crater (see entry; 9 miles/15 km) with its mines. Just beyond the fork is seen on the left the site of **Mamshit** (see entry), another Nabataean city in the Negev. Via *Dimona* (4 miles/7 km), which was founded in 1955 and now has a population of 28,000, the route leads back to Beersheba (23 miles/ 37 km).

Beit Lahm

see Bethlehem

Belvoir

Northern District.
ⓘ **Government Tourist Office,**
Casanova Street,
Nazareth;
tel. (0 65) 7 05 55.

The ruins of the great Crusader castle soar high above the Jordan valley. On account of its view out over the valley the French Templars called it "Belvoir", and in Hebrew it is called "Kokhav Hayarden" (Star of the Jordan).

There are two routes to Belvoir. Coming from the N and leaving the Tiberias–Bet Shean road just beyond the valley of the Tavor (8 miles/13 km S of the Sea of Galilee), it is possible to turn right up a twisting track which winds its way up to the castle some 550 yd/500 m higher up. The castle can also be reached by taking the Bet Shean–Afula route, forking right near En Harod (9 miles/14 km) and following a road which passes the villages of Ramat Zevi and Bene Brit on the summit of Ramot Yissakhar and leads to Belvoir (8 miles/13 km from En Harod).

SIGHTS. – The **Crusader castle** of Belvoir was constructed about 1130 on the site of Gerofina, which was destroyed by the Romans. Materials from the ancient city were, to a certain extent, used in the new work. It occupies a quadrilateral 110 yd by 153 yd/100 m by 140 m, with four towers at the corners and a fifth tower in the middle. The double gate at the entrance is on the E side where the cliff falls away steeply. The other three sides are protected by deep moats. The castle was strong enough to withstand in 1187 an assault by Saladin, who had won a great victory at the battle of the Horns of Hittim (see entry). Having been given an assurance of safe passage to Tyre, the knights then surrendered the castle which was destroyed in 1219. Its impressive ruins have now been partially restored.

Benot Ya'akov

Northern District.
ⓘ **Government Tourist Office,**
Town Hall,
Safed;
tel. (0 67) 3 06 63.

5 miles/8 km N of Rosh Pinna the Jordan is crossed by the bridge called Benot Ya'akov (Daughters of Jacob). It owes this name to the local legends according to which the patriarch Jacob passed through this area with his family. It is said it was at Jacob's ford that his daughters foretold the fate in store for his son Joseph.

According to tradition Joseph was flung by his brothers into the well in the caravanserai of Gov Yosef (Joseph's Well) and subsequently sold to Midianite traders who took him off to Egypt. *Gov Yosef* is the name given to the ruins of the caravanserai near the *Ammiad* kibbutz which lies 4 miles/6 km S of Rosh Pinna, W of the road to Tiberias.

The Bible, however, speaks of only one daughter of Jacob, Dinah, and does not place this incident here. When Jacob sent Joseph away, he went from Hebron along the old royal highway through Samaria to Sechem and then on into the Dothan Valley which reaches its end near Jenin. It was there he found his brothers who then sold him into slavery (Genesis 37, 12–28).

The Crusaders, harking back to the old tradition, named the place Jacob's ford and claimed it was here that Jacob wrestled with the angel, though this, too, was in contradiction to the Bible which states that the event took place at the "ford Jabbok" (now called Nahr ez Zarqa) between the villages of Amman and Djerash in present-day Jordan (Genesis 32, 24ff.). In 1178 King Baldwin IV built the fortress of Chastellet to protect the crossing, but it was destroyed again by Saladin as early as 1179.

In the 20th c. the Benot Ya'akov bridge, the sole crossing of the upper reaches of the Jordan, became strategically important for a number of reasons. The British twice set out from here to attack Syria which, in the First World War, was occupied by the Turks, and, in the Second World War, by the Vichy government of France. In June 1946 it was dynamited, as were ten other bridges, by Hagannah, the Jewish underground organisation, as a protest against British policy in the Mandated territory. – When the British had been building a bridge earlier on, an elephant's tusk and other prehistoric items were discovered.

Bet Alfa

Northern District.
Population: 800.
(i) Government Tourist Office,
Casanova Street,
Nazareth;
tel. (0 65) 7 05 55.

The Bet Alfa kibbutz stands at the foot of Mount Gilboa, 4 miles/6 km W of Bet Shean and 12 miles/19 km E of Afula. It was founded in 1921. The place became famous when the almost intact **mosaic pavements of a 6th c. synagogue were discovered here.

When an irrigation channel was being dug in the nearby Hefzi Bah kibbutz in 1928 a mosaic pavement was found by chance. It is considered, along with that at Tiberias-Hammat (see Tiberias), to be the most important evidence available about synagogue architecture in the Byzantine period. – The synagogue lies on land belonging to the Hefzi Bah kibbutz. But it is called Bet Alfa, though that is the next kibbutz, because the site of the synagogue used to belong to the old Bet Alfa.

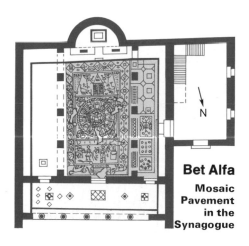

Bet Alfa
Mosaic
Pavement
in the
Synagogue

SIGHTS. – **Mosaic pavements* are preserved in the nave and right-hand aisle of the **synagogue** which has been given a new roof. The building comprises a nave with two side aisles and a semicircular apse with a Torah cupboard at the S end. The mosaic side aisle to the right has ornamental motifs, the mosaic in the nave is dominated by figurative designs. By the entrance may be seen, between a lion and a steer, a Graeco-Aramaic consecration inscription.

Bet Alfa – Abraham sacrificing Isaac (detail of the mosaic pavement in the synagogue)

The mosaic pavement in the nave is divided into three panels. Behind the old center portal is portrayed the sacrifice of Isaac by Abraham. On the left two men are driving Abraham's ass. In the middle stands Abraham, bearded and in a long cloak, holding the sacrificial knife in his right hand and grasping little Isaac with the left. Behind the patriarch the ram can be seen, tied to a tree, and over it appears the hand of God which indicates to Abraham that he should offer up the ram instead of his son. On the right the altar can be seen, prepared for a burnt offering.

A cosmological design dominates the middle panel. Its central circle portrays frontally the sun-god Helios in his chariot which is drawn by four horses. All around the twelve signs of the Zodiac are shown, as are the seasons of the year in the four corners.

In the S panel a closed Torah cupboard is depicted in the middle, flanked by menoras, incense scoops, two birds and two animals. On each side of the picture hang curtains.

These two fields of imagery, the circle of animals and the Torah cupboard, are also found in the mosaic pavements in the Hammat synagogue at Tiberias. But while the mosaics there are works of consummate artistry, those at Bet Alfa are rather in a simple style typical of local craftsmanship.

Bet Guvrin

Southern District.
ⓘ **Government Tourist Office,**
Afridar (Shopping Center),
Asqelon;
tel. (0 51) 3 24 12.

Bet Guvrin kibbutz lies in the W part of the Judean highlands, 22 miles/36 km E of Ashqelon on the road to Jerusalem via Qiryat Gat and Bet Shemesh.

The village was founded in 1949 to protect the border between Israel and Jordan. It stands on the ruins of an Arab village and has been given an ancient Hebrew name.

HISTORY. – In the 6th c. B.C. Bet Guvrin was a suburb of Maresha (see entry), the capital of the Edomites, which lies just 1 mile/2 km away. In the 2nd c. B.C. it was conquered, along with Maresha, by the Maccabees. Under Roman rule it developed, from the 1st c. B.C. onwards, into an important fortified settlement. The Emperor Septimius Severus (193–211) gave it the name of *Eleutheropolis* (i.e. Free City). Even in the Byzantine era it was the administrative center of the largest district – it stretched as far as Gaza – in Palestine. To protect the route S to Jerusalem the Crusaders built Gibelin Castle here. It was captured by Saladin in 1187, won back by the Crusaders, and finally taken by the Mamelukes in 1244.

SIGHTS. – In the course of excavations ½ mile/1 km SE of the village two *mosaic pavements belonging to Christian churches of the 5th–6th c. were uncovered in 1921. In them are depicted deer, birds, symbols of the seasons and a hunting scene (for a guided tour, ask in the kibbutz).

Further on there stands a *synagogue* of the 3rd c. On one of the pillars there was formerly a Hebrew inscription, and a menora was carved on the capital of another. Most of these antiquities are now kept in the Rockefeller Museum, Jerusalem.

Beside the road there stands a ruin dating from Crusader days which was inhabited by Arabs until 1948.

Bethany

see El-Azariye

General view of Bethlehem

Bethlehem/ Beit Lahm

West Jordan.
Altitude: 2,462 ft/750 m.
Population: 20,000.
Telephone code: 02.
ⓘ **Government Tourist Office,**
Manger Square;
tel. 74 25 91.

HOTEL. – *Bethlehem Star*, Al Baten Street, II, 54 r.; *Handel*, II, 40 r.

**Bethlehem (Beit Lahm in Arabic) is famous in the Bible as the town of David and of Jesus. It has an Arab population, half Christian and half Moslem. Its religious center is the Church of the Nativity, a 6th c. basilica which has survived to the present day.

BIBLICAL HISTORY. – In and around Bethlehem there are several places that figure in Scriptural tradition. – It is first mentioned in connection with the death of Rachel, the wife of Jacob. On her way from Bethel she died when giving birth to Benjamin, her second son, and "was buried in the way to Ephrat, which is Bethlehem" (Genesis 35, 19).

Centuries later, Ruth, after being left a widow, came with her mother-in-law Naomi back from Moab to her home-town of Bethlehem. When she was gleaning corn in the field belonging to Boaz, she met him. He married her, and she bore him Obed, who was "the father of Jesse, the father of David" (Ruth 4, 17). David, the youngest son of Jesse, was anointed king of Bethlehem by Samuel (1 Samuel 16, 13).

Finally Jesus was born of the lineage of David in Bethlehem. His parents had come there from Nazareth where they normally resided because of a census

conducted in the days of the Emperor Augustus (Luke 2, 1–7). The angels proclaimed the birth to the shepherds in the fields (Luke 2, 10).

HISTORY. – After the Bar Kochba uprising had been put down, the Emperor Hadrian erected a shrine to Adonis over the Grotto of the Nativity in 135. The latter is not mentioned in the gospels, but Justin Martyr does speak of it around 155. By about 200 it had already become "a firm concept for the pilgrims" (Hollis/Brownrigg). In 325 the Emperor Constantine had a church built above the grotto in place of the shrine dating from Hadrian's time. From descriptions and the results of excavations carried out in 1934 the plan can be reconstructed as follows (according to R. W. Hamilton). Entry was through an atrium surrounded by arcades; it stood below the present-day courtyard in front of the church. The basilica had a central nave and two aisles on each side; there were mosaic pavements, and the walls were clad with marble. At the E end of the basilica three stairs led up to an octagonal room. This was located directly above the grotto, and an opening in the middle allowed pilgrims to look down into it. It is not certain whether the entrance to the grotto was to the E or the W. In 386, a few decades after the construction of this building, St Jerome, who was born in Dalmatia, came to Bethlehem and settled in a grotto near the Grotto of the Nativity. It was here that he prepared the Vulgate, his Latin version of the Bible. At that time pilgrims were coming to Bethlehem in great numbers from many different lands. As Jerome put it: "People hymned God's praises in every imaginable tongue."

Samaritans destroyed Constantine's church in the course of a revolt in 529. St Sabbas, who resided in the nearby Monastery of Sabbas (see Mar Saba), journeyed to Constantinople and sought to persuade Justinian, who had been emperor for two years, to rebuild the church. Justinian's architect took over from the older church the basic pattern of a central nave and double aisles on either side, but replaced the octagon with a trefoil plan and omitted the atrium.

This church has survived to the present day, which must be accounted something of a miracle. The Persians advancing on Byzantium spared it in 614 because they believed they could recognise their fellow countrymen in the figures of the Three Kings in oriental garb in a relief over the entrance. – In the time

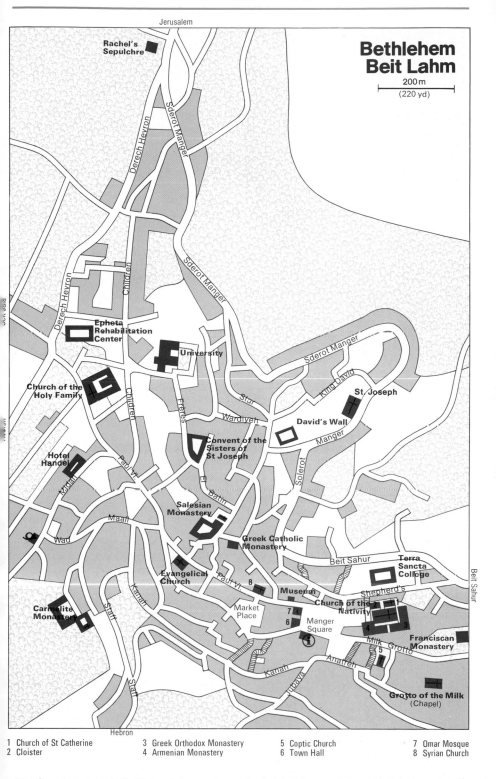

Bethlehem Beit Lahm

200 m
(220 yd)

Jerusalem

Rachel's Sepulchre

Derech Hevron

Sderot Manger

Derech Hevron

Children

Sderot Manger

Epheta Rehabilitation Center

University

Sderot Manger

King David

Church of the Holy Family

Children

Frères

Star

Wardiyeh

St. Joseph

David's Wall

Manger

Convent of the Sisters of St Joseph

Hotel Handel

Paul VI

Soleron

Batin

Salesian Monastery

Maali

Wad

Greek Catholic Monastery

Beit Sahur

Terra Sancta College

Evangelical Church

Paul VI

Museum

Shepherd's

Beit Sahur

Kanah

Market Place

8

Church of the Nativity

Carmolite Monastery

Staff

7

6

Manger Square

4

3

Milk Grotto

Franciscan Monastery

Staff

Kanah

Anatreh

Lubaya

5

Grotto of the Milk
(Chapel)

Hebron

1 Church of St Catherine	3 Greek Orthodox Monastery	5 Coptic Church	7 Omar Mosque
2 Cloister	4 Armenian Monastery	6 Town Hall	8 Syrian Church

of the Crusaders who took Bethlehem before capturing Jerusalem, the Byzantine Emperor Manuel had the church thoroughly restored between 1161 and 1169. At an earlier date, on Christmas day 1100, Baldwin I was crowned first king of Jerusalem here. – The Mamelukes did not destroy the church in the 13th c. either, though in later years it did fall into serious decay. In 1497 the roof had to be shored up. After 1516 the Turks used the marble cladding of the walls

for their buildings on the Temple site in Jerusalem. In 1670 Greek Orthodox Christians, with the approval of the Osman authorities, commenced the restoration of the church.

In the 18th and 19th c. there were often bitter and sometimes even violent conflicts between Christians of various churches – Greek Orthodox, Catholics and Armenians. These were further aggravated by the

mpanile in Bethlehem

Entrance to the Church of the Nativity

intervention of Russia and France, both countries claiming the right to protect one side or the other. The Sublime Porte sought to control these troubles by means of a settlement of proprietorial rights (the status quo) in 1757. The agreement was renewed in 1852 and survived the termination of Osman rule, remaining in force to the present day.

SIGHTS. – **The **Church of the Nativity** when seen from the square in front is a building that seems like a fortress. It is only on careful inspection that the gable over the nave can be made out. There were originally three entrances, but those on either side have been walled up. Passing

through the *central portal* it is possible to see how the building evolved over the centuries. The original door surrounds can be seen, as well as the carved roof beams of the 6th c. building of Justinian's time, resting on stone brackets. The Crusaders reduced the size of this entrance by inserting a portal with a pointed arch and walled up the upper parts. This portal was itself made even smaller, in order to prevent the Mamelukes from riding on horseback into the church. The headroom is at present only 4 ft/1·20 m, which means that visitors have to bend low on entering the church.

The interior still displays in essence the original tranquil monumentality of the 6th c. The view towards the wall where the altar stands is unimpeded; the British General Allenby had the tall screen erected by the Greeks between the nave and the choir removed in 1917.

Four rows each of 11 monolithic columns, the Corinthian capitals of which were originally gilded, support the roofs of the side aisles and the clerestory of the **nave** which is 177 ft/54 m long and 151 ft/46 m wide. Through two openings in the floor of the nave it is possible to see, 2 ft/60 cm below, the mosaics on the floor of the church erected by Constantine in 325. The *baptismal font* in the right-hand aisle dates from the time of Justinian.

Church of the Nativity   Bethlehem

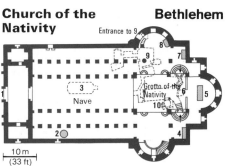

1	Entrance	6	Iconostasis
2	Baptismal Font	7	Altar of the Three Kings
3	Mosaic Pavement	8	Altar of Our Lady
4	Altar of the Circumcision	9	Grotto of the Innocents
5	High Altar	10	Altar of the Crib

Portions of the marble cladding brought here in the Crusader era (1261–69) remain on the clerestory walls. On the S side are portrayed, above the forebears of Christ, the first seven General Councils of the Church which were recognised by the Eastern Christians; the explanation is that the artists who worked here were not Western, but Greek. The Emperor Manuel of Byzantium was related by marriage to Baldwin III, the fourth king of the Crusader state, and had the mosaics executed by Basilios and Ephremos, two master craftsmen from his capital city. – Painted decoration from the Crusader period still remains on the shafts of the pillars. There are, for instance, pictures of saints such as King Canute of Denmark and St George, and the helmet of Baldwin I with a swan on it. (Baldwin, who was crowned first king of Jerusalem in the Church of the Nativity in 1100, was held to be a descendant of Lohengrin, the knight of the swan.)

Nave of the Church of the Nativity

A few steps lead up into the *crossing*. Both choir and transepts have semicircular end walls. In the N part stand the Armenian altars of Our Lady and of the Three Wise Men. In the S part the altar of the Circumcision which, like the high. altar that stands beyond the iconostasis, belongs to the Greeks.

Leaving by the *S transept* (right), from the semi-circular end of which a door leads into the adjacent Greek Orthodox monastery, and passing through a very finely carved portal under a pointed arch from the Crusader period, it is possible to go down stairs to the *Grotto of the Nativity. It is 40 ft/12.30 m long and 10 ft/3.15 m wide. The actual place where Jesus was born is marked by a *silver star* with a Latin inscription: "Hic de virgine Maria Jesus Christus natus est" (Here Jesus Christ was born of the Virgin Mary). Above it there is an altar in a niche with 12th c. mosaics which can hardly be made out. Opposite is the altar of the manger, three steps lower, and nearby stands the *Altar of the Three Wise Men*. – The further part of the Grotto is not open to the public. The door leading to the system of caves which link up with the other grottos is opened only for processions.

The Grotto of the Nativity in the Church of the Nativity

From the Grotto of the Nativity a second flight of stairs leads up to the *N. transept* and into the nearby Catholic **Church of St Catherine** which was built by the Franciscans in 1881 on the site of an earlier church. – A stairway in the N right-hand aisle leads down to the N part of the network of grottos. On the left is the *Chapel of the Innocents*, which commemorates the slaughter of the children of Bethlehem by Herod, and the *Chapel of St Joseph* lies straight ahead. On the right is the Chapel of Eusebius and the graves of St Paula and her daughter Eustachia and, further along, the *Grave of St Jerome* who came to Bethlehem with these two women. On the wall at the back can be seen the stone bench on which the body of the saint was laid after his death in 420 until his bones were conveyed to Rome and buried in Santa Maria Maggiore. The room that lies to the N of the

bench is considered to be the one in which Jerome composed the Vulgate.

The way out of the Church of St Catherine is through the **crossing** and across the square in front of the Church of the Nativity. By Manger Square, which serves as a car park, there are cafés, restaurants and souvenir shops in which gaily coloured embroideries and carvings out of olive wood (including crib figures) may be purchased. The Government Tourist Office is also here.

From the square in front of the Church of the Nativity a street goes SW between houses and the Greek monastery with its dependencies. After five minutes' walk the so-called *Grotto of the Milk* or *the Women's Cave* is reached. It is a cave, measuring 16 ft/5 m by 10 ft/3 m by 8 ft/2·5 m, which has been converted into a chapel. It is said that the Holy Family hid here before the Flight into Egypt. At that time a drop of Mary's milk is supposed to have fallen on to the ground.

From Manger Square Paul VI Street leads to the Market and the various commercial parts of the town. – W of Manger Street (Sderot Manger) which runs N, quite near St Joseph's Church, *David's Well* is found. It consists of water cisterns hewn out of the rock. Excavations are being carried out in the area of David's Wall which surrounds it.

SURROUNDINGS. – To the N of the town, just where the road leaves it, the *Grave of Rachel* can be seen on the left. She died when giving birth to Benjamin; it is a place of pilgrimage for pious Jews. 1 mile/2 km N of Bethlehem the **Monastery of Elijah** rises up on a hill on the right-hand side. The building was put up in the 6th c., restored by the Crusaders in the 11th c. and again by the Greek Orthodox in the 17th, and still survives. From here there are fine *views looking back over Bethlehem. The settlement of **Ramat Rahel**, with a name referring to the grave of Rachel, lies ½ mile/1 km further along the road. It was founded in 1926, destroyed in 1948 and rebuilt in 1950 right on the frontier with Jordan. On the 2,685 ft/818 m high mountain near the kibbutz a fortified palace of the Kings of Judah has been excavated. It was built in the 9th–8th c. B.C. and occupied until the time of King Joachim (608–598 B.C.). It was restored after the Babylonian captivity after 535 B.C. and it was probably destroyed by the Romans under Titus.

SE of Bethlehem lies the village of *Beit Sahur*. A certain field here is said to be the field of Boaz; he married Ruth who had come from Moab (Ruth 4). There is also the so-called Field of the Shepherds where the angels proclaimed the birth of Jesus (Luke 2, 7). Near the remains of a Byzantine church there is a Franciscan church built in 1954. ½ mile/1 km further along is a Greek Orthodox church where archaeologists discovered in the course of excavations in 1972

Monastery of Elijah near Bethlehem

a 4th c. church which was known from references in literature; it has very fine mosaic pavements. On the eastern outskirts of Beit Sahur the road forks; the left fork leads by way of the Monastery of Theodosius to the desert monastery of **Mar Saba** (see entry), while the right fork passes through the village of *Za'tara*, which was founded for Bedouin of the Taamara tribe in the 1960s, and leads to the fortress of **Herodeion** (see entry).

The road SW out of Bethlehem towards Hebron (see entry; 15 miles/24 km) soon passes the Pools of Solomon (on left). They are three vast open-top cisterns which were constructed in antiquity to provide water for Jerusalem; a reliable tradition attributes the work to King Solomon in the 10th c. B.C. "I build for me pools of water wherewith to water the wood of green trees." (Wisdom of Solomon 2, 6.)

A side road which turns off left 3 miles/5 km S of Bethlehem leads to the pools, near which the Turks built a small fort in 1540, and then runs along a valley with luxuriant vegetation to the village of **Artas** (1 mile/2 km). The nunnery in the lower part of the village bears the name "Hortus conclusus"; it serves as a reminder that with reference to this area the Bible does not only speak of pools and trees but also of the "garden enclosed" (Song of Solomon 4, 12), that is to say the "Hortus conclusus" which later became a metaphor of virginity and an emblem of the Virgin Mary. The present-day name of the village – Artas – is derived from the Latin word "hortus".

Just before the turn off to Artas on the Bethlehem–Hebron road, another road goes off to NW. It goes through the village of **Khadr**(2¼ miles/4 km), whose name comes from el Chodre, i.e. St George. A Greek Orthodox church ½ mile/1 km away is also dedicated to this saint. – ½ mile/1 km beyond Khadr a right turn leads to **Battir** (2½ miles/4 km). This village – the Betar of former times – is on the slopes to the S of the Ephraim Valley, through which runs the Tel Aviv–Jerusalem railway. Thanks to the abundance of water in the well here agriculture could develop on a large scale. Above the village there are ruins which await excavation; the Arabs call them "Khirbet el Yahud", that is "the Jews' ruins". A fortification which used to stand here held

out to the very end during the rebellion against the Romans in 132–135, and it was here that the leader of the revolt, Bar Kochba, met his death.

Bet Oren

Haifa District.
Population: 250.
ⓘ **Government Tourist Office,**
18 Hertzl Street,
Haifa;
tel. (04) 66 65 21.

ACCOMMODATION. – *Guesthouse*, II, 76 r, SP (tel. (04) 22 21 11).

Bet Oren (house in the pinewoods) is a kibbutz founded in 1939. It lies 12 miles/19 km S of Haifa in the Carmel mountains.

There are two routes to Bet Oren, either S along the coast from Haifa until turning left at the Atlit crossing (8 miles/13 km) or directly from Haifa over Carmel, turning right after 12 miles/19 km. – Bet Oren is situated in the mountains but is only 4 miles/6 km from the sea, so holiday-makers can enjoy a marked difference in environment.

SURROUNDINGS. – In caves 4 miles/6 km W of the village remains have been found of Carmel man who lived here 130,000 years ago in the Old Stone Age; finds in the Rockefeller Museum, Jerusalem.

Bet Shean

Northern District.
Altitude: 322 ft/98 m below sea level.
Population: 13,000.
Telephone code: 0 65.
ⓘ **Government Tourist Office,**
Casanova Street,
Nazareth;
tel. (0 65) 7 05 55.

*Bet Shean lies 16 miles/26 km S of the Sea of Galilee on the banks of the River Harod in the eastern part of the Plain of Jezreel which, thanks to carefully regulated irrigation, is now fertile. In the Talmud it says "if the Garden of Eden is in the Land of Israel, then its gate is surely in Bet Shean". The sights include such buildings as the Roman theater, and there are indications that the history of the town goes back beyond Roman times to the 4th millennium.

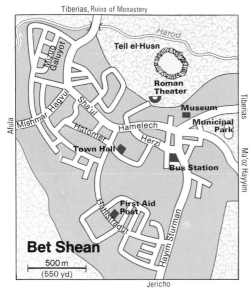

Tiberias, Ruins of Monastery

Tell el-Husn

Roman Theater

Museum

Municipal Park

Town Hall

Bus Station

First Aid Post

Bet Shean

500 m
(550 yd)

Jericho

Among the historical connections is a link with the fate of King Saul.

HISTORY. – In the course of excavations between 1921 and 1923 archaeologists from the University of Pennsylvania in America succeeded in identifying 18 layers belonging to distinct periods of settlement here. The oldest, from a period about 3500 B.C., was found at Tell es Husn, N of the present town. The *Canaanites* worshipped, together with other deities, the God Mekal, as is shown by a limestone stele carved about 1500 B.C. and which is now in the Rockefeller Museum in Jerusalem. As the town was under Egyptian suzerainty at the time, the inscription is in hieroglyphics.

Another temple was dedicated to Astarte (Ashtoreth), and an image of her was found on a second stele. This temple was taken over by *Philistines* who advanced

from the coast to Bet Shean in the course of the 12th c. After defeating King Saul and his sons in the battle on nearby Mount Gilboa in 1010 B.C. they brought Saul's armour "in the house of Ashtaroth, and they fastened his body to the wall of Bethshan". Then, after nightfall, men from Gilead, on the other side of the Jordan, came and took away the body and buried it (1 Samuel 31).

Saul's successor subjugated the Philistine town which was, for reasons that remain obscure, abandoned in the 8th c. B.C. It was only in the 3rd c. that it was reoccupied, by Scythian veterans, receiving the new name of *Skythopolis*. Jewish inhabitants started returning to the town in the Hashmonean era (2nd and 1st c. B.C.). Pompey made it a free city in 63 B.C., and it became part of the Decapolis league. Under Roman rule Bet Shean enjoyed, thanks to its flourishing agriculture and textile industry, a new period of prosperity. The Roman theater is evidence of this. Monuments of the Byzantine era include a round church, a monastery (567) and a synagogue (508). This period ended with the Islamic conquest of 639. In the 12th c. Bet Shean became an apanage (dependency) of Tancred, prince of Galilee. After Saladin had conquered it in 1183, the town had a Jewish population and among the inhabitants was Rabbi Ashtori Haparphi who wrote the first geography of Palestine in Hebrew. Later on Arabs settled here in increasingly large numbers, and they changed the name of the town to *Beisan*. The administrative building (Serail) erected in 1905 is a reminder of the Turkish era; it stands in what is now the Municipal Park. Jews came back to Bet Shean in 1937, and more and more have been coming since 1948.

SIGHTS. – The road from Tiberias first comes to the small *Municipal Park* with a modest open-air museum. Here stands the Turkish *Serail*, built in 1905, with its entrance which incorporates ancient pillars. King Saul Street goes off to the left, passing through a district in which parts of a Roman hippodrome were found. A left

Bet Shean – Roman theater

turn leads down to the *theater. Built towards the end of the 2nd c. during the reign of the Emperor Septimius Severus, it is the best preserved Roman theater in Israel. It originally held 5,000 spectators. The lower part of the semicircular building with rows of seats for spectators was dug out of the hillside, and the upper part is supported on massive foundations. Entry is by nine so-called vomitoria which debouch on to the diagoma, or *walkway* round the auditorium. Short, narrow passages lead off from the vomitoria towards small rooms with cupolas which have now disappeared. The function of these rooms is unclear. – The upper rows of seats have been partially destroyed, but the 14 rows below the walkway are still in a very good state of repair. There are likewise still impressive remains of the wall behind the stage. In the area behind this wall which was once richly decorated with pillars and statues there are numerous fragments of architectural interest.

Immediately N of the theater rises up lofty **Tell el Husn**. There temple buildings from the Canaanite era and other remains of ancient Bet Shean have been excavated. In the S part lay the *Temple of Astarte*, in which Saul's armour was hung up, while the *Temple of Dagon* is in the N part. Most of the finds are at present in the Rockefeller Museum in Jerusalem. Among them are the Mekal stele (about 1500 B.C.), a stele of the time of the Pharaoh Sethos I (1318 B.C.), a stele depicting Anat, the war-goddess (1250 B.C.), and an anthropomorphic earthenware sarcophagus (about 1280 B.C.).

Finds of a far more recent epoch came to light N of Tell es Husn, on the other side of the valley of the Harod. In 567, during the Byzantine period, a **monastery** was founded here by a noblewoman, Maria, and her son, Maximus. It has important mosaics which are now protected under a roof.

The entrance leads into a large, trapezium-shaped courtyard. Its *mosaic pavements* depict animals and birds, with two Greek inscriptions, and in the middle, within a circular band made up of animals with a Greek inscription, the sun-god Helios and the moon-goddess Selene are portrayed. – On the left there is a rectangular room where the mosaic, according to the inscription was "completed in the time of George, priest and abbot, and Komitas, his successor". In a little chamber opposite the entrance to the monastery, in the E part of the monastery grounds, in the narthex and in the *church* itself, further mosaics may be seen (vine tendrils, hunters and animals). Peacocks are

Convent of Our Lady   Bet Shean

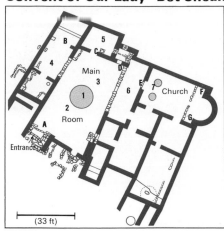

(33 ft)

MOSAICS
1 Circle with animals,
   Sun-God, Moon-Goddess
2 Animals and Birds
3 Animals and Birds
4 Ornamental Pavement
5 Grape Motives, Human
   Beings, Birds
6 Ornamental Pavement
7 Two Peacocks

A, B, C, D, E, F, G: Greek inscriptions

depicted in mosaics behind the entrance, and in the sanctuary there are Greek funerary inscriptions.

SURROUNDINGS. – **Bet Alfa** (see entry) lies 4 miles/6 km W of Bet Shean. It is famous for the mosaic pavements in its ancient synagogue. – The name of the *Gan Hashelosha* National Park (Park of the Three) which is situated on the road between Bet Shean and Bet Alfa commemorates three settlers who died when the area was conquered in 1938. The waterfalls (in Arabic called Sakhne) are impressive, and upstream there is a bathing pool with a picnic place.

7 miles/12 km N of Bet Shean lies the **Neve Ur** kibbutz. Its inhabitants are Jews from Iraq, and that is why it takes its name from Abraham's home town in Mesopotamia. A little further NW, on the left, the ruins of the Crusader castle of **Belvoir** (see entry) tower up. A zig-zag road leads up to it.

A secondary road goes E of Bet Shean by way of *Neve-Etan* (i.e. Seat of Power), a settlement founded in 1939, to the two-year older settlement of **Ma'oz Hayyim** (i.e. Rampart). Some 2 miles/3 km further S is the site of **Kefar Ruppin** at an altitude of 820 ft/ 250 m above sea level and 5 miles/8 km from the banks of the River Jordan.

The Jericho road S of Bet Shean has a turn half left (2 miles/3 km) which goes by way of *En Hanatziv* and *Sede Eliahu* to *Tirat Tsevi* (7 miles/12 km) which was founded in 1938. It is near Tell Sheqafim and is a typical frontier settlement for Orthodox Jews.

The Necropolis at Bet Shearim – entrance to catacomb No. 20

Bet Shearim

Northern District.
ⓘ **Government Tourist Office,**
18 Herzl Street,
Haifa;
tel. (04) 66 65 21.

The archaeological site of *Bet
Shearim 12 miles/20 km SE of Haifa,
near the road to Nazareth, is important in the Jewish rabbinical tradi-

tion. The catacombs are especially
impressive. They were excavated by
B. Mazar in 1936 and subsequently
by N. Avigad.

HISTORY.   Bet Shearim took on particular importance when in 135, after the failure of the Bar Kochba
uprising, Rabbi Juda Hanassi moved his seminary
here from Yavne (see entry), making the place the
spiritual center for the Jews. It was for this reason that
the High Council had its seat here for a time. Juda was
at its head, which entitled him to the title of Hanassi
(or Prince). Many members of this council were

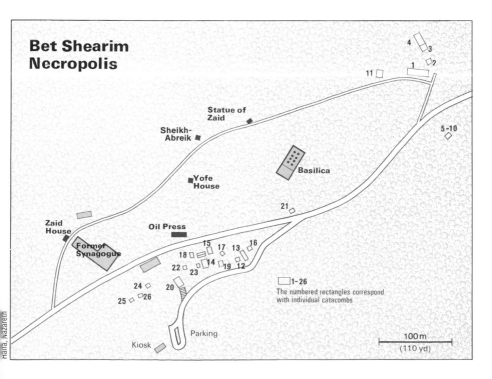

**Bet Shearim
Necropolis**

Statue of
Zaid

Sheikh-
Abreik

Yofe
House

Basilica

Zaid
House

Oil Press

Former
Synagogue

Parking

Kiosk

☐1-26
The numbered rectangles correspond
with individual catacombs

100 m
(110 yd)

Haifa, Nazareth

Relief with the menora in the Museum at Bet Shearim

From here it is a short walk to the *necropolis, which consists of catacombs in the hillside. A few of the catacombs are open to visitors. – In one of the caves there is a *museum* with a number of finds, including a relief depicting a menora of remarkably modern appearance.

Catacomb 20 has a façade which has been partially restored; there are three stone doorways under a triple arch. Inside there is a broad central gangway with several passages leading off to the side. At the far end of the first passage off to the left may be seen, with other remains, the *Hunting Sarcophagus*, with a lion hunting a gazelle, and the *Lion Sarcophagus*. In the rather narrow passage off to the right is the *Eagle Sarcophagus*. In the next on the right is the *Sarcophagus of the Bearded Man*, while the third on the right contains, at the far end, the artistically decorated *Mussel Sarcophagus*.

The façade of **Catacomb 14** likewise has a triple arch. In it are found most informative inscriptions, on the sarcophagus of a certain Simon and Gamaliel, presumably the sons of Rabbi Juda Hanassi who was himself buried in Bet Shearim.

buried at Bet Shearim. The fame of the place was such that other pious Jews also asked to be laid to rest here.

SIGHTS. – The road from Haifa bears right from the route to Nazareth in Qiryat Tavon and as it comes into Bet Shearim there may be seen on the left first the ruins of a large *synagogue* with central nave and side aisles which dates from the 2nd or 3rd c. and then, a little further on, *an oil press* with two rooms. Just round the next bend there is a car park, with refreshment kiosk.

Bet Shemesh

Jerusalem District.
Population: 11,600.
ⓘ **Government Tourist Office,**
24 King George Street,
Jerusalem;
tel. (02) 24 12 81.

Bet Shemesh stands S of the Tel Aviv–Jerusalem railway near the Biblical town of the same name. It was founded in 1950 and has developed from a tented camp for newly arrived immigrants into a modern settlement.

Bet Shemesh lies 19 miles/31 km W of Jerusalem. It is reached by turning off S from the Tel Aviv–Jerusalem road either 3 miles/5 km E of Latrun (see entry) or else 6 miles/10 km E of Abu Gosh and taking the road that goes via Bet Guvrin (see entry) to Qiryat Gat and Ashqelon (see entry).

HISTORY. – The new city took its name from the Biblical Bet Shemesh which in 1838 was identified with the Tell W of the present settlement and which was excavated before and after the First World War. The existence of a Hyksos and Canaanite city dating from the 18th c. B.C. was proved. The name Bet Shemesh means "House of the Sun" and is probably connected with the Canaanite temple the foundations of which have been discovered there. Joshua conquered the city in the 13th c. B.C. (Joshua 21, 16). In the 11th c. B.C. the *Philistines* captured the Ark of the Covenant from the Israelites in the battle of Ebenezer.

One of the Bet Shearim catacombs

But it brought them misfortune, and they handed it back. The two-ox wagon on which they had loaded the Ark stopped for a while in Bet Shemesh (1 Samuel 6, 12). From here the Ark was transported to Qiryat Yearim, near present-day Abu Gosh. – About 800 B.C. there were two battles between Jehoash, king of Israel, and Amaziah, king of Juda (2 Kings, 14, 11).

As excavations have proved, the city was also occupied in the Hellenistic and Roman periods. In the 13th–14th c. the Mamelukes built a caravanserai over the ruins.

As most of the people who have migrated to Bet Shemesh since 1950 are engaged in forestation, there are many conifer plantations in the area. – Limestone from the quarries in the Judaic Highlands provides raw material for a cement factory.

SURROUNDINGS. – The monastery of **Beit Jimal** (*Bet Gamal*) lies 2½ miles/4 km S, to the left of the road. It was founded by Salesian monks in 1881. They practise agriculture on a large scale and have vineyards. The monastery also maintains an orphanage. – In the cloisters fragments from the Byzantine period are preserved, including the mosaic pavement from a church which was erected in the 5th or 6th c. over the grave of the protomartyr St Stephen. His body was, according to a legendary tradition, laid to rest in Yavne (see entry) by Rabbi Gamaliel, Head of the Supreme Council, who was born here

Caesarea

Haifa District.
ⓘ **Government Tourist Office,**
18 Herzl Street,
Haifa;
tel. (04) 66 65 21.

HOTELS. – *Dan Caesarea* (k), Golf hotel, L, 110 r., Sauna, tennis (tel. (0 63) 6 22 66); *Chalets*, in Sedot Yam kibbutz.

RESTAURANTS. – *Charly's* (Oriental meals and sea food); *Harbour* (fish).

EVENTS. – *Concerts* in the Roman theater (in summer).

LEISURE and SPORT. – Golf (18-hole course), swimming.

*Caesarea, a classical city with Crusader associations, lies half-way between Tel Aviv and Haifa. Its ruins and other buildings are well worth a visit, and it also has facilities for holidays and leisure activities. In summer there are concerts in the restored Roman theater under the aegis of the Israeli Music Festival.

HISTORY. – The first settlements date back to the *Phoenicians*. They constructed a harbour here in the 4th c. B.C. After Alexander the Great had conquered the region in 332 B.C., Greeks lived here. In 22 B.C. Herod the Great began building work on a city which he called Caesarea in honour of Augustus. With a temple dedicated to Augustus, a theater, a hippodrome and a good water supply, Caesarea became a considerable city with a lively port and was inhabited by Jews, Romans and other gentiles. When Judea became a Roman province, its governors resided here from A.D. 1 onwards. Among them were Pontius Pilate under whose governorship Jesus was crucified and who lived here from 26 to 36, and Felix who held St Paul captive in the city for two years (Acts 23, 35) and who lived here from 52 to 60. About 35, also under the governorship of Pontius Pilate, Peter had baptised Cornelius, the Roman centurion (Acts 10); this caused some stir as it was the first time a gentile had been baptised, and it was the cause of the first "council of the apostles" (Acts 11, 1–18). Conflicts between the Jewish and Greek population of the city sparked the Jewish uprising in 66 which was put

Caesarea – fort on the Mediterranean port

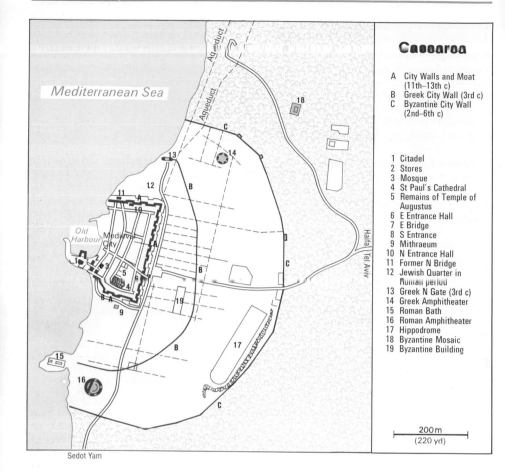

Sedot Yam

Caesarea

A   City Walls and Moat (11th–13th c)
B   Greek City Wall (3rd c)
C   Byzantine City Wall (2nd–6th c)

1   Citadel
2   Stores
3   Mosque
4   St Paul's Cathedral
5   Remains of Temple of Augustus
6   E Entrance Hall
7   E Bridge
8   S Entrance
9   Mithraeum
10   N Entrance Hall
11   Former N Bridge
12   Jewish Quarter in Roman period
13   Greek N Gate (3rd c)
14   Greek Amphitheater
15   Roman Bath
16   Roman Amphitheater
17   Hippodrome
18   Byzantine Mosaic
19   Byzantine Building

200 m
(220 yd)

down by Vespasian and his son Titus in 70. In 69 Vespasian was proclaimed Emperor in Caesarea and raised the status of the city to that of a Roman colony. After the failure of the second Jewish uprising against Roman rule to which the name of Bar Kochba is linked, its spiritual leader, Ben Aikba, was tortured to death in Caersarea in 135.

The apostle Philip founded a Christian congregation here as early as the 1st c. At the end of the 2nd c. Caesarea was a bishopric. In the 3rd c. Origen, the Father of the Church who came from Alexandria, taught here and founded his famous library. Between 313 and 340 Eusebius, who was probably born in the city and was the first historian of the Church, became the first bishop of Caesarea. Procopius, the historian of the Justinian age, was likewise born in Caesarea, in about 500.

This period came to an end with the capture of the city by the *Arabs* in 637. From then on the harbour lost its importance. The Crusaders came in 1101, but it was not until 1254 that the French king Louis IX fortified the city once again. The buildings he erected occupied only a fraction of the land covered by the ancient city. Just 21 years later the Sultan Baibars took the city, and its harbour began to silt up. – It was only in 1940 that new settlement began with the foundation of the Sedot Yam kibbutz.

In 1951 archaeological investigations of the huge site were begun; they are still far from completion. A few major finds, such as a 3rd c. B.C. head of Artemis and an important Byzantine mosaic, are preserved in the Israel Museum, Jerusalem.

SIGHTS. – A left turn from the Tel Aviv–Haifa road leads into the city, and the first thing to be seen on entering the site of Herod's city is, to the left, the **Hippodrome** (or horse racing track). It is overgrown with vegetation and awaits excavation. It is 252 yd/230 m long and 88 yd/80 m wide and could accommodate 20,000 people. Some 220 yd/200 m further on, on the left by the kiosk, there is a *building from the Byzantine period.* From the N a stairway leads to a porch in which there is a mosaic with a Greek inscription to the effect that Flavius Stategius constructed the stairway and the building under the governorship of Flavius Entolius. The entry, which is formed with pillars, was later walled up. Beyond it are two decapitated statues of the 2nd to 3rd c. One is of white marble, the other of porphyry, and the latter at least may be considered, on account of the purple material used, to be the statue of an emperor, perhaps Hadrian (117–138).

After this the *Crusader city is reached. It is protected by walls which are strengthened with bastions that jut out. The walls, which are now covered with brushwood, stand on the far side of a deep moat. These fortifications were built by Louis IX of France in 1254 on a unified plan in the course of a short period of time. They are rectangular in outline, with one long side along the shore to the W. Entry is by the E side, through a vaulted *gatehouse*. On the left-hand side the remains of houses can be seen with water cisterns provided with marble spouts. Pillars, shafts and other fragments can be seen lying all packed together on the ground here; it shows that the Crusaders used ancient material for the foundations of

Pointed arches in the Crusader castle

Roman statues

the city was taken on May 17, 1101. William of Tyre, the chronicler of the First Crusade, describes it as a flat, round dish carved out of a great emerald and records that it is the Holy Grail ("sacro catino"), that is to say the vessel used by Christ at the Last Supper. King Baldwin was considered to be a descendant of Lohengrin and thus stood in the tradition of the Knights of the Grail. He was, however, obliged to cede this precious trophy to the Genoese to recompense them for providing a fleet. That is how the "sacro catino", which served as corroboration for the Saga of the Grail and inspired poetry up to the time of Wolfram von Eschenbach, was taken to Genoa where it is preserved in San Lorenzo. (It has, however, since been established that it is a Roman glass dish.)

their streets and buildings. A *passage with pointed arches* leads across to the SE corner where it is possible to climb the wall; and there is a good view of the site from here, too.

A view down over the *old port's* warehouses can be had by walking from the

Inside the precinct of the fortress the land rises. Higher up the remains of the ancient water supply system can be seen, as well as the ruins of the Herodian *temple dedicated to Augustus*. Nearby is the **Crusader cathedral** whose three semicircular apses still stand. It was built by the Crusaders as the Cathedral of St Paul on the site of a former Byzantine church. It is probable that a famous object came from here, which King Baldwin seized when

Apses of the Crusader cathedral

Caesarea – Roman Theater

cathedral towards the sea. There are a few other remains, too. It is possible to go out to the bastion on the tongue of land where once the Phoenician's "Straton tower" stood. Pillar shafts protrude from the sea-washed wall of the Crusaders' port.

S of the Crusader city, close to the Herodian S wall, is the Roman theater. At the entrance to the precinct there stands, on the right, a copy of a stone found in Caesarea which bears the only inscription bearing the name of Pontius Pilate, governor here from 26 to 36: it runs "Tiberieum (Pon)tius Pilatus (praef)ectus Juda(eae)". The theater, restored some time ago, is so designed that from the seats the audience can look out over the orchestra and the remains of the stage buildings and see the sea. A peculiarity of the theater is the fact that a second semicircle has been added to the semi-circular orchestra; this was done only at a later date after the completion of the main building and involved the removal of the original stage wall. This provided, how-ever, an elliptical surface of the type familiar in amphitheaters and suitable for gladiatorial combats and fights with animals.

The site of the Crusader city and the theater which lies ½ mile/1 km S form a single *National Park*.

There is a further monument from Hero-dian times in the N of the ancient site. It is the **Aqueduct**, now partially buried in drifting sand, by means of which water was brought to Caesarea from a spring 4 miles/6 km to the N. It consists of a pair of conduits. From the remains at the S end it is clear that the right-hand channel was built first and that the left-hand one was added later. A second aqueduct was constructed about 110 yd/100 m further inland.

Cana/Kafr Kanna

District: North.
ⓘ **Government Tourist Office,**
Casanova Street,
Nazareth;
tel. (0 65) 7 05 55.

The village of Cana (Kafr Kanna), 5 miles/8 km N of Nazareth on the road to Tiberias, is famed as the place where Jesus worked his first miracle, the changing of water into wine at the "Wedding of Cana" (John 2, 1–11).

SIGHTS. – This friendly village, whose inhabitants are Christians and Moslems, has two churches commemorating this event. In the *Greek Orthodox Church* are

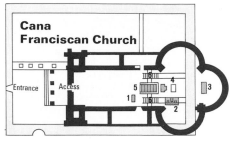

Cana
Franciscan Church

Entrance   Access

1 Hebrew Inscription   3 Altar   5 Stairs to the Crypt
2 Well   4 Old Jar 6 Steps

Capernaum/ Kefar Nahum

District: North.
ⓘ Government Tourist Office,
8 Elhadef Street,
Tiberias;
tel. (0 67) 2 09 92.

two stone jars said to be connected with the miracle. According to tradition the Catholic **Franciscan Church** stands on the site of the house where the wedding took place. In the nave, just in front of the steps to the crypt, is an inscription in Hebrew in memory of "Joseph, Tanhum's son" (3rd or 4th c.). This church also has an old jar which is said to be one of the six in which the water became wine.

Nearby is the *Nathanael Chapel* which also belongs to the Franciscans. It was built as a tribute to Nathanael of Cana who was initially prejudiced against Jesus ("Can there any good thing come out of Nazareth?") but then worshipped him as the son of God (John 1, 46–49) and who was also present at the miraculous draught of fishes when the risen Christ appeared (John 21, 2).

The wine sold here labelled "wine from Cana" also continues the Christian tradition.

*Capernaum (Kefar Nahum in Hebrew – village of the Nahum, Tell Num in Arabic) on the N bank of the Sea of Galilee is closely linked to the works of Jesus who after leaving his home town of Nazareth mostly taught in this fishing town and the surrounding area. Since 1894 there has been a Franciscan monastery here, and the monks, together with several archaeologists, have studied the old town and helped in the reconstruction of two important buildings, Peter's house and the synagogue.

BIBLICAL HISTORY. – "Leaving Nazareth, he came and dwelt in Capernaum, which is upon the sea coast, in the borders of Zabulon and Nephthalim." (Matthew 4, 13.) It was here that he called his first disciples, who were all fishermen: Simon Peter and his brother Andrew, James and his brother John (Matthew 4, 18–22). He preached in the synagogue where he healed a man possessed by the devil (Mark 1, 32). He also healed the lame and crippled (Matthew 15, 29–31), the servant of the centurion of Capernaum (Luke 7, 5–10) and raised the twelve-year-old daughter of Jairus, one of the rulers of the synagogue (Mark 5, 21–43). Near Capernaum he fed the five thousand with five loaves and two fishes (Matthew 14, 13–21; Mark 6, 35–44) and on another occasion fed the four thousand with seven loaves and a few little fishes (Matthew 15, 32–39; see Tabgha). It was in Capernaum that he taught in parables of the sower,

Capernaum – view of the synagogue

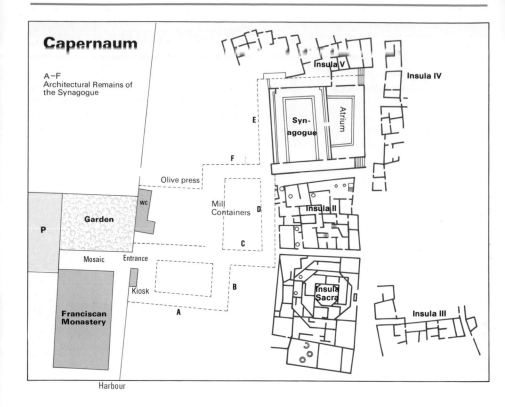

Capernaum

A–F
Architectural Remains of
the Synagogue

Insula V
Insula IV
E
Syn-
agogue
Atrium
F
Olive press
WC
Mill
Containers D
Garden
Insula II
P
C
Mosaic   Entrance
Kiosk   B
Insula
Sacra
Franciscan   A
Monastery
Insula III

Harbour

of tares among the wheat, of the grain of mustard seed, of leaven, of the treasure hid in a field, of the fishing net, etc. (Matthew 13). Above all it was here that on a nearby height he preached the Sermon on the Mount (Matthew 5–7; see Mount of Beatitudes).

HISTORY. – Finds of coins suggest that the town, though not mentioned in the Old Testament, was founded in the 2nd c. B.C. Capernaum was a small unfortified town which did not take part in the insurrections against Rome in the 1st and 2nd c. and consequently survived unscathed. Later on the original town, which stretched from the synagogue to the lake, was extended in the 4th c. by new quarters that grew up E and N of the synagogue. The fact that the synagogue was not built of the local black basalt but of imported limestone is proof of the wealth of the inhabitants. S of the synagogue an octagonal church was built about 450 on top of older houses to commemorate Peter who had lived on this spot. After the Islamic invasion in the 7th c. the town declined. The pilgrim Burchardus noted in the 13th c.: "The once renowned town of Capernaum is now a sad sight to behold and numbers but seven fisherfolk's hovels."

It began to develop anew when the American Robinson identified the place in 1838. Charles Wilson carried out the first investigations in 1866. In 1894 the Franciscans took custody of the ruins. In 1905 the German archaeologists Kohl and Watzinger discovered the nave and E aisle of the synagogue, brought down by an earthquake; the Franciscan monk Wendelin Hinterkeuser then spent until 1914 excavating the rest of the synagogue and the courtyard and investigated the adjoining area. Between 1921 and 1926 the Franciscan friar Gaudentius Orfali excavated residential areas and the octagonal Church of St Peter.

Further excavation work began in 1968. The archaeological investigations of Stanislao Loffreda have

furnished proof that after the time of the Apostles Capernaum and the surrounding area were continuously inhabited by Judeo-Christians. They passed on their knowledge of these holy places to the pilgrims who, from the 4th c. onwards, came to the Holy Land from the west and told stories of the town when they returned to their own countries. Today Capernaum's black basalt walls are overgrown with bougainvillea and cluster around fascinating remains of buildings dating from the 1st c. B.C. to the 5th/6th c. A.D.

SIGHTS. – A little beyond the entrance, which is between the Franciscan monastery and the garden, is the ticket-kiosk where slides and specialist literature, including the excellent guide "A Visit to Capernaum" by Stanislao Loffreda, are also on sale. Laid out like a park, the site is full of sculpted architectural fragments together with mosaics, with the Octagon of St Peter straight ahead in the background and the partly reconstructed synagogue on the left.

An anticlockwise route brings the visitor first, on the S side, to a *mosaic pavement* from Cana and a mass of remains from the synagogue, including columns from a window, a relief with vine-leaves, grapes and palm branches, a cornice with a seahorse and two eagles carrying a garland, a column with an inscription in Aramaic "Alphäus, son of Zebedee, son of John made the column as a blessing unto himself", a relief with a cart which probably depicts the portable Ark of the Covenant, a cornice with grapes and figs, a shell in a wreath (keystone of an arch in the façade), bits with swastikas or the Star of David and a second mosaic from Cana.

After turning left and then right the visitor arrives at the **Octagon of St Peter**. Its authenticity has been borne out by literary sources and archaeological investigations. It stands on the site of houses, originally arranged in squares (insulae), which can be traced back, in the case of the oldest ones, to the 1st c. B.C. These humble dwellings – tiny rooms enclosing a small yard and a hearth – appear from the number of fishing-hooks found in them to have belonged to fishermen.

One of the houses was subsequently replastered at least three times. The 131 inscriptions pieced together from the plaster fragments frequently contain the names of Jesus Christ and Peter which means that it can be supposed that at the end of the 1st c. the house had already assumed holy status as the *House of the Apostle Peter*. – About 350 it received a wall around it and was covered by an arched roof. The Spanish pilgrim Etheria noted at the end of the 4th c. that the house of the prince of the Apostles in Capernaum had become a church and that its walls had remained intact, which means that it was then a "domus ecclesia", a private house used for religious services.

About 450 an octagonal church was finally erected over this building (round or octagonal buildings were mainly used for baptistries or, as here, for memorials).

The mosaic pavement has a peacock in the middle as a symbol of immortality. The semicircular apse to the E was used as a baptistry.

N of the insula sacra with the Octagon is another insula and then the *synagogue. A few steps lead into an open porch from which three doors open into the body of the synagogue and another two into the courtyard adjoining it to the E. Consoles with palm trees have now been fixed back on to the middle door. Inside rows of columns separate the aisles from the nave and continue round the back of them. There are stone benches against the left-hand wall. On one of the Corinthian columns at the back is an inscription in Greek: "Herod, son of Monimos, and Justus, his son, and their children, erected this column." The synagogue presumably had a women's gallery. There is no Torah recess. The Torah must have been placed on the S side facing Jerusalem, i.e. at the entrance, for services. – To the E is a courtyard which could be reached from the synagogue as well as from the porch.

Historical and architectural considerations led Watzinger to date the building of the synagogue to the 2nd or early 3rd c. but more recent research, based on finds of coins and pottery under the paved floor of the synagogue, has led to the conclusion that it was not built until about 400. While the more ancient level of the St Peter Octagon can probably be looked upon as the rooms where Jesus stayed and where he healed Peter's mother-in-law (Matthew 8, 14–17; Mark 1, 29–31; Luke 4, 38–41), the synagogue is undoubtedly a building of a later date.

It is hoped that future excavations will unearth the actual synagogue where Jesus "taught as one that had authority, and not as the scribes" and where he worked several miracles (Matthew 12, 9–13; Mark 1, 21–22).

Detail of main portal in the synagogue in Capernaum

Carmel/ Har Karmel

District: Haifa.
(i) **Government Tourist Office,**
18 Herzl Street,
Haifa;
tel. (04) 66 65 21.

*Mount Carmel (Karmel=God's vineyard; 1,812 ft/552 m) is one of the foothills of the mountains of Samaria. 5 to 6 miles/8 to 10 km across, it stretches for 14 miles/23 km NW until it falls away steeply to the sea at Cape Carmel. In the NE its

precipitous slopes border on the Jezreel Plain (see entry) while in the SW it drops gently down to the Plain of Sharon (see entry).

HISTORY and SCRIPTURE TRADITION. – Finds in the caves on Mount Carmel, e.g. at Bet Oren (see entry), have shown that this area was inhabited 130,000 years ago, in the Old Stone Age (finds in the Rockefeller Museum, Jerusalem).

The Baal of Carmel was worshipped on its heights as the god of the region at least as far back as the Canaanite period. David brought Mount Carmel into his kingdom about 1000 B.C. but it was not until the 9th c. B.C. that, owing to the prophet Elijah, the worship of Yahweh was to prevail over the worship of Baal favoured by King Ahab of Israel (1 Kings 18). In an act of theological rigorism and of great significance for the development of strict monotheism and for Jewish history, the zealous prophet confronted the 450 priests of Baal and the 400 priests of Astarte of the kingdom of Ahab on the heights of Mount Carmel. He and his adversaries offered up sacrifices in the sight of the people at one of the old High Places and each waited for his god to "answer by fire". From Baal there was no response, but "the fire of the Lord fell" on to Elijah's altar. After this ordeal Elijah led the priests of Baal and Astarte down to the plain and the brook of Kishon where he slew them.

This is supposed to have taken place on the rocky crag of Muhraqa ("place of burning" in Arabic, 1,582 ft/ 482 m) in the SW part of Mount Carmel, where in 1886 a Carmelite monastery was built on the remains of an older church while Tell el Kassis (Priests' Hill) on the plain below is the putative grave of the priests. – According to another version the ordeal took place on Cape Carmel where the Carmelite monastery stands near the grotto of Elijah (see Haifa).

The form of religious life brought about by Elijah came to an end only a hundred years or so later with the Assyrian conquest in 732 B.C. The Baal of Carmel, once again the object of worship, was equated with Zeus by the Greeks after the rule of the Diadochi had been established and was called Deus Carmelus by the Romans. In the 2nd–3rd c. there was an offshoot here of the cult of Jupiter of Heliopolis, i.e. Baalbek (which also harks back to a Baal), and a citizen of Caesarea paid for the erection of a statue of this "Heliopolitan Zeus of Carmel". A fragment of one of the feet of this statue, authenticated by its inscription, is kept in the Carmelite monastery.

During the time of the Crusades Christians settled on this ancient sacred mountain for the first time. The Carmelite Order was founded here in 1150, and its monastery, which had been destroyed several times, underwent its final rebuilding in 1828 (cf. Haifa).

Mount Carmel has two ridges and consists of hard limestone and dolomite. Its lower slopes are covered with a host of different plants and shrubs thanks to abundant rainfall. Because of the unique beauty of its landscape Mount Carmel has been declared a *National Park* (several

camp sites). – In the 20th c. the rapidly expanding city of Haifa has encroached further upon the NW slopes of Mount Carmel and the University tower on the hill is visible from a long way off; the Druse villages on the wooded slopes are popular for excursions (see surroundings of Haifa).

Chorazin

Northern District.
ⓘ Government Tourist Office,
8 Elhadef Street,
Tiberias;
tel. (0 67) 2 09 92.

The ruins of the *synagogue of Chorazin, a little Jewish town mentioned in the New Testament, lie some 2½ miles/4 km N of the Sea of Galilee and 1 mile/2 km E of the road from Tiberias to Rosh Pinna.

The road N from Tiberias to Rosh Pinna runs past the Mount of the Beatitudes (see entry), and a right turn (12 miles/19 km) leads up a by-road to Almagor kibbutz. 1 mile/2 km along it a direction sign on the right (with no name indicated) points towards an ancient Jewish town the remains of which are reached after a few minutes' walk along a footpath. On the left there is an Islamic sepulchre, and then, further along, are the remains of the houses of the town of Chorazin which was founded about the time of the Second Temple and is mentioned in the New Testament as one of those places where lack of faith is deplored by Jesus (Matthew 11, 21).

SIGHTS. – Amidst other debris lie the ruins of the *synagogue which was constructed in the 2nd or 3rd c. out of local black basalt. It had – like the synagogues in Capernaum (see entry) and Bet Alfa (see entry) – a nave and side aisles. The entrance was S. Parts of the walls of the rectangular prayer chamber, the floor and the bases of ten of the original fourteen columns which divided off the side aisles still remain. The synagogue had rich architectural decoration, like the synagogue in Capernaum. But, on account of the brittle material employed the forms are less graceful.

Beams may be seen with tendrils, fruits, animals and human faces.

A beautifully crafted stone sedilia with a Judaic-Aramaic dedicatory inscription was rated an especially interesting find. Such seats were provided in the old synagogues as places of respect for the head of the congregation. The chair is now to be found in the Jerusalem Museum for Antiquities.

Dan

Northern District.
Population: 450.
ⓘ **Government Tourist Office,**
Town Hall,
Safed;
tel. (0 67) 3 06 33.

The Dan kibbutz lies 5 miles/8 km E of Qiryat Shemona close to the N frontier of Israel. It was founded in 1939, taking its name from the Tell of the ancient city of Dan, ½ mile/1 km N. The Dan, one of the three head-waters of the Jordan, rises at the foot of the Tell.

HISTORY. – On the Tell once stood the Canaanite city of Lais (Lajish) which is mentioned in Egyptian texts of the 18th and 15th c. B.C. Seeking for a place to settle, the Jewish tribe of Dan conquered it: hence the name by which it is still known. The Danites erected a graven image which they had stolen from Mount Ephraim and built a shrine around it (Judges 18, 27 01). A further shrine, not dedicated to Jehovah, was raised by Jeroboam I, first king of the Northern Kingdom of Israel from 933 B.C. As the Temple in Jerusalem was in the possession of the kingdom of Judah he ordered the building of two shrines, one in Bethel and the other in Dan (1 Kings 12, 28–30); in them a golden calf was worshipped. He also constructed in Dan a palace which was uncovered during excavations in 1955 and 1966. This city was destroyed 200 years later by Tiglatpilesar III.

In the kibbutz there is a museum with finds from the Hule Valley. There is an interesting nature trail through the *Dan nature reserve*. It leads through thick vegetation, across wooden bridges and past caves to the head-waters of the Dan, which remain unspoilt.

Dead Sea/ Yam Hamelach

District: Judean Desert.
ⓘ **Government Tourist Office,**
24 King George Street,
Jerusalem;
tel: (02) 24 12 81.
Government Tourist Office,
Shopping Center,
Arad;
tel: (0 57) 9 81 44.

HOTELS. – *Moriah Dead Sea* (tel. 0 57/8 42 21), L, 220 r., SP; *Shulamit Gardens* (tel. 0 57/9 06 51), I, 184 r., SP; *Galei Zohar* (tel. 0 57/8 43 11–5), I, 160 r., SP; *Ein Bokek* (tel. 0 57/8 43 31), I, 96 r., SP, tennis. – *Guest house* in the kibbutz of En Gedi (tel. 0 57/8 47 57), 91 r., SP. – YOUTH HOSTEL in Neve Zohar. – CAMP SITE in Neve Zohar.

The *Dead Sea (Yam Hamelach (=salt sea) in Hebrew, Bahr Lut (=sea of Lot) in Arabic) is 1,306 ft/ 398 m below sea level and is therefore the lowest place on the earth's surface. 47 miles/76 km long and up to 10 miles/16 km wide, it covers an area of about 386 sq. miles/ 1,000 sq. km. A peninsula jutting out into it from the E divides it into the small S part, only 13–20 ft/4–6 m deep, and the larger N part which reaches a depth of 1,420 ft/433 m. The most important river flowing into the salty lake is the Jordan. The N section of the W shore belongs to the Israeli-occupied West Bank.

View of the Dead Sea from Massada

BIBLICAL HISTORY. – The salt landscape with its salt caves at the S end of the Dead Sea is the scene of the Biblical story of Sodom and Gomorrah, destroyed by fire and brimstone because of their vices. At Abraham's intercession God spared only his nephew Lot and his daughters; they went to Zohar (W of the Dead Sea) and thence to a cave in the hills where, by their father, the sisters conceived Moab and Bar Ammi, the founders of the tribes of the Moabites and the Ammonites (Genesis 19). Above a salt cave near present-day Sodom stands a pillar of salt which is said to be Lot's wife.

En Boqeq on the Dead Sea

The Dead Sea, in any case, has a considerably higher salt content (about 25%) than the Mediterranean (3·5%). As a result its water contains no living organisms and bathers cannot sink in it. The high iodine, sulphur and mineral content has led to the treatment of skin diseases in its waters. In the last few years several hotels with bathing facilities have sprung up on the S part of the W shore. The eyes, nose and mouth have to be protected from the water when swimming and bathers must shower thoroughly afterwards.

The Egyptians and Nabataeans took advantage of the deposits of asphalt that from time to time are washed up from

No waters flow out of the Dead Sea but it has such a rapid rate of evaporation because of the hot climate that up till now the water level has remained almost constant (there is often a veil of mist over the countryside). In the last few years, however, so much water has been taken from the Sea of Galilee that the amount of water reaching the Dead Sea from the Jordan has been reduced and there are times when the lake is completely divided into two parts by the peninsula that juts out from the E shore. The reduction in the flow of fresh water is also leading to increased salinity. To offset the loss of water a canal is to be built from the Mediterranean through the Gaza Strip; this will also supply cooling water for future nuclear power stations and its fall will be used for generating hydroelectric power. Egypt and Jordan, the neighbouring Arab countries affected, are opposed to the project.

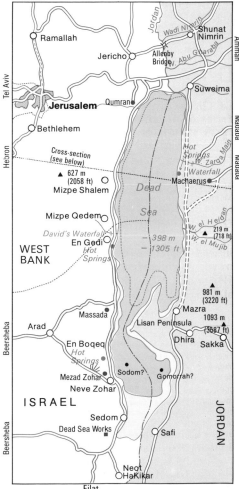

Dead Sea
Yam Hamelach

☐ 1930 Waterline

⬤ Waterline in Biblical times

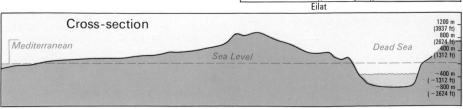

Cross-section

under the Dead Sea. Today the *Dead Sea Works* in the S mine potash and bromine.

Massada (see entry), *En Gedi* (see entry) and *Qumran* (see entry) are interesting places to visit on the W shore of the Dead Sea. There are also some ruined castles in the hills near the W shore. The furthest S of these castles, *Mezad Zohar* which dates from the Byzantine period, is on a small rocky outcrop on the valley road through a wild mountainous area. The road to Arad up into the hills from *Neve Zohar* near the S end of the Dead Sea passes, just before the sign indicating sea level, two vantage points, each with a small pavilion; from the top one it is possible to look down on to Mezad Zohar and from the bottom one there is a breathtaking *view, especially at sunset, of the Dead Sea and the Jordan hills.

Dor

Haifa District.
Population: 200.
ⓘ **Government Tourist Office,**
18 Herzl Street,
Haifa;
tel. (04) 66 65 21.

ACCOMMODATION. – *Hof Dor* (Igloo hotel) on Mediterranean coast, 75 r. (tel. (0 63) 9 95 33).

Dor is a commune with a beautiful beach. It was created in 1949 by immigrants from Greece on the ruins of the Arab village of Tantura. It lies 18 miles/29 km S of Haifa, on the shores of the Mediterranean.

HISTORY. – The hill on which stood ancient Dor lies on the far side of the present settlement. It was one of the 31 cities taken by Joshua about 1200 B.C. (Joshua 12, 11). One of the four offshore islands takes its name from Tafat, the daughter of a man appointed governor here by Solomon (1 Kings 4, 11). After the Assyrian conquest (8th c. B.C.) Tantura belonged for a time to the Phoenician kings of Sidon. From the 4th c. A.D. the city was inhabited by Christians, until it was destroyed by Moslems in the 7th c. In the 12th c. the Crusaders built a castle here, naming it after the de Merel family. It was destroyed by the Mamelukes in 1291.

Dor is reached by turning right off the Haifa–Tel Aviv road and crossing the railway. On the right may be seen Nahsholim kibbutz, beside the remains of a glassworks built by Baron de Rothschild, and then the Dor moshav.

SIGHTS. – There are remains of the old port, of **Merel Castle** and a 6th c.

Byzantine church. In 1979 a 1,196 sq. yd/ 1,000 sq. m *basilica* of the 5th c. was excavated; an object of veneration there used to be a piece of rock from Golgotha which had been fixed in a marble pillar.

Eilat/Elat

Southern District.
Altitude: 66 feet/20 m.
Population: 21,000.
Telephone code: 0 59.
ⓘ **Government Tourist Office,**
Merkaz Mischari Rechter (Shopping Center),
Hatemarim Street;
tel. 7 22 68.

HOTELS. – *King Solomon Palace* (k; tel. 65 12 58), 460 r., SP, sauna, tennis (opening spring 1984); *Aviva Sonesta Eilat* (k; tel. 7 61 91). L, 326 r., SP, tennis; *Laromme Eilat* (k), Coral Beach (tel. 7 41 11), I, 286 r., SP, sauna, tennis; *Lagoona* (k), Coral Beach (tel. 7 65 83), I, 253 r., SP; *Caesar* (k), North Beach (tel. 7 61 61), I, 240 r., SP, tennis; *Shulamit Gardens* (k), North Beach (tel. 7 51 51), I, 224 r., SP; *Moriah Eilat* (k), North Beach (tel. 7 21 51), I, 190 r., SP, tennis; *Red Rock* (k), North Beach (tel. 7 31 71), I, 114 r., SP; *Neptune* (k), North Beach (tel. 7 31 31), I, 100 r., SP; *Queen of Sheba* (k), North Beach (tel. 7 21 21–6), I, 92 r., SP, tennis; *Moon Valley* (k; tel. 7 51 11–8), II, 200 r., SP; *Americana Eilat* (k), PO Box 27 (tel. 7 51 76–9), II, 104 r., SP; *Etzion* (k), Hatemarim Street (tel. 7 41 31–3), II, 97 r., SP, sauna; *Eyal* (k), North Beach (tel. 7 61 11), II, 90 r., SP; *Center* (k), Hatemarim Street (tel. 7 31 76–8), II, 31 r.; *Caravan Sun Club* (k), Coral Beach (tel. 7 13 45–7), III, 108 r., SP, tennis; *Bel* (k), PO Box 897 (tel. 7 61 21–3), III, 84 r.; *Dalia* (k), North Beach (tel. 7 51 27–8), III, 52 r., SP; *Red Sea* (k), Hatemarim Street (tel. 7 21 71–2), III, 41 r., SP; *Adi*, Tzofit (tel. 7 61 51–3,–5), III, 32 r.; *Hadekel*, Hativat Hanegev Street (tel. 7 31 91), IV, 17 r.; *Coral Sea* (k), Coral Beach (tel. 7 41 84), 144 r., SP; *Galei Eilat*, North Beach (tel. 7 31 21–5), 106 r., SP; *Melony Tower* Aparthotel, Zolit Elite Center (tel. 7 51 35–6), 48 apartments; *Melony Club* Aparthotel, 6 Los Angeles Street (tel. 7 31 81–5), 36 apartments; *Sun Bay* holiday camp, with camp site, North Beach (tel. 7 31 05–6), 91 r.; *Blue Sky Caravan* holiday camp (tel. 7 39 53–4), 74 r.; *Les Coraux* Club Méditerranée holiday camp, North Beach (tel. 7 39 76–7).

YOUTH HOSTELS. – *State Youth Hostel* (tel. 7 23 58); *Nophit Youth Hostel* (tel. 7 22 07).

RESTAURANTS. – *Arizona*, Main Street; *Au Bistrot* (French) Elot Street; *La Bodega* (Spanish), 259 Chorev Street; *Luxemburg* (French), Yeelim Street; *Nophit* (local specialties), near the New Tourist Center; *Rimini* (pizzeria), New Tourist Center.

EVENTS. – Touring theater companies and orchestras.

LEISURE and SPORT. – Scuba (equipment hire: "Elat – Aqua Sport" Club, Coral Beach; Red Sea Divers, Caravan Hotel; Lucky Divers, Moriah Hotel; Nature Reserves Authority, Coral Beach), swimming, sailing, wind surfing.

BOAT TRIPS. – Tour Yam Co., New Pier (Coral Beach), round trips in glass-bottomed boats; Sherutey Yam, Marina (North Beach); Gery Services, Marina (North Beach); Red Sea Flotilla, New Tourist Center.

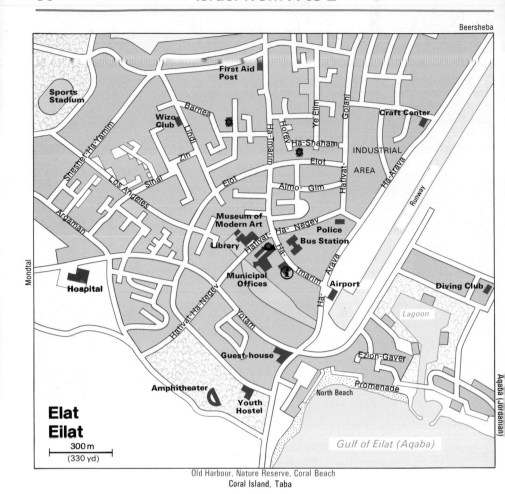

Beersheba

Elat
Eilat

300 m
(330 yd)

Gulf of Eilat (Aqaba)

Aqaba (Jordanian)

Old Harbour, Nature Reserve, Coral Beach
Coral Island, Taba

HOW TO GET THERE. – Several flights each day by Arkia Israel Inland Airway between Eilat, Jerusalem, Tel Aviv and Haifa (Arkia Office, New Tourist Center, tel. 7 61 02). – Long-distance buses (Egged Co.) from the bus station, Hatemarim Street (tel. 7 31 48). – Sherut taxis are run by Yael Daroma, Rehov Almogim (tel. 7 22 79). – Local buses depart bus station, Hatemarim Street, for North Beach, where most of the hotels are, every 20 minutes, and for Coral Beach every 30 minutes.

*Eilat is the southernmost town in Israel. Founded as recently as 1949, it has quickly grown from a police station into a township, which still has something of the pioneer spirit about it. Thanks to its situation at the northern end of the Red Sea it has a lot to offer those in search of relaxation. With its dry, hot climate – only about eight days with rain a year, a winter minimum temperature of 50°F/10°C and summer temperatures over 104°F/40°C – Eilat attracts holiday-makers from Israel and from abroad. It is possible to reach Eilat either by driving through the Negev or by flying.

Eilat is situated on a coastal strip some 7 miles/11 km long between the mountains of Sinai in the W and those of Edom to the E. It became part of the newly founded state of Israel in 1949. Since 1964 Eilat has been a port for overseas trade, serving as a staging point for oil, being linked to Ashqelon on the Mediterranean. In general Eilat still gives the impression of being a new town. The Eilat region and the nearby Jordanian port of Aqaba have, however, a history that goes back to remote times.

HISTORY. – Leaving Egypt under the leadership of Moses, the Israelites wandered through Sinai and then came "from Elath and from Ezion-Geber" and "passed by the way of the wilderness of Moab" which was inhabited by the sons of Lot (Deuteronomy 2, 8–9).

Elat, no doubt on the site of present-day Aqaba, and Ezion-Geber, which was excavated at Tell-al-Khalayfa in 1934, were neighbouring townships even in pre-Israelite times. Ezion-Geber, the so-called "harbour of Solomon", was presumably founded by the Edomites or else by the Midianites who inhabited the coastal region to the S which is now part of Saudi Arabia. It was also frequented by Egyptian shipping which transported the copper mined in Timna (see entry). In the 10th c. B.C. Solomon had ships built in Ezion-Geber, manning them with his own sailors and with Phoenicians placed at his disposal by King Hiram of Tyre. They brought to Ofir "six score talents of gold" (1 Kings 9, 26–8). At the same period the Queen of Sheba is supposed to have landed at this port before journeying to Jerusalem to "prove Solomon with hard questions" (1 Kings 10, 1 ff.).

The Israelites lost the port in the 8th c. B.C. In the 3rd c. it fell into the hands first of the Egyptian Ptolemies, then of the Nabataeans. Eventually it became a Roman possession, receiving the name of Aila. The architect of the 6th c. A.D. Monastery of St Catherine on Mount Sinai (see entry) was a native of Aila.

In 1116 the crusaders under King Baldwin I built a fortress on the island which now stands offshore from present-day Eilat. After being captured by Saladin in 1170, it was won back by Rainalt of Châtillon. But then it came into Moslem possession once more, belonging first to the Mamelukes, then to the Turks.

After the First World War Eilat was in the British Mandated Territory and in 1949 it became part of Israel. In that year a new Jewish settlement was founded, the kibbutz Elot which was later moved 2 miles/3 km further inland.

SIGHTS. – S of the port, on Coral Beach, there is a **Nature Reserve**. The main attraction is the ***Underwater Observatory**. A 330 yd/300 m long path leads down to this building. Through its twenty observation panels it is possible to view life 20 ft/6 m beneath the surface of the water. In this complex there is also an excellent *Aquarium*, with hundreds of the different kinds of fish that live in the Red Sea on display, as well as a *Dolphinarium* (under construction). – Further inland is the Texas Ranch.

The **Museum of Modern Art** (Sat, Sun.–Thurs. 5–8 p.m., Tues. and Thurs. also 10 a.m. – noon, Sat. and Sun. 11 a.m. – 1 p.m. – with exhibitions by contemporary artists is worth a visit. So is the

Public Library, with works in Hebrew, English and French (Sun., Thurs, 5–9 p.m., Fri. 1–4 p.m.). Both are opposite the Town Hall in Hativat-Hanegev Street.

In the Aquarium at Eilat

SURROUNDINGS. – 12 miles/20 km NW of Eilat is **Moon Valley**, rising to 2,626 ft/800 m. Its granite hillsides are quite denuded of vegetation. The *Gorge of the Inscriptions*, so called on account of the Nabataean, Greek and Hebrew inscriptions carved on the rocks, is reached by turning off left from the road to Moon Valley 14 miles/22 km E of Eilat.

5 miles/8 km S of Eilat lies the oasis of *Taba* with its palm trees ("Nelson Village" and beach facilities). – About 4 miles/7 km S of the holiday center is the *coral island* (Egyptian territory; special permit required!) which was an Egyptian harbour in classical times. The ruins of the Crusader fortress cover most of the island. The tiny harbour is full of starfish.

Shores of Eilat Bay, Gulf of Eilat (Aqaba)

On the road through the Arava Depression

El-Azariye (Bethany)

Jerusalem District.
Population: 2,200.
ⓘ **Government Tourist Bureau,**
24 King George Street,
Jerusalem;
tel. (02) 24 12 81.

The Arab village of El-Azariye (or Eizariya) was just a handful of houses a few decades ago. Now it has more than 2,000 inhabitants. It is situated on the eastern slopes of the Mount of Olives, and today just as in times past it is the last stopping place before Jerusalem for those who are making the journey from Jericho. It is the Bethany mentioned in the New Testament.

From Eilat to Neve Zohar on the Dead Sea (114 miles/183 km). – An excursion from Eilat towards the N goes through the Arava Depression, across which the Israeli-Jordan border runs. Near Gav Zaarava an altitude of 660 ft/200 m is reached, gradually falling to the N in the direction of the Dead Sea (1,306 ft/398 m below sea level). 16 miles/25 km further on, a short distance beyond the copper mines (at present not worked) the road leads off into the valley of **Timna** (see entry) with the so-called Pillars of Solomon, sandstone columns 164 ft/50 m high. – Further N is seen on the right-hand side of the road the 1,500 acre *Bar Hay* wildlife park. It was created in 1963 as a sanctuary for wild donkeys, and other desert animals. 10 miles/16 km N of the fork comes the date palm oasis of the kibbutz *Yotvata* which was founded in 1951 as a military settlement. It takes its water from the abundant spring called En Yotvata (Arabic: Ain Radian). Refreshment kiosk by the roadside. "Yotbata, a land running with springs" is mentioned in the Old Testament (Deuteronomy 10, 7). Near *Gerofit* (5 miles/8 km) a road leads off towards Beersheba. If the road towards the Dead Sea is taken, the route passes (28 miles/45 km further on) the broad *Wadi Paran* (see entry) and then the *Wadi Zin* (40 miles/65 km) which feeds the En Avdat spring (see entry). From here the route leads past the Dead Sea Works and the salt-mines of Sodom, close by *Neve Zohar* (see En Boqeq: 15 miles/24 km), to the **Dead Sea** (see entry).

From Eilat to Beersheba (144 miles/231 km). – The route leads N, turning left near Gerofit (30 miles/49 km), and rising out of the Arava Depression climbs into the Negev highlands (see entry). The road, the surface of which is mainly good, but with indifferent sections, passes through an austere, bare landscape. 31 miles/50 km on it crosses the upper reaches of the *Wadi Paran* (see entry), goes through Maktesh Ramon and climbs in zig-zags up to the settlement at *Mizpe Ramon* (28 miles/45 km). Via *Avdat* (see entry; 14 miles/23 km) and *Sede Boqer* (see entry; 14 miles/23 km) the route takes us through to **Beersheba** (see entry; 32 miles/51 km).

BETHANY IN THE BIBLE AND HISTORY. – The sisters Mary and Martha who "received Jesus into their house" lived in Bethany (Luke 10, 38), and he raised their brother Lazarus from the dead (John 11, 11–45). When he was going up for the last time from Jericho to Jerusalem where he was to suffer his Passion, Jesus visited the house of Lazarus and his two sisters again six days before the feast of the Passover, and Mary anointed his feet (John 12, 1–4). The next day he went on across the Mount of Olives to Jerusalem, riding on an ass from Bethphage.

In the village of El-Azariye, whose name is derived from Lazarus (Arabic: el Azar), there are a few reminders of events in the time of Jesus. In the 4th c. a chapel was built over the sepulchre which is ascribed to Lazarus. It fell into disrepair, and was restored by the Crusaders. They also built a monastery in commemoration of Mary and Martha. Later on a mosque was erected by the Moslems over the grave of Lazarus, and it was only in the 17th c. that Christians were again allowed to visit the site.

In the 19th and 20th c. the Christians were permitted to restore the religious buildings. In 1953 the Franciscans built a new church dedicated to Lazarus just below the sepulchre on the land which had been acquired in 1858. It stands near remains dating back to the Byzantine and Crusader periods.

SIGHTS. – The new **church** dedicated to **Lazarus** is built on the plan of a Greek cross, and takes the form of a mausoleum surmounted by a dome. Inside it has Latin inscriptions, the words which Jesus spoke in Bethany. Thus, on the wall above the altar, may be read: "Ego sum resurrectio et vita" ("I am the resurrection and the life"), and in the vault of the dome the text continues: "Whosoever believeth in me, though he were dead, yet shall he live, and whosoever liveth and believeth in me, shall never die." (John 11, 25.)

Close to the church is the entrance to the *sepulchre of Lazarus*, down 24 steps. It is the property of the Moslems. There is also to be found in El-Azariye a modern *Greek Orthodox church*; it is recognisable by its light blue dome and four-storey tower with light lantern.

Emeq Hefer
see Hefer Plain

Emeq Hula
see Hula Plain

Emeq Sharon
see Sharon Plain

Emeq Yizre'el
See Jezreel Plain

En Avdat

Southern District

ⓘ **Government Tourist Office,**
Bet Tnuat Hamoschavim,
Nordau Street,
Beersheba;
tel. (0 57) 3 60 01.

*En Avdat, the spring near the ruined city of Avdat, is one of the most

The pool at En Avdat

astounding natural phenomena in the Negev. In an austere highland landscape whose grim outlines are relieved only by a few settlements, four springs are found between Avdat and Sede Boqer.

The water from the En Avdat spring falls into a pool and drops into a deep gully. This is the source of the Nahal Zin which then flows through the *Zin Desert* (Midbar Zin). After the tribe of Judah had taken over the territory, this formed the extreme southern boundary of the kingdom (Joshua 15, 1). The desert is bordered by mountains 1,640 ft/500 m high to the N and nearly 2,625 ft/800 m high to the S. The land falls away to the Arava Depression towards the S of the Dead Sea.

BIBLICAL HISTORY. – Moving on from the Paran Desert the people of Israel under the leadership of Moses wandered into the Desert of Zin where they ran short of water. Scripture recounts how Moses at God's command struck the rock with his staff, "and the water came out abundantly, and the congregation drank, and their beasts also" (Numbers 20, 1–11). It is not recorded whether this was the En Avdat spring, but the account shows the importance of any spring in an arid region such as the Negev.

SIGHTS. – Access to the spring is from near the Negev High School, 2 miles/3 km S of Sede Boqer (see entry); allow a good hour.

Going up towards the school, the route turns off to the right just before the first houses and, with the surface getting worse and worse, leads down into the

The rocky valley of En Avdat

deep gully. Keeping always to the right, one comes eventually to a car park in the valley. From here it is possible to reach the *spring on foot. The valley gets narrower and narrower, its rocky walls reflect the sun, and the water flows along amidst the scree and brushwood.

Finally the pool is reached. The spring water flows into it over a wall of rock. At morning and nightfall the goats that live nearby come down to drink. The water has, however, a somewhat bitter taste.

The spring and its vicinity have been declared a *National Park* in order to conserve the unusual landscape.

On the way back to the car park the Library Building of Negev High School can be seen in a commanding position on the high rocky cliff. In front of it are the trees around David Ben Gurion's grave. A short distance to the S lie the ruins of the city of Avdat (see entry).

En Boqeq

Southern District.
Telephone code: 057.
ⓘ **Government Tourist Office,**
Shopping Center,
Arad;
tel. (0 57) 9 81 44.

HOTELS. – *Moriah Dead Sea* (k), spa hotel (tel. 8 43 21), L, 220 r., SP, tennis; *Shulamit Gardens* (k; tel. 9 06 51), I, 184 r., SP; *Galei Zohar* (k; tel. 8 43 11–5), I, 160 r., SP; *Ein Bokek* (k; tel. 8 43 31), I, 96 r., SP, tennis; *Lot* (k; tel. 8 43 21–8), 200 r., SP; *Tsell Harim* (k; tel. 8 41 21–2), 160 r., SP. – YOUTH HOSTELS in New Zohar. CAMPING in Neve Zohar.

En Boqeq is a center for foreign tourists and a spa on the SW shore of the Dead Sea. It has a warm mineral spring which has been used for therapeutic purposes ever since ancient times.

The kings of Judah built a **fortress** here as protection against the Moabites. Its ruins may be seen near the spring.

In En Boqeq there are just a few hotels and hydropathic institutions which are mainly concerned with the treatment of skin diseases. – The extremely salty deeper layers of water in the lake here are utilised as reservoirs for heat from the sun and thus help in energy conservation.

SURROUNDINGS – 5 miles/8 km S on the shore of the Dead Sea (see entry) lies **Neve Zohar** with several hot sulphur springs; it, too, is visited by many in search of medical and other therapeutic treatment. There is a restaurant on the beach and a filling station. The Bet Hayozer Museum has informative displays illustrating the natural life and economic development of the Dead Sea.

The gully of the River Zohar which flows out near Neve Zohar leads by way of a 2 mile/3 km long footpath to **Mezad Zohar**, a Nabataean fortress that was later used by the Byzantines. It stands on a conical rock in magnificent mountain scenery. A fine view of the fortress may be had when coming from Neve Zohar towards Arad (see entry) as far as the second, higher vantage point (on the right). The lower vantage point offers a magnificent prospect of the Dead Sea and the Jordanian Highlands.

The fortress of Zohar, near En Boqeq

From En Boqeq to Qumran (38 miles/61 km). – The road N from En Boqeq, with the Dead Sea on the right-hand side, comes in 7 miles/12 km to the fortress of **Massada** (see entry). It stands on cliffs 1,300 ft/ 400 m high. In the 1960s it was excavated under the direction of Y. Yadin and partially restored. From the N palace there is a good *view (access either by the twisting pathway or by funicular).

The highway back to the Dead Sea follows the E edge of the Judaic Desert, passing (11 miles/17 km) through the oasis of **En Gedi** (see entry: kibbutz with guest house), with palm trees and gardens. The nearby David waterfall is worth a visit; the water tumbles down nearly 330 ft/100 m over the rocks. – The final stage leads from En Gedi to **Qumran** (see entry; 19 miles/31 km). Here in 1947 a young Arab shepherd discovered in a cave ancient scrolls which had presumably been hidden here by Essenes, a sect which prophesied the coming of the Messiah.

En Gedi

Southern District.
Telephone code: 0 57.
(i) **Government Tourist Office,**
Shopping Center,
Arad;
tel. (0 57) 9 81 44.

ACCOMMODATION. – *Guest house* (tel. 8 47 57–8), 91 r., SP.

YOUTH HOSTEL: *Bet Sara*, 200 b. – CAMPING.

RECREATION AND SPORT. – Swimming (bathing beach on the Dead Sea).

Thanks to the "Goats' Spring" (En Gedi) which was known in Old Testament times and after which the settlement takes its name, the En Gedi kibbutz and the area around it support rich vegetation. The large *natural park with its historic relics, plants and animals is, with Massada, the most important tourist attraction on the W bank of the Dead Sea.

HISTORY. – There was a settlement on this site as early as the Chalcolithic Age, that is to say, the period of transition between the Stone Age and the time when metals began to be used, in the 4th millennium B.C. At this time a temple was built over the Schulamite spring. During an Egyptian campaign in Palestine the inhabitants concealed their valuables in a cave at Nahal Mishmar (7 miles/12 km S of En Gedi). During excavations the finds included the heads of 240 staffs of office and five ebony carvings which no doubt came from the Chalcolithic temple.

After the Israelites took over the Promised Land En Gedi was listed as a city in the territory of the house of Judah (Joshua 15, 62). When David was fleeing before the wrath of the aging King Saul he sought refuge in the fortress near En Gedi. Saul set out with 3,000 men to capture David and his followers, and matters came to a head dramatically. Saul "went in to cover his feet. And David and his men remained in the

sides of the cave." But, contrary to the urging of his followers, David did not touch the Lord's anointed but "cut off the skirt of Saul's robe privily". When Saul left the cave, David approached him and showed him the skirt which he had cut off to demonstrate that he had not had evil intentions towards him. Saul said to him: "Thou art more righteous than I; for thou hast rewarded me good, whereas I have rewarded thee evil." Then he acknowledged David as his successor: "And now, behold, I know well that thou shalt surely be king, and that the kingdom of Israel shall be established in thine hand." (1 Samuel 24, 2–23.) The name of the river – Nahal David – recalls these events.

En Gedi, as a place of great beauty, figures in the love poetry which is known as the Song of Solomon, David's son. The girl sings: "My beloved is unto me as a cluster of camphire [camphor] in the vineyards of En-gedi." (Song of Solomon 1, 14.)

In the course of excavations begun in 1961 at Tell Goren to the N of the kibbutz, evidence of five successive settlements has been found. These date from the 7th c. B.C. to the 5th c. A.D., a period of some 1,200 years.

The first settlement was destroyed by Nebuchadnezzar in 582 B.C., four years before the fall of Jerusalem. It was rebuilt after the return from the Babylonian captivity, and this second city flourished in the 5th and 4th c. B.C. The Hashmoneans built the third, Hellenistic city (2nd to 1st c. B.C.). This was destroyed in the course of the conflict between the Hashmoneans and Herod. The latter built the fourth city, which fell during the Judean War in 68. The fifth and last city lay a little NE of the Tell, the remains of a synagogue marking the site. Why it was abandoned in the 5th c. is not known.

In the course of the Bar Kochba uprising which was put down by the Emperor Hadrian in 135 the numerous caves in the vicinity of En Gedi took on a certain importance, as has been shown by Yigael Yadin's excavations. In the Nahal Hever valley (3 miles/5 km E of En Gedi) finds bear witness to the fate of the Jewish rebels who had fled here. For instance, in the 465 ft/150 m deep Cave of the Epistles the finds included 15 letters by Bar Kochba, a fragment of a psalm, metal vessels, keys from abandoned dwellings, skulls of dead men, scraps of clothing and sandals. The "Cave of Horrors" opposite it takes its name from the remains of the fugitives who died here.

The En Gedi site remained unoccupied from the 5th c. until in 1949, at a distance of only 2½ miles/4 km S of the border between Israel and Jordan, an Israeli military camp was set up. From this an agricultural settlement developed in 1953.

SIGHTS. – Immediately to the N of the kibbutz the *Nahal Arugot* valley runs from W to E. To the N of this, close by the sea shore, are large new palm plantations, and rather further inland rises *Tell Goren*. NE of it amidst the palm trees is the **Synagogue**, dating from the period of the fifth settlement at En Gedi. In the central circle and in the corners of the mosaic pavement there are several pairs of birds, the star of David and an inscription of which eighteen lines remain.

Waterfall in the En Gedi Nature Park

quadrilateral Roman fort, and a round Israelite fortress (to the W).

Journey times: (1) from the entry to the waterfall and back – 1 hr 15 min.; (2) to En Gedi Spring, the Bronze Age Temple and Dodim Cave – 4 hr; (3) via the temple to the Dry Canyon – 5 hr. – Further information can be obtained from the wardens of the Nature Park and at the agricultural college, situated to the N of the entrance, which carries out research into the plant and animal life of the Judaic desert and the Dead Sea region. For longer tours it is advisable to take a local guide, for the hot, dry desert nearby can be dangerous.

En Gev

Northern District.
Population: 300.
ⓘ **Government Tourist Office,**
8 Elhadef Street,
Tiberias;
tel. (0 67) 2 09 92.

ACCOMMODATION. – *Guest house* (chalets: tel. (0 67) 5 11 67). – CAMPING.

RESTAURANT. – Fish restaurant on sea shore.

EVENTS – Each year a festival is held in the large concert hall at Passover.

The En Gev kibbutz, founded on the E bank of the Sea of Galilee in 1937, is situated at the foot of the hill on which stood the city of Susita.

From Tiberias, the kibbutz can be reached by road (17 miles/28 km) or by water (5 miles/8 km). Until 1967 access was possible only by sea. The road connection which had been made in 1941 was broken in 1948 when the Syrians advanced up to the shore of the lake.

SURROUNDINGS. – 1 mile/2 km E of En Gev, at the top of a steep slope 1,150 ft/350 m above the Sea of Galilee, lie the ruins of the city of **Susita**. Its name, derived from the Hebrew word "sus" which means "horse", became "Hippos" in the Hellenistic period. In the 1st c. the city was a possession of the Decapolis, later becoming part of Herod's kingdom. In the Byzantine era it was a Christian bishopric. It was finally destroyed either by the Persians or the Arabs in the 7th c. At the summit ruins are found which date from the Judaic, Roman and Byzantine periods.

The most noteworthy attraction, however, is the *Nature Park** in which water plants grow beside desert vegetation and in which goats, hyenas, leopards and birds of every sort are kept. The entrance to the park is situated on the track turning off from the road along the sea shore N of the palm plantations (plans of the park on sale; car parking). A shady lane leads up Nahal David into an area with vegetation that becomes more and more luxuriant, in stark contrast to the desert zone here, until it reaches a pool into which the stream tumbles over perpendicular rocks. The track, which sometimes becomes quite difficult, leads up further from the *waterfall* and, bearing S all the time, it comes to *En Gedi Spring*, near which the remains of an old water mill have been found. Continuing to the N, the track leads to the remains of the Early Bronze Age *Temple* (4th millennium B.C.); it was dedicated to the cult of the moon and the spring. In the middle of the building there still lies a round moon stone. The two gates of the sacred precinct point towards the En Gedi spring in one direction and towards the Shulamit spring, which lies to the N, in the other. N, beyond the Shulamit spring, is the *Dodim Cave* above the waterfall which has just been mentioned. – On the other side of the Bronze Age temple lies the "Dry Canyon" (to the NW), with a

En Sheva

see Tabgha

Galilee/Galil

Northern District.
ⓘ Government Tourist Office,
Town Hall,
Safed;
tel. (0 67) 3 06 33.
Government Tourist Office,
Casanova Street,
Nazareth;
tel. (0 65) 7 05 55.

Galilee (Galil in Hebrew) is the northernmost part of Israel. It borders on the Mediterranean, the valley of the Jordan and the plain of Jezreel (see entry). It comprises a coastal strip to the W and the mountains of Upper and Lower Galilee around Safed and Nazareth respectively. Agriculturally it is very marginal land, only just able to support crops.

HISTORY. – When the Israelites came into the Promised Land the tribes of Naphtali, Sebulon and Asser settled in Galilee (Joshua 19), being joined later by the tribe of Dan (Judges 18, 27). In the 8th c. B.C. the Assyrians occupied the area, followed later by the Babylonians, Persians and Greeks. After the Hashmonean conquest in 163 B.C. the Jews were excluded from the coastal plain and lived in the mountainous parts. After the Roman annexation of Galilee, it was placed, together with Judea (see entry), under the rule first of the Hashmonean Hyrkanos II and then of Herod the Great. Subsequently, during the lifetime of Jesus, it was part of the tetrarchy of Herod Antipas who made Tiberias (see entry) his capital. Next it came under the sway of Herod Agrippa. In 66 Galilee was a stronghold of the Jewish rebellion against the Romans. After the

Bar Kochba uprising in 135 it replaced Judea as the center of Judaic feeling, with the cities of Bet Shearim (see entry), Sepphoris (Zippori, see entry) and Tiberias taking on particular importance in this connection. In the 16th c. Safed (see entry) developed into a hub of religious renewal. – After the 7th c. Arab settlement in Galilee increased steadily. It was in Rosh Pinna (1878) and Metulla, the most northerly village in Israel, that the first Jewish settlements of the modern period were founded. Galilee became part of the newly founded state of Israel in 1948.

The N section of the area, *Upper Galilee*, reaches an altitude of 3,958 ft/1,208 m at Hare Meron. The S part, *Lower Galilee*, does not reach such altitudes (Mount Tabor: 1,845 ft/562 m). The border between Upper and Lower Galilee is the plain of *Bet Kerem.*

Gilboa, Mount
see Mount Gilboa

Golan/ Golan Heights

The area of the Golan Heights was annexed by Israel in 1981. Situated E of the Jordan and the Sea of Galilee, it stretches 31 miles/50 km from N to S, from the mouth of the Hermon to the mouth of the Yarmuk River, and 12 miles/20 km away towards the E

Herds of goats on the Golan Heights

Memorial on the Golan Heights

from the Jordan. At Mount Avital (Har Avital), W of Quneitra, the high plateau reaches an altitude of 3,952 ft/1,204 m.

HISTORY. – In ancient times there were Jewish settlements in the region of the Golan Heights. In the 1st c. A.D. the area formed part of the territory of Herod's son, Philip, who founded Caesarea Philippi (see Banyas). In the south of the Golan, on the Yarmuk, Gadara (see Hamat Gader) had some significance as a capital of Greek culture and was a frequented spa.

After 1948 the Israel–Syria border followed the Jordan. After the Israeli occupation of the Golan Heights in 1967 several Jewish settlements were founded. UN troops are stationed in a buffer zone. Israel annexed the Golan late in 1981.

The Golan stands mainly on volcanic basalt. The area is cut up by a large number of wadis. Nowadays the area is inhabited by Jews, a few remaining Arabs and some 10,000 Druse peasants. Since the settlement of Israelis here much has been done to improve the infra-structure, including the building of schools and the improvement of medical services.

Hadera

Haifa District.
Population: 36,500.
ⓘ Government Tourist Office,
7 Mendele Street,
Tel Aviv;
tel. (03) 22 32 66–7.

Hadera is a town on the N–S road between Haifa and Tel Aviv, and is equidistant (30 miles/49 km) from both. It is situated in the Plain of Sharon, at the turning when the road goes off to Afula in the valley of the Jezreel.

This town developed from a caravanserai which was bought, together with the surrounding land, in 1890. The old building has been restored and today houses the community center with a *synagogue*.

In 1891 an agricultural settlement sprang up. It was called after the old Arab name of the place, "Hudaira", meaning green. The earliest settlers had to contend with great difficulties in this malaria-infested region. Better living conditions came only after the marshes had been drained, with financial help provided by the Baron de Rothschild. In 1911 when the township was twenty years old it already had 500 inhabitants, including immigrants from Russia and the Yemen.

In 1920 Hadera acquired a rail link to the new line built by the English between Tulkarm and Haifa. The connection with Tel Aviv was constructed after 1948. This triggered off substantial development in the area. Several places in the vicinity were incorporated in the township, and plant was built for the paper and rubber industries.

Caesarea, Haifa Caesarea, Haifa

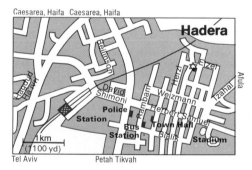

Tel Aviv   Petah Tikvah

SURROUNDINGS. – **Caesarea** (see entry), with its ancient and medieval ruins, lies 6 miles/10 km NW of Hadera. 5½ miles/9 km N is the village of *Binyamina*, so called after the Hebrew forename of Baron Edmond de Rothschild whose monumental grave is found 3 miles/5 km further on, just before *Zikhron Ya'ahov*.

HaEmeq
See Jezreel Plain

Haifa/Hefa

Haifa District.
Altitude: 0–985 ft/0–300 m above sea level.
Population: 227,000.
Telephone code: 04.

ⓘ **Government Tourist Office,**
Herzl Street;
tel. 66 65 2.
Haifa Port;
tel. 66 39 88.
Municipal Information Office:
in Town Hall (Center: tel. 64 53 59);
23 Haneviim Street (Hadar: tel. 66 30 56);
119 Hanassi Boulevard (Carmel: tel. 8 36 83);
at the Central Bus Station (tel. 51 22 08).

HOTELS. – *Dan Carmel* (k), 87 Hanassi Boulevard, L,
220 r., SP, sauna; *Nof* (k), 101 Hanassi Boulevard, I,
100 r.; *Zion* (k), 5 Baerwald Street, I, 94 r.; *Shulamit*
(k), 15 Kiryat Sefer Street, I, 70 r.; *Vered Hacarmel* (k),
1 Heinrich Heine Square, I, 23 r.; *Yaarot Hacarmel* (k),
Mount Carmel, II, 103 r., SP; *Carmelia* (k), 35 Herzliya
Street, II, 50 r.; *Dvir* (k), 124 Yefe Nof Street, II, 39 r.;
Ben Yehuda (k), 154 Hayam Street, II, 22 r.; *Beth
Shalom Carmel*, 110 Hanassi Boulevard, III, 31 r.;
Talpiot, 61 Herzl Street, III, 24 r., *Nesher*, 53 Herzl
Street, III, 15 r.

YOUTH HOSTEL. – *Carmel*, 400 b.

RESTAURANTS. – *Bankers Tavern*, 2 Habankim
Street (continental); *La Trattoria*, 119 Hanassi
Boulevard (Italian/French); *Neptune*, 19 Margolin
Street (fish dishes); *Balfour Cellar*, 3 Balfour Street (k;
Jewish continental).

CONNECTIONS. – Haifa is connected by shipping
routes with the rest of the Mediterranean. Air routes:
inland flights by Arkia Company to Tel Aviv. – Buses:
many city and long-distance services: Central Bus
Station, corner of Jaffa Street and Heyl Hayam Street
(tel. 51 52 11); Egged Tours, 4 Nordau Street (tel. 64
31 31–2). – The Carmelite Line (underground railway)
runs between the harbour area and the upper town.

*Haifa (Hefa) is Israel's chief port. It
lies on the N slopes of *Mount
Carmel which juts out into the sea
here, gradually rising from the sheltered W corner of the Bay of Haifa.
The city is an important staging post
for the export of agricultural
produce, an industrial center and has
a Technical High School and a University. Sites such as the Bahai
Shrine and the "School of the
Prophets" are reminders of the significance of the place for the faithful
belonging to various religions.

HISTORY. – Haifa is not mentioned in the Bible. At
this spot there were at first two settlements. *Salmona*
lay towards the E, beside the River Kishon, at Tell Abu
Hauwam which was flattened in the modern period to
provide space for industrial developments. To the W
lay *Shiqmona* the remains of which have been
excavated S of the Oceanographic Institute. The
settlement dates back to the era of Solomon (10th c.
B.C.), and finds are displayed in the Haifa Museum of
Ancient Art.

Between these two places lay *Haifa*, which is referred
to in the Talmud. In the Byzantine period the name
came to be applied to the entire settlement. Despite its
destruction in the 7th c., Haifa was renowned in the
11th c. for shipbuilding and the Talmud school. In
1099 it withstood a six-month siege by the Crusaders,
but was then sacked. Sultan Saladin captured it from
the Crusaders in 1187, but Richard the Lion-Heart
won it back in 1191. In 1265 the Crusaders were
definitively expelled by Sultan Baibars. The *Carmelite*
monastery, which belonged to an order founded here
in 1150 by the monk Berthold, was destroyed after the
fall of Akko (Acre) in 1291, and the monks fled to
Europe.

Under the *Mamelukes* and (after 1517) the Osmans,
Haifa was no more than a fishing village. In 1740 it
was captured by Dahir el Umar, the lord of Galilee. He
instituted a new settlement which is the present "Old
City" between Paris Square (Kikar Paris) and the Post
Office, and he developed the harbour for the grain
trade with Egypt. Under Pasha *Ahmed Jezzar*, who
succeeded Dahir in 1775, the Carmelites were allowed
to return to the grotto of Elijah. During Napoleon's
advance on Acre in 1799 the monastery served as a
hospital, but Ahmed Jezzar had the wounded soldiers
slaughtered after Napoleon withdrew. On the outbreak of the Greek War of Independence, Jezzar's
successor, Abdallah Pasha, had a lighthouse (Stella
Maris) constructed 345 ft/105 m above sea level,
close to the grotto of Elijah. He persecuted the Greek
Orthodox Christians, but in 1828 allowed the Franciscan Carmelites to rebuild their monastery dedicated
to Elijah close by the lighthouse.

The importance of Haifa as a port increased with the
coming of steamships for which the harbour of Acre
was too small. In 1868 German settlers, the *Templars*
from Wurtemberg, came to join the Jewish population. Their houses remain on either side of Ben Gurion
Street, and their burial ground is to the N, on Jaffa
Street. When the Templars wanted to expand on
Mount Carmel they came into conflict with the French
Carmelites who put up a boundary wall on the
mountain. This is the origin of the name "French
Carmel" for the W part.

When the Emperor William II visited the city in 1898 a
jetty was constructed and this marked the start of the
development of the port. The Emperor supported the
idea of linking Haifa with the Hedscha railway, which
led to the opening up of the hinterland. With the
upturn in economic activity the Old City began to
expand to the NW, towards the German colony. It was
as early as 1881 that the first Jewish school was
opened. Christians from Lebanon and Arabs came to
the area, too, and Haifa was chosen as a center by the
Bahai and Admediya sects which broke away from
Islam, the former coming from Persia, the latter from
India.

At the beginning of the 20th c. it was Jewish initiatives
which were the decisive influence. In his book
"Altneuland" ("The Old New Country") Theodor
Herzl hailed Haifa as the "city of the future". The Tel
Aviv suburb Herzliya dates from 1903. In 1906 three
Russian Zionists founded the Atid (i.e. "Future") silk
mills. The Technical Institute was created in 1912, and
its buildings were used by the Turks as a military
hospital in 1914. When the Institute was able to open
again in 1925, Hebrew was introduced as the
language of instruction; the German Zionist founders
had a preference for German, and this started a bitter
conflict about the language question. The Technical
Institute developed subsequently so considerably that

General view of the Mediterranean harbour at Haifa

in 1953 a larger site (Qiryat Hatechnion) had to be opened.

On September 23, 1918 the *British* occupied the city. They established a rail link via Gaza to Egypt. 1920 saw the formation in Haifa of the Workers' Cooperative. Soon new suburbs were being laid out; in 1920 Hadar Hakarmel ("Carmel's fame"), Ahusat Samuel in 1921, Bat Galim ("Sea Maiden") in 1922, Geula ("Deliverance") and Neve Sha'an ("Home of peace") in 1922. New industrial plant was installed, too. These developments went forward despite differences between the Jewish and Arab populations. In 1933 the new deep-water harbour was completed. 1934 saw the completion of the oil port at the end of the Iraki pipeline.

In 1935, following a further outbreak of violence, the Jewish population left the E sector of the lower city and concentrated in Hadar Hakarmel. As a consequence Haifa was all but partitioned. In the Second World War the German Templars were evacuated. In the post-war period there were conflicts between the Jewish underground organisation called "Haganah", the British naval base and the Arabs. The Haganah emerged victorious. – After the proclamation of the state of Israel, Haifa took on great importance as the port of entry for immigrants from Europe. The economic up-turn left its mark on the city, and tourism was developed in a planned fashion.

Planning Your Visit

Bahai Shrine and Bahai Garden
(Persian Gardens),
Zionut Avenue.
Gardens: 8 a.m.–6 p.m. (5 p.m. in winter).
Bab's Mausoleum: Sun.–Thurs. 9 a.m.–noon.
Shoes must not be worn when the mausoleum is visited; photography is forbidden.

Dagon-Silo and Museum
down by the harbour.
Sun., Mon., Wed., Thurs. 8.30 a.m.–3 p.m.; Tues. and

Fri. 8.30 a.m.–noon. Guided visits daily at 10.30 a.m. (not Sat. or on public holidays).
Museum: cultivation and treatment of crops.

Grotto of Elijah
at the foot of the ridge on Mount Carmel (opposite the lighthouse).
Sun.–Thurs. 7 a.m–5 p.m.

Ethnographical Museum
See Haifa Museum.

Gan Ha'em Park
on Hanassi Boulevard (Central Carmel).
Flower shows from April to May.

Haifa Museum
26 Shabtai-Levi Street.
Sun., Tues., Wed. and Thurs. 10 a.m.–5 p.m.; Mon. 10 a.m.–1 p.m. and 5–10 p.m.; Sat. 10 a.m.–1 p.m.; closed on Fri.

Carmelite Monastery
near the lighthouse.
Church and museum.
Mon.–Sat. 8 a.m.–1.30 p.m. and 3.30–5.30 p.m.

Marine Museum
204 Allenby Street.
Sun., Wed., Thurs. 9 a.m.–3 p.m.; Mon. and Tues. 9 a.m.–4 p.m.; Fri. and the day before public holidays 9 a.m.–1 p.m.; closed on Sat. and public holidays.

Museum for Biology and Pre-History
in Gan Ha'em Park.
Sun.–Thurs. 8 a.m.–4 p.m. (in July and August 6 p.m.); Fri. and the day before public holidays 8 a.m.–1 p.m.; Sat. and public holidays 9 a.m.–4 p.m. (in July and August 6 p.m.).

Museum of Modern Art
See Haifa Museum.

Mane Katz Museum
89 Yefe-Nof Street.
Mon.–Thurs. 10 a.m.–1 p.m. and 4–6 p.m.; Fri. 10 a.m.–noon; Sat. and public holidays 10 a.m.–1 p.m.
Collection of pictures and sculptures by the Jewish artist Mane Katz.

Tikotin Museum of Japanese Art
89 Hanassi Boulevard.
Sun.–Thurs. 10 a.m.–1 p.m. and 4 p.m.–7 p.m.; Sat.
and public holidays 10 a.m.–2 p.m.; closed Fri.

Music Museum
23 Arlosoroff Street.
Sun.–Fri. 10 a.m.–1 p.m. and Sun.–Wed. 4–7 p.m.
Collection of folk-music instruments from Asia, Africa,
Europe and South America.

Maritime Museum
198 Allenby Street.
Mon.–Thurs. 10 a.m.–5 p.m.; Fri. and the day before
public holidays 9 a.m.–1 p.m.; Sat. 10 a.m.–2 p.m.
Objects concerned with the history of seafaring,
especially models of ships.

School of the Prophets
See Cave of Elijah.

Tell Shiqmona
near the Oceanographic Institute on the W outskirts of
the city.
Sun.–Thurs. 9 a.m.–5 p.m. (in winter 9 a.m.–4 p.m.).
Archaeological sites.

Description of the City

The city rises up in three tiers. The lowest
is the Old City with the harbour and
coastal strip. The middle tier is formed by
the Hadar Hacarmel district, at an altitude
of between 197 and 394 ft/60 and 120 m,
and at the top comes the High City
(Carmel Merqazi and Ahusa) between
820 and 985 ft/250 and 300 m above sea
level. The zones have been linked since
1959 by an underground railway 1 mile/
1·8 km long. From the station at the foot of
the slopes in Paris Square (Kikar Paris) it
rises at a gradient of one in eight and a half
via four stations in the Hadar district to
Gan Haem (920 ft/280 m), close to the
viewing promenade of Yefe Not.

Between 1929 and 1933 the **harbour** of
Haifa was developed into a deep-water
port. It is protected by two moles.

The space necessary for administrative
buildings, forwarding warehouses and
stores, roads and railways has been
provided by land reclamation schemes
which have altered the coastline considerably. The most remarkable installations are a 10,000-ton wet dock and the
223 ft/68 m high **Dagon silo** which holds
100,000 tons of grain. – Entry permits for
visits to the harbour are available at the
information bureau to the right of the
entrance. It is also possible to take a boat
trip round the harbour. (Photography is
forbidden in the harbour area.)

Opposite the Dagon silo is Ben-Gurion
Street (formerly Shderot Hacarmel). It
was once the main street of the *colony of
German Templars* which was founded in
1868 and survived until the Second World
War. The houses with their tiled roofs are
characteristic. The Templars' graveyard –
the only one, apart from that in Jerusalem,
that still exists – is NW of the settlement on
Lot 150, Jaffa Street, next to the British
First World War Military Cemetery.

Jaffa Street leads back to Paris Square
(Kikar Paris), with the station at the foot of
the Carmel underground railway. Han-
evi'im Street goes N to Masaryk Square
(1,313 ft/400 m), turning left into
Shabtai-Levi Street, where the *Haifa
Museum (No. 23) is situated. Since
1977 its exhibition rooms have housed
the *Museum of Modern Art* and the
Museum of Ancient Art, which formerly
occupied premises in the Town Hall. The
Haifa Museum also has *ethnographical
and folklore displays* as well as objects
belonging to Jewish ritual art. Among the
exhibits at the Museum of Ancient Art are
finds from Caesarea and Byzantine
mosaics from Shiqmona. Pictures by
Israeli and foreign artists (Western European, American and Japanese) from the
18th c. to the present day may be viewed
in the Museum of Modern Art. – There is a

Portrait bust of Nero, Haifa Museum

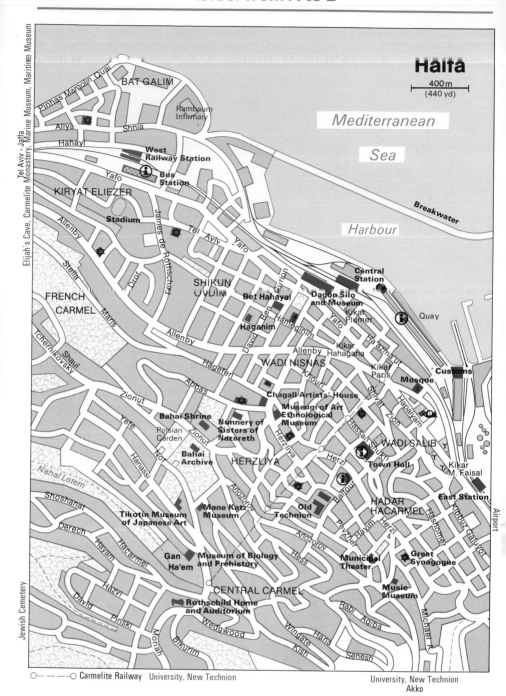

○————○ Carmelite Railway   University, New Technion

University, New Technion
Akko

lecture-room, a reading-room and several galleries for temporary exhibitions. In the evenings there are lectures illustrated with slides. – Opposite the Museum stands the *Chagall Artists' House*.

From Paris Square the narrow Khatib Street leads to Shivat Sion ("Return to Sion") Street which runs in an easterly direction. Side-roads go uphill to the HADAR HACARMEL district. On one of them, Bialik Street, stands the **Town Hall**, on the W side.

Opposite, at an altitude of 197 ft/60 m, lies *Gan Haziqaron*, memorial gardens on the site of the citadel which was built here by Dahir el Umar (1740–75), the Lord of Galilee. An old cannon is a relic of former times. Herzl Street is the main thoroughfare of the district, and a tourist information office is to be found at the corner leading into Balfour Street. Rather further up along Balfour Street stands the *Old Technion* (Polytechnic) whose construction began in 1912 and which was opened in 1925. (The enlarged *New*

Technion is in the SE part of the city: Qiryat Hatechnion.) Opposite, Pevzner Street leads away to the *Municipal Theater*, the rabbi's offices and the *Music Museum*.

From here it is possible to climb to CENTRAL CARMEL, to Gan Ha'em Park with its little zoo and to Hanassi Boulevard (No. 89: the Japanese *Tikotin Museum*) and the viewing promenade of Yefe Not from which a wonderful *view may be enjoyed over the city and the harbour and across to Akko.

Down from Yefe Not, in UN Avenue (Hazionut), lie the *Persian Gardens* with the *Bahai Shrine* whose golden dome dominates the whole townscape. Inside is the grave of the founder of the Bahai faith; it has become an object of veneration to the faithful.

In 1844 the Persian Mirsa Ali Mohammed declared he was "Bab" ("Gateway to God"). He was shot dead in Tabris in 1850. His successor, Mirsa Hussein Ali, took the name Baha-u-illah and fled to the Ottoman Empire where he proclaimed himself Iman in 1868. He was held in captivity in Acre for 24 years, died in 1892 and was buried near the present-day Shamerat kibbutz N of Acre. His disciples brought the body of his predecessor, Mirsa Ali Mohammed, secretly to Palestine from Persia and in 1909 they buried him in Haifa. The monumental dome over his grave was completed in 1953. Nearby in beautifully tended gardens stands the classical archive building of the Bahai religious community whose faith has spread into Europe and America.

There is another building worthy of a visit on the ridge of Mount Carmel, the Carmelite monastery. From the harbour it can be reached by taking Allenby Street and Stella Maris, or from the Gan Ha'em Park by taking Hanassi Boulevard and Tchernikovsky Street. The monastery is next to the *Stella Maris* (Star of the Sea) lighthouse. It is owned by the Carmelite order which takes its name from this place.

The order was founded here in 1150. The first monastery was destroyed in 1291 after the fall of Acre. It was rebuilt in the latter part of the 18th c., under the reign of Ahmed Jezzar, destroyed again in 1821 and rebuilt once more in 1828. In front of the monastery are buried the wounded soldiers from Napoleon's army whom Ahmed Jezzar had slaughtered in 1799. The monastery is dedicated to the Prophet Elijah and his disciple Elisha. Their lives are illustrated in pictures in the *church*. There is also a figure of the Virgin made of cedar with a porcelain head and dating from 1820; it is Our Lady of Mount Carmel. Steps lead down to a grotto described variously as the dwelling and the grave of Elijah. – There is a small *museum* in a room by the entrance to the monastery.

Opposite the monastery a track leads up to the **School of the Prophets**. The cave at the foot of the ridge is held to be the one in which Elijah hid from the kings of Israel and is, according to Zev Vilnay, "the holiest Jewish site in Haifa". Elijah is also revered by the Moslems as el Khidr (the "Green Prophet"), and they had a temple here until 1948. From the cave the track leads down to Jaffa Street.

The *Oceanographic Institution* lies $\frac{1}{2}$ mile/ 1 km further out of town. Nearby the old settlement of Shiqmona has been excavated. 550 yd/500 m beyond there is a bathing beach, close to Jewish and Christian burial grounds. – In the direction of the city the **Maritime Museum** can be seen on the right; it was moved out to here from its old site by the harbour. With model ships, maps and prints, etc., it presents the history of seafaring and the harbours of the Holy Land.

SURROUNDINGS. – From Central Carmel by way of Moriah Street and Horev Street SE past the Biran Cadet School (to the left), the hamlet of *Hod Carmel* (to the right), and the campus of the new University of Haifa (to the left), one route climbs right up to the highest summit of *Mount Carmel* (1,792 ft/546 m). It next reaches the village of *Isfiya* (9 miles/14 km) with a population of Christians and Druse and then comes to *Daliyat* (2$\frac{1}{2}$ miles/4 km) whose inhabitants are exclusively Druse. Another road goes SE to *Mount Muhraka* (2$\frac{1}{2}$ miles/4 km; 1,582 ft/482 m high) where the **Carmelite monastery of St Elijah stands**. According to tradition this is the place where Elijah erected his altar when he was in conflict with the priests of Baal (1 Kings 18, 30).

From Haifa via Caesarea to Tel Aviv-Yafo (Jaffa) (59 miles/95 km). – The road to Jaffa goes around the ridge of Mount Carmel and leaves the urban area at the Oceanographic Institution. – After 11 miles/18 km a side road goes off to the right towards *Atlit* (see entry). The castle, laid out by the Knights Templar in the 13th c., was the strongest in Palestine. It was abandoned in 1291 after the capture of Acre and gradually fell into decay. There still remain, however, very impressive ruins. In 1903 Baron de Rothschild founded an agricultural settlement of the same name just 1 mile/2 km S. Salt is still obtained here by the evaporation of sea water.

Inland from the castle and further along the Jaffa road, a turning heads off to the left (12 miles/19 km) to *En Hod*. Formerly an Arab village, it is now inhabited by artists.

Alternatively it is possible to travel further S from Atlit by the new road along the coast. A side road (5$\frac{1}{2}$ miles/ 9 km) leads to Dor. On the other side of the railway can be seen the *Nahsholim* kibbutz near the remains of a glassworks put up by Baron de Rothschild and, to the left, the village of **Dor** (see entry; 10 miles/16 km) which was brought into existence by Greek immigrants.

1 mile/2 km S of Dor the road bears left to the town of **Zikhron Ya'ahrov** (see entry; 4 miles/7 km). On the

Monastery of Elijah on Mount Muhraka near Haifa

southern outskirts of the village a track leads off to *Ramat Hanadiv* ("The Hill of the Benefactor") where Baron Edmond de Rothschild and his wife Ada are buried.

Before coming to the village of *Binyamina* 3 miles/5 km S, the road passes an Arabic building (to the right) which stands over a Roman theater. The road turns away to the right in Binyamina, then to the left, and right again a mile/2 km further on, before reaching the environs of the ancient city of **Caesarea** (see entry), the residence of the Roman viceroy in the 1st c. and the site of the fortifications put up by the Crusaders. – The route continues via *Natanya* (11 miles/18 km) to **Tel-Aviv-Yafo** (6 miles/10 km).

From Haifa to Bet Shean and back (round trip of 90 miles/145 km). – Leaving Haifa by the Bar-Yehuda Street in a right fork (8 miles/13 km), the route then takes us into the Plain of Jezreel. – 20 miles/ 32 km further on **Megiddo** Tell is reached (see entry); on account of its advantageous strategic situation it was fortified as early as the 3rd millennium B.C. There is an instructive museum and important excavations.

The route next passes by way of *Afula* (see entry; 6 miles/10 km) in a SE direction to **Bet Alfa** (see entry; 11 miles/18 km), with a mosaic pavement from a 6th c. synagogue, and to **Bet Shean** (see entry; 4 miles/ 6 km), with sites dating back to the Canaanite, Roman, Byzantine and Turkish periods.

Turning back N from Bet Shean towards Afula (16 miles/26 km), the route leads to **Nazareth** (see entry; 7 miles/11 km). Another road goes off to Mount Tabor (7 miles/12 km). 13 miles/21 km W of Nazareth lies **Bet Shearim** (see entry; 13 miles/21 km). It was very important in the 2nd and 3rd c. as the seat of the High Council (Sanhedrin), and has catacombs containing the graves of members of the Sanhedrin. It is possible to return to Ḥaifa (11 miles/18 km) by way of *Qiryat Tiv'on* (3 miles/5 km).

From Haifa via Nazareth to Tiberias (45 miles/73 km). – Leaving Haifa by Bar Yehuda Street and taking the left-hand fork 8 miles/13 km further on, the road

bears right beyond *Qiryat Tiv'on* (3 miles/5 km) towards the catacombs at *Bet Shearim* (see entry; 3 miles/5 km). The route then returns to the main road and, after crossing the plain, reaches **Nazareth** (see entry, 13 miles/21 km). In this township situated high up above the plain various sites recall Jesus and his parents – the Church of the Annunciation, Mary's spring, etc.

NE of Nazareth lies the village of *Cana* (see entry; 4 miles/7 km), where the "Wedding in Cana" took place. 7 miles/12 km further on is the volcanic formation of the "Horns of Hittim", in the vicinity of which the Crusader army was annihilated by Sultan Saladin in 1184. Tiberias (see entry) lies 6 miles/10 km beyond, on the W shore of the Sea of Galilee.

From Haifa via Nahriya to Rosh Hanikra (26 miles/42 km). – The route skirts the Bay of Haifa with its industrial plant and provides an opportunity for a visit to the old sea port of **Akko** (see entry; 14 miles/22 km) with its picturesque harbour and buildings dating back to the Crusaders and the Osman periods.

Further N (left turn, 4 miles/7 km) the village of *Shave Zion* lies beside the sea. It was founded in 1938 by immigrants from Rexingen in Württemberg. In an early Christian (pre-422) basilica nearby a mosaic pavement has been uncovered. Next comes (2 miles/3 km) the seaside village of **Nahariya** (see entry) which was founded by German immigrants in 1936. The village of **Rosh Hanikra** (6 miles/10 km) is right on the Lebanese border. A funicular goes up to its caves which are well worth a visit.

A road leads inland from Nahariya to *Mi'ilya* (9 miles/ 15 km), near *Montfort Castle* (see entry) which belonged to the German Knights, through delightful scenery to *Safed* (see entry; 19 miles/31 km) and *Tiberias* (see entry; 22 miles/36 km). Near the village of *Sasa* (11 miles/17 km – beyond Mi'ilya) a road branches off past *Kfar Biram* (1 mile/2 km – with the ruins of the largest synagogue in Galilee), runs close to the Lebanese frontier, following it through Qedesh-Naphtali (11 miles/17 km) and goes down into the Hule basin.

Hamat Gader

Northern District.

(i) **Government Tourist Office,**
8 Elhadef Street,
Tiberias;
tel. (0 67) 2 09 92.

Hamat Gader (Arabic: El-Hamma) lies in the lower Yarmuk Valley not far from the E bank of the Sea of Galilee. In antiquity an important spa grew up with medicinal sulphur springs. It belonged to the city of Gadara on the opposite, S bank of the Yarmuk which is now in Jordanian territory. In Hellenistic times it became a center for Greek culture in the E portion of the Jordan area.

HISTORY. – The satirist Menippos and the poet Meleagros came from Gadara. In Roman times the town formed part of Decapolis, to which Skythopolis (i.e. Bet Shean) on the W bank of the Jordan belonged as well as nine cities on the bank, among them Damascus, Philadelphia (i.e. Amman), Pella and Gerasa (Djerash). Gadara served as capital for a while. Decapolis survived until the 2nd c. This area comprising ten cities is first mentioned in the New Testament (Matthew 4, 25 and Mark 5, 20; 7, 31).

The route to **Hamat Gader** goes S from Tiberias across the Jordan and through Ma'agan before turning off beyond Sha'at Hagolan (12 miles/20 km from Tiberias).

In **Hamat Gader**, on the N bank of the Yarmuk, in Syrian territory occupied since 1967 by the Israelis, Yizhak Hirschfeld (of the Hebrew University of Jerusalem) is conducting archaeological investigations into the spa buildings of Hamat Gader on a site which now covers some 4,784 sq. yd/4,000 sq. m.

In **Gadara**, on the river bank belonging to Jordan, there are various remains from the Greek, Roman and Byzantine periods, among them two theaters, several *temples*, a *gymnasium*, Byzantine *churches* and several graves. Within the city area excavations are being carried out, under the auspices of King Hussein, by Dr Ute Lux-Wagner, director of the German Evangelical Archaeological Institute in Jerusalem. At present an important burial place is being excavated.

Har Gilboa
See Mount Gilboa

Har Carmel
See Carmel

Har Tavor
See Mount Tabor

Hazor

Northern District.

(i) **Government Tourist Office,**
Town Hall,
Safed;
tel. (0 67) 3 06 33.

ACCOMMODATION. – *Guest house* in Ayelet Hashahar kibbutz, I, 144 r., SP (tel. (0 67) 3 53 64).

*Hazor Tell dominates the road N from Tiberias to Metulla at the spot where it comes down from the high land and comes into the plain of Hula. The first investigations were carried out by John Garstang in 1928, and further excavations by Yigael Yadin between 1955 and 1969 have revealed in detail the history of this Tell.

HISTORY. – In the course of excavations it has been established that there were 21 different settlements on this site. The most recent is dated 3rd–2nd c. B.C. (Hellenistic period), while the oldest goes back to the early Bronze Age (about 2600 B.C.). This Canaanite city enjoyed its first period of great prosperity in the 18th and 17th c. B.C. (level 17). At this time it is named in the archives of Mari on the Euphrates (E Syria), and it is noteworthy that it is mentioned along with Qatna, Babylon and other cities of similar size.

This information, taken along with the considerable size of the site and the number of buildings of the Canaanite period, is in accord with the information given in the Bible according to which Hazor was the capital city of many pre-Israelite kings (Joshua 11, 10). The last king, Jabin, formed a combined army with the troops of several kings from the area between Dor (see entry) and the Mediterranean and Mount Hermon in the N when the Israelites under Joshua took over the region in the 13th c. B.C. Joshua, however, defeated the Canaanites "at the waters of Merom" (the present-day Hula region), captured their cities and slew the defeated soldiers. The only city he burned down was Hazor (Joshua 11, 13).

The first Israelite settlement in the vicinity of the city which they had destroyed dates from the 12th c. It was, however, fortified strongly only in the 10th c. under Solomon when gates and bulwarks were constructed. Further works were undertaken during the reign of Ahab who resided in Samaria (9th c. B.C.). Level 8 in the citadel and the large storeroom with its rows of pillars (once assigned to the time of Solomon) are testimonies to the architectural achievements of Hazor in the days of King Ahab and to the economic significance of the city.

Ruins of the Canaanite Royal Palace

This city was destroyed by the Assyrian Tiglatpilesar III in 732 B.C. Afterwards the fortress continued to exist, but without any economic importance, until the 2nd c. B.C.

SIGHTS. – The entry to the large site of the Tell is on the W side. The caretaker who sells entry tickets also gives information. Further information is also provided by large display boards with coded plans at each of the excavation complexes. Tourists generally find Sections A, B, H and L the most impressive.

First a general impression of Section A may be gained from a viewing platform. It is here that the Canaanite royal palace stood, with a wide ceremonial stairway leading up. After it had been destroyed by Joshua in the 13th c. B.C., Solomon built a *gate-house* in the style typical of the period with three rooms on each side of the entry as well as a bulwark adjacent (left of the stairs) and a barracks. In the next century it was covered over by the large storehouse which Ahab erected here, its other end being identified from the viewing platform by two clearly visible rows of pillars.

Section B is the **citadel**. Here was found, among other relics, an Israelite prayer booth of the 11th c. The citadel was reconstructed in monumental style during the reign of Ahab, but later additions and changes have also been identified.

In Section H a **temple** in three parts was discovered over the remains of three earlier temples. It was built during the reign of the last king of Canaan, Jabin, and was destroyed when Joshua burned down the city. In the narthex stand two pillars. In the sanctuary, which is surrounded by orthostatai (large stone slabs), many finds have been made – an incense altar, drink offering tables, a basalt vessel with a spiral design, a sitting figurine (of the king?), a bronze bull, aureoled panels. This all serves to indicate that the temple was dedicated to the weather god Hadad. According to Yadin, this Canaanite building, which has an analogue in the 20th–19th c. B.C. temple in Megiddo, was the prototype of Solomon's temple. If this is true, it is especially important since the latter is known ex-

Hazor – remains of the pillared hall in the Palace of King Ahab

Museum at Ayelet Hashahar, near Hazor

clusively thanks to descriptions which are not backed up by archaeological finds. – In Section F a temple was also discovered, with a 5-ton altar stone dating from the 12th c. B.C. In Section C a 14th c. temple was found with numerous steles; these indicate that the temple was dedicated to the moon-god.

In Section L the *water supply system* has been uncovered. It is an astonishing piece of engineering from the days of Ahab (9th c. B.C.), like the tunnel for supplying water at Megiddo. It consists of a channel cut down through the early settlements and the bed rock, with a width at the top of 62–82 ft/19–25 m and a depth of 98 ft/30 m. On each of its four sides are 10 ft/3 m wide steps going down the lowest portion; a fifth stairway, at the bottom, occupies the entire shaft, leading into a tunnel 82 ft/25 m long. This debouches into a pool 16 ft/5 m across and 33 ft/10 m deep which extends down below the water table. Consequently Hazor's water supply was assured even when the spring outside the Tell was inaccessible to the inhabitants during a siege. It is possible to get down to this lowest rocky chamber by means of a modern stone stairway of 150 steps built over the old steps.

The finds from Hazor are to be seen nowadays in the Israel Museum in Jerusalem. Some, however, may also be seen in the Hazor Museum at the entrance to the kibbutz Ayelet Hashahar ($\frac{1}{2}$ mile/1 km).

Hebron/Hevron

West Jordan.
Altitude: 3,039 ft/926 m.
Population: 38,500.
Telephone code: 02.
(i) Government Tourist Office,
2 King George Street,
Jerusalem;
tel. (02) 24 12 81.

HOTEL. – *Eshkolot Hebron* (k), Kiryat Arba, 45 r.

The city of *Hebron (Arabic: El Khalil; Hebrew: Hevron) is situated in the Judaic Highlands between Jerusalem (23 miles/37 km) and Beersheba (30 miles/48 km). It is the religious center of Islam in the S portion of the West Bank of the Jordan, like Nablus in the N. The monumental sepulchre constructed over the grave of Abraham at Machpelah makes this one of the great sights for tourists with an interest in Scriptural history.

HISTORY. – Hebron is very ancient city. Ever since its foundation by the Canaanites it has always been occupied. The religious tradition associated with the place goes back to Abraham, the ancestor of the Jews as well as of the Arabs. When his aged wife Sarah died here, he bought from Ephron, son of Zohar, the field called Machpelah, to the E of Mamre, together with the "cave that was therein and all the trees" (Genesis 23, 17–20). After the burial of Sarah, Abraham himself, his son Isaac and his wife Rebecca and his grandson Jacob together with the latter's wife Leah were likewise buried here. It was from Hebron that Jacob set off to find his brothers who were conspiring to kill him (Genesis 37, 14).

Hebron – Haram el-Khalil, over the Cave of Machpelah

After the death of King Saul (end of 11th c. B.C.) the thirty-year-old David was anointed king of Judah in Hebron. For seven and a half years – up to the capture of Jerusalem – he resided here with his six wives (among them Ahinoam from Jezreel, mother of his firstborn son Amnon; Abigail from Carmel, mother of Caleb; and Masha, mother of Absalon). It was during this period that his general Joab slew Saul's general Abner in Hebron (2 Samuel 3, 27). It was at the pool in Hebron that David had executed the two men who had murdered Ish-bosheth, the last son of Saul. They had brought him the prince's head, which had been cut off. He placed it in Abner's grave (2 Samuel 4, 7–11).

After the Jews were forced into exile in Babylon, Edomites from the Negev settled in Hebron in the 6th c. B.C. They ruled there until in 163 B.C. Judas Maccabaeus attacked them (1 Maccabees 5, 65). Herod the Great (37–4 B.C.) rebuilt the city and constructed the great building over the Machpelah Cave which exists to the present day.

In the 6th c. the Emperor Justinian of the East erected a church over Machpelah and in the 7th c., after the end of Byzantine rule, this was converted into a mosque. In 1215 Crusaders broke open the sepulchre and, it is recounted, glimpsed the remains of the prophet. The city was captured in 1267 by the Mameluke Sultan Baibars. Jews and Christians alike were denied entrance to the sacred site.

Non-Moslems were prohibited from entering until modern times. In 1862 the Prince of Wales and in 1869 Crown Prince Frederick William were allowed to enter, but only after a special order had been obtained from the Turkish sultan.

At that period Hebron had barely 10,000 inhabitants, including 500 Jews. The Jewish community grew larger when at the end of the 19th c. Chassidic Jews from East Europe settled in Hebron, to be followed by immigrants from Russia. In 1929, however, there was a pogrom which cost many Jews their lives. In 1980 there were serious conflicts between Arabs and Jews.

The latter gained access to the shrine at Machpelah for the first time for 700 years, and in 1968 they founded the city of Qiryat Arba on the heights towards the NE.

SIGHTS. – The landscape is dominated by the shrine over the cave of Machpelah, the *Haram El-Khalil ("Shrine of the Friend"), so called because, for Moslems, Abraham is "al-Khalil er-Rahman" ("the Friend of the Lord"). It rises up close by the *Sultan's Pool* (Birket es-Sultan), where David had the murderers of Ish-

Joseph's Grave in Haram el-Khalil

bosheth, King Saul's last son, executed. (2 Samuel 4, 7–12). The Jordanian authorities razed the hovels around the Haram in 1960, and visitors now have an unimpeded view of the impressive building. The boundary wall was constructed by Herod the Great; it encloses a quadrilateral 213 ft/65 m by 115 ft/35 m. Low down an inner area can be seen, divided up by pillars. The upper portion of the wall with its round battlements dates from the Islamic period, as do the two minarets. Originally there were four of them.

A flight of stairs leads up to the entrance on the NE side and gives access to the courtyard. There are four **sepulchral monuments** here; underneath lie the graves of the patriarchs in the burial cave which is not open to visitors. To the right stand the *mausoleums* which were put up over the cenotaphs of Jacob (to the left) and his wife Leah (to the right). Opposite is the cenotaph of Abraham (right) and Sarah (left). Richly embroidered canopies hang over the monuments.

it was allocated to the Jews after 1967 as a place for prayer and is no longer considered to form part of the mosque. In the floor there is an opening through which pious Jews lower into the Cave of Machpelah slips of paper with prayers written on them.

From the W side of the mosque a door leads out to a long passage which serves as a *mosque for women*. On the left Herod's wall has been breached, and a rectangular room has been built on. The sarcophagus standing here is venerated by Moslems as being that of Joseph. The Jews, however, rely on the testimony of the Bible and assert that Joseph's bones when brought out of Egypt were buried not at Hebron but at Sechem (See Surroundings of Nablus) (Joshua 24, 32).

Near Haram el-Khalil are the densely populated *market alleys* of Hebron where food, pottery and glassware are offered for sale.

Before acquiring the Cave of Machpelah, Abraham had dwelt in the Grove of **Mamre**. It was there that he had built an altar (Genesis 13, 18), and "The Lord appeared unto him", as did, too, the three men who came to him and whom he welcomed into his abode

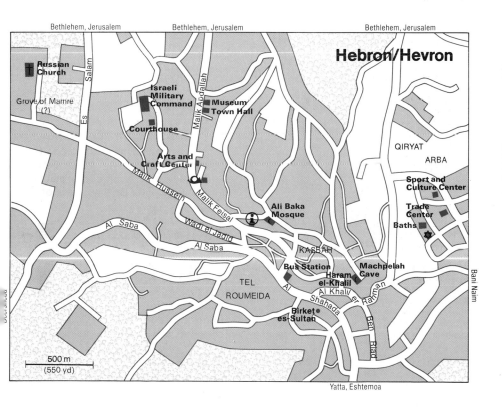

Nearby is the entrance to the inner building. It is 99 ft/ 28 m wide and 79 ft/24 m long, and is divided into three aisles. It presumably is a survival of the church erected by Justinian and the Crusaders. It took on its present appearance as a **mosque** in the 14th c. under the Mamelukes. The roof is supported on four pillars. In the middle of the SE aisle stands the prayer niche (Mihrab), and to the right of it is the richly carved pulpit (Mimbar), erected in 1191 at the behest of Sultan Saladin. Here, too, are two more cenotaphs, for Isaac (right) and Rebecca (left). – There are small carpets on the floor of the right-hand part of the room;

(Genesis 18, 1–2). It was here also that his wife died, and he buried her in the cave which lay "east of Mamre" (Genesis 23, 17; 49, 30). Consequently the Mamre of the Bible must have been W of Hebron, and this supposition finds expression in the siting of the Russian orthodox community of *Moskalia* with its church dating from 1871 $\frac{1}{2}$ mile/1 km W of the new ring road, close to the old "Oak of Resting" (Balut es Sebat).

There is also another place 3 miles/5 km N of Hebron which has links with the Mamre tradition. It is *Beit*

Ilanim, at an altitude of 3,952 ft/1024 m, 550 yd/500 m W of the Jerusalem road. Here are remains of buildings with large blocks from the age of Herod. Excavations were carried out in 1926, and it was shown that the Herodian building was destroyed by Titus in A.D. 70. In 135 Hadrian rebuilt it, providing a temple which Constantine replaced with a church in the 4th c. Up to its destruction by Persians or Arabs in the 7th c. Christians made pilgrimages to what they thought to be the former abode of Abraham.

SURROUNDINGS. – The highlands S and E of Hebron are rich in ruined sites. This shows that even after the destruction of Jerusalem in 70 it was not only Galilee (as was previously supposed) but also Judea which had a relatively large and prosperous Jewish population. Certain of their settlements were taken over by the Byzantines, and several survive to the present day as Arab villages.

4 miles/6 km E, at an altitude of 3,121 ft/951 m, lies the Arab village, of *Bani Naim*. In the mosque which has been built on top of a Byzantine church is to be found, according to the tradition of the village, the grave of Lot. There are good views of the Dead Sea.

From Hebron the road to Beersheba has a left turn (4 miles/6 km) to the large Arab village of **Yatta** (4 miles/6 km), the Jutta of the Old Testament. Some of the houses there are built of stones from older buildings. There are ruins of a 6th c. synagogue.

3 miles/5 km SE of Yatta lies the large and as yet unexcavated site of *Carmel* with all its ruins. The property belonged, together with *Maon* (1 mile/2 km) further S which also has extensive ruins that await archaeological investigation, to Nabal. He was a rich man whose wife Abigail left Carmel after his death and married David who was being persecuted by Saul (1 Samuel 25, 2–42).

Another road goes S from Yatta to **Sammu**, the Eshtemoa of the Bible (Joshua 21, 14). In the vicinity of the mosque a synagogue was excavated in 1935. Dating from the 3rd c. it presumably survived during the Islamic period until the 7th c.

E from Sammu a track leads to *Horvat Suseya* (Sussia; 3 miles/5 km). A few years ago a large synagogue was excavated on the heights. It had a marble entrance, women's galleries, Menora mosaics and inscriptions. It survived as late as the 10th or 11th c. – With regard to the agricultural practices handed down from generation to generation, the flocks owned by the inhabitants and the life style of the people in this remote highland area, Hans Kühner remarks on the village of Sussia: "Here may yet be seen the totally undisturbed world of our forefathers."

Hefa
see Haifa

Hefer Plain/ Emeq Hefer

Central District, Haifa District.
ⓘ **Government Tourist Office,**
7 Mendele Street,
Tel Aviv;
tel. (03) 22 32 66–7.

ACCOMMODATION. – *Youth Hostel* in Kefar Vitkin.

The Plain of Hefer, formerly known as Wadi Hawarit, is a prolongation of the Plain of Sharon which stretches down between Hadera and Netanya to the Mediterranean coastline. With streams coming down from the mountains of Samaria, it is a fruitful area with many settlements.

HISTORY. – The king of Hefer, along with 30 other Canaanite princes, was defeated by Joshua when the Israelites conquered the Promised Land (Joshua 12, 17). The Tell near the Mabarot kibbutz corresponds with the Hefer of the Bible. In the 10th c. Solomon's court was provided with victuals from the Plain of Hefer (1 Kings 4, 19). Later the Plain degenerated into marshland, and as malaria spread it became impossible to maintain permanent settlement here. Only a few impoverished Egyptian peasants, brought here by Ibrahim Pasha in 1830, lived in this inhospitable region.

The Jewish National Fund acquired the property in 1929, and draining operations began in the marshes in 1930. Soon the region began to develop into one of the most fruitful parts of the country. Many settlements sprang up, the first being *Kefar Vitkin* in 1933, and an agricultural college was founded. Some of the villages take their names from famous personalities. *Kefar Monash* was called after the well-known First World War general, and *Kefar Yadidia* after the Jewish philosopher Philo (or Yedidia, in Hebrew) of Alexandria. At *Mabarot* kibbutz there is a museum with local archaeological finds.

Herodeion/ Herodion

West Jordan.
Altitude: 2,488 ft/758 m.
ⓘ **Government Tourist Office,**
Manger Square,
Bethlehem;
tel. (02) 94 25 91.

The mountain *Herodeion (Herodion) is visible from afar, rising on

Herodeion

the West Bank of the Jordan 7 miles/ 11 km SE of Bethlehem to a height of 2,488 ft/758 m. Its peculiar shape, which recalls a volcano with its crater levelled off at the top, dates back to the time of King Herod after whom it is named and who had a fortified palace built there.

HISTORY. – In 40 B.C. when in the course of the Roman-Parthian War the Hashmonean Antigonos became High Priest and king, Herod had taken refuge with Mariamne and the rest of his family in this castle, before withdrawing to Massada (see entry). After confirming his rule by his victory over Antigonos, he commanded the completion of the fortress which he intended should be his mausoleum. After the death of Herod in 4 B.C., his son Archelaus conveyed the body from Jericho (see entry) to the mausoleum in a magnificent cortège.

Excavations conducted from 1962 onwards have confirmed the impressive descriptions given by Josephus in his Jewish Wars (1 21, 10). Herod had the top of the hill cut away and dug out, and the spoil was

allowed to tumble down the rounded slopes. The plateau thus created was surrounded with an immense double wall, strengthened in between with four semicircular towers in which magazines were placed. On the level ground within the walls he set "magnificent palaces which were glorious to look upon not only from within, but also from without, with walls, battlements and roofs decorated with extravagant splendour." There were gardens inside a peristyle, apartments, baths and a synagogue. The so-called "Pools of Solomon", S of Bethlehem, provided the necessary water. To reach the only entrance it was necessary to mount a stairway of 200 white marble steps.

The grave of the monarch has, however, not so far been located. Presumably it was destroyed at an early date, probably during the Judaic War (66–70), when Jewish zealots took refuge here or during the Bar Kochba rebellion in 132–135 when Bar Kochba installed his headquarters here. – Later a handful of Byzantine monks lived in Herodeion, turning the synagogue into a church. Israeli troops occupied this region, and the rest of West Jordan, in 1967.

Arcaded hall in the Palace of Herodeion

Nowadays a wide footpath leads up to the **palace and its grounds** in a broad curve. It will be noticed that the walls of the palace still have some of their original decoration. From the top of Herodeion visitors have an extensive view of the surroundings. Beyond the territory at the foot of the hill where the city which Herod had laid out to supply the needs of his court still awaits excavation, it is possible to see, looking N across the Judaic highlands, as far as the towers on the Mount of Olives near Jerusalem and, looking E, as far as the Dead Sea which lies 3,774 ft/1150 m below.

Herodeion (Herodion)   Djebel Furadis
Fortress

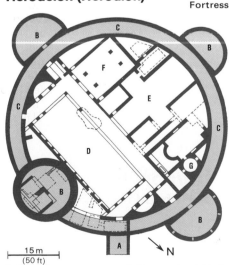

15 m	
(50 ft)	↘N

A Access Ramp
B Defensive Towers
C Double Wall in form of a circle, with the gangway between the walls used as stores
D Peristyle (Hall with Pillars)

E Synagogue (erected by the zealots, later used as a church)
F Synagogue (formerly a Triclinium)
G Hot baths

Herzliya/Herzliyya

Tel Aviv District.
Altitude: 33–130 ft/10–40 m.
Population: 61,000.
Telephone code: 03.
ⓘ **Government Tourist Office,**
7 Mendele Street,
Tel Aviv;
tel. (03) 22 32 66–7.

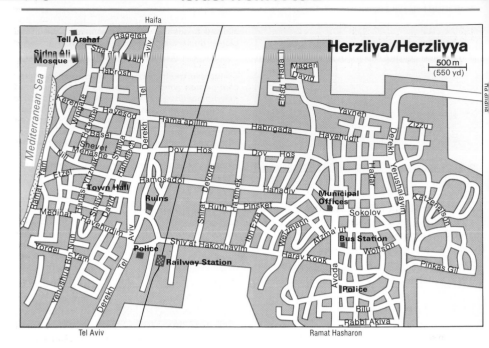

HOTELS. – *Sharon & Sharon Towers* (k), by the sea, L, 210 r., SP, sauna, tennis; *Dan Accadia* (k), by the sea, L, 192 r., sauna, tennis; *Daniel-Tower Sonesta* (k), by the sea, L, 180 r., sauna; *Tadmor* (k), 38 Basle Street, III, 63 r.; *Cymberg,* 29 Hamaapilim Street, III, 12 r.; *Eshel* (k), by the sea, 49 r.

COMMUNICATIONS. – Herzliya is a station on the Tel Aviv–Haifa railway line. – Bus and Sherut taxi connections with Tel Aviv.

*Herzliya (Herzliyya) is named after Theodor Herzl. It was founded in 1924 9 miles/15 km N of Tel Aviv. Its population was about 500 in 1948 and has increased more than a hundredfold. Its hotels and bathing facilities have made it a favourite seaside resort.

SIGHTS. – The town is divided into two parts. The older of the two lies E of one of the sandstone ridges which separate the Plain of Sharon from the coast. In ancient times this ridge was broken through to allow water to flow away more easily into the sea, thus preventing the land from turning into marshes. After the foundation of the settlement the drainage channel was cleared of the detritus which had accumulated over the centuries. It is possible to see where it emerges E of the coast road near the Herzliya crossing. E of this spot lies the center of the old city, while the new districts are on the W, up from the beach.

On the NW beach, beyond the small suburbs of Nof Yam and Reshef, the minaret of the Islamic Shrine of *Sidna Ali* (Our Lord Ali) rises up, and still further N *Tell Arshaf* can be seen.

The ruins of Arshaf belong to the ancient port of *Rishpon* which is mentioned in Assyrian texts. It was dedicated to Reshef, the Canaanite god of fire and fertility. He was identified by the Greeks, who had been settled here since the late 4th c. B.C., with Apollo, so they called the city *Apollonia.* The Hashmonean king Alexander Jannaios captured the city in 95 B.C. Greek influences became strong once again, however, as a result of its annexation by Pompeius in 63. The Arabs made use of the harbour from the 7th c. onwards. They called the place *Arsuf,* whence the name "Arsur Castle" applied by the Crusaders in the 12th c. In 1191 Richard the Lion-Heart defeated Sultan Saladin here. The Mamelukes destroyed the city in 1265. – In 1950 Roman buildings, including a theater, were uncovered.

With its long, wide, sandy beach, Herzliya is a favourite place for excursions from Tel Aviv and Yafo. Buses run between Tel Aviv and Herzliya every day, including the Sabbath.

Hevron
see Hebron

Horns of Hittim/ Qarne Hittim

Northern District.
ⓘ **Government Tourist Office,**
8 Elhadef Street,
Tiberias;
tel. (0 67) 2 09 92.

6 miles/10 km W of Tiberias stands this hill. It is not particularly high, but it has a curious conformation as a consequence of the collapse of its crater. On account of this it has been given the name of "Horns of Hittim" (or in Hebrew, Qarne Hittim). It was here that a decisive battle took place during the Crusader period.

HISTORY. – Sultan Saladin inflicted an annihilating defeat on the Crusading knights at the Horns of Hittim on July 4, 1187. The kingdom of Jerusalem, which had been set up by the Crusaders, maintained itself in the city for only 88 years. After the loss of Jerusalem and much of the territory close by, the kingdom survived only in the coastal strip, with Acre as its capital.

Saladin, a Kurd, ruled over Egypt from 1171 and brought Syria under his sway in 1174. In 1187 he crossed the Jordan with a great host which he quartered in the vicinity of Tiberias in order to provoke the Crusaders to do battle. The Crusaders had concentrated on July 2, 1181 near Sephoris (see Zippori), 4 miles/6 km NW of Nazareth, where there was an adequate supply of water for themselves and their horses. In a council of war the Grand Master of the Templars, Gerhard, and the adventurer Rainald of Châtillon prevailed over the more circumspect majority. Under their influence King Guy de Lusignan ordered the heavily armoured army to advance in great heat across an arid region towards Hittim, some 12 miles/20 km distant as the crow flies. Almost dying of thirst they found that the spring there was dried up, and, to make matters worse, the Moslems set fire to the shrivelled undergrowth.

They launched an attack the next morning. The knights fought with desperate courage, and a few

broke through to Tripolis. The bishop of Acre, who had carried the Holy Cross into the battle, was slain, and the relic was lost. Most of the Crusaders and the king were taken captive. Saladin offered King Guy a drink of water, but he had Rainald of Châtillon decapitated after reproaching him for his countless acts of brigandage – attack on a caravan during a truce, for instance, and stealing from pilgrims going to Mecca. The fanatical Sufis slaughtered the knights Templar and the knights of St John, but the secular barons were kept as captives. The infantry and other followers were despatched to the slave markets of Damascus where prices plummeted as a consequence of over-supply.

The Horns of Hittim is then a place which recalls an absurd military enterprise which had fateful consequences for those who initiated it. Saladin went on to conquer Jerusalem and Acre, too, but the latter was won back by the Christians four years later and held for another century.

A footpath leads up from the main road to the top of the hill (barely half an hour's walk). There are Bronze Age *ruins* here, and visitors have fine *views across Eastern Galilee and the Sea of Galilee.

Hula Plain/ Emeq Hula

Northern District.
ⓘ **Government Tourist Office,**
Town Hall,
Safed;
tel. (0 67) 3 06 33.

ACCOMMODATION. – *Guest house* in Ha Gosherim kibbutz, II, 121 r., SP, tennis, tel. (0 67) 4 01 37–9.

The Hula Plain (Emeq Hula) is in the N part of Israel, stretching from Dan on the Lebanese frontier and S to Hazor. Its E border is formed by the Golan Heights, its W border by the Lebanese highlands. The valley is

View over the Plain of Hula

one of the largest land drainage areas in Israel, and it is an important agricultural zone.

For centuries the Hula Plain consisted of malaria-infested marshes. When the Egyptian Ibrahim Pasha took Palestine from the Turks between 1830 and 1840, he had some of the volcanic rocks to the S of the bridge of Benot Ya'aqov (see entry) blasted away so that the water could flow away more readily down into the Jordan. His plan for bringing the land into cultivation with the aid of resettled impoverished Egyptian peasants could not, however, be brought to fruition because of political developments. Just a few Bedouin with their water buffaloes subsisted in the area.

In 1883 Jewish immigrants founded the village of *Yesud HaMa'ala* (9 miles/15 km NE of Rosh Pinna). In the early difficult days financial support from Baron de Rothschild made it possible to lay out gum-tree plantations in 1890. Large-scale land drainage schemes were, however, only set in train when the land was acquired by the Jewish National Fund in 1934. Between 1951 and 1958 the work was taken a stage further forward in a planned fashion, and this time one of the objects was to supply the southern parts with water from Galilee. The digging of drainage ditches, the deepening of the Jordan and the regulation of water flow by altering the gradients have led to the disappearance of the marshes, and they have been replaced by fertile land. As well as fields there are also fish farms here. N of the oldest settlement (Yesud HaMa'ala) there is now a **nature reserve** devoted to the conservation of the plant and animal life of the region.

Improved conditions have led to the foundation of several agricultural communities. The villages of *Amir* and *Sede Nehemya* (4 miles/6 km NE of Qiryat Shemona) on the rivers Hazbani, Dan and Banyas, which flow into the Jordan, date from 1940, as does *Bet Hillel* (2½ miles/4 km S of Qiryat Shemona). *Ne'ol Morde-khay* (5 miles/8 km S of Qiryat Shemona) was founded in 1946, and *HaGosherim* in 1948. The latter is on the N edge of the Hule area 3 miles/5 km E of Qiryat Shemona on the road to Dan (see entry) and Banyas (see entry).

Qiryat Shemona, which is now a town of 15,500 inhabitants, came into life in 1949 as a camp for immigrants. It was placed amid the ruins of a deserted Arab village on the NE edge of the Hula region. From Qiryat Shemona two roads lead S, one in the valley and the other, further W, skirting the Lebanese border. From it there are fine views of the landscape of Hula.

In Upper Galilee (3 miles/5 km W of Qiryat Shemona) there is an extensive National Park in the valley of *Horeshat*. It has camping facilities and a lake, fed with water from the Dan; in it swimming is permitted.

Jaffa

See under Tel Aviv-Jaffa

Jenin

West Jordan.
Population: 13,200.
ⓘ **Government Tourist Office,**
Casanova Street,
Nazareth;
tel. (0 65) 7 05 55.

Near the Arab town of Jenin, between Afula (7 miles/12 km) and Nablus (26 miles/42 km), in West Jordan which has been under Israeli occupation since 1967, the old highway which runs from Jerusalem up over the Samarian Mountains goes through the valley of the Dotan into the Plain of Jezreel. On account of its position Jenin has been able to control this important line of communication ever since ancient times.

In the 13th c. the Mamelukes were afraid of further incursions by the Crusaders. So they destroyed all the cities on the coast and developed Jenin as a starting post for caravans between Damascus and Egypt. In the First World War Jenin became a station on the railway between Afula and Nablus which was planned to link with Jerusalem and eventually the Suez Canal. As the area fell to the British work was, however, interrupted. – The Germans, who fought on the side of the Turks in the First World War, built an aerodrome in Jenin. A memorial on the W outskirts of the town commemorates the German aviators who gave their lives here.

The main road from Jerusalem to Haifa and Galilee used to run through Jenin right up to the 1930s. When the coast road via Hadera was opened in connection with the development of the port of Haifa, Jenin lost most of its importance as a communications center.

Jericho/Yeriho

West Jordan.
Altitude: 820 ft/250 m above sea level.
Population: 7,000.
Telephone code: 02.
ⓘ **Government Tourist Office,**
   24 King George Street,
   Jerusalem;
   tel. (02) 24 12 81–4.

*Jericho (Arabic: El-Riha; Hebrew: Yeriho) lies 22 miles/36 km NE of Jerusalem and 9 miles/15 km NW of the Dead Sea on the West Bank of the Jordan. It is an oasis city with agriculture supported by irrigation. On account of the abundant quantities of fresh water and the mild climate, bananas, dates and oranges do well here. In antiquity Jericho was said to be the most ancient city in the world. It was the winter residence of various rulers, among them Herod and the Caliph Hisham.**

HISTORY. – Archaeological investigations of the Tell at Jericho began in 1860, at first without positive results. When J. Warren drove his trial trenches, he just failed to locate a stone tower. The work was continued by Sellin and Watzinger, but it was not until 1930–31 that British archaeologists achieved significant results. The work of investigation was completed by Kathleen Kenyon only in the early 1950s.

K. Kenyon established that there were 20 successive layers indicating different settlements. The earliest dates from about 8000 B.C. It was then, in the Middle Stone Age, that a nomadic population erected a remarkable rectangular building measuring $11\frac{1}{2}$ ft by 21 ft/3·5 m by 6·5 m. They raised stone walls on a foundation made by putting a 1 ft/30 cm layer of soil over the chalk. Two of the $2\frac{1}{2}$ ft/75 cm high blocks of stone were bored through vertically, to receive posts which supported ritual poles. Archaeologists consider that the building was the shrine of these nomads.

Another complex of buildings on the middle of the Tell dates back to the Neolithic period. On top of a 13 ft/3·90 m high ash pile which resulted from occupation over a period of 8 millennia the archaeologists discovered houses built of hand-made convex tiles, some round in plan, others rectangular with semicircular roofs. This settlement had strong fortifications, which gave it the true character of a city. The wall is 6 ft/1·95 m thick and, in the W, its height is still 12 ft/3·60 m. Up against the wall on the inside there is a round stone tower which is 29 ft/9 m high. Rather later on a moat was dug in front of the wall: it is 9 ft/2·70 m deep and 27 ft/8·10 m across. The city wall was raised to 25 ft/7·60 m. These improvements to the city's defences were completed about 7000 B.C..

Between 8000 and 7000 B.C. a population of hunters and gatherers completed here the transition to a sedentary life style. From now on they practised agriculture and animal husbandry. This meant that one individual could provide the food needed for many of his fellows, and this led to a division of labour as not everybody had to be concerned with ensuring there was enough to eat. These two are the essential preconditions for the development of an advanced civilisation.

Jericho – Columns in the Great Arcaded Hall in the Omaijadi Palace of Qirbat al-Mafyar (Palace of Hisham)

"The descendants of the Mesolithic hunters who had erected the sanctuary by the spring at Jericho made remarkable progress. In the course of a period which Carbon-14 evidence suggests is about a thousand years they had made the entire transition from a wandering to a settled existence. As the imposing defensive works show they built up a hierarchical communal system with communal organisation that worked well . . . The most ancient village settlements known elsewhere are probably to be assigned to a period two thousand years later, and the pyramids in Egypt, the first major stone buildings in the Nile Valley, are 4,000 years younger than the great tower of Jericho." (Kathleen Kenyon.)

At this period the inhabitants of Jericho practised fertility rites and the cult of the dead. They placed over the heads of their dead thin slabs of stone and kept them in their homes (finds in the Rockefeller Museum, Jerusalem, and the Archaeological Museum in Amman).

After the destruction of the city, by war or an earthquake, the place was inhabited in the 6th millennium by another race. Its members were already acquainted with the art of pottery, but they built only very simple houses.

In the Bronze Age (5th millennium) the settlement moved at first somewhat to the W, towards the entrance to Wadi Qilt (see entry), possibly because the spring had changed position. But a return to the original site soon followed. Rectangular houses were constructed within a strong city wall. – From the period about 2000 B.C. archaeologists have found pottery jugs in the form of human faces. In the Hyksos period (18th–16th c. B.C.) a new city wall was erected. It was made of beaten earth and was covered with scrub. This city was destroyed about 1400 B.C.

The Bible (Joshua 2–6) provides a detailed account of the capture and destruction of Jericho by Israelites who came out of East Jordan under the leadership of Joshua ("trumpets of Jericho" episode). This used to be assigned to the 15th c. B.C., but nowadays the 13th c. is considered a more likely date (period of Pharaoh Ramses II). When the Promised Land was apportioned between the tribes, Jericho came into the territory of Benjamin (Joshua 18, 21). Under King Ahab of Israel (9th c. B.C.) the ruined city was reconstructed. It was at this time that the city received a visit from the prophet Elijah and his disciple Elisha (2 Kings 2). Elijah crossed the Jordan, and "there appeared a chariot of fire, and horses of fire . . . and Elijah went up by a whirlwind to heaven" (2 Kings 2, 11). Elisha returned to Jericho where the inhabitants complained to him that the spring water was harmful to crops. "Then he went forth unto the spring of the water, and cast the salt in there, and said, 'Thus saith the Lord, I have healed these waters: there shall not be from thence any more death or barren land.' And the waters were healed unto this day." (2 Kings 2, 21–22.) It is on account of this episode that the spring is called the Spring of Elisha.

In 586 B.C. the Babylonians brought to Jericho the last King of Jerusalem who had fled from Jerusalem. They put out his eyes, and he was then taken away into exile in Babylon (2 Kings 25, 7). – During the Persian period the Tell at Jericho was once again abandoned as it had been in the 5th millennium.

After 332 B.C. Hellenistic Jericho grew up further S, near the entrance to Wadi Qilt. It was captured by the Maccabees in 161 B.C. The oasis was presented by Octavian (later the Emperor Augustus) to Herod in 30 B.C. Herod reconstructed the place to turn it into a winter residence, and for its defence the fortress of Kypros (named after his mother) was built. It was here that he died in 4 B.C., and his body was conveyed to Herodeion (see entry) in a ceremonial cortège.

It was near Jericho that Jesus, as he was coming through the Jordan valley for the last time on his way from Galilee to Jerusalem, was hailed as "the son of David" by two blind men. He restored their sight, and "they followed him" (Matthew 20, 30–34).

Hellenistic-Herodian Jericho was destroyed by the Romans in A.D. 70. Subsequently a settlement evolved on the present site, SE of the Tell. Several churches and a synagogue have been identified as belonging to the Byzantine period. A new era opened with the Arab conquest in 634. The Omayyaden caliphs who resided in Babylon erected a fortress and a mosque. Caliph Hisham built a palace (Qirbat al-Mafyar) in 724. After this Jericho gradually lost importance, eventually becoming a modest village.

Under the British Mandate in the inter-War period the old Roman road through Wadi Qilt was replaced by a new road from Jerusalem to the Dead Sea and Jericho. In 1940 Jericho had 4,000 inhabitants who made a living by selling the bananas and citrus fruits produced around the oasis. Between then and the present day the population has risen to 7,000. Jericho was occupied by the Israelis in 1967.

SIGHTS. – The *Tell of Old Jericho lies $1\frac{1}{2}$ miles/2·5 km NW of the central point of the present-day oasis, opposite the spring which is known variously as the well of Elijah and the Sultan's well (Ain es-Sultan). It stands 69 ft/21 m high and occupies an area of 47,800 sq. yd/40,000 sq. m. The most obvious feature is the deep, broad trench which the archaeologists have driven right across the hill in order to make it possible to investigate the settlements right down to ground level. In this trench may be seen remains of the Neolithic city (about 7000 B.C.); these consist of a portion of the city wall and the 30 ft/9 m high round tower which nestles up against it. On the E side the entrance can be seen: it gives access to a spiral stairway of 22 treads. There is also an opening at the top. – N of this K. Kenyon found the shrine constructed by Mesolithic nomads a thousand years earlier (about 8000 B.C.). N of the Well of Elijah, along a road which turns right in about $\frac{1}{2}$ mile/1 km through an avenue of cypresses, there stands a house in the cellar of which the mosaic pavement of a Jewish synagogue from the Byzantine era (5th–6th c.) is still to be seen. In the middle there is a medallion containing a menorah, a palm bough, a ram's horn and the Hebrew inscription "Shalom al Israel" (Peace be unto Israel).

Tower in Neolithic Jericho

The palace of *Qirbat al-Mafyar lies 1 mile/2 km N of the Well of Elijah, on the other side of a dried-up river bed. It was constructed in 724 by Hisham, the 10th Omayyaden caliph and the last significant representative of the dynasty. The building work was never completed, and some of it was destroyed by an earthquake as early as 746. The site was covered over with sand and remained quite forgotten until English archaeologists came upon it in 1937 and laid bare an area 175 yd by 142 yd/160 m by 130 m. Numerous finds with designs typical of early Islamic art are at present on show in the Rockefeller Museum, Jerusalem.

The palace is laid out on a quadrilateral plan, like a Roman camp. Four ranges of buildings are placed all round an inner court; they all open on to it while the complex is closed to the outside. Adjacent to these buildings, to the N, there is a large bath-house.

Entry to the palace is through a spacious forecourt with a four-sided cistern which was once surmounted by a dome, and through a gate-house which leads into the quadrilateral inner courtyard. Here a round window can be seen which once was fitted in one of the rooms overlooking the courtyard. Opposite, in the W wing, steps go down to a subterranean *bath-house*. The big, rectangular *bath-house* lies to the N, just beyond the ruins of a mosque. The bath-house measures 130 ft by 130 ft/40 m by 40 m, and the bareness of its outside walls is relieved by semicircular niches in which stand alternately male and female figures. The roof was supported on 16 pillars. Parts of the *mosaic pavement* have survived. In the NW corner there is a small chamber with an apse at one end. It was no doubt the place where the caliph rested, or else received visitors. It is famous on account of its perfectly preserved *mosaic*. It shows an orange tree and three gazelles, one of which is being attacked by a lion. It is a choice piece of craftsmanship.

NW of Old Jericho rises a striking mountain. According to Christian tradition it is the **Mount of the Temptation**. It was here that Jesus fasted for forty days after being baptised by John. Then the Devil tempted Him: "If thou be the Son of God, command that these stones be made bread. But He answered and said, Man shall not live by bread alone, but by every word that proceedeth out of the mouth of God." (Matthew 4, 1–4.)

The Arab name for the mountain is "Qarantal". Saint Chariton built a chapel on its summit in 340, and another was set

Jericho
Qirbat al-Mafyar
(Hisham Palace)

|———— 50 m ————|
(164 ft)

1 Gate-house
2 Small Mosque
3 Underground Bath-house
4 Bath-house
5 Room with mosaics
6 Calidarium (steam bath)
7 Large Mosque
8 Cistern

Inner Courtyard

Forecourt

Mosaic, Qirbat al-Mafyar

up in the cave in which Jesus sheltered. – The Greek Orthodox Church acquired the site in 1074, and the Jaranduarion Monastery (taking its name from the 40 days' fasting) was built half-way up in 1895. A steep pathway leads up from the monastery to the summit where the remains of Chariton's chapel and of the Hashmonean village of Dok may be seen. There is also a fine view from here.

1½ miles/2·5 km W of Jericho, Wadi Qilt enters the Plain of Jordan. Recent Israeli excavations of Yehud Netzer have unearthed an extensive **palace**, which shows clear signs of Hellenistic influence. Presumably it was laid out by the Hashmonean king Alexander Jannaios (103–76 B.C.) and occupied by the last Hashmonean monarchs and by Herod. The latter had the building completed in magnificent style. He died within its walls. Unlike the Palace of Massada (see entry) which is more intimate in character, these apartments were designed for state occasions.

The palace stood in a park with terraces which are supplied with water by an irrigation system. The buildings were constructed symmetrically around a vast courtyard. Among the finds were a grand *audience chamber*, apartments with frescoes, and Roman and Jewish ritual baths. The most striking is a swimming *bath* which is 105 ft/32 m long, 59 ft/18 m wide and 13 ft/4 m deep. According to Netzer, it was the scene of a frightful episode in King Herod's life. It was here that Herod had Aristobulos, his 18-year-old son-in-law, drowned while he was bathing. This occurred just a year after Herod had nominated him as High Priest (Josephus 1, 22, 2). A little later on he also ordered the death of Mariamne, a Hashmonean princess and the sister of Aristobulos.

Jerusalem/ Yerushalayim

District: Jerusalem.
Altitude: 1,989–2,711 ft/606–826 m.
Population: 415,000.
Telephone code: 02.
ⓘ **Government Tourist Office,**
24 King George Street,
tel. 24 12 81.

City Information Centers:
34 Jaffa Street;
tel. 22 88 44.
Jaffa Gate;
tel. 28 22 95–6.

HOTELS. – IN THE W OF THE CITY: *Jerusalem Hilton* (k), Givat Ram, L, 420 r., tennis; *Jerusalem Plaza* (k), 47 King George Street, L, 414 r., SP, sauna; *King David* (k), 23 King David Street, L, 258 r., SP, sauna, tennis; *Laromme*, 3 Jabotinsky Street, 312 r.; *Ramada Shalom* (k), Bayit Vegan, I, 288 r., SP, sauna; *Kings* (k), 60 King George Street, I, 214 r.; *Jerusalem Moriah* (k), 39 Keren Hayessod Street, I, 170 r.; *Ariel* (k), 31 Hebron Street, I, 140 r.; *Holyland* (k), Bayit Vegan, I, 116 r., SP, tennis; *Central* (k), 6 Pines Street, I, 77 r.; *Tirat Bat Sheva* (k), 42 King George Street, I, 70 r.; *Sonesta Jerusalem* (k), 2 Wolfson Street, 172 r.; *Ram* (k), 234 Jaffa Street, II, 156 r., sauna; *Jerusalem Tower* (k), 23 Hillel Street, II, 120 r.; *Eilon Tower* (k), 34 Ben Yehuda Street, 120 r., panoramic restaurant on 21st floor; *YMCA*, 26 King David Street, II, 68 r., SP, tennis; *Jerusalem Tadmor* (k), 1 Hagai Street, Beit Hakerem, II, 51 r.; *Neveh Shoshana* (k), 5 Beit Hekerem Street, II, 27 r.; *Orgil* (k), 18 Hillel Street, III, 50 r.; *Palatin* (k), 4 Agrippa Street, III, 28 r.; *Ron* (k), 42A Jaffa Street, III, 22 r.; *Vardi Rosenbaum* (k), 21 Mekor Haim Street, III, 20 r.; *Har Aviv* (k), 16A Bet Hakerem Street, III, 12 r.; *Jerusalem Forest Recreation Center* holiday camp, PO Box 3353, 40 r., SP, tennis.

IN THE E OF THE CITY: *Diplomat* (k), 6 Etzion Street, L, 500 r., SP; *Intercontinental*, Mount of Olives Street, L, 200 r., tennis, *King Solomon Sheraton* (k), 22 King David Street, L, 150 r.; *St George International*, Salah-ed-Din Street, L, 150 r., SP; *Mount Scopus*, Sheikh Jarrah Street, L, 65 r.; *Ambassador*, Sheikh Jarrah Street, I, 118 r.; *American Colony*, Nablus Street, I, 102 r., SP; *National Palace*, 4 Az-Zahra Street, I, 108 r.; *Ritz*, 8 Ibn Khaldoun Street, I, 103 r.; *Panorama*, near the Garden of Gethsemane, I, 74 r.; *Capitol*, 17 Salah-ed-Din Street, I, 54 r.; *Windmill* (k), 3 Mendeli Street, II, 133 r.; *Holyland East*, 6 Rashid Street, II, 99 r.; *Pilgrims' Palace*, King Suliaman Street, II, 95 r.; *Palace*, Mount of Olives Street, II, 68 r.; *Gloria*, Jaffa Gate, II, 64 r.; *YMCA – Aelia Capitolina*, 29 Nablus Street, II, 57 r., tennis; *Strand*, Ibn Jubeir Street, II, 55 r.; *Shepherd*, Mount Scopus, II, 52 r.; *Commodore*, Mount of Olives, II, 45 r.; *Alcazar*, 6 Almutanbi Street, II, 38 r.; *YWCA*, Wadi Jose, II, 30 r.; *Jordan House*, Nur El Din Street, II, 25 r.; *New Metropole*, 8 Salah-ed-Din Street, II, 25 r.; *Christmas*, Salah-ed-Din Street, III, 24 r.; *Mount of Olives*, Mount of Olives Street, III, 63 r.; *Victoria*, 8 Masudie Street, 54 r.; *Vienna East*, Sheikh Jarrah Street, III, 39 r.; *Rivoli*, 3 Salah-ed-Din Street, III, 31 r.; *Lawrence*, 18 Salah-ed-Din Street, III, 30 r.; *Azzahra*, 13 Azzahra Street, III, 24 r.; *New Regent*, 20 Azzahra Street, III, 24 r.; *Astoria*, Mount of Olives Street, III, 23 r.; *City*, Mount Scopus, III, 22 r.; *New Orient House* (k), 10 Abu-Obideah-El-Jarrah Street, III, 22 r.; *Zion* (k), 4 Luntz Street, III, 22 r.; *Park Lane*, Mount Scopus, III, 20 r.; *Pilgrims' Inn*, Rashidia Street, III, 15 r.; *New Imperial*, Jaffa Gate, IV, 50 r.; *Knights' Palace*, New Gate, IV, 42 r.

CHRISTIAN HOSPICES. – *Casa Nova*, Old City; *Christ Church Hospice*, Jaffa Gate; *Dom Polski*, Damascus Gate; *Ecce Homo Convent*, Via Dolorosa; *Lutheran Hospice* (German), Old City (near Church of the Redeemer); *Notre-Dame de France*, opposite New Gate; *St Andrew's Hospice*, railway station; *St George's Hospice*, Nablus/Saladin Street; *St Karl Borromaeus Hospice*, German Colony; *Sisters of the Rosary*, 14 Agron Street; *Sisters of Zion*, En Karem; etc.

YOUTH HOSTELS. – *Bet Bernstein*, 1 Keren Hayesod Street; *En Karem*, in En Karem; *Ivy Yehuda Youth Center*, in the Jerusalem Forest (groups only); *Louise Waterman-Wise Youth Hostel*, Bayit Vegan; *Moreschet Yahadut*, in the Jewish Quarter of the Old City; *Ramot Shapira*, Beth Meir; and others in the Jerusalem area.

CAMP SITE. – *Bet Netofa* (7 miles/11 km W of Jerusalem).

RESTAURANTS. – *Abu Thor* (vegetarian), 5 En Rogel Street; *Alla Gondola* (Italian), 14 King George Street;

Chez Simon, 15 Shammai Street; *City Restaurant* (oriental), 181 Agrippas Street; *Cohen* (oriental), Veshajahu Street; *Fink's* (European), 13 King George Street; *Georgia* (k, Russian), 4 King David Street; *Goulash Inn* (Hungarian), En Karem; *Yemeni Restaurant* (Yemeni), 181 Agrippas Street; *La Bidule* (French), 12 Shmuel Hanaggid Street; *Leviathan* (fish), 11 Al-Rashid Street; *Mandarin* (Chinese), 2 Shlomzion Hamelka Street; *Mishkenot Sha'anaim* (k, French), in the Yemin Moshe quarter; *Mifgash Bavli* (vegetarian), 54 Haneviim Street; *Philadelphia* (oriental), Haphraim Street; *Sea Dolphin* (fish), Al Rashid Street; *The Khan Restaurant* (Rumanian), David Remez Square.

EVENTS. – *Concerts* (Israeli Philharmonic Orchestra, Chamber Music Ensemble); *plays:* every evening, except Fridays and the evenings before public holidays, performances of the history of the Biblical old city in the David Tower near the Jaffa Gate (8.45 p.m. in English; not in winter); *folk-dancing:* Wednesday evenings in the Khan theater in David Remez Square (opposite the station); *illuminations:* Mount Zion, Jaffa Gate and Citadel, Damascus Gate, Cross Monastery and major portions of the city wall are floodlit each evening; the Knesset building is illuminated on Monday and Tuesday evenings and the Israel Museum on Tuesday evenings.

SPORTS AND LEISURE. – Swimming (Jerusalem Swimming Pool, 43 Rehov Emek Refaim; Bet Taylor Swimming Pool, 25 Zangwill Street, Qiriat Hayovel), tennis (tennis courts: A.A.C.I., 9 Rehov Alcalay; Halpool Tennis Club, Qiriat Hayovel; YMCA hostels).

TRANSPORTATION. – Arkia has daily flights to Tel Aviv, Haifa, Rosh Pinna (Galilee) and Eilat. *Atarot* airport is to the N of the city. Information: Arkia, 9 Heleni Hamalkha Street (tel. 22 58 88). Sightseeing bus trips by Egged Tours: Zion Square (tel. 22 34 54); 224 Jaffa Street, central bus station (tel. 53 45 96).

The "high city" of **Jerusalem, in Hebrew Yerushalayim (Dwelling of Peace), in Greek and Latin Hierosolyma, in Arabic El-Quds ("holy"), once the capital of the Jewish Kingdom, is the capital of the State of Israel and the See of a Greek Orthodox, an Armenian and a Roman Catholic patriarch and of an Anglican bishop. As the city of the Temple of David and Solomon, the site of Christ's passion and the place from which Mohammed ascended into heaven Jerusalem is revered by Jews, Christians and Moslems alike. Its status as a "holy" city is uniquely evidenced by the abundance of holy places sacred to the three monotheistic religions. Consequently every year the city is visited by pilgrims and tourists from all over the world.

Jerusalem lies 31°47' N and 35°14' E on the eastern slope of the *Highlands of Judea* on a dry chalk plateau which overlooks the Kidron Valley to the E and the Hinnom valley to the S like a peninsula

Jerusalem in Classical times·

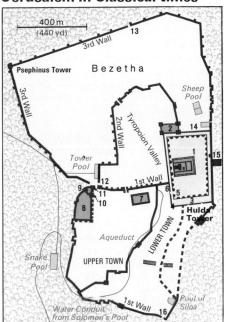

1 Temple	7 Hashmonean Palace	13 Women's Gate
2 Antonia Fort	8 Herod's Palace	14 Israel Pool
3 Stoa Basilica	9 Phasael Tower	15 Susa Gate
4 Robinson Arch	10 Marianmne Tower	16 Ennener Gate
5 Barclay Gate	11 Hippicus Tower	
6 Wilson Arch	12 Garden Gate	

and is divided into a narrow E hill (2,442 ft/744 m), the old Mount of the Temple, and the W hill (2,550 ft/777 m) which contains the former Upper Town. The NW side, connected to the range of hills, rises even higher. The old city is surrounded by a circular wall 40 ft/12 m high and about 2½ miles/4 km long, which is fortified with towers and was erected in its present form by Sultan Suleiman the Magnificent in 1537. Two main streets, David Street leading from the Jaffa Gate eastwards (called Street of the Chain in the E), and Suq Khan ez-Zeit leading southwards from the Damascus Gate, intersect in the middle of the old city and divide it into four quarters: the Christian quarter in the NW, the Armenian quarter in the SW, the Moslem quarter in the NE and the Jewish quarter in the SE. The alleys are winding and are often vaulted. The new city, adjoining the old city to the W, has developed in a very modern way, with public agencies, ministries and parliamentary buildings. The city is still expanding northwards with the building of new residential area.

History of the city

The discovery of flint tools (in the Ephraim Valley near the station) and of graves indicates that men were

Jerusalem: view of the old city looking northwards

living here as early as the Old Stone Age. From the third millennium B.C. the center of the settlement was Mount Ophel, S of the Mount of the Temple. There was an early Canaanite town here, near the vitally important Gihon spring. In the time of Abraham (presumably in the 18th c. B.C.) the town was called *Salem*; its priest-king Melchizedek welcomed the wandering Abraham (Genesis 14, 18). Towards the end of the 2nd millennium B.C. the town belonged to the Jebusites, whom *David* conquered around 1000 B.C. (2 Samuel 5, 6–10). He erected the "City of David", again on Mount Ophel, and made Jerusalem the political and religious center of the Kingdom of Israel.

His son *Solomon* (965–928) erected a palace and a temple to Yahweh (1 Kings 6–8). After Solomon's death Jerusalem became the capital of the southern Kingdom of Judah. Queen Athaliah (845–840) introduced the cult of Baal into the Temple and under King Ahaz (733–727) Assyrian gods were also worshipped. His son Hezekiah (727–698) purified the Temple and built walls to defend the city and a tunnel for the water supply. In 628 B.C. Josiah made Jerusalem the only legitimate Israelite holy place (2 Kings 22). In 587 the King of the Babylonians *Nebuchadnezzar* seized the city and removed a large part of the population. After the end of the "Babylonian Captivity" the second Temple was built (520 B.C.). Nehemiah built a new city wall.

In 332 B.C. Jerusalem came under Greek domination and became increasingly Hellenised. The desecration of the Temple by Antiochus IV triggered off the Maccabean revolt in 167 B.C. Under the Maccabees and the Hashmoneans the city grew westwards as far as today's Mount Zion. In 63 B.C. it came under the Roman sphere of influence. In 37 B.C. the Idumee *Herod* became ruler. He reconstructed the Temple square magnificently and provided the city with palaces, a citadel, theaters, a racecourse and an agora

on the Graeco-Roman pattern. After his death (4 B.C.) Jerusalem was the city of the High Priests – under Roman procurators. From A.D. 41 to 44 King Agrippa I enlarged the city northwards (3rd wall). In the year 70 Jerusalem was destroyed by *Titus* and after 135 restored as *Aelia Capitolina* by Emperor *Hadrian*.

Jerusalem became a Christian city in 326 when the Emperor *Constantine* and his mother Helena had churches built. The Empress Eudoxia, consort of Theodosius II, who lived in Jerusalem from 444 to 460, and the Emperor Justinian (527–565) also encouraged the building of Christian churches. This era ended in 614 with the Persian conquest; from 627 to 638 the Byzantines held the city once again.

In 638 Jerusalem was conquered by Islamic armies. The *Omayyad Caliphs* had the Dome of the Rock and the El Aqsa Mosque built. Another era of Christian rule began on July 15, 1099 with the capture of the city by the *Crusaders* who embellished it with numerous

buildings (churches, palaces, hospices). When Sultan Saladin conquered Jerusalem in 1187 Islam again became predominant and this situation continued under the Egyptian *Mamelukes* (1291–1517) and the *Ottomans* (1517–1917) under whose rule the present city wall was built in 1537.

In the 19th c. the Christian powers of Europe, having supported the Turkish sultan against the Egyptian Ibrahim Pasha, gained increasing influence from 1840 onwards, and this was shown in the construction of churches, schools, hospitals and orphanages. The Pope renewed the Latin patriarchate which had been founded in 1099 and dissolved in 1291. An English-Prussian diocese was set up in 1845. In 1873 the German Templars founded a settlement (near the station) and in 1881 members of an American-Swedish religious group founded the American Colony (N of the Damascus Gate).

After centuries of being forbidden to live in the city,

Jews began to return in the 13th c. In 1267 Ramban (Rabbi Nachmanides) founded a synagogue, in 1488 Jews arrived from Egypt, and after 1492 Sephardic Jews came from Spain. Ashkenazi Jews arrived in 1701: Rabbi Hanassi came from Poland with 500 followers. By the 18th c. there were about 1,000 Sephardis (the Jewish elite) and 700 Ashkenazis. Immigration increased in the 19th c. In 1854 the first Jewish hospital was founded and in 1855 Sir Moses Montefiore set up the first Jewish settlement outside the old town, still identifiable today by its windmill. In 1868 Jews from North Africa built Makhane Israel (on the corner of King David Street and Agron Street). In 1874 the settlement of Mea Shearim was set up. The Sephardic Chief Rabbi was the official representative of the divided Jews. The year 1891 saw the opening of the rail link with the port of Jaffa.

On December 11, 1917 the *British* entered Jerusalem under General Allenby. From July 1, 1920 Jerusalem was the headquarters of the British High Commissioner for the Palestinian Mandate. In 1925 the Hebrew University was opened. In 1947 the United Nations decided to divide the country between Arabs and Jews and to make Jerusalem an international city. In 1948 when the Mandate came to an end Israel and Jordan fought over the city which was divided during the 1949 ceasefire. In 1950 the Israelis made West Jerusalem their capital; East Jerusalem was annexed after the 1967 Six-Day War. In 1980 Jerusalem, including the Arab old town, was declared "the capital of Israel for all time", and this led to renewed unrest.

Sights

Most museums and public institutions are closed on Saturdays, the Jewish sabbath. Special arrangements apply for Fridays and the day before public holidays.

Abu Gate
(Giv'at Hananiya)
Viewpoint near the station.

Agricultural Museum
13 Helena Hamalka Street.
Summer Sun.–Fri. 8 a.m.–1 p.m.; winter Sun.–Thurs. 8 a.m.–2 p.m. and Fri. 8 a.m.–1 p.m.

Allenby Monument
Elit Square.

American Institute for Exploration of the Holy Land
On Mount Zion.

Antonia Fortress
In the old town.

Artists' House
12 Shmu'el Hanaggid Street.
Sun.–Thurs. 10 a.m.–1 p.m. and 4–7 p.m.; Fri. 10 a.m.–1 p.m.; Sat. 11 a.m.–2 p.m.
Regular exhibitions.

Bezalel Art School
10 Shmu'el Hanaggid Street.
Regular exhibitions.

Biblical Zoo
10 Brandeis Street.
8 a.m.–6 p.m. daily in summer (4 p.m. in winter).

Binyanei Ha'ooma
(Assembly hall)
Opposite the Central Bus Station
Israeli Song Festival, etc.

Chuzot Hayozer
Jerusalem Brigade Street.
Center for art and handicrafts.

Citadel
Near the Jaffa Gate.
Sun.–Thurs., Sat. 8.30 a.m.–4.30 p.m.; Fri. and the day before a public holiday 8.30 a.m.–2 p.m.
Museum of Jewish history in the basement.

David Palombo Museum
Mount Zion.
Sun.–Thurs. 10.30 a.m.–4.30 p.m.; Fri. 9.30 a.m.–1 p.m.

Dorva Dor Museum
(in the Chief Rabbinate)
Sun.–Thurs. 9 a.m.–1 p.m.; Fri. 9 a.m.–noon.
Jewish ecclesiastical folk art.

Ecce Homo Arch
Old town.
Part of a Roman triumphal arch.

En Karem
SW suburb of Jerusalem.
Artists' colony, art gallery.

Garden of Gethsemane
At the foot of the Mount of Olives.
Sun.–Thurs. 8.30 a.m.–noon and 3–7 p.m.

Gihon spring
In Siloam Street.
Start of the Hiskia tunnel.

Hall of Heroes
Russian Square.
Sun.–Thurs. 9 a.m.–4 p.m.; Fri. and Sat. 9 a.m.–1 p.m.
Testimony to the Jewish struggle for independence.

Hebrew University
(Qiryat HaUniversita)
In the W of the city.
Guided tours Sun.–Fri. 9–11 a.m.

Heikhal Shelomo
(Chief Rabbinate; Sir Isaac and Lady Wolfson Museum) 58 King George Street.
Sun.–Thurs. 9 a.m.–1 p.m.; Fri. 9 a.m.–noon.

Hiskia Tunnel
Mount Ophel.

House of Caiaphas
In the Armenian Monastery of the Redeemer.

Islamic Museum
On the Mount of the Temple.
Sun.–Thurs. 8.30–11.30 a.m. and 1.30–4.30 p.m.
Arabic books and manuscripts, weapons.

Israel Museum
(Book Shrine, Bezalel Art Gallery, Archaeological Museum, Billy Rose Sculpture Garden)
Ruppin Street.
Sun., Mon., Wed., Thurs. 10 a.m.–5 p.m.; Tues. 4–10 p.m.; Fri. and public holidays 10 a.m.–2 p.m.
Closed on some public holidays.

Jeremiah's grotto
Opposite Herod's Gate in Saladin Street.

Jerusalem Theatre
20 David Marcus Street.
Modern building opened in 1972.

Jerusalem – ancient sarcophagus in front of the Israel Museum

Jishuw Museum
(Museum of the old Jewish community), in the Jewish quarter.
Sun.–Thurs. 10 a.m.–5 p.m.

Kennedy Memorial
W of the city center.

Khan Center
Near the station.
Old caravanserai, now center for cultural events.

Knesset
Ruppin Street.
Sun.–Fri. 8.30 a.m.–2.30 p.m.; Sun. and Thurs. free guided tours.
Passport required.

Model of ancient Jerusalem
In the garden of the Holy Land Hotel in the suburb of Bait Vegan.
Summer Sun.–Fri. 8 a.m.–5 p.m.; winter Sun.–Fri. 8 a.m.–4 p.m.

Mount Herzl
Herzl Boulevard.
Park: 8 a.m.–6.30 p.m. daily (5 p.m. in winter).
Museum: Sun.–Tues. and Thurs. 9 a.m.–5 p.m.; Fri. and Sat. 9 a.m.–1 p.m.

Museum of Islamic Art
2 Hapalmach Street.
Sun.–Tues., and the day before a public holiday 10 a.m.–12.30 p.m. and 3.30–6 p.m., Wed. 3.30–9 p.m.; Sat. 10.30 a.m.–1 p.m.; closed on public holidays.

Museum of Musical Instruments
7 Smolenskin Street.
Sun.–Fri. 10 a.m.–1 p.m.

National Archives
In the Prime Minister's offices in the Hakirya quarter.
Sun.–Thurs. 9 a.m.–1 p.m.

Natural History Museum
6 Mohilever Street.
Sun.–Thurs. 10 a.m.–1 p.m., Mon. and Wed. also 4–6 p.m.; Sat. 10.30 a.m.–1 p.m.

Papal Bible Institute
3 Paul Botta Street.
Visits by arrangement.

Rockefeller Museum
NE of Herod's Gate.
Sun.–Thurs. 10 a.m.–5 p.m.; Fri., Sat., the day before a public holiday and on public holidays 10 a.m.–2 p.m.

Rubin Academy of Music
Smolenskin Street.
Sun.–Fri. 9 a.m.–1 p.m.; closed Sat.
Exhibition of musical instruments.

Shoken Library
Balfour Street.
Sun.–Thurs. 9 a.m.–1 p.m.
Rare Hebrew prints and precious manuscripts.

Square of the Temple
(Haram esh-Sharif)
Sat.–Thurs. 8 a.m.–5.30 p.m. (4 p.m. in winter).
The Dome of the Rock and the El Aqsa Mosque have different visiting hours.

Tax Museum
32 Agron Street.
Sun., Tues., Thurs. 1–4 p.m.; Mon., Wed., Fri. 10 a.m.–noon.

Via Dolorosa
In the old town.

Wailing Wall
(West Wall)
In the old town.

Yad Vashem
Near Mount Herzl.
Sun.–Thurs. 9 a.m.–5 p.m.; Fri. 8 a.m.–4 p.m.
Monument to the victims of the Second World War.

CHURCHES and MONASTERIES

Abyssinian Church
Abyssinia Street, in the Mea Shearim quarter.

Alexandra Hospice
In the Christian quarter.
Mon.–Sat. 8 a.m.–1 p.m. and 3–5 p.m.; closed Sun. and during the holiday period.

Cathedral of St James
In the Armenian quarter.

Church of the Holy Sepulchre
In the Christian quarter.
Open daily 4.15 a.m. until sunset
Greek Orthodox service: 1 p.m.; Armenian service:
2.30 p.m.; Roman Catholic service: 4–7 p.m.

Church of the Nations
In the Garden of Gethsemane.

Church of the Redeemer
In the Christian quarter.

Church of St Anne
Near the Bethesda pool.

Church of St Mary Magdalene
On the Mount of Olives.
Tues., Thurs., Sat. 9 a.m.–noon and 2–7 p.m.;
Sun. 10 a.m.–noon.

Church of the Sisters of Zion
Opposite the Antonia fortress.
Mon.–Sat. 8.30 a.m.–12.30 p.m. and 2–5.30 p.m.;
closed on Sun.

Dominus Flevit
On the Mount of Olives.
Sun.–Thurs. 8.30 a.m.–noon and 3–6 p.m. (2–5 p.m.
in winter).

Dormitio Sanctae Mariae
On Mount Zion.
Closed Sun.; open Mon.–Sat. (closed 1–3 p.m.).

Monastery of Constantine
W of the Church of the Holy Sepulchre.

Monastery of the Cross
Boulevard Ben Zwi.
Mon.–Fri. 8 a.m.–noon.

Pater Noster Church
On the Mount of Olives.

Russian Orthodox Cathedral
E of Bar Kochba Square.
9 a.m.–4 p.m. daily (until 1 p.m. Fri. and Sat.).

St John the Baptist
In the suburb of En Karem.
10 a.m.–noon; 2 p.m. until sunset.

Tomb of the Virgin
(church cut in the rock)
Near Gethsemane.

Visitatio Mariae Church
In the suburb of En Karem.
9 a.m.–noon and 3–6 p.m.

SYNAGOGUES

Eliahu Hanavi Synagogue
In the Jewish quarter.

Emtzai Synagogue
In the Jewish quarter.

Hadassah Synagogue
In the Hadassah Medical Center to the W of the city.
Sun.–Fri. 9 a.m.–noon and Sun.–Thurs. 1.30–4 p.m.;
closed Sat. and public holidays.
Twelve stained-glass windows by Marc Chagall.

Hurva Synagogue
Hayehudim Street.
Jewish quarter (being restored).

Istanbul Synagogue
In the Jewish quarter.

Porat Josef Synagogue
By the Wailing Wall.

Ramban Synagogue
In the Jewish quarter.

Teshurun Synagogue
King George Street.
9 a.m.–2 p.m. daily.
Important library (Judaica).

Yohanan Ben Zakkai Synagogue
In the Jewish quarter.

MOSQUES

Dome of the Rock
On the Mount of the Temple.
Sat.–Thurs. 8–11.30 a.m. (11 a.m. in winter),
12.15–2.45 p.m. and 3.45–5.30 p.m.
(12.15–2.15 p.m. and 3–4 p.m. in winter); closed
on Fri. and Moslem holidays.

El Aqsa Mosque
On the Mount of the Temple.
Sat.–Thurs. 8–11 a.m., 12.15–3.15 p.m. (2.45 p.m. in
winter), and 3.45–5.30 p.m. in summer.
(3.15–4.30 p.m. in winter); closed on Fri. and Moslem
holidays.

TOMBS

Bnei Hezir
In the Kidron Valley.
Known as *Jacob's Grotto* in Christian times, tomb of
a Hashmonean family of priests according to the
inscription in Hebrew.

Garden Tomb
N of the Damascus Gate.
Mon.–Sat. 8 a.m.–12.30 p.m. and 3–5.30 p.m.;
closed Sun.

Jacob's Grotto
See Bnei Hezir.

Jason's Tomb
10 Alfasi Street.

Tomb of Absalom
In the Kidron Valley.

Tomb of David
On Mount Zion.
Sun.–Thurs. 7 a.m.–5 p.m.; Fri. 7 a.m.–4 p.m.;
Sat. 6 a.m.–4 p.m.

Tomb of Herod
Abu Sikhra Street.

Tomb of Hulda
On the Mount of Olives.

Tomb of Josaphat
In the Kidron Valley.

Tombs of the Kings
Saladin Street.
Sun.–Thurs. 8.30 a.m.–5 p.m.

Tombs of the Prophets
On the Mount of Olives.

Tombs of the Sanhedrin
In the northern suburb of Sanhedria.
Open daily from 9 a.m. until sunset; closed on Sat.

Tomb of Simon
Near the Sheikh Jarrah quarter.

Tomb of the Virgin
On the Mount of Olives.

Tomb of Zachariah
In the Kidron Valley.

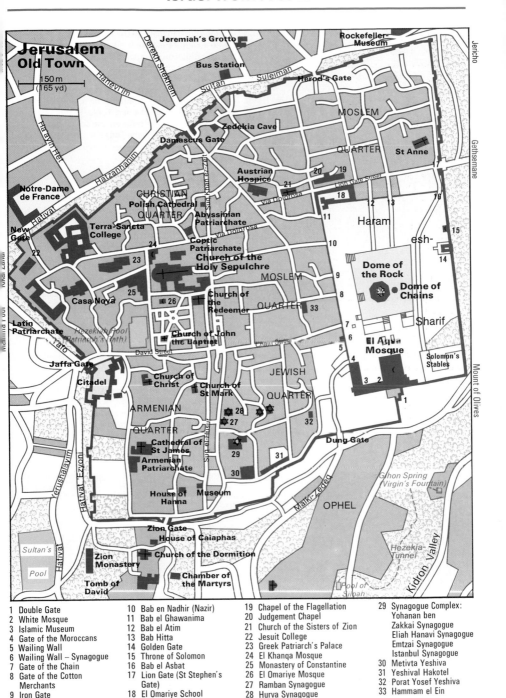

Jerusalem Old Town

150 m
(165 yd)

Jeremiah's Grotto
Rockefeller-Museum
Bus Station
Herod's Gate
Suleiman
Sultan
Zedekia Cave
Damascus Gate
MOSLEM QUARTER
St Anne
Notre-Dame de France
Austrian Hospice
CHRISTIAN QUARTER
Polish Cathedral
Abyssinian Patriarchate
via Dolorosa
Haram
Terra-Sancta College
New Gate
Coptic Patriarchate
via Dolorosa
esh-
Church of the Holy Sepulchre
MOSLEM
Dome of the Rock
Dome of Chains
Casa Nova
Church of the Redeemer
QUARTER
Sharif
Latin Patriarchate
Hezekiah Pool
Church of John the Baptist
Chain Street
El Aqsa Mosque
Solomon's Stables
Jaffa Gate
David Street
JEWISH
Church of Christ
Church of St Mark
QUARTER
Citadel
ARMENIAN
Dung Gate
QUARTER
Cathedral of St James
Armenian Patriarchate
House of Hanna
Museum
OPHEL
Gihon Spring (Virgin's Fountain)
Zion Gate
House of Caiaphas
Hezekia Tunnel
Sultan's Pool
Zion Monastery
Church of the Dormition
Kidron Valley
Tomb of David
Chamber of the Martyrs
Pool of Siloah

1 Double Gate	10 Bab en Nadhir (Nazir)	19 Chapel of the Flagellation	29 Synagogue Complex:
2 White Mosque	11 Bab el Ghawanima	20 Judgement Chapel	Yohanan ben
3 Islamic Museum	12 Bab el Atim	21 Church of the Sisters of Zion	Zakkai Synagogue
4 Gate of the Moroccans	13 Bab Hitta	22 Jesuit College	Eliah Hanavi Synagogue
5 Wailing Wall	14 Golden Gate	23 Greek Patriarch's Palace	Emtzai Synagogue
6 Wailing Wall – Synagogue	15 Throne of Solomon	24 El Khanqa Mosque	Istanbul Synagogue
7 Gate of the Chain	16 Bab el Asbat	25 Monastery of Constantine	30 Metivta Yeshiva
8 Gate of the Cotton	17 Lion Gate (St Stephen's	26 El Omariye Mosque	31 Yeshival Hakotel
Merchants	Gate)	27 Ramban Synagogue	32 Porat Yosef Yeshiva
9 Iron Gate	18 El Omariye School	28 Hurva Synagogue	33 Hammam el Ein

Sightseeing in Jerusalem

From the Jaffa Gate to the Wailing Wall

Named after the road to the port of Jaffa which begins here, the **Jaffa Gate** connects the old town and the Jewish new town of Jerusalem and, apart from the Damascus Gate, is the most important access to the **OLD TOWN**, which UNESCO declared in 1981 to be "a protected cultural monument". Entering the old town through the Jaffa Gate and crossing Omar ben Qattab Square one reaches David Street and its continuation, the Street of Chains, leading to the Wailing Wall and the Square of the Temple. To the N of these streets lie the Christian and Moslem quarters and to the S the Armenian and Jewish quarters.

Jaffa Gate

The Arabs call the gate Bab el Khalil (Hebron Gate) and the Jews call it Shaar Yafo. It is part of Suleiman the Magnificent's defensive wall (16th c.). The gap to its right was made by the Turks in 1898 to enable the German Emperor and Empress to enter the city in procession. Today it allows trucks to pass through.

Immediately to the S of the Jaffa Gate is the **Citadel**, also popularly known as "David's Tower".

It does not date back to David, however, but to Herod who about 24 B.C. built his palace surrounded with fortifications on the site of the C of its lla named the three towers after his brother, his friend and his wife – Phasael, Hippicus and Mariamne. After the city was taken by Titus in A.D. 70 the Romans set up a garrison in the fort. Later it fell into decay and was rebuilt by Crusaders, Mamelukes and Turks. In the 14th c. the David's Tower was built on the foundations of the Phasael Tower and in the 16th c. a minaret was added; the NW tower stands on the site of the Hippicus Tower.

The Citadel is today a museum of the history of the city and a folklore museum. There is a view over the city from the top.

Opposite the entrance to the Citadel is the Anglican *Church of Christ* (1849). Now turn southwards to the ARMENIAN QUARTER and follow the Street of the Armenian Patriarchate. After passing a police station (right) turn left into St Jacob's Street and then left into Ararat Street to the Syrian *Monastery of St Mark*.

According to tradition the richly ornamented 12th c. *church* stands on the site of the house of Mary, the mother of Mark the Evangelist, where Peter went when he fled from the prison of Herod Agrippa I (Acts 12, 12–17). Behind the church portal on the right there is an Aramaic inscription and in the body of the church a silver-mounted font over which is an icon of the Virgin which the monks ascribe to Luke the Evangelist (in the Orthodox Church Luke is the painter

Jerusalem – Citadel

of the first and hence authentic icon of the Virgin). The richly carved patriarchal throne is also worth seeing.

Return to the Street of the Armenian Orthodox Patriarchate and turn to the S to reach the **Monastery of the Armenian Patriarchate** (left), the largest monastery building in the city and the spiritual center of the 35,000 Armenians who live here.

House of Hanna (chapel)

Armenian Quarter

The **Cathedral of St James**, open to visitors only during services, dates from the period of the Crusades (12th c.). The S porch has a fine portal dating from that time.

The relationship with its patron James is twofold. A chapel to the left of the entrance is supposed to be the site where James the Elder, the son of Zebedee, was put to death on the orders of Herod Agrippa I in A.D. 44 (Acts 12, 2); legend has it that after the Arab conquest his body was taken to Spain where from the 11th c. onwards it became the focus of the cult of Santiago de Cóostela. Under the altar of the Cathedral there is also the tomb of the first bishop of Jerusalem who had the same name and is supposed to be Jesus' oldest brother and the author of the Epistle of James in the New Testament who was stoned to death in A.D. 62.

A gate in the S side leads into the *Etshmiadsin Chapel* which houses stones from Sinai, Mount Tabor and the Jordan.

Near the entrance to the district a staircase leads to the *residence of the Armenian Patriarch* which has a treasury and library housing some 4,000 illuminated manuscripts from the 10th to 17th c., the sceptre of the last Armenian king (14th c.) and rich liturgical vestments, crowns and objects from the last three centuries.

On the other side of the site, past the *Gulbenkian Library*, through an archway and then to the right, is a *chapel* (1300) on the site of the "House of Hanna", the father-in-law of the high priest Caiaphas, and the *Deir ez-Zeituni Convent* (Olive Tree Convent) which has an olive tree to which Jesus is supposed to have been bound before he was questioned by the high priest.

Then go further S, along the city wall eastwards and through the **Zion Gate**, from where the road leads to the Hinnom and Kidron Valleys and to Mount Zion. Continue inside the wall into the JEWISH QUARTER.

The fighting between Jews and Arabs in 1948 and subsequent events left this district in ruins and it was rebuilt after 1967. In the second wide street, the Street of the Jewish Quarter (Rehov Ha-Yehudim), turn N. On the right are several synagogues which have been rebuilt in the last few years.

The first one, on the right, is the *Ramban Synagogue*, which was the first to be built in the old town in 1267, by Rabbi Moshe ben Nahman Ramban (Nachmanides) who had come to the Holy Land from Spain. Immediately to the N is the *Hurva Synagogue*, the reconstruction of which began in 1977. It dates back to Rabbi Yehuda Hanassi who came from Poland in 1701 with 500 Ashkenazi disciples, whereupon the Jewish community of the city split and the Ashkenazi built their own

In the Jewish Quarter

Prayers in the Wailing Wall

Wall ("Kotel Hama'aravi") on the SW side of the Temple district, the largest of the sites venerated by the Jews. Since 1967 the densely built site has been made into a huge open square. Where it borders the Wall it is cut off by a railing and this area is used as a synagogue, the right-hand part being for women and the left-hand part for men. This is where great religious ceremonies take place and where recruits are sworn in.

synagogue. After the Rabbi died it fell into decay (hence the name Ha-Hurva=ruin) and was not rebuilt until 1856, when it once more became a center for the Ashkenazi Jews until its destruction in 1948. The street runs N to David Street and continues as the Khan ez-Zeit bazaar which leads to the Damascus Gate.

A short distance S of the Ramban Synagogue to the left is an alley leading to the **Metivta Yeshiva** complex which has four synagogues. The recently reconstructed Sephardic *Yohanan ben Zakkai Synagogue* is named after a rabbi of Roman times. The *Elia hu Hanavi Synagogue* is a reminder that the Prophet Elias stayed here. The *Emtzai Synagogue* (middle synagogue) is the smallest of all. The *Istanbuli Synagogue*, named after Jews from Turkey, is today used by the pupils of the Metivta Yeshiva.

NE of this complex lie the ruins of the main Chassidic synagogue *Tipheret Israel* (glory of Israel) and opposite to the NW is the courtyard of the Jewish Caraite sect.

In the large square in front of the Wailing Wall are the Porat Josef Synagogue and its Talmud school. This is now being reconstructed next to Yeshivat Hakotel, the Torah school by the Wailing Wall.

Next there is the 158 ft/48 m long and 60 ft/18 m high ****Wailing Wall** or *West*

A vaulted passage in the NE corner leads along the Herodian wall to the so-called Wilson Arch (below the present-day Chain Gate), which was once an entrance to the Temple over the Tyropoion Valley. Under this arch one can look down the square shaft excavated by Wilson's assistant Warren; there are 14 ashlar layers under the present level right down to the natural rock, which gives an idea of how massive this wall is.

The Wailing Wall gets its name from the lamentation of the Jews for the destruction of the Temple. It was the only part of the Temple that was almost always accessible to them. Today pious Jews do not take advantage of the possibility of going into the Temple square itself since

Wailing Wall (West Wall)

the position of the Holy of Holies where none but the high priests may go is not precisely known.

Now go along an alley in the NW of the square to the Street of Chains. Turn left, cross the Street of the Bazaar and return to the Jaffa Gate along crowded David Street with its cafés and shops.

Or turn right into the street of the bazaar (Khan ez-Zeitun) and follow it to the Damascus Gate.

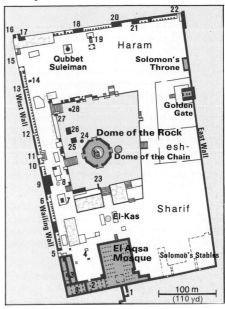

Temple Mount   Jerusalem

1 Double Gate	15 Bab el Ghawanima
2 White Mosque	16 Minaret
3 Islamic Museum	17 Medresse el Malakiyeh
4 Jussel Dome	18 Bab el Atim
5 Gate of the Moroccans	19 Sebil es-Sultan Suleiman
6 Chain Gate	20 Bab Hitta
7 Qubbet Musa	21 Medresse el Gahdiriyeh
8 Qaitbay Spring	22 Bab el Asbat
9 Medresse	23 Pulpit
10 Bab el Mastarak	24 Prayer Niche of the
11 Gate of the Cotton	Prophet
Merchants	25 Ascension Dome
12 Iron Gate	26 Hebron Dome
13 Bab en-Nadhir (Nazir)	27 St George's Dome
14 Sebil Ala ed-Din el Basir	28 Dome of the Spirits

Between Jaffa Gate and the Citadel

Temple Mount

To the E of the Wailing Wall is the *Temple Mount. Israel's old Temple Square (called Haram esh-Sharif, "the noble sanctuary", by the Arabs) is the most important Islamic shrine after Mecca and Medina.

Nowhere else do holy places of the three monotheistic world religions lie so close together as here. The spot is holy for Moslems and no less so for Jews whose Temple used to stand here; it is also important for Christians for it was in the Temple that Jesus was presented as a baby (Luke 2, 22), it was here that the twelve-year-old boy argued with the scribes (Luke 2, 46), it was from the courtyard that he later cast out the merchants and the moneychangers (Matthew 21, 12), and it was on a pinnacle of the Temple that he was tempted by the Devil (Matthew 4, 5).

History of the Temple Mount

The history of this place, in which myth, miracle and history combine to form the great unit imbued with religion, begins with *Abraham*. Arriving from Ur on the lower Euphrates, he and his tribe were living in Beersheba when God ordered him (Genesis 22) to sacrifice his son Isaac on Mount Moriah. It is generally accepted that this Mount was the place where the Temple was later built. Abraham obeyed the instructions, covered the 53 miles/85 km back to Jerusalem in three days, and prepared the sacrifice. God intervened to prevent the human sacrifice and a ram appeared in Isaac's place; this can be regarded as an allegory for the redemption of man through animal sacrifice. This event, which probably took place in the 18th c. B.C., sanctified for all time the steep rocky summit which reared up between what were then the valleys of the Kidron and the Tyropoion.

About 1000 B.C. *David* captured the town, which at the time belonged to the Jebusites, built an altar on the threshing-floor of the Jebusite Ornan, and placed there the Ark of the Covenant containing the Tablets (2 Samuel 6).

His son *Solomon* (960–926 B.C.) then had the **First Temple** built on this spot in conjunction with his palace (1 Kings 5 and 6). It was the Israelites' first large building, and as they had no experience in this field Solomon engaged the help of the Phoenician king Hiram of Tyre. In return for 20,000 measures of wheat and 20 measures of pure oil a year Hiram sent him cedarwood from the Lebanon and his masterbuilder. Thus the Temple displayed the features of Phoenician architecture; details such as the two copper columns, Boas and Jachin, in the courtyard have their exact counterparts in temples of the pre-Israelite people of Canaan (e.g. the 20, 10th c. B.C. temples which have been excavated in Hazor, see entry), as well as in a great many later temples to Baal as in Palmyra.

The Temple was begun in the fourth year of Solomon's reign and was completed in seven years, i.e. 950 B.C. It was 33 ft/10 m wide, 46 ft/14 m high and 89 ft/27 m long. It had a porch about 15 ft/4.5 m deep and side chambers for the Temple treasures and ecclesiastical vestments. The main chamber (hekal) was 59 ft/18 m long and the adjacent oracle (debis) 30 ft/9 m long. The walls were clad with cedar and gilded. In the main chamber stood the altar and in the oracle the Ark, watched over by two huge gilded cherubim whose wings stretched from one wall to the other.

It was in the sumptuously appointed Temple that the priests appointed by Solomon, the Zadoks, offered up prayers and sacrifices. The altar for burnt offerings was the top of the Moriah rock which was incorporated into the Temple.

Solomon's building stood for almost 400 years until it was destroyed by the Babylonian Nebuchadnezzar in 587 B.C. On their return from captivity in Babylon the Israelites removed the rubble and built the **Second Temple** which was completed in 516 B.C. Its dimensions are given in the Book of Ezra (Ezra 6, 3); it was obviously less sumptuous than the first Temple.

In the course of time, especially in the conflicts with the Seleucid rulers which led to the Maccabean uprising, this Temple was probably severely damaged, which is why Herod (37–4 B.C.), wishing to appear a true believer in the eyes of the Jews, had it rebuilt. As when the first Temple was built ideas were borrowed from another culture. Herod combined the requirements of the Jewish religion with elements of the Graeco-Roman style, as was also the case in other Semitic temples such as Palmyra and Petra.

First he extended the area of the Temple to its present size of about 985 ft by 1,575 ft/300 m by 480 m. This called for in-filling with soil and the construction of massive piles (the so-called "Solomon's stables") since the site falls away to the S. The land gained in this way was surrounded by huge ashlar walls which are still visible on the S and E sides and on the S half

of the W side. In the SE corner they reach a height of 213 ft/65 m over the Kidron Valley.

Stoas were built along the outside walls. The Royal Stoa (Stoa basilike) on the S side was particularly magnificent with its four rows of Corinthian columns. There were several entrances to the Temple: in the E there was an entrance where the Golden Gate stands today; in the S excavations after 1967 brought to light the Hulda Gate under the Royal Hall; in the W are the Warren and Barclay Gates, named after their discoverers, and the Wilson Arch which spanned the Tyropoion Valley; in the SW corner one can now see the Robinson Arch which was reached by a staircase.

The outer forecourt was for temporal business and merchants and was open to anyone. The inner forecourt was on a higher level and only Jews were allowed access. It was divided into three parts: the Women's Courtyard, the Courtyard of the Israelites (for men only) and the Priests' Courtyard. In the Priests' Courtyard, probably above the holy rock, stood the large horned altar on which animals were sacrificed. Finally, in the very centre, there was the actual Temple, as described in detail by Flavius Josephus in his "History of the Jewish War" V, 4–6. The white marble façade had golden capitals and a golden door lintel ornamented with vine tendrils. The façade was about 165 ft by 165 ft/50 m by 50 m and the building behind it was 66 ft/20 m less in width. There were no gates on the front part because "it was to symbolise the infinite dimensions of Heaven". The adjacent room was divided into two. The first part contained the seven-branched candlestick and the censer. A curtain separated the empty Holy of Holies, the dwelling-place of the invisible God. "The outside of the Temple was a delight to the eye and to the heart. Sheathed in heavy gold plate on all sides, it shimmered in the gleam of the sunrise and matched the sun in its brilliance." Thus spake Flavius Josephus, who also described the Temple service of his time and, the destruction of the Temple, for the Herodian Temple, which lasted barely 100 years, was destroyed by the Romans in A.D. 70.

That was the end of the Jewish Temple. It was the end of the sacrificial rites, the rabbis replaced the priests, the synagogue became the place of prayer, and the Wailing Wall stayed on as the reminder of the Temple. The Temple square is today a holy place for Moslems.

Jerusalem – Dome of the Rock in the Temple square

Before, however, the Moslems gained control of Jerusalem, the city stood in the shadow of the Cross. After Emperor Constantine the Great had built churches over the Holy Sepulchre and on the Mount of Olives in the 4th c., Justinian (527–564) had a church to the Virgin built in Jerusalem. According to Prokop of Caesarea ("De Aedificiis" V, 6) this basilica with its roof built from the trunks of huge cedars stood on the Temple square.

When the armies of Islam conquered Jerusalem in 638, the city was visited by Omar, originally a vehement opponent of Mohammed and then his second successor (caliph). Accompanied by Archbishop Sophronius and arrayed in the simplest of clothing he proceeded to the Temple square where he prayed at Abraham's rock. This rock was sacred to the Moslems. The 17th sura of the Quran tells of the miraculous journey which the Prophet made by night "from the mosque of the sanctuary (Mecca) to the distant mosque" (at Aqsa, i.e. Jerusalem); it was from the Moriah rock that Mohammed ascended into the seven Heavens and then returned to Mecca.

Because of this the Moslems ascribe great importance to the Haram esh-Sharif. It has become even more important during the 20th c.: it was here that King Hussein I (1853–1931), a pioneer of the Arab movement in this century, was buried, and it was here that his successor Abdullah was assassinated in 1951.

In the magnificent period of the Omayyad Caliphs, whose seat was in Damascus, the two buildings which have since become symbols of the city were built in the Haram: between 687 and 691 Abd el Malik built the *Dome of the Rock* over the Moriah rock and his son Al Walid I (705–715) turned Justinian's church dedicated to the Virgin into the *El Aqsa Mosque*.

Islamic rule over the Temple Mount was interrupted by the Crusaders, whose rule in Jerusalem lasted from 1099 until 1187. The Crusaders plundered the Dome of the Rock and the El Aqsa Mosque (contrasting with Caliph Omar who had embellished the Church of the Holy Sepulchre). The first kings of Jerusalem lived in the El Aqsa Mosque, then handed it over to the Templars whose order was founded in 1149 and who took their name from Templum Salomonis (El Aqsa) and Templum Domini (Dome of the Rock).

After it was recaptured by Saladin for Islam in 1187 the Haram was the site of further building, particularly by the Egyptian Mamelukes. – Damaged by grenades during the 1948 Israeli-Arab conflict, the Dome of the Rock was reconstructed by Jordan, Egypt and Saudi Arabia in 1958–64 and was given a new golden dome. Israeli soldiers regained the Wailing Wall during the Six-Day War on June 7, 1967 and since that time Jews have been able to visit it.

In order to get a complete impression of the Temple square and its buildings it is advisable first to make a tour of the surrounding walls from E to W via the southern side.

The **East Wall** looks out most impressively over the Kidron Valley. Set in the wall is the *Golden Gate* erected in the 7th c. on the site of Herod's Susa Gate. The Arabs call the S entraance Bab er-Rameh

Golden Gate (inside)

(Gate of Salvation) and the N entrance Bab el Tobeh which refers to the expectation (of Jews as well as Moslems) that the Kidron Valley and the Mount of Olives will be the site of the Last Judgement. The Jews believed that the Messiah would enter the city here. For this reason (and certainly also for strategic reasons) the Arabs walled up the entrances and also laid out a cemetery in front of the gate.

The wall reaches its greatest height (213 ft/65 m) in the SE corner. Here one can clearly see the massive ashlar blocks that characterised Herodian buildings and the smaller-scale repair work added at a later date.

Excavations on the **South Wall** have uncovered the staircases which led to the Hulda Gates. From here one climbed up under Herod's Royal Stoa to the Temple Square. Adjoining this to the W is a large archaeological dig where Israeli archaeologists led by Benjamin Mazar have been making important finds since 1968. In 1975 they discovered the remains of a two-storey palace covering 1,196 sq. yd/

West Wall (Wailing Wall)

In the El Aqsa Mosque

below the upper limit of the outer wall. In Mazar's opinion it had been hurled to the ground when the Temple was destroyed in A.D. 70. This cornerstone, mentioned by Flavius Josephus, has a recess in which the priest presumably stood when proclaiming the beginning and end of the sabbath. – Next comes the *Dung Gate* which is the entrance to the Jewish quarter. – Not far from the SW corner of the wall is the *Robinson Arch*, named after its discoverer, which in fact was not an arch at all but a staircase leading up to the Temple square.

Through a checkpoint one arrives at the **Wailing Wall** (see above), the S section of the West Wall.

Besides the Bab el Magharibeh, the 536 yd/490 m long West Wall, which extends to the former Antonia Fortress, has six gates, the most important of which are the Chain Gate (Bab es-Silsile), the Gate of the Cotton Merchants (Bab el Qattanin), decorated with stalactites, the Iron Gate (Bab el Hadid) and the Bab en-Nadhir, which gives access to the Temple square for anyone arriving from the Damascus Gate via King Solomon Street and Ala ud-Din Street.

On the West Wall and **North Wall** of the Haram esh-Sharif there are four *minarets* – in the SW corner (1278, restored 1622), over the Silsile Gate (1329), in the NW corner (1297) and, finally, the most recent on the North Wall (1937).

Entering the *Temple Square (*Haram esh-Sharif*) through the *Gate of the Moroccans* (Bab el Magharibeh) one finds oneself in the spacious Moslem area. The western side of the square has arcades dating from the Mameluke period in which Moslem events are held. In the building between Bab el Qattanin and Bab el Hadid are some *tombs*, including that of King Hussein I Ibn Ali (1853–1931).

Hussein I was a member of the Hashemite family, named after Mohammed's grandfather Hashem, which from 960 onwards held the office of Grand Sherif of Mecca. In 1916 he announced his independence from the Ottoman Empire and declared himself King of Arabia (recognised only as King of the Hejaz) and also, after 1924, Caliph. On October 3, 1924 he renounced both titles in favour of his son Ali, who, at the end of 1925, was forced to cede Arabia to the Wahabis under Ibn Saud. Hussein's second son Abdullah (b. 1882), who became ruler of Transjordan in 1921 and King of Jordan in 1948, was assassinated

1,000 sq. m which has been identified as that of Queen Helena from Adiabene in northern Mesopotamia, who converted to Judaism around A.D. 50 and settled in Jerusalem. A 6 ft/2 m high stone from the SW corner of the Temple square had already been found in 1971 115 ft/35 m

El Aqsa Mosque　　Jerusalem

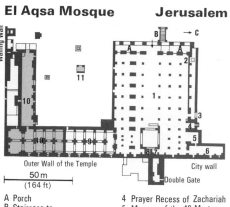

Outer Wall of the Temple
City wall

50 m
(164 ft)

Double Gate

A Porch
B Staircase to Basement
C Staircase to "Christ's cradle"

1 Prayer Room
2 Well
3 Elias Gate

4 Prayer Recess of Zachariah
5 Mosque of the 40 Martyrs
6 Omar Mosque
7 Prayer Niche (Mihrab)
8 Pulpit
9 White Mosque (Women's Mosque)
10 Islamic Museum
11 Jussef Dome

El Kas purification fountain

in 1951 when entering the El Aqsa Mosque in the presence of his grandson, now King Hussein II of Jordan. His younger brother Faisal (1883–1933) became King of Syria in 1920 and King of Iraq in 1921.

The main buildings in the Temple square are related to each other: the Dome of the Rock as the place for the veneration of the holy rock and the El Aqsa Mosque.

The *El Aqsa Mosque (Mesjid el Aqsa), together with its neighbouring buildings, the *Museum for Islamic Art* next to the Gate of the Moroccans and the women's prayer rooms, takes up most of the S side of Haram esh-Sharif. Prayers are said facing S, towards Mecca. It was built on the site of Justinian's basilica, dedicated

to the Virgin by the Omayyad Caliph Al Walid I (705–715). The Crusaders looked upon it as the Temple of Solomon and the Jews call it Solomon's School (Midrash Shelomo). The building has been restored several times, most recently in 1938–43 when it received the white Carrara marble columns presented by Mussolini and the ceiling donated by King Farouk of Egypt.

The Mosque is 263 ft/80 m long and 180 ft/55 m wide, excluding the adjoining buildings. In 1951 King Abdullah of Jordan (grandfather of King Hussein) was shot when entering the Mosque. In 1967 the Mosque was damaged by gunfire and in 1969 by fire (now restored).

Main portal and dome of the El Aqsa Mosque

In the Islamic Museum

The Dome of the Rock (Qubbet es-Sakhra)

Dome of the Rock   Jerusalem

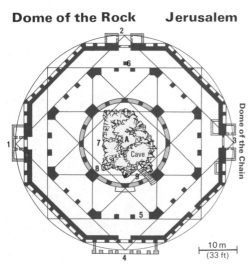

Dome of the Chain

10 m
(33 ft)

A Holy Rock (Es-Sakhra)

1 West Door (Bab el Gharb)
2 Door to Paradise (Bab ed Jenneh)
3 David's Gate of Judgement
4 South Door (Bab el Quibleh)
5 Prayer Niche (Mihrab)
6 Slab which covered Solomon's tomb and into

which Mohammed is said to have knocked twelve gold nails
7 Fingerprints of the Archangel Gabriel who is said to have held back the rock when Mohammed ascended into Heaven
8 Footprint of a Prophet
9 Steps to the "Fountain of Souls" (Bir el Arwah)

The INTERIOR of the El Aqsa Mosque with its seven naves is astonishing. The 12th c. carved wooden pulpit, which suffered considerable damage in the 1969 fire (restored), was a gift from Saladin, who also gave the beautiful mosaic on a gold ground in the drum of the dome. The prayer recess with its elegant marble columns also dates from the same period. – Adjoining the transept to the W is the *White Mosque* for women which dates from the time of the Templars.

Going N from here one passes the large round Purification Fountain (El Kas) and climbs a broad flight of steps to the upper platform. Like the steps on the other sides of the platform these are spanned by beautiful Mameluke pointed arches. Immediately to the left of the top step is the marble *Summer Pulpit* which was built during the Mameluke period, using the columns from a Crusader building.

One is now standing in front of the ****Dome of the Rock** (Qubbet es-Sakhra), one of the most important monuments of Islam, still incorrectly called "Omar Mosque" although it is not a mosque and does not date back to the Caliph Omar. It is much more likely to have been built by Abd el Malik (685–705), the fifth Caliph of the house of the Omayyads. It is a round building consisting of an octagonal lower storey surmounted by a dome over the holy Moriah rock. The impressive effect of the Dome of the Rock results from a combination of sumptuous furnishings, well-designed proportions and an apparently simple ground plan.

The ground plan is based on three concentric circles: a circular colonnade around the rock which supports the dome; then an octagonal colonnade, separated from the first circle by a wide ambulatory, and then, finally, after a narrow ambulatory, the octagonal outer wall.

Cupola of the Dome of the Rock

K. A. Cresswell discovered how the proportions were worked out. According to Jerry M. Landay in "The Dome of the Rock" they took two squares in the inner circle with the second square at an angle of 45° to the first. If the sides of these squares were extended in both directions they met at eight points – the pillars supporting the octagonal colonnade separating the two ambulatories. Then if the sides of this octagon were extended, they met again at eight points thus giving two larger squares whose sides were parallel to those of the inner squares. If an outer circle were then drawn around the two larger squares and the sides of the inner octagon extended outwards until they intersected this circle, a larger octagon was obtained – the outer walls of the Dome of the Rock.

Other proportions are also simple. The diameter of the inner rotunda, the height of the drum and the height of the dome are almost the same (65 ft/19·8 m and 66 ft/20·1 m). The overall height (177 ft/54 m) is only slightly more than the overall diameter (171 ft/52 m) of the building. The ratio of the outer octagon to the height of the dome is 1:3.

Interior of the Dome of the Rock

On the outside of the Dome of the Rock one's gaze is first drawn to the magnificent coloured tiles with which the Ottoman Sultan Suleiman (1520–66) covered the octagon and the elegance of the gilded aluminium dome which was restored in 1958–64.

Entering the INTERIOR by one of the four doors, whose copper plating was a gift from Qaitbay (1468–96), one is struck by the exquisite decoration: richly-ornamented wooden ceilings in both ambulatories, pillars and columns of precious marble with Classical gilded capitals, two-colour arches above the inner colonnade, stained-glass windows filtering the light, *mosaics on a gold ground* in the ambulatories and especially in the inner rotunda and above this the luxuriant decoration of the cupola. – There is a clear contrast between the coloured tiles which emphasise the substantial structure of the external façade and the almost insubstantial lustre of the Byzantine mosaics in the interior.

Façade of the Dome of the Rock

At the center of the inner ambulatory the **Holy Rock** (*Es-Sakhra*) rises to 4 ft–6½ ft/1·25 m–2 m above floor level. Possibly the altar for the burnt offerings of the Jews, it is almost 59 ft/18 m long and 44 ft/13·25 m wide. The best view of it is from the high bench near the NW door in the grille which was erected by the Crusaders in the 12th c. to prevent collectors of relics from breaking off bits of the Rock. The Jews and Moslems believe that the Rock marks the spot where Abraham intended to sacrifice Isaac and where Mohammed was carried up into Heaven on the miraculous horse Burak.

Under the Rock is a cave which the Moslems call "Bir el Arwah" (Fountain of Souls) and which they believe is where the souls of the dead gather to pray.

Solomon's Stables

Haram esh-Sharif – the square of the Temple

Immediately to the E of the Dome of the Rock is a small circular domed building called "David's Court" (Mehkemet Daud) or **Dome of the Chain** (*Qubbet es-Silsile*) because Solomon is supposed to have hung up a chain in the court of his father David from which, when a perjurer took the oath, a link would fall out. The large prayer recess in the S side (towards Mecca) was added in the 13th c.

In the NW part of the platform bearing the Dome of the Rock there are several monuments: the *Prayer Niche of the Prophet* (Mihrab en-Nebi), built in 1538, the *Hebron Dome* (Qubbet el Khalili), built as a prayer room in the 19th c. by the

View from the Temple Mount to Mount Zion

Sheikh of Hebron, the *Cupola of St George* (Qubbet el Khodr) and the *Ascension Dome* (Qubbet el Miraj) on the spot where, according to Islamic tradition, Mohammed prayed before ascending into Heaven. W of the Dome of the Rock next to the broad steps is a *covered well*, a gift from the Mameluke Qaitbay in 1455.

In the SE corner of the Haram is a staircase leading down to **Solomon's Stables** (usually closed), the substructures built by Herod when the Temple square was being enlarged. 88 huge pillars connected by arches form 12 parallel passages which, as can be seen by the rings for tethering animals in many of the pillars, were used by the Crusaders as stables in the 12th c.

Up in the Temple square once again, there are a few steps up to the sentry-walk leading along the E wall to the SE corner. From here one has a view beyond the El Aqsa Mosque and the new excavations below the S wall to the Dormition Abbey on its dominating site, but what is particularly impressive is the *view over the Kidron Valley with its Hellenistic tombs (including "Absalom's Tomb") to the Garden of Gethsemane and the Mount of Olives.

Following the E wall northwards one comes to the two portals of the Golden Gate and the small mosque called *Kursi Suleiman* (Throne of Solomon). From here it is possible to return to the entrance in the SW or to leave the Temple square by the Bab Hitta in the N leading into the "Street of the Lion Gate" which leads W to the Via Dolorosa.

From St Stephen's Gate to the Citadel

In the northern section of the E old town wall is **St Stephen's Gate** where, according to Christian tradition, St Stephen suffered his martyrdom. It is also known as the "Lion Gate" because of the reliefs of lions on the exterior, and in Arabic is called *Bab Sitti Maryam* (Gate of the Virgin Mary). Going from St Stephen's Gate towards the town after a few yards one comes to the **Church of St Anne** on the right. It dates from the time of the Crusades and remains intact. It was built in 1142 by Avda, the widow of Baldwin I, the first king of Jerusalem, on the spot

St Stephen's Gate (Lion Gate)

where Joachim and Anne, Mary's parents, are supposed to have lived. After Sultan Saladin conquered Jerusalem he turned the church into a Quran school in 1192. In 1856 it was given to Napoleon III by the Ottoman Sultan Abdülmecit in gratitude for French support during the Crimean War and Mauss subsequently cleared the interior of later additions.

A good view of the exterior, especially the triangular protruding main apse, the transept and the flat dome can be obtained from the E by climbing some steps in the town wall N of St Stephen's Gate. It is built of compact ashlar masonry and has small narrow windows. The entrance to the church is formed by a severe portal with pointed arches between two flying buttresses. The tympanum contains an Arabic inscription dating from the period when it was used as a Quran school. The upper of the two windows above the portal has the same decoration as the portal of the Church of the Holy Sepulchre.

Church of St Anne

Excavations near the Church of St Anne

St John's comment that there were five porches here can be explained by the fact that there were two pools, each measuring 164 ft by 164 ft/50 m by 50 m and with a depth of 43 ft/13 m, separated by a dam, with a porch on each side of the pool and a fifth porch on the dam. The water had healing properties – "an angel went down at a certain season into the pool and troubled the water" – which indicates the presence of an intermittent spring.

This must have originally been used as a cistern for supplying the Temple area with water and was visited by the sick in Jesus' time. Here in the 2nd c. there was a shrine to Asclepius, the God of Healing, whose cult had spread from Epidaurus throughout the Classical world. During the excavations begun in 1871 several votive offerings to Asclepius were found, including a relief with the snake of Asclepius and a votive offering in the shape of a foot from Pompeia Lucilia.

In the 5th c. the Byzantines erected a three-aisled basilica here. Its W section stood on the dam of the former central porch, though the dam had first to be widened by deep foundations, and the E section was on dry ground. This church was destroyed in the early part of the 11th c. The Crusaders built a chapel in the ruins of the N aisle in the 12th c.

The design of the INTERIOR is Burgundian Romanesque with strong simple pillars supporting a vaulted three-aisled nave. Three yokes lead to the crossing which is surmounted by a cupola. To the rear, a few steps lead to the raised sanctuary with the *high altar* carved by the French sculptor Philippe Kaeppelin in 1954. Its front panel shows the Annunciation (right), the Birth of Christ (left) and the Deposition (center). The side panels are Mary's upbringing by her mother Anne (left) and the Presentation of Mary in the Temple (right).

Decoration is completely subordinated to the architecture and is limited to the capitals. On the first pillar on the left is a small cask, on the first pillar on the right two sandals, and over it a scroll (perhaps signifying the marriage contract between Joachim and Anne). On other capitals are volutes, tendrils and leaves, almost giving the effect of Corinthian capitals. On the left and right of the main apse there is a human figure and a bull (the symbols of the evangelists Matthew and Luke); animal figures can be seen on both sides of the apse windows at the top of the pilasters.

A staircase leads from the aisle on the right into the *crypt* which is in a grotto. This was thought by the Crusaders to be Mary's birthplace, which according to tradition immediately adjoined the Pool of Bethesda.

The **Pool of Bethesda** is in the area being excavated just NE of the Church of St Anne. It was here that Jesus, who had come to Jerusalem from Galilee for a Jewish feast, healed a man who had been crippled for 38 years (John 5, 1–9). "Jesus saith unto him, Rise, take up thy bed, and walk. And immediately the man was made whole." Jesus thus incurred the wrath of the pious Jews because this took place on the sabbath.

The pool by which the sick man lay was near the Sheep Gate and therefore known in Latin as piscina porbatica (sheep pool).

Alley in the Moslem Quarter

The excavations confirmed the description in the Bible and exposed remains of various periods. These included the dried-out pool, with parts of the central dam, columns from the Asclepium of the Roman period, the foundations and an arch from the façade of the Byzantine church and a mosaic with a gem-stone cross from the martyrium of this church. – The French White Friars who look after the site have provided a plan and labelling in French to help the visitor find his way round.

Now follow the Street of Mary's Gate (Tariq Sitte Maryam) W to the **Antonia Fortress**, built by Herod (37–4 B.C.) and named after Mark Antony, ruler of the Roman Empire in the E at that time.

Ecce Homo Arch at the start of the Via Dolorosa

The higher land here immediately over-looks the Temple Mount to the S which is why Herod decided to build a strong fortress in the corner between the W and N walls of the Temple on the site of Baris, the Hashmonean castle.

The Antonia Fortress was a 100 yd by 175 yd/ 100 m by 160 m complex surrounded by high crenellated walls. Flavius Josephus says in his "History of the Jewish War" (V 5, 8) that the Antonia Fortress stood on a rock about 108 ft/33 m high which had slabs laid on its flanks up to a height of 89 ft/27 m. At the four corners were towers, the one in the SE being the highest at almost 164 ft/50 m "so that from it one can overlook the whole Temple area. Where the fortress adjoined the Temple, steps led downwards to enable armed squads from the Roman garrison permanently stationed in the Antonia Fortress to move

throughout the Temple on feast days to check on any possible acts of sedition by the people." The interior, according to Josephus, had, "the spaciousness and furnishings of a palace, for it was divided into rooms of all kinds and for all purposes, halls, baths and great courtyards for the troops so that the fortress . . . seemed as magnificent as a palace."

This fortress lasted only a few decades since Titus had it dismantled after the city was conquered in A.D. 70. Yet even then major portions of it must have remained, since behind the main entrance on the W side a triumphal arch was erected for the visit of the Emperor Hadrian in A.D. 135 and, now known as the Ecce Homo Arch, this still spans the Via Dolorosa. Other parts of the triumphal arch, together with other remains from the Antonia – its cisterns and pavement – can be seen when visiting the Church of the Sisters of Zion.

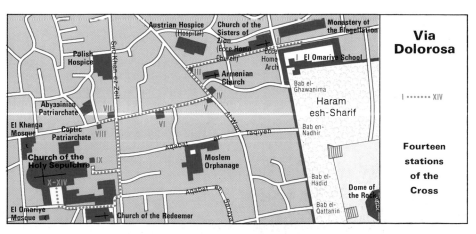

I Jesus is condemned to death by crucifixion by Pontius Pilate

II Jesus takes up the Cross

III Jesus falls for the first time under the burden of the Cross

IV Jesus meets his mother

V Simon of Cyrene helps Jesus to carry the Cross

VI Veronica hands Jesus the handkerchief

VII Jesus falls for the second time

VIII Jesus comforts the women of Jerusalem

IX Jesus falls for the third time

IN THE CHURCH OF THE HOLY SEPULCHRE

X Jesus is disrobed

XI Jesus is crucified

XII Jesus dies on the Cross

XIII Jesus' body is taken down from the Cross

XIV Jesus' body is laid in the tomb (Holy Sepulchre)

Walking W past, on the right, the *Chapel of the Flagellation*, built in 1927, and, a little further on, the *Judgement Chapel*, recalling events from Christ's Passion that took place here, one arrives at the **Ecce Homo Arch**, named after Pilate's words "Behold the man!" (John 19, 5.) On the right is the entrance to the **Church of the Sisters of Zion** (in French, *Basilique des Dames de Sion*).

In the INTERIOR there is an explanatory model of the Antonia Fortress. Part of Hadrian's triumphal arch is incorporated to great effect into the choir of the church. Particularly impressive is a passageway in the basement leading past a large Herodian cistern into the *crypt*. Here one is at the original street level and the floor of the crypt is the pavement of one of the courtyards of the Antonia Fortress, the "lithostrotos" of the gospel, bearing the scratches made on it by the Roman soldiers. This was certainly the pavement on which Jesus stood before Pilate, where he was judged, mocked and crowned with thorns (unless, as some have recently suggested, Pilate lived in the Citadel near the Jaffa Gate and not in the Antonia Fortress).

For this reason close to the Antonia Fortress, the Gate of the Virgin Street becomes the **Via Dolorosa**, the first part of which runs parallel to the E–W axis of the Antonia Fortress. It is called "Street of Sorrows" because this was the path that Jesus must have taken, after his judgement, to Golgotha, the place of execution. At 3 p.m. every Friday a procession led by Italian Franciscan monks makes its way along the Via Dolorosa which is divided up into the 14 Stations of the Cross, some of which are mentioned in the gospels and some of which are traditional. Stations I–IX are located along the road and Stations X–XIV are inside the Church of the Holy Sepulchre which was built over Golgotha and the Holy Sepulchre.

In the bazaar

The *Stations of the Via Dolorosa* should not be considered as historical sites so much as points marking stages in the procession. Centuries of rubbish deposits have raised the street level far above what it was in Jesus' time and the roadline has been altered in some details by later building. However, the start and the finish of the Via, the Antonia Fortress and Golgotha, are historically accurate so that in the main, if not in detail, the Via Dolorosa does correspond to the path taken by Jesus on that first Good Friday.

The first Station (Jesus is condemned to death) is on the S side of the Via Dolorosa in the courtyard of the Islamic Al Omariye Medrese which is reached by steps. This is where the Franciscan monks gather on Fridays for their procession. From window recesses in the S wall, which corresponds to the S wall of the Antonia Fortress, there is a very fine view of the Temple square.

Station II (Jesus takes up the Cross) is on the other side of the street near the entrance to the Judgement Chapel. Leaving the precincts of the Antonia Fortress and proceeding W, Station III (Jesus falls for the first time) is on the left at the turning into King Solomon Street. Station IV (Jesus meets his mother) is further up this street on the left. The Via turns right immediately after this and in this street are Stations V (Simon helps Jesus to carry the Cross) and VI (Veronica hands Jesus the handkerchief).

Crossing a crowded bazaar street (Suq Khan ez-Zeit) we came to Station VII (Jesus falls for the second time) and Station VIII (Jesus speaks to the weeping women). Here we have to make a detour because the direct route to Golgotha through a gate is blocked up as it was in the Middle Ages, and turn right into the bazaar just crossed. After some 65 yd/60 m a broad flight of steps on the right leads to Station IX (Jesus falls for the third time).

Station IX is marked by a Roman column between the Coptic Patriarchate (right) and the entrance to the *Monastery of the Abyssinian Monks* (left) which is built over the Helena Chapel of the Church of the Holy Sepulchre. The monks live in huts forming a laura (the name for an orthodox monastery). They celebrate Christmas on the 24th of every month. It is possible to walk through the Abyssinian Monastery, admiring the examples of Abysinnian folk art in the chapels on the way, to the square in front of the Church of the Holy Sepulchre. Or one can turn back into the bazaar and turn right once again into the next street. Here on the right is the Russian Orthodox *Alexandra Hospice* which at the time of Christ was the site of the city wall (nuns show visitors round the excavations). Opposite is the Church of the Redeemer and the Muristan district. Leaving the Muristan on the left and walking a little further W we come to the narrow path to the forecourt of the Church of the Holy Sepulchre.

Jerusalem – Church of the Holy Sepulchre

The ** **Church of the Holy Sepulchre** (in Arabic *Keniset el Kijame*, "Church of the Resurrection") built on the site of the Crucifixion and entombment and with a gilded cross on top of the main dome which can be seen from afar, is one of the holiest places in Christendom. – This comes as a disappointment for many visitors when they do not find a building as monumental and as imposing as St Sophia or St Peter's but a medium-sized building which will be undergoing restoration for years to come.

HISTORY. – The question has constantly been asked whether Christ's tomb really was on the spot indicated in the Church of the Holy Sepulchre. General Gordon, famous for his Egyptian campaigns in the 19th c., queried the authenticity of the tomb in the Church of the Holy Sepulchre because it was within the city walls. He was correct in thinking that tombs were considered unclean and were therefore always outside the walls of Jewish cities, but overlooked the fact that the 16th c. Ottoman wall, on whose N side he found the "garden tomb" in 1882, is further N than the second wall of Jerusalem which existed in Jesus' time. Research has since clearly proved that this second wall ran S and E of Golgotha, so that the place of execution was outside the wall and hence outside the city.

Further arguments in favour of the authenticity of the site of the Holy Sepulchre can be deduced from historical tradition dating right back to the very first Christians. The original community of Christians knew where their master was crucified and buried. Since these Christians were Jews they, like all Jews, were not allowed to enter Jerusalem after Titus destroyed the city in A.D. 70. Yet there is no gap in the list of the bishops of Jerusalem for this period and the site of

Christ's death was known even at a later date. Hence Emperor Hadrian's (117–138) decision to do away with the Christian churches can only be explained by the fact that veneration of the holy places had already become very widespread in his time. The Romans erected a temple to Venus on the site of the tomb and a statue of Jupiter on Golgotha. – Yet the Christians still knew of the existence of these places, so that Makarios, the Bishop of Jerusalem, was able to give directions to the Empress Helena, mother of Constantine the Great, during her visit in 326 which resulted in the temple of the emperor Hadrian having to be demolished on the orders of a new emperor (Constantine), so that the main shrine of Christendom could be built (cf. Hollis/Brownrigg).

HISTORY OF THE BUILDING. – The removal of the Temple and its terrace exposed a tomb cut into the slope of a rock, the hill of Golgotha, and, to the E, a subterranean Roman cistern into which several crosses of execution had been thrown. Empress Helena identified one of these as the True Cross and it became one of the most important relics. This is commemorated on May 3 by the Catholic Festival of the Finding of the Cross.

Enough of the hill was removed to leave a flat building site but the rocks of Golgotha and the Holy Sepulcre remained and the Church of the Holy Sepulchre was built over them.

The major form of church built during Constantine's reign was the three- or five-aisled basilica with a broad nave and lower side-aisles. The nave and side aisles were separated by a horizontal architrave or a row of arches (archivolt), with an atrium in front of the entrance and at the other end, usually the E, the transept and an apse with the altar.– There was also the domed round or octagonal central building, usually a chapel for a tomb or a baptistry.

Emperor Constantine combined both these ground plans in the Church of the Holy Sepulchre. The rock

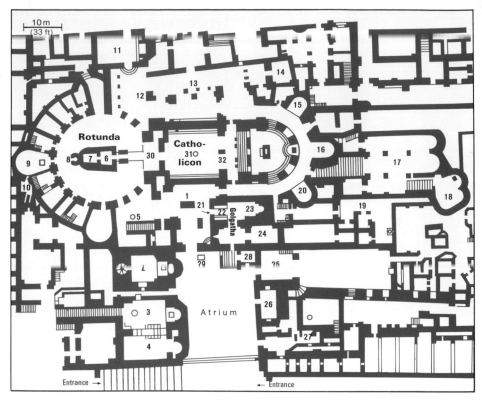

Church of the Holy Sepulchre   Jerusalem

1 Stone of Unction
2 Chapel of Forty Martyrs and Belfry
3 Chapel of St John and Baptistry
4 Chapel of St James
5 Stone of the Three Women
6 Chapel of the Angel
7 Holy Tomb
8 Chapel of the Copts

9 Chapel of the Jacobites
10 Tomb of Joseph of Arimathea
11 Franciscan Chapel
12 Mary Magdalene Altar
13 Archway of the Virgin
14 Christ's Prison (chapel)
15 St Longin
16 Sharing of the Raiment
17 Crypt of St Helena

18 Crypt of the Finding of the Cross
19 Medieval Cloister
20 Oratory of the Insults
21 Chapel of Adam
22 Site of tombs of Godefroy de Bouillon and Baldwin I
23 Crucifixion Altar and Stabat Mater Altar
24 Chapel of the Crucifixion

25 Chapel of St Michael
26 Chapel of St John (Armenian)
27 Abraham's Chapel
28 Chapel of the Sorrows (Mary the Egyptian)
29 Tomb of Philippe d'Aubigny
30 Latin Choir
31 Navel of the World (omphalos)
32 Greek Choir

with Christ's tomb became the center of a rotunda. A five-aisled basilica adjoined this to the E and then came an atrium. The façade was in line with a double row of columns which stood where Khan ez-Zeit stands today. In the open space between the basilica and the rotunda was the Rock of Golgotha with the Holy Cross towering above it.

This building, begun in 326 and completed about 335, was destroyed in 614 when the Persians conquered the country under Chosroes. After the Byzantines under Emperor Herakleios reconquered the country, Abbot Modestus was able to rebuild it in 629 in accordance with the original plan. The Cross, which the Persians had carried off as plunder, was returned and erected on Golgotha again (Festival of Raising the True Cross, September 14).

380 years later, 683 years after it was first built, the church was almost completely destroyed in 1009 by the fanatical Fatimid Caliph El Hakim.

In 1048 the Byzantine Emperor Constantine IX Monomachos rebuilt the Church of the Holy Sepulchre, but on a much smaller scale. Constantine's basilica was abandoned. Only the rotunda remained

and this was joined on the E by a courtyard surrounded by small rooms.

The Crusaders came to Jerusalem in 1099 and re-established the bipolar character of the site by completing their church in 1149. On the site of the original basilica the French architect Jourdain erected a shorter nave which had a semicircular E end and was vaulted in the style of the time. The rotunda with the Tomb was retained. Golgotha, which up till then had been outside in the open, was incorporated in the main body of the church as a raised side chapel, and tombs for the conqueror of Jerusalem, Godefroy de Bouillon, and Baldwin I, the first king of the Crusader kingdom, were made in a grotto under the rock of Golgotha.

Thus to this day the Church of the Holy Sepulchre, though somewhat altered, has retained its two sacred focal points and its two related buildings, as can be seen from outside from the two domes of the building. – Since over the centuries the church had become shabby and was seriously damaged in the 1927 earthquake, the various Christian communities involved with the Church of the Holy Sepulchre decided in 1958 on its restoration.

Ownership of the church is shared by six religious communities:
The Greek Orthodox Church has the Catholicon (nave), the N section of Golgotha, Chapel of Adam underneath and "Christ's Prison".
The Roman Catholic "Latins" own the S section of the rock of Golgotha, the choir between the rotunda and the Catholicon, the Epiphany Chapel with the adjoining Franciscan monastery, the Mary Magdalene Altar and the Chapel of the Finding of the Cross.
The Place of the Three Marys, the E chapel in the ambulatory and the Chapel of St Helena are Armenian. Then there are the Copts with the chapel behind the Holy Tomb, the Syrians with the W chapel in the rotunda and the Abyssinians with the "Tomb of Joseph of Arimathea" which is reached through the W chapel. The Stone of Unction and the Tomb of Christ are owned in common.

Entrance to the Holy Sepulchre

At the entrance, the S side of the Church of the Holy Sepulchre, the *façade* is dominated by two portals with pointed arches erected during the Crusades. Saladin blocked up the right-hand one in 1187. Over the arches is a profusely decorated Corinthian modillion which was part of the church built by Constantine.

Between the two portals is a coat of arms divided into four sections. It commemorates the tomb of Philippe d'Aubigny, who fell in 1236 and was tutor to King Henry III of England. This knight's epitaph is the only one that remains from the many tombs which used to encircle the church.

INTERIOR of the Church of the Holy Sepulchre.
– Entering through the left-hand portal one passes the recess (left) for the Moslem doorkeepers of the Nuseibeh family who for centuries have held the privilege of keeping the keys to the church. In order to get an idea of the lay-out of the church it is a good idea to go into the nave (catholicon) first of all or, if it is closed, into the small choir between the catholicon and the rotunda, as this is the center.

To the right of the entrance is a staircase leading up to **Calvary** (*Golgotha*). The top of the rock is 16 ft/5 m above floor level and excavations below the floor have shown that the rock is 33 ft/10 m overall. On the rock are two chapels rich in mosaics. First is the Catholic chapel with the *Altar of the Crucifixion* which has copper reliefs dating from 1588. The realistic mosaics, done in 1937, show how Jesus was nailed on to the Cross on this spot. A window in the right-hand wall looks through into the Chapel of Sorrows, also Catholic.

Turning left past the *Stabat Mater Altar*, which according to tradition is where Mary stood while her son was being crucified, one comes to the Greek Orthodox Crucifixion Chapel. On the wall above the altar Christ on the Cross is depicted between Mary and

his disciple John, the figures being almost life-size. Under the altar is the hole in the rock which held the Cross. On the right of the altar a metal rail hides the crack in the rock which according to the Bible (Matthew 27, 51) appeared at the moment of Christ's death.

From here the N staircase leads down again under Golgotha to the Chapel of Adam (Greek Orthodox) where one can again see the crack in the rock. The chapel gets its name from the legend which says that Adam's skull was discovered here at the moment of Christ's crucifixion. On each side of the entrance stone slabs represent the tombs of the first rulers of the Crusader Kingdom, Godefroy de Bouillon and Baldwin I, which were broken up by fanatical Greek monks in 1808 after Moslems had already removed the bones in the 13th c. We know from drawings that these tombs had low pillars supporting saddle stones which

Holy Sepulchre

Architectural details of the Church of the Holy Sepulchre

carried Latin inscriptions, and we also know the text of these inscriptions. According to Zev Vilnay one of them read: "Here lies the famous Duke Godefroy de Bouillon who won this whole land for the Christian faith. May his soul rest in Christ. Amen." The other ran: "Here lies King Baldwin, a second Judas Maccabeus, the hope of his country, the pride of the Church and its strength. Arabia and Egypt, Dan and haughty Damascus feared his might and humbly brought him gifts and tributes. Oh suffering! This wretched sarcophagus covers him."

Going W from here one passes the stone slab or "Stone of Unction" on which, according to the Catholic belief, the body of Jesus lay after it was taken down from the Cross and embalmed (Matthew 27, 59); past the place of the three Marys (Armenian) one comes next to the *rotunda* which contains the *Holy Sepulchre*. After the fire of 1808 the exterior of the Sepulchre was rebuilt by Kalfa Komnenos, a Greek from Smyrna, in the over-ornate Turkish rococo style. Before the façade stand large candelabra and above the portal hang 43 lamps, the Greeks, Latins and Armenians each having 13, and 4 owned by the Copts. The Sepulchre makes it impossible to see the rock, but this can be seen on the other side of the Sepulchre in the Coptic chapel.

In an anteroom, THE CHAPEL OF THE ANGEL, stands a stone on which the angel who announced the Resurrection to the three women is said to have sat. It probably came from the round stone that once sealed the Tomb. A low door leads into the small *sepulchral chamber* where on the right-hand wall a marble slab covers the location of the body. Without the marble slab this would be just like any other of the many tombs found in Jesus' time. The rock rolled over the entrance was round (like a mill-stone), and its diameter also determined the height of the entrance. – On Easter Eve the Holy Sepulchre is the scene of an oft-described religious ceremony when the Greek Orthodox patriarch of Jerusalem symbolises the Resurrection by lighting the "holy fire" in the Chapel of the Angel which has been sealed since Good Friday.

Restoration work in the rest of the rotunda has already met with visible success. Some of the massive pillars encircling the Holy Sepulchre have given way to a less substantial colonnade.

There are semicircular conchas on the S, W and N sides of the rotunda. In the W concha, opposite the Coptic chapel, is a chapel belonging to the Syrian Christians (Jacobites) which has the entrance to a rock tomb on the left. This is supposed to be the tomb of Joseph of Arimathea who also provided the Tomb for Jesus (Matthew 27, 60). It is still in its original condition, with no marble slabs.

Going from here into the N section of the rotunda one enters the Latin part of the church. Here one finds the church of the Franciscans that serves their adjoining monastery, and the Altar of Mary Magdalene. One is now in the N aisle of the church containing columns from various periods, including a few ornate Corinthian columns from the original 4th c. building. These are known as the *Archway of the Virgin* because it is said that the risen Christ appeared to his mother on this spot. At the E end of the aisle there is a small square room known, without any historical foundations, as *Christ's Prison*.

Passing through an ambulatory at the E end of the nave, past the Chapel of St Longin and the Chapel of the Raiment, one comes to steps leading down to the Armenian Chapel of St Helena. The rock wall on the right is covered with small crosses scratched by pilgrims at the time of the Crusades.

The CHAPEL OF ST HELENA is an almost square chamber with four squat Byzantine columns supporting the high arches of the roof. Through the dome light falls from above on to the large central square and gives this chapel its own special atmosphere which is intensified by the lamps, ornamental cloths and the altar.

To the right of the main apse is a recess from which Empress Helena is said to have directed the search for the Roman cistern in which the True Cross was found. More steps lead down to what was once the cistern but is now the unpretentious Catholic CHAPEL OF THE FINDING OF THE CROSS whose walls still bear witness to its original purpose. There is a statue commemorating St Helena which, together with the altar, was a gift from the ill-fated Maximilian of Habsburg who later became Emperor of Mexico.

On leaving the Church of the Holy Sepulchre turn right out of the forecourt into Christian Street. About 44 yd/40 m S on the right is the entrance to the **Church of John the Baptist** built by Crusaders about 1170. It is in a square reached by a portal marked with a cross. In the façade are Roman spoils of war.

The church, with its three conchas but no nave, is today used for Greek Orthodox services. It is entered from the W side opposite the broad richly carved iconostasis behind which are the altar and the E apse. The other two semicircular shell-shaped conchas are in the N and the S.

This church was preceded by a 5th c. chapel which is now the *crypt* but, as the old window-openings show, it was originally at ground level. A crystal reliquary found here that had been hidden from the Arabs is now kept in the treasury (not open to the public) of the Church of the Holy Sepulchre. This first church was dedicated to John the Merciful, Patriarch of Alexandria.

The church belongs to the *Pilgrims' Hospice* which was founded here in 1073, before the First Crusade, by merchants from the Italian seafaring republic of Amalfi. It was here that at a later date the Order of the Knights of St John of Jerusalem was founded (Ordo militiae Sancti Ioanni Baptistae hospitalis Hierosolymitani) which was ratified by Pope Paschalis II in 1113 when John the Baptist replaced the original patron of the church. The church is revered by the English Knights of St John as their mother church. The hospice complex covers the area between David Street and the Church of the Holy Sepulchre, Christian Street and Khan ez-Zeit. The vaults of the Knights of St John are still to be found along David Street. The hospice tradition lived on after the end of the Crusader period in Jerusalem (1187) and the area N of David Street is still called "Muristan", which is a Persian-Arabic word for "hospital".

The MURISTAN is reached by turning left from David Street into the street leading to the Church of the Redeemer, where it is on the left.

In 1868 the Ottoman sultan gave the E part to the Crown Prince of Prussia, Friedrich Wilhelm; the W part was awarded to the Greek Orthodox patriarchate so that both Western and Eastern churches would be represented. Nowadays it is the Greek bazaar with mainly leathergoods on sale. In the middle of the bazaar is a 19th c. ornamental fountain and in the N part is the Omar Mosque which was built in 1216 to commemorate the visit of the Caliph Omar in 638.

On the E edge of the Muristan is the Lutheran **Church of the Redeemer**. It was consecrated by Kaiser William II on Reformation Day 1898 and occupies a site rich in tradition.

The land was given to Charlemagne by the country's ruler at that time, Caliph Harun ar-Rashid, and it

became the site of the Church of St Mary Latina which was destroyed by El Hakim in 1009 and rebuilt later in the 11th c. Both church and cloister fell into decay over the centuries and after Prussia acquired the site in 1868 the foundation stone for a new church was laid in 1893. It was to continue the old Western tradition in close proximity to the Holy Sepulchre, henceforth the spiritual heart of Protestantism in the Holy Land. Since then the church and the adjoining buildings have been the headquarters of the Lutheran provostship for Jerusalem.

Imperial eagle in the German part of the Muristan

The simple interior was renovated a few years ago. To the right behind the entrance is the door to the tower which is well worth climbing, as from it there is a view over the whole of the old town and the Mount of Olives. The reconstructed cloister, containing some elements of the medieval building, is also worth visiting.

If on leaving the Church of the Holy Sepulchre one takes the steps on the right to Christian Street and follows this N, one comes to the *Khankha Mosque*, the palace of the patriarchate of the Crusaders, on the right-hand corner of Khankha Street.

Just before this there is a turning to the left, the Street of the Greek Orthodox Patriarchate, which takes its name from the *Greek Patriarch's Palace* on the right. Opposite is the Greek Orthodox **Monastery of Constantine**; there are precious icons in the Chapel of Constantine. In a small museum in the monastery the items on display include the slim sarcophagus of Queen Mariamne who was murdered by her husband Herod I in 29 B.C. The side on view is decorated with tendrils and rosettes. It was transferred here with a second sarcophagus during the Second World War from Herod's tomb near the King David Hotel. – N of the monastery was the palace where the kings of Jerusalem resided after they had handed over their original residence, the El Aqsa Mosque, to the Templars.

View from the tower of the Church of the Redeemer

Turning left at the end of Christian Street one comes to the Catholic ("Latin") district. Past the Terra Sancta Church (on the right) and the turn-off to the New Gate is the *Latin Patriarchate* directly behind the town wall. Through narrow alleys is David Street, opposite the Citadel, right beside the Jaffa Gate.

From the Mount of Olives to Mount Zion

The walk on the **Mount of Olives** begins at a bend in Jericho Street below St Stephen's Gate. Past a monument to Israeli parachutists who were killed here in 1967 is the **Tomb of the Virgin** (on the left of the street) with its 12th c. Gothic Crusader façade. It is one of the many buildings in this area which were built during three periods: in the early-Christian 4th and 5th c., at the time of the Crusader state (12th c.) and in the 19th–20th c.

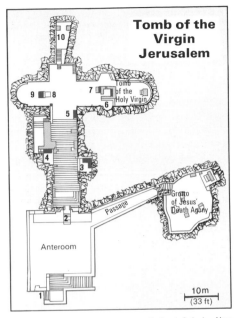

Tomb of the Virgin Jerusalem

A flight of 47 wide marble steps leads into the dark underground shrine. Half-way down are two recesses: the one on the right contains the tombs of Joachim and Anne, Mary's parents, and the one of the left contains an altar over the tomb of Joseph. At the bottom, 40 ft/12 m below the level of the square, behind a Greek Orthodox altar on the right, is the **Tomb of the Virgin**, hewn out of the rock at the E end of a long chamber. It is flanked by an Armenian altar (left) and a medieval Islamic prayer recess (right). In the W part of the room is a cistern containing water that is supposed to have healing powers, and an altar belonging to the Abyssinian Christians. The first building here in the 5th c. was a chapel of devotion. Ephesus, in Asia Minor, has a house which Mary is supposed to have lived in but, according to early Christian tradition, she spent her last years in Jerusalem, died 22 years after her son and was buried in the Josaphat Valley. The site of the Tomb of the Virgin is also known as the "Church of the Assumption" as it was believed that it was from here that Mary was carried up to Heaven by angels.

At the exit from the Tomb of the Virgin a passage on the left of the portal leads to the *Grotto of the Death Agony* adjoined to the S by the *****Garden of Gethsemane**

1 Access from the Jerusalem to Jericho road	5 Greek Orthodox Altar
2 Entrance	6 Islamic Prayer Niche (mihrab)
3 Chapel with the tombs of Anne and Joachim, Mary's parents	7 Armenian Altar
	8 Cistern
4 Chapel with the tomb of St Joseph	9 Abyssinian Altar
	10 Vault

with eight ancient olive trees ("Gethsemane" comes from the Hebrew Gath-Shamma=oil press).

After Jesus had celebrated the Last Supper with his disciples on the day later known as Maundy Thursday he went with them "as was his wont . . . unto a place called Gethsemane" (Matthew 26, 36). "And he was withdrawn from them about a stone's cast, and kneeled down, and prayed . . . and being in an agony

Jerusalem – the Garden of Gethsemane

he prayed more earnestly." (Luke 22, 41 and 44.) The disciples slept and left him alone at this hour. Shortly afterwards he was taken and brought into the city

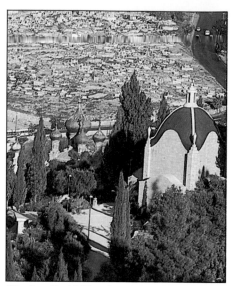

"Dominus Flevit" Chapel

Emperor Theodosius I, as early as the 4th c., built a basilica in the Garden of Gethsemane over the rock on which Jesus is supposed to have prayed. Its ground plan is visible in the floor of the modern church which was built in 1924 on the same spot. Like its predecessor the church has three aisles but is bigger. In distinct contrast to its colourful façade the interior of the church is gloomy. Six columns support the roof which consists of twelve small mosaic-covered domes. In front of the altar is the rock, surrounded by a low railing resembling the Crown of Thorns. The pictures of the church are gifts from several countries, hence the name **Church of the Nations**.

Church of the Nations

On the right is the Russian **Church of Mary Magdalene**, a magnificent building with seven domes. It was built by Alexander III in 1888 in memory of his mother Maria Alexandrovna, a princess of Hesse. Grand-Duchess Elizabeth (b. 1864, assassinated 1918), sister of the last Tsarina, also a Hessian princess and wife of Grand-Duke Sergei, is buried here.

About 220 yd/200 m further up is the entrance (left) to the site of the **Franciscan Dominus Flevit Chapel** ("The Lord wept"). It was built in 1955 on the foundations of a 5th c. church from which there is a mosaic on the left of the entrance. Inside in a large window above the altar is the outline of a chalice. The name of the chapel is a reminder that when he came to Jerusalem for the last time Jesus wept over the future of the city (Luke 19, 41). – During the building work

in 1953 Jewish and Byzantine tombs were exposed near the chapel.

About 220 yd/200 m further on to the right is a large area containing the **Tombs of the Prophets**. The owner of the land will open the vault in the rock (agree on the price beforehand!), which holds burial recesses ascribed, among others, to the prophets Haggai and Malachi and their disciples. From here or from the nearby terrace there is a marvellous *view over Jerusalem: the Temple Mount and the old town with its domes, minarets and church towers and the blocks of apartments in West Jerusalem; in the foreground down the slope of the hill is the large *Jewish cemetery*, with graves dating back to Biblical times which were badly damaged by Arabs in 1948. Since according to Zachariah 14 it is near what Jews expect to be the site of the Last Judgement, this place has for centuries been much in demand as a burial ground.

Further N to the right of the path is the **Pater Noster Church**. It stands on the site of Constantine's Eleona Basilica (326–333) which was destroyed by the Persians in 614; the Crusaders built a new chapel. In 1874 the Princesse de la Tour d'Auvergne acquired the neglected site and founded a convent for Carmelite nuns. She was buried here in 1957, long after her death. The chapel commemorates Jesus teaching his disciples the Lord's Prayer (Luke 11, 2–4) which is written in 80 languages on tablets of coloured tiles.

From the Pater Noster Church one can make a 985 yd/900 m detour to the E to *Bethphage*. A church in Bethphage commemorates the fact that it was here that Jesus ordered his disciples to untether the ass on which he rode into Jerusalem on Palm Sunday (Luke 19, 29). Remains of a Crusader church were discovered in 1876. A painted stone cube from this building, an interesting example of early Gothic painting, is now in the more recent Franciscan church.

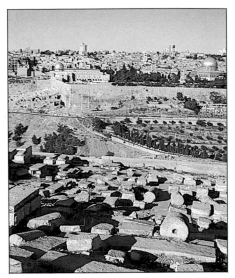

Next comes the Arab village of Et-Tur where one finds the **Ascension Chapel** within the precincts of a mosque. It lies on the route from Jerusalem to Bethany (see El Azariye) and it was on this road that Jesus ascended into Heaven, according to Luke 24, 50–51. The Crusaders built a chapel here in the 12th c. which was later converted by the Moslems into a domed building. The chapel was octagonal and its open sides were spanned by eight pointed arches which supported a narrow frieze to indicate the upper limit of the building which was also open to the sky, thus representing the Ascension in its architecture.

View of Jerusalem from the Mount of Olives

The Moslem caretaker also has the key to a tomb a little to the W opposite the Pater Noster Church. The Jews believe it to be the "Tomb of the Prophetess Huldah" who lived in Jerusalem at the time of King Josiah (639–609 B.C.) (2 Kings 22; the S gates to the Temple square are named after her). According to the Christian tradition (the two do not necessarily contradict each other) it is the grotto of St Pelagia of Antioch who lived here as a penitent and died in 280.

To the E of the Ascension Chapel is the Russian **Ascension Monastery** the 197 ft/60 m high tower of which dominates the whole area (view!).

From the village of Et-Tur, by taking one of the Mount of Olives paths, one can return to Gethsemane.

A little to the S of the Gethsemane church the narrow Siloah road turns right into the **Kidron Valley** which continues S into the **Josaphat Valley** and separates Mount Moriah (Temple square) from the Mount of Olives ("Jehosaphat" means "God will judge").

This area and its name are referred to in two prophecies made in the Old Testament, by Zachariah and Joel. According to Joel: "For, behold, in those days, and in that time, when I shall bring again the captivity of Judah and Jerusalem, I will also gather all nations, and will bring them down into the valley of

Tomb of the Princess

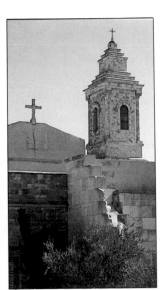

Pater Noster Church

The Lord's Prayer in Esperanto

Tombs in the Kidron Valley

Jehoshaphat, and will plead with them for my people and for my heritage Israel . . ." (Joel 3, 1–2). "Multitudes, multitudes in the valley of decision: for the day of the Lord is near in the valley of decision." (Joel 3, 14.)

It is here, therefore, that the Jews expect the Last Judgement, and this is also the belief of Islam: a rope will be stretched from the Temple battlements over the valley to the Mount of Olives, the just, supported by their guardian angels, will cross over, the unjust will fall down into damnation.

The desire to be here on the Day of Judgement is the reason why Jews and Moslems have laid out cemeteries on each side of the Kidron Valley – on the slope of the Mount of Olives and in front of the wall of the Temple Mount. The large **Jewish Cemetery** dates back to Biblical times, and the great tombs that can be seen on its lower fringe are also connected with it. They are on the left of the road and are named after figures in the Old and New Testaments, but all date from the Hellenistic-Herodian period. Almost entirely hewn from the rock, they display the mixture of Hellenistic and Roman features typical of that period.

The first in the row is the *Tomb of Absalom* which used to be pelted with stones in memory of Absalom's revolt against his father David, but its ascription to Absalom is not based on historical fact. The square burial chamber has a Doric frieze above Ionic half- and quarter-columns in a typical mixture of styles. This substructure supports an attic and a low cylinder terminating in a conical pointed roof of individual square stones and slabs. To the left is the *Tomb of Josaphat*.

A little further S is a loggia-type façade with two Doric columns and a Doric architrave. Christian tradition has it that James hid here after Jesus was arrested. This *Grotto of James* is a Jewish family tomb, according to an inscription on the architrave in Hebrew, for the Hezir family of priests (1st c. B.C.). Inside is a central chamber with small burial chambers leading off it. Finally there is the *Tomb of Zachariah*, a cube of rock crowned by a pyramidal roof. To the right is another loggia-type tomb which was never finished.

440 yd/400 m further on one comes to the Gihon spring which is at the foot of the E slope of **Mount Ophel**. This extends from the S wall of the Temple Mount to where the Kidron and Hinnom valleys meet and was the site of the "City of David" and of the Jebusites before him.

Recently a group of archaeologists under Yigal Shiloh of the Archaeological Institute of the Hebrew University has been excavating in this area. They have got down as far as the stratum of the period when David founded the city in 1000 B.C. David's Jerusalem was built on terraces on the hillside, like the present-day Arab village of Silwan opposite. Its four man-made terraces were connected by steps. The remains of buildings and a sewage system have been discovered. Individual finds from later periods show that Jews returning home from captivity in Babylon settled here and that it was also inhabited in the Persian, Hellenistic and Roman periods. The city of David was not abandoned until the Middle Ages, by which time Jerusalem had moved further W to the area of the present-day old town and the hill then known as "Mount Zion".

Immediately to the E of the town wall lay the Gihon spring. It was there that David had his son Solomon anointed king (1 Kings 1, 33–34 and 39). Several centuries later King Hezekiah (727–698) ordered the construction of a tunnel 590 yd/540 m long, 13 ft/4 m high and 3 ft/1 m wide which ran under the SW part of Mount Ophel and brought water from the Gihon spring into the town at the Pool of Siloah. Thus the inhabitants of Jerusalem had a supply of water even when enemies were besieging the town. The entrance to the **Pool of Siloah** is just 550 yd/500 m to the right of the road, below the minaret of a mosque belonging to the Arab village of Silwan. In 1880 an inscription in Hebrew (now in Istanbul) was found here which confirmed the Biblical report of the building of the tunnel. It was at this pool, which nowadays measures 20 ft by 56 ft/6 m by 17 m, that Jesus healed the man who had been blind from birth (John 9, 7). A Christian church was built here in the 5th c. and some sections of its columns can still be seen in the pool.

S of the Pool of Siloah is the **Hinnom Valley**. It is reached by returning from Siloah to the road, following it for 220 yd/200 m and then turning off to the right.

At the time of the Canaanites this valley was a site for the worship of Baal and Moloch in which children were made to "pass through the fire", i.e. they were burned as sacrifices. The Books of Moses contain various edicts against this gruesome cult which prevailed in the Phoenician kingdom as far as Carthage. Yet the worship of Moloch existed even in the time of the Israelites: Manasseh, the son and successor of King Hezekiah who had the water tunnel built, not only erected altars to Baal and Astarte but also "made his son pass through the fire" (2 Kings 21, 6). The place where this happened later came to personify evil. Thus from the word "Hinnom" comes the Arabic "gehennah" (hell). The hill in the NW is called "Mount of Evil Counsel" because this is where the high priest Caiaphas is supposed to have held the assembly which resolved that Jesus was to be put to death (John 11, 42–53). And near the Onuphrios monastery is the field of blood (hakeldama) bought with the 30 pieces of silver that the repentant Judas Iscariot threw down in the Temple (Matthew 27, 6–8).

From the Pool of Siloah a path with steps dating from the Roman period leads up to Mount Zion. The tradition that Jesus celebrated the Last Supper in a house in the upper town is probably correct and he would then have taken this path when he went to Gethsemane. It leads to the Catholic church of **St Peter in Gallicantu** (*St Peter at Cockcrow*) which commemorates Peter's third denial of Christ (Matthew 26, 69–75). The monastery church built in 1931 contains finds dating from the Jewish and early Christian periods. "Christ's Prison" can also be visited here.

From here the road leads N to the Dung Gate and Wailing Wall, and NW to the Zion Gate. Turning left just before this and right at the next fork in the road, one comes to **Mount Zion** with its Jewish, Christian and Moslem shrines. This hill was part of the upper town at the time of Herod.

Since the 4th c., as is evidenced by churches built at that time, this has been revered as the place where Jesus celebrated the Last Supper with his disciples and established the Eucharist (Matthew 26, 17–30; Mark 14, 12–25; Luke 22, 7–20) and where the Holy Ghost came down upon them at Pentecost (Acts 2); according to the 7th c. patriarch Modestos this is where Mary spent the end of her life and where she died. – Since the 12th c. the tomb of King David has been venerated on Mount Zion although one would have expected to find it in the old City of David on Mount Ophel.

The churches, erected in the 4th/5th c., had already fallen into decay when the Crusaders arrived in 1099. They rebuilt the Zion Minster and built a two-storey Romanesque house. On the ground floor was the Room of the Footwashing and on the first floor the Room of the Last Supper. Both the church and the Room of the Last Supper were destroyed by Egyptians in 1219. The Room of the Last Supper was rebuilt in its present-day Gothic style by the Franciscans, to whom Pope Clement IV transferred the care of this site in 1342. A small monastery on the S side also dates back to the Franciscans. In the 16th c. Sultan Suleiman drove out the Franciscans and the Moslems built a mosque. Finally the older buildings were joined by the *Dormition Abbey* when Kaiser William II had been able to acquire the site in 1898 after he had consecrated the Protestant Church of the Redeemer. He transferred the piece of land on the NW side of the old group of buildings "to the German Holy Land Association free of usufruct for the benefit of German Catholics". The Tomb of David was opened for the Emperor and Empress by order of the sultan; normally Christians and Jews were not allowed in, and this remained the case until the British Mandate after the First World War.

The remains of buildings dating from the time of Herod have been discovered at one site on the hill. To the right of the road is

Pool of Siloah

View from the W to the Dormition Church on Mount Zion

the entrance to the "Room of the Foot-washing" (John 13, 1–11) which is now used as a synagogue. In the adjoining room is the **Tomb of David**. The dating of the stonework in this room is uncertain. There are three interpretations: it was part of the 12th c. Romanesque Crusader building; or it was part of an early Christian church mentioned by the pilgrim Etheria in 384; or it was part of the ancient synagogue reported by the pilgrims of Bordeaux in 333 as being the only one in this region not destroyed (this interpretation is based on the fact that the apse

recess points N, towards the Temple). In front of this apse, which is 8 ft 1 in./2·48 m wide and 8 ft/2·44 m high, is the cenotaph which is supposed to be the real tomb of the king. It is covered with

King David's empty tomb

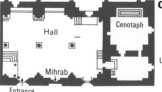

Coenaculum: Room of the Last Supper

Coenaculum

Hall

Cenotaph

Mihrab

Entrance

Under the Coenaculum is the ROOM OF THE FOOTWASHING with the **Tomb of David** embroidered cloths and on it stand silver Torah crowns and Torah rolls. Jewish pilgrims pray here, especially on Shavuot, the traditional day of the death of the king. – Left of this room is a *Martyrs' Room* (Martef Hashoa) built in memory of the Jews murdered by the Nazis.

Turning right into an alley on leaving David's Tomb, past an archway, again on the right, one comes to the steps leading to the *Room of the Last Supper* (Coenaculum) over the Room of the Footwashing and David's Tomb. The 33 by 53 ft/10 by 16 m room, with two Gothic columns supporting the vaulted ceiling, was renovated by the Franciscans in the 14th c. A large square stone opposite the Moslem prayer recess is supposed to be the place where Jesus sat at the Last Supper.

Daniel, Isaiah, Jeremiah and Ezekiel, and the second the names of the twelve apostles. Around the outside are the signs of the zodiac and an inscription (Proverbs 8, 25–26). A mosaic on the vaulted ceiling of the apse shows the Mother and Child. The surrounding chapels are dedicated to the English Benedictine monk St Willibald, the Three Wise Men from the East, St Joseph and Jesus' ancestors and John the Baptist. In the center of the crypt, under a mosaic dome, is a sculpture of Mary on her deathbed. Surrounding the crypt are chapels endowed by several countries.

From here one arrives back at the Zion Gate, or, along the outside of the W part of the old town wall, at the Citadel and the Jaffa Gate.

Dormitio Sanctae Mariae Church

The same alleyway leads to the neo-Romanesque Catholic **Dormitio Sanctae Mariae Church** (Dormition of the Virgin Mary), designed by Heinrich Renard and consecrated in 1908. It is in a dominant position and is cared for by German Benedictine monks. The building has a central plan and is influenced by the rotunda in the Church of the Holy Sepulchre. The lovely mosaic floor has three interlocking circles in the middle as a symbol of the Trinity. From this center lines radiate outwards to the next two (concentric) circles, the first of which contains the names of the four prophets

From the Damascus Gate to Mount Scopus

The **Damascus Gate** connects the new quarter of the town in the N with the old town in the S. This is the beginning of the road to Damascus via Nablus and Sichem which is why the first part of the road is called Nablus Street by the Arabs and the gate is called "Shaar Shekhem" (Sichem Gate) by the Jews; the Arabs call the gate "Bab el Amud" (Pillar Gate) after a pillar from which the distance to Damascus was measured.

The gate, built in 1537, is the finest and most extravagant of the gates dating back to Suleiman the Magnificent. With its side towers and decorative battlements its aesthetic appeal is as great as its defensive value. Beneath the gate can be seen the remains of the columns and walls of a 2nd c. city gate.

E of the Damascus Gate a garden extends along the foot of the wall. 164 yd/150 m from the Gate in the base of the wall there is an iron gate that is part of *Solomon's Quarry*, a cave with many tunnels that extends a long way under the old town. According to an ancient tradition this is where Solomon quarried his building stone. The Jews call it "Zedekiah's Cave" since they believe that Zedekiah, the last king of Judah, hid here from the Babylonian troops in 587 B.C. before being captured and taken to Babylon with most of his people.

Garden Tomb

with the sepulchral chamber on the right. There is one burial place on the left and another, unfinished, on the right under a small window. The tomb dates back to the Roman or Byzantine period.

This was discovered in 1882 by General Gordon who thought it was Christ's tomb since it lay outside the city wall in accordance with the Jewish laws on the siting of tombs; in the outline of the hill he saw the likeness of a skull (Golgotha=place of the skull). Gordon's theory was disproved, however, partly because the line of the city wall in Jesus' time was different from what it is today. Nevertheless, some Christians, especially Anglicans, believe that the "Garden Tomb" is where Jesus was buried and rose again.

Opposite this cave is a short alley leading to *Jeremiah's Grotto*; it is said to be the prison in which around 605 B.C. the prophet Jeremiah wrote his lamentations on the imminent fall of the city which actually occurred in 587 B.C. (Jeremiah 38, 6).

Returning to the Damascus Gate and bearing right into Nablus Street one finds an alleyway just on the right leading to the so-called **Garden Tomb**. Here there is a kind of garden in front of a low cliff which contains a tomb. A door hewn out of the rock leads into a rectangular anteroom

Following Nablus Street one comes on the right to the French *Dominican Monastery of St Stephen* on the site of the stoning of St Stephen, the first Christian martyr.

A little further on a street forks off to the left and the point where it meets St George Street was the site of the *Mandelbaum Gate*. From 1948 to 1967 this was the only crossing point between the Israeli and Jordanian sectors of Jerusalem. Despite its poetic name there was neither a real gate nor an almond tree (Mandelbaum= almond tree in German) here, but only a passage between tangles of barbed wire, and the name refers to the owner of the house next to it, S. Mandelbaum (commemorative plaque). Further along St George Street the next alley on the right

Damascus Gate

Tombs of the Kings

Capitals in the Tombs of the Kings

leads past the Anglican *St George's Church* to Nablus Street. Immediately to the N of this church, where Saladin Street leads into Nablus Street, on the right one finds the *Tombs of the Kings*, which are well worth visiting, in the American Colony which was founded in 1881. On the right at the bottom of 26 broad steps cut in the rock are two water channels leading to cisterns. Through a round arch in the rock and to the left is a large courtyard in front of the entrance to the tombs which are hewn out of the rock. Three steps lead into an anteroom which has a Doric frieze. In the left-hand corner of this room is the low entrance to the interior which was once sealed by a round stone which can still be seen. Inside, several burial chambers on two levels lead off from a central chamber.

The site was purchased in 1874 by a French Jewess and after her death passed to the French nation. The sarcophagi were placed in the Louvre. The name "Tombs of the Kings" is based on the assumption that the kings of Judah were buried here. In fact the site is of considerably later date. It was laid out by Queen Helena of Adiabene, now Kirkuk between Mosul and Baghdad, after her conversion to Judaism and her move to Jerusalem about A.D. 45. Adiabene had gained its independence in the 2nd c. on the fall of the Seleucid empire and its governors became kings. Helena, who did great service to the people of

Jerusalem, took the Jewish name of Sarah Maleka (Queen Sarah); this name is written in Aramaic on one of the sarcophagi in the Louvre.

Turning now towards the town once again along Saladin Street one reaches the town wall at *Herod's Gate*. Following the town wall eastwards opposite the NE corner one sees the group of buildings, dominated by a huge tower, of the *Archaeological or Rockefeller Museum, named after John D. Rockefeller who endowed it in 1927 with a gift of 2 million dollars. It is situated on the raised square from which the Crusaders under Godefroy de Bouillon stormed the city on July 15, 1099. It contains a collection of finds from every period in the history of Palestine.

Beyond the entrance hall is the *Tower Room* with casts of reliefs from the palace of Nineveh showing the capture of Lakhish in 701 B.C. by the Assyrian king Sennacherib whose siege of Jerusalem was unsuccessful. To the left is the *South Octagon* with Egyptian and Mesopotamian objects found in Palestine, including a stele of the pharaoh Seth I (1319–1304 B.C.). The long *South Gallery* contains finds dating back to c. 200000 B.C. The "Galilee skull" (case A, right) dates from this early period, remains of a person from Mount Carmel (case B) are attributed to c. 100000 B.C., and a skeleton from a crouched burial (case II) is attributed to the period c. 10000 B.C. Case I contains heads from Jericho (c. 6000 B.C.); there is also a skull which has added modelling (other examples are in Amman Museum, Jordan) and

Archaeological Museum
Rockefeller Museum Jerusalem

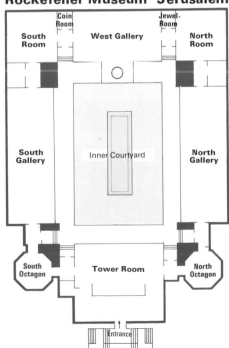

Romanesque capital in the Rockefeller Museum

another made of clay. Also worth seeing are a copper sword (c. 3500 B.C., case L), a clay mould for bronze casting (c. 1600 B.C., case W), a games board with pottery figures (also c. 1600 B.C., case AA), a vase from Cyprus (c. 1400 B.C., case AA) and a Hittite battleaxe made of bronze (c. 1500 B.C., case HH). Through the square *South Room* (18th c. wood-carvings from the El Aqsa Mosque) is the *coin room* and then rooms containing finds from the palace of Khirbat al Mafyar built near Jericho in 724 by the Omayyad caliph Hisham. There are windows and reconstructions of vaulted ceilings with rich ornamentation and many figures (animal and human) which display the special features and high quality of early Islamic art in the Omayyad period: the artists were inspired by the art of the great powers of the time, Byzantium and Persia; the non-pictorial Islamic art of the Arabesque came later. – In the small room next door is a carved elephant's tusk and Classical jewelry, including large gold earrings from the Roman period. Through a *room containing jewelry and precious stones* and the *North Room* is the long *North Gallery*, the contents of which are post-1200 B.C. and therefore follow on chronologically from those in the South Gallery. They include a clay sarcophagus in the shape of a human being (c. 1100 B.C., left), human and animal figures on a clay incense burner (1100 B.C., case B), then the "Lakhish letters" (fragments of clay with inscriptions in Hebrew, case C) dating from 588 B.C., ivory pieces from the palace of King Ahab of Israel in Samaria (c. 850 B.C., case C) and iron tools (c. 1000 B.C., case D); also Phoenician, Greek and Roman articles, including a bronze statue of Heracles (2nd c. B.C., case N), a

Nabataean bowl (from about the time of the birth of Christ, case R), Roman glasses (2nd–3rd c., case S) and a Justinian bronze coin (6th c. case X). Finally there is a family tomb from the time of the Hyksos (c. 1600 B.C.), found in Jericho in 1954 and given to the museum. The North Gallery leads into the North Octagon which contains displays of Jewish objects from all periods, especially candlesticks and reliefs, and a mosaic from the synagogue of En Gedi.

There is a fountain in the museum's inner courtyard which is surrounded with other archaeological finds (sarcophagi, capitals, mosaics, etc.) and modern depictions of the history of Palestine.

From the Rockefeller Museum proceed W along Shmuel Ben Adiya Street and eventually turn left into Mount of Olives Street. Going N one reaches **Mount Scopus** (2,668 ft/813 m) and the old *Hebrew University* (opened in 1925; also new buildings). A little further N one finds the old *Hadassah Clinics* and the huge building of the *Augusta-Victoria Home* which was endowed by Kaiser William II.

NW and SW quarters of the old town

In front of the NW corner of the old city wall, 330 yd/300 m from the Jaffa Gate, is Zahal Square (Kikar Zahal). This is the beginning of Hazanhanim Street which runs along the wall to the Damascus Gate, past the New Gate, opposite which is the enlarged complex of *Notre Dame de France*, built in 1877. This is also the start of Jaffa Street which leads NW into the center of the **NEW TOWN**, to Bar Kochba Square and Zion Square. In Bar Kochba Square a street leads off to the right to the RUSSIAN QUARTER where one can see the green domes of the **Russian Orthodox Cathedral**.

This cathedral originated about 1860 as a large walled complex to house the Russian pilgrims visiting Jerusalem, mostly at Easter. The buildings on the NE side were the Consulate and a women's hostel. On the SW side there used to be the hospital, the mission house with rooms for the archimandrites, the priests and wealthy pilgrims and, on the other side of the cathedral, a large hostel for men. Nowadays these are official buildings including the police headquarters and the law-courts.

In Classical times this place was a stone quarry, which accounts for the 40 ft/12 m column that broke when it was being quarried and was therefore unfinished and which lies, still joined to the rock, in a hollow opposite the entrance to the cathedral. It was intended either for the colonnade of the Herodian Temple, or, as seems likely from several capitals found here, for a building in the Theodosian period (2nd half of the 4th c.).

Rockefeller Museum

A side door leads NW to the Street of the Prophets (Rehov Haneviim), on the far side of which begins the Mea Shearim quarter. Turn left into the Street of the Prophets and then immediately right into the Street of the Abyssinians (Ha Habbashim). This gets its name from the Abyssinian Monastery, founded and enlarged by the Emperor John (1872–89) and Menelik (1889–1913). The monastery's **Abyssinian Church** is a round building with a green dome.

The lion reliefs above the gate recall the title "Lion of Judah" borne by the rulers of the Ethiopian dynasty descended from the Queen of Sheba; they believed that the Queen of Sheba was also queen of Abyssinia and that Solomon granted the queen the coat of arms with the lion of Judah when she visited Jerusalem ("Abyssinia" is the former name of "Ethiopia"). – The church contains simple Abyssinian icons.

Next to the monastery is the *House of Eliezer Ben Yehuda* who played a large part in the creation of Modern Hebrew (Ivrit) (commemorative plaque).

N of the monastery is the MEA SHEARIM quarter, founded in 1875 as the second Jewish settlement outside the old town. At the access points are signboards requesting that the customs of the strict orthodox Jews living here be respected, especially on the sabbath. It is also inadvisable to wear "indecent clothing" (e.g. shorts, short-sleeved blouses and dresses) or to take photographs of the inhabitants. The name Mea Shearim refers to "Isaac's hundredfold harvest" (Genesis 26, 12) but also means "100 gates". In the narrow streets can be seen the orthodox Jews in their old east-European costumes with peyot (side-locks), streimel (fur-trimmed hat) and black clothing. They speak mostly Yiddish, since they regard Hebrew as a holy language reserved for religious services. The Neturei Karta extremists do not recognise the state of Israel because it was not created by the Messiah and therefore regard themselves as a ghetto of true orthodoxy within the Jewish state. There are very many synagogues, "mikvot" (ritual baths), Talmud schools and workshops of Torah scribes in this quarter. The shops, especially those around the market place, sell religious articles, silverware, etc.

Walking N from here into Ezekiel Street and then turning left into Rehov Habuharim, one arrives at the BOKHARA QUARTER (quarter of the Jews from Bokhara) which was founded in 1892 and where the old picturesque costumes are still worn, especially on holidays.

Following the Street of the Prophet Samuel (Rehov Shmuel Hanavi) N one comes to a fork. Turning right one reaches the **Tombs of the Sanhedrin**, 1st c. rock tombs. The pediment over the entrance, like the one over the door, is finely decorated with acanthus leaves and pomegranates. The main chamber is on two levels and steps lead down to a third level. The recesses used to hold coffins. Since this is all very imposing it is assumed that the members of the Sanhedrin, the High Council of the Jews, were buried here.

Return to the fork and turn right into Bar Ilan Street which eventually becomes Jeremiah Street (Rehov Yermiyahu). Shortly before the ROMEMA quarter a path goes off to the right to the **Biblical Zoo** where there is a collection of the animals mentioned in the Bible. By going further S from there and then turning right into Sarei Yisrael Street one returns to Jaffa Street near the memorial to the British conqueror of Jerusalem, General Allenby (1917).

From Zahal Square the short Shelomo Street leads SW to King David Street (David Hamelekh). There on the right is the *YMCA Building*, built in 1928, with its 150 ft/46 m high tower which is popular as a viewing point. The floor of the entrance hall has a copy of the 6th c. map of the Holy Land, the original of which is in Madaba (Jordan).

YMCA Building

Opposite is the **King David Hotel**. During the Second World War and after it was used as administrative headquarters by the British troops, which is why the Jewish Underground blew up one wing in 1946. Since 1948 it has again been used as a hotel.

Right next to the hotel, in a narrow side street, is one of the city's old burial places the *Herodian Tomb*. Herod I had a monumental tomb built for himself on Mount Herodian near Bethlehem (see Herodeion), but for his family he had a separate tomb built above the Hinnom

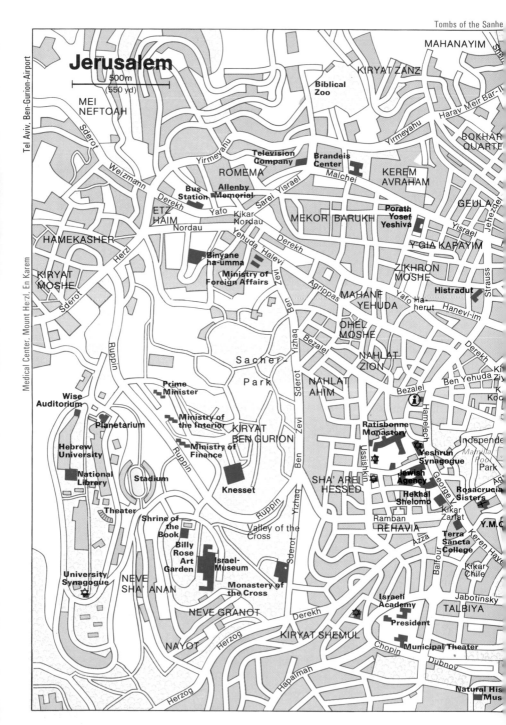

Tombs of the Sanhe

Jerusalem

| 1 | Dome of the Rock | 3 | El Aqsa Mosque | 5 | Wailing Wall | 7 | Bab en-Nadhir |
| 2 | Chain Dome | 4 | Moroccan Gate | 6 | Silsile Gate | | |

Valley. His wife Mariamne and other victims of his violent temper and paranoia were buried here.

The foundations of a pyramid have been discovered left of the entrance. Steps lead down first to the courtyard hewn from the rock and then into the entrance gallery which still contains the round stone which, as in the Tombs of the Kings, was used to seal the entrance. The first chamber is square and the second is smaller and has three burial chambers leading off from it. Until the Second World

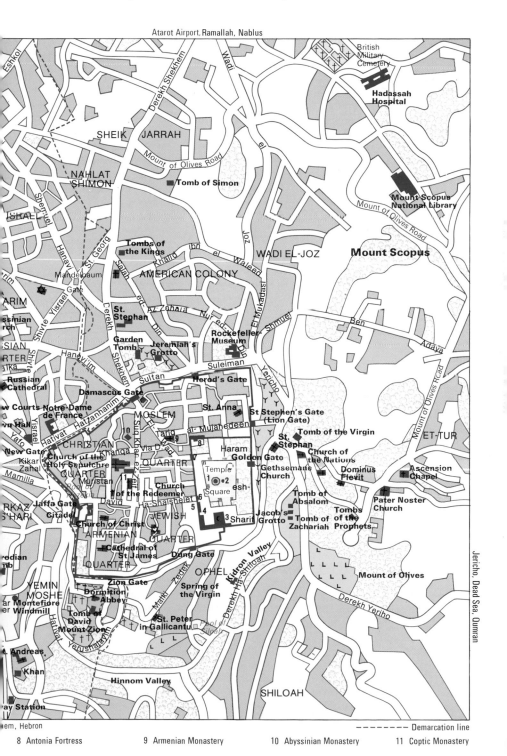

------- Demarcation line

| 8 Antonia Fortress | 9 Armenian Monastery | 10 Abyssinian Monastery | 11 Coptic Monastery |

War the sarcophagi stood here in their original positions. When the British, stationed in the nearby King David Hotel, used the tomb as an air-raid shelter, the sarcophagi were taken to the Greek Orthodox Constantine Monastery near the Church of the Holy Sepulchre.

Montefiore Windmill

Further S along King David Street on the left is the *windmill* built by Sir Moses Montefiore in 1857. At the same time a New Orleans Jew, Juda Touro, paid for apartment buildings to be built near this windmill and the new quarter was given the name of Mishkenot Shaanaim (dwellings of peace). The buildings were rebuilt after 1967 and are now placed at the disposal of writers, artists and musicians.

A little further S on the far side of the crossroads is the Scottish *Church of St Andrew* (1927) on the left, and next to it the *Khan*, a former Turkish caravanserai, which has been converted into a theater. E of here is the hill of Abu Gate from which Titus stormed Jerusalem in A.D. 70. From here there is a fine view of the Hinnom Valley, Mount Zion and the old town.

S of the Khan is the **railway station**, the last station on the line from Jaffa to Jerusalem, which was built in 1891. Leave the station on the left and turn into Emek Refaim Street. This is the site of the *Colony of German Templars* founded in 1873. The parish hall, with its apse and small belfry, and the houses with gardens are still the main features of the locality. At the end of the Colony, adjoining the American cemetery, is the Templars' cemetery which was laid out in 1878.

Returning to the start of Emek Refaim Street, take a side street on the left immediately in front of the *Natural History Museum*. This street leads past the rose garden to Chopin Street which runs NE into Hanassi Street. Here on the right is the modern Jerusalem **theater** opened in 1972, the *residence of the State President* and the *Academy of Sciences*. Balfour Street on the left leads to Zarefat Square (Kikar Tsarfat) with, in the right-hand corner, the *Terra Sancta Building* of the Franciscans.

Turn left from Kikar Tsarfat into Ramban Street and then left again into Alfasi Street, where the *Tomb of Jason*, a Hellenistic tomb, was found in 1956 at No. 10 during excavations. Its name was on an inscription. The façade is made of freestone blocks and the entrance is divided into two by a stout column. The top is closed by a pyramidal roof. Inside the 2nd c. tomb is a passage from which chambers containing burial recesses lead off.

Returning to the Kikar Tsarfat turn left into King George Street (Hamelekh George) where there are some important modern buildings on the left. The first is the **Chief Rabbinate** *(Heikhal Shelomo)*, the supreme religious body in the country. It is the headquarters of the Sephardic and Ashkenazi Chief Rabbis who are responsible for questions of Jewish law. The building was endowed by Sir Isaac Wolfson. On each side of the entrance are the scales of Justice surrounded by the Hebrew inscription "and they shall judge the people with just judgement" (Deuteronomy 16, 18). A representation of the seven-branched candlestick (menorah) decorates the façade. Inside is a synagogue with an ark of the covenant from Padua, a museum of Jewish ecclesiastical and folk art and a library.

Next comes the **Building of Zionist Institutions**. Its central wing houses the *Jewish Agency*, created in 1897 by Theodor Herzl, and the side wings the *Jewish National Fund* (Keren Kayemet), the task of which used to be land purchase and is now land reclamation, and the Foundation Fund (Keren Hayesod). The Zionist Archives and the Golden Rolls of Honour can be seen here.

A little further on is the **Yeshurun Synagogue**, the largest in the city.

Behind it is the Monastery of the French Pères de Sion, founded in 1874 and named after its benefactor Alfonso Ratisbonne.

Opposite this section of the street is the broad expanse of **Independence Park** (Gan Ha'atsmaut). It contains the "Lion's Cave", in which according to legend a pious lion guarded the bones of martyrs, and in the E part, near an old Islamic cemetery, the Mimilla pool, a cistern which was part of the water supply system for Classical Jerusalem.

Until a few decades ago the Monastery of the Cross lay far to the W of the city but it has now lost its isolation with the rapid expansion of modern Jerusalem.

One enters the monastery through a low portal leading to courtyards, terraces and rows of cells grouped around the **church**. Its tower is Baroque but the building itself dates back to the 12th c. and possibly earlier.

A silver ring in the sanctuary indicates the site of the tree of the Holy Cross. The paintings, most of which have survived but have, unfortunately, in some cases, been badly restored, show Biblical themes, Georgian kings and saints. At the bottom is a painting of Shotha Rustaveli, the most important of the Georgian poets. Sent here as a monk by Queen Tamara (1184–1211), it was here that he wrote "Vapkis Takossani" (The Man in the Panther Skin), about 1187. He is shown as a small kneeling figure at the feet of Maximos the Confessor and John of Damascus.

Western part of the new town and suburbs

Whereas the tours described so far can be done on foot, visits to the W districts of the city, which extend beyond the village of En Karem, have to be made by bus, car or taxi.

Between the district of REHAVIA and the Israel Museum is the **Valley of the Cross**. On the Boulevard Ben Zvi (Sderot Hanassi Ben Zvi) the huge fortress-like **Monastery of the Cross** (in Arabic Deir el Musalliba), a medieval fortified monastery, rises up out of the olive trees of the valley.

Knesset (Parliament building)

Legend has it that Lot settled here after his separation from his two daughters and planted the seeds of cedar, cypress and pine; they germinated and grew together to form the tree that supplied the wood for Christ's cross. The monastery gets its name from this legend, which probably recalls an old cult of tree worship. Its early history is not altogether clear. According to Greek Orthodox tradition Helena, the mother of Emperor Constantine the Great, founded it when she visited Palestine. Another tradition has it that Constantine gave the site to the first Christian king of Georgia, Mirian (d. 342), who built the monastery. Over a long period there grew up a strong connection between Georgia and the Monastery of the Cross, which for the Christians of Transcaucasia was similar in its meaning to that of the Georgian Monastery ("Iviron") on Holy Mount Athos. During the period of the Crusades and in the following Islamic period until the 18th c. the monastery remained Georgian. In the 16th c. there were cells for 365 monks and another 220 in the 18th c. The monastery got into financial difficulties when Georgia lost its independence in the late 18th c. and it became the property of the Greek Orthodox patriarchate of Jerusalem to whom it still belongs today. The Georgian manuscripts have since been kept in the library of the patriarchate. In 1843, a few years after the founding of the University of Athens, the Greeks built a college here where Orthodox priests could devote themselves to general and theological studies, and this college, the first rector of which was the Greek monk Dionysius Cleophas, existed until the First World War.

Following the Ben Zvi Boulevard N one reaches Ruppin Street where the *Knesset, the Israeli parliament and the most striking building in the HAKIRYA government quarter, is situated. In front of the entrance is a *menorah*, a 16 ft/5 m high seven-branched candlestick, symbol of the State of Israel, designed and cast in bronze by Benno Elkan. Twenty-nine reliefs show figures and events from Jewish history. The candlestick was a gift from the British parliament. – The Knesset was inaugurated in 1966; mosaic and tapestry by Marc Chagall. There are guided tours when parliament is not sitting, and during sessions the visitors' gallery is usually accessible (passports must be shown).

To the NW of the Knesset stand three long government buildings: the *Ministry of Finance*, the *Ministry of the Interior* and the *Prime Minister's Office*. In the park to the N there is a replica of the United States Liberty Bell and in a nearby pool a 6th c. Christian mosaic can be seen.

Interior of the Shrine of the Book

SW of the Knesset are the pavilions of the **Israel Museum** containing the Shrine of the Book, Archaeological Museum, Bezalel Art Gallery, Billy Rose Art Garden and Department of Antiquities. The museum, which is on a hill, was opened in 1965 and is the only one in the country that collects and displays archaeological finds as art objects.

Right of the entrance is the *Shrine of the Book. Its pale concrete dome is shaped like the lid of one of the jars in which the "Dead Sea Scrolls" were discovered in 1947. Found in caves near the monastery of the Essene sect of Qumran (see entry), they came to Israel through the mediation of the archaeologist Yigael Yadin (others are in the Amman Archaeological Museum). The scrolls, originally in clay jars with lids, are the oldest manuscripts of the Old Testament in the Hebrew language. In the center of the round building are displayed the scrolls containing the main sections of the Book of Isaiah. Written about 100 B.C., they vary only slightly from the later manuscripts. This oldest extant text of the Old Testament is proof of the accuracy of the Biblical manuscript tradition. Other texts are displayed on the outside walls. The cases on the lower floor contain finds from Massada (see entry), dating from the period when the uprising by the Jewish Zealots was put down by the Roman siege in A.D. 73, and which were found during excavations in 1964 and 1965, and the Kochba letters discovered on the Nahal Hever in 1960 and 1961.

In the pavilion-type sections of the long main building are the Archaeological Museum (see below) and the *Bezalel Art Gallery which has an impressive collection of Jewish religious art. A lot of the exhibits are from the Diaspora and have obviously been influenced by the host countries concerned.

Room 105: impressionists and post-impressionists. – Room 201: Jewish objects from all over the world, including Torah containers, candlesticks and Kiddush cups; old Hebrew manuscripts. – Room 203: articles for Jewish festivals, including Chanukkah candlesticks. – Room 204: objects connected with

ceremonies such as circumcision, Bar Mitzvah (roughly corresponding to confirmation) and marriage. – Room 205: "Erna Michael Synagoque" from Vittorio Veneto (Italy), completed in 1700 according to an inscription under the Torah shrine, with Baroque interior. – Room 206: synagogue from Horb near Bamberg. – Room 208: folk art, including festive clothing from Morocco, the Yemen, Bokhara and other Diaspora countries; brides' jewelry. – Room 210: Israeli art. – Room 211: paintings and prints. – Room 212: contemporary art, including the triptych "The Gates of Jerusalem" made to commemorate the 20th anniversary of independence. – Rooms 213 and 214: modern Israeli painters (Agam, Arikha, Aroch, Dagan, Engelsberg, Kupferman, Mokady, Paldi, Rubin, Tumarkin, Witkin, Zaritsky, etc.). – Room 215: (Rothschild Room): "Grand Salon" in the Louis XV style purchased by Baron Rothschild in 1887. – Room 216: Empire furniture, Sèvres porcelain. – Room 217: "Italian pavilion" with 18th c. Venetian furniture; paintings (including a Veduta of Venice ascribed to Michele Marieschi). – Room 219: Old Masters. – Room 221: 18th c. English dining room.

The *Archaeological Museum is also in the main building (Samuel Bronfman Museum of Biblical Archaeology).

Room 102: coins. – Room 103: American pre-Columbian art. – Room 104: African art (under construction). – Room 301: prehistory; including photographs of excavations, animal remains, tools from the Old Stone Age to the New Stone Age (1000000–4000 B.C.). Room 302: Chalcolithic Age. (Copper Stone Age); pottery and bronze items mainly from Beersheba and En Gedi. – Room 303: early Canaanite period (3000–2000 B.C.); photographs of remains of settlements in Megiddo. – Room 306: middle Canaanite period (2000–1750 B.C.); pottery jars and lamps (grave furnishings). – Room 307: late Canaanite period (1750–1200 B.C.); jar, steles, a life-size stone lion from Hazor. – Room 309: period of the Judges (1200–1020 B.C.); including part of a bronze axe from Afula, pottery figurine in the Mycenaean style. – Room 310: period of the first Temple (1020–586 B.C.); including religious artefacts, grave furnishings from the N (Phoenician influence). – Room 311: period of the second Temple (538 B.C.–A.D. 70); Persian-, Hellenistic- and Roman-style objects. – Room 312: Roman period (63 B.C.–A.D.324); sarcophagi, a stone with the name of Pontius Pilate, sculpture, mosaic floors. – Room 313: Byzantine period (A.D. 324–638); remains of synagogues, mosaic floors from Galilee, sarcophagi. – Room 315: documents from the Arab and Crusader periods and later; including marble altar cupboards from Christian churches. – Room 316: neighbouring cultures; large wall-maps showing the areas concerned.

Room 401: Children's section: from December to May there are educational exhibitions with themes ranging from ancient history to modern art. – From May to November children's work is on display.

The Billy Rose Art Garden, named after its founder and designed by the Japanese architect Isamo Noguchi, is laid out on the slopes of the Neveh Shaanan. Most of the sculptures here are modern, by artists such as Henry Moore, Victor Vasarely, Fritz Wotruba, Jacques Lipchitz, Aristide Maillol, Pablo Picasso, Jean Tinguely, Menashe Kadishman and Yehiel Shemi.

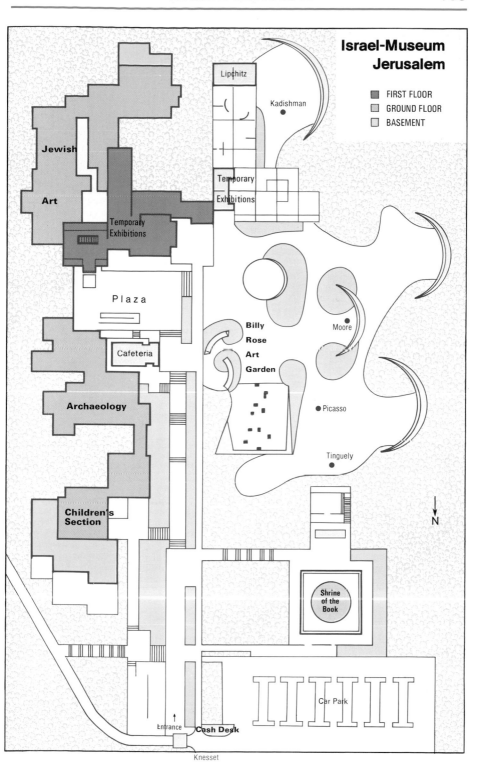

Israel-Museum Jerusalem

- ■ FIRST FLOOR
- ▨ GROUND FLOOR
- □ BASEMENT

Lipchitz

Kadishman

Temporary Exhibitions

Jewish

Art

Temporary Exhibitions

Plaza

Cafeteria

Billy
Rose
Art
Garden

Moore

Archaeology

Picasso

Tinguely

N

Children's
Section

Shrine
of the
Book

Car Park

Entrance Cash Desk

Knesset

Along Ruppin Street to the W is the **Hebrew University** with its large campus of Giv'at Ram. To the right of the entrance is the administration building with a 5th–6th c. mosaic from the Jezreel plain in the lobby. Nearby is the Wise auditorium. In the middle of the site is the Jewish National and University Library, and in the S one's gaze is drawn to the white dome of the synagogue designed by Rau, a German architect, and built in honour of Rabbi Israel Goldstein.

Clay scroll jar   Sculptures in the Israel Museum's Billy Rose Art Garden

Ruppin Street leads out of the city to Herzl Boulevard (Sderot Herzl) which in turn leads to the cemetery for Israeli soldiers killed since 1948 and **Mount Herzl**, named after the founder of Zionism.

Theodor Herzl was born in Budapest on May 2, 1860 and died in Edlach (Lower Austria) on July 3, 1904. In his book "The Jewish State", published in 1896, he called for the creation of an independent Jewish state, an idea which he reiterated in his novel "Altneuland" (1903) and at the Zionist World Congress for which he was responsible. In 1949, a year after the founding of the state he had prophesied, his mortal remains were brought to Israel and placed in a freestanding sarcophagus on Mount Herzl. There is also a replica of Herzl's study and library near the main entrance. – Nearby are the tombs of Herzl's parents and several leading Zionists, and Prime Ministers Levi Eshkol and Golda Meir are buried near the road leading to the military cemetery.

From Mount Herzl Hazikaron Street leads to the *Hill of Remembrance* (Har Hazikaron) with the **Yad Vashem Memorial** to the Jews murdered by the Nazis.

The name "Yad Vashem" means "a monument and a name"; it refers to a saying of the prophet Isaiah (Isaiah 56, 4–5): "For thus saith the Lord: Even unto them will I give in mine house and within my walls a place and a name, that shall not be cut off." Voted for by the Knesset in 1953 and built by the Office for the Commemoration of Martyrs and Heroes, Yad Vashem has become a monumental memorial to the millions of victims of National Socialism.

First is the *Avenue of the Righteous*, devoted to non-Jews who risked their own lives to save Jews. Israel bestows on them the honorary title of "one of the Righteous" and they can have a carob-tree planted here bearing their name. – The *Memorial Hall* is built of boulders with a huge concrete slab on top. Inside a wide windowless hall the floor is inlaid with the names of the extermination camps in Hebrew and Roman lettering while an everlasting flame keeps the memory

of their victims alive. The rooms that adjoin the hall document the names of the victims and contain an exhibition of photos and a special library.

Back in the main street, En Karem Street leads down into the valley of *En Karem* (2½ miles/4 km).

According to a Christian tradition going back to the 5th or 6th c., this terraced village is where Zacharias and Elizabeth lived, where Mary visited her pregnant cousin Elizabeth (Luke 1, 39–56) and where Elizabeth's son, John the Baptist, was born (Luke 1, 57–66). – A street leads off the main street to the right to the Franciscan Monastery of St John. The Church of St John was built in the 17th c. over the grotto where John the Baptist was born. Near the entrance, in a grotto, is a 5th or 6th c. mosaic with peacocks and doves; the Greek inscription means "Greetings, martyr of God". In the church are fine wrought-iron grilles. Steps lead down into the crypt where there is a marble tablet with the inscription "Hic Praecursor Domini natus est" (the Lord's precursor was born here). Reliefs show events from the life of John the Baptist.

On the far side of the main street in the middle of the village is a spring which since the Crusades has been known as the Spring of the Virgin Mary. Near it stands the *mosque* of the Arabs who left the village in 1948. Stone steps lead to the **Franciscan Visitatio Mariae Church** on the site of a cottage in which Mary is supposed to have visited Elizabeth. The two-storey modern building, its façade decorated with a mosaic of the Visitatio, was built in the ruins of a basilica dating from the Crusades. There is an old cistern on the lower floor and the upper church contains remnants of the apse of the Crusader building with, next to this, pilgrims' crosses scratched into the masonry. The furnishings are modern.

Franciscan church in En Karem

A road leads NW out of En Karem to Eitanim. 1 mile/2 km out of the village on the left is the **Hadassah Medical Center** (University Clinics). The Center was opened in 1962 and is part of the Hebrew University. Its synagogue with twelve *stained-glass windows by Marc Chagall showing the tribes of Israel is worth visiting. Down below in the valley is the small *Franciscan Monastery of St John in the Wilderness* which recalls the youth of John the Baptist (Luke 1, 80).

The **Kennedy Memorial** can be seen high on a hill in the S. This memorial to the assassinated U.S. president was paid for by American citizens and can be reached by driving SE from Hadassah and taking the turning on the right to Ora. It then lies 2 miles/3 km beyond the village.

From Mount Herzl another road, Rav Uziel, leads S to the *Holyland Hotel* in the W suburb of BAIT VEGAN. In the grounds of this hotel there is a ***model of ancient Jerusalem.**

The project was the brainchild of Hans Broch, the owner of the Holyland Hotel, who also paid for it. To make sure it was accurate Michael Avi-Yonah (author of "Topography of Jerusalem at the time of the Second Temple") was commissioned to design it. His wife was responsible for the plans and elevations of the buildings and these were put into effect first by E. Scheffler, the sculptor, and then by R. Brotze. Their work, which was begun in 1965 and practically completed by 1968, has resulted in an imposing layout combining scientific accuracy with visual impact: this is what Jerusalem must have looked like "at the time of the Second Temple, shortly after the rule of Herod the Great", in other words at the time of Jesus.

On the 1,196 sq. yd/1,000 sq. m area (=1 dunam) the original contours of the site have been reproduced in

From the Spring of the Virgin a narrow rocky path through the trees leads to the *Russian Lavra* with its small colourful church. There is an unfinished basilica above the nuns' dwellings.

Stained-glass windows by Marc Chagall in the Hadassah Medical Center

reinforced concrete and correctly oriented as well, which is important for the effect of light and shade. The scale of 1:50 was chosen for the buildings, so about ¾ in./2 cm on the model equals 1 yd/1 m in reality. This large scale did away with the usual distortions of the ratio of height to width. Between the highest point, the Psephinus Tower (2,675 ft/815 m above sea level), and the lowest point in the Kidron Valley (1,989 ft/606 m above sea level) there is a difference in altitude of about 13 ft/4 m on the model. The original building materials have been used (stone, marble, metal) so it did not need to be roofed over. This helps to make it even more likelike but means that the details are not as accurate as they could have been if modelled in plaster or plastic.

So far as the details of the model are concerned, Michael Avi-Yonah has explained in several publications that a careful assessment was made of the archaeological findings and written sources. The main sources were, for the appearance and furnishings of the Temple, the Mishna Tracts "Midot" ("survey") and "Tamid" ("the daily Temple sacrifice"), written soon after the Temple was destroyed, and, for the city, the description by Flavius Josephus in his "History of the Jewish War". There are still gaps, however, in what is known of the city before it was destroyed in A D 70, concerning details of its lay-out and, more particularly, what styles were used for the larger buildings. This meant looking for clues in similar sites so that the Hashmonean palace (2nd–1st c. B.C.) and the Herodian buildings (1st c. B.C.) were modelled on Hellenistic palaces, while the palace of Queen Helena of Adiabene, who came from Mesopotamia, was based on Parthian buildings in that region.

The entrance to the site (portable recorded commentaries are available) is on the W side of the model and affords a view of the whole city looking over towards the Temple Mount. In the N can be seen the lines of the Second Wall and the Third Wall (built by Agrippa I) with an almost open space between them. In the NW corner is the octagonal Psephinus Tower. In the middle of the W side stand the three towers of the Herodian citadel or "David's Tower": in front is the rectangular Phasael Tower, named after Herod's older brother, with two storeys above the lower sentry-walk, then a little nearer the center of the city, the Hippicus Tower, named after a friend of Herod and recognisable by a tall row of pillars on each of the four sides and a round superstructure with a small dome, then, S of this, the Mariamne Tower, named after the Hashmonean princess who was Herod's wife, which has a square base and three storeys of different heights surrounded by columns, topped by a pointed cone.

N of the Citadel is the tomb with pyramidal roof of the Hashmonean high priest John Hyrkanos (135–104 B.C.). Immediately to the S is Herod's rectangular palace with its gardens and rows of rooms in what is now the Armenian quarter. The adjoining upper town is shown as a wealthy quarter with a street pattern based on Hippodamos of Miletus' grid system. Along the wall leading from the Citadel to the Temple Mount (where David Street and Chain Street run today) is the rectangular complex of the Hashmonean palace. A little to the S (near the wall separating the upper and the lower town) one can see Herod's theater, which was in the Roman style.

The anti-clockwise route goes around the S and E sides and overlooks the lower town, reconstructed "as a warren of little houses", with its shops and workshops. To the E is the narrow strip of what was the City of David on Mount Ophel, in which Avi-Yonah depicts not only a Roman racecourse but also palatial villas. To the N is the vast group of buildings on the Temple Mount, separated from the city in the W by what was then the Valley of the Cheesemakers (Tyropoion) (and which has since been filled in). In the SW corner is the flight of steps leading to the top of the Robinson Arch with, a little further N, the Wilson Arch. The Huldah Gates, one of the main ways into the Temple (exposed by recent excavations) can be seen in the S wall. The top of the S wall is dominated by the Royal Stoa (stoa basilike). More stoas can be seen on the other sides of the large square which has in the center the Herodian Temple with its courtyards to the E. The exterior of the tall building is decorated with small columns, pilasters, a richly ornamented acroterion and stepped merlons.

In the N the massive Antonia Fortress, also a Herodian building, with towers at its four corners, dominates the Temple square. Further N there are various markets within the inner (Second) wall. Behind the outer (Third) wall the Bethesda pool is the most obvious feature; four Hellenistic stoas surround the pool and a fifth divides it in two. Here as at other points the model of the city clearly shows that in the 1st c., when Jesus lived here, Jerusalem's architecture was largely Hellenistic and that Graeco-Roman features were combined with local styles to produce the typical blend of cultures that was also to be found elsewhere in the Middle East at that time.

Tomb of Rachel

SURROUNDINGS of Jerusalem. – The Hebron road (Derech Hevron), which starts at the railway station, goes S to Bethlehem. After 4 miles/6·5 km on rising ground on the left is the 12th c. Greek Orthodox *Elias Monastery* (Deir Mar Elias) which was restored in the 17th c. 1 mile/1·5 km further on, on the right of the road, is the **Tomb of Rachel** (Qubbet Rahil), a small 18th c. domed building supposedly built over Rachel's tomb in which Jacob laid her to rest when she died shortly after the birth of Benjamin. – A little further on the road forks: right to Hebron, left to **Bethlehem** (1 mile/2 km; see entry), the birthplace of David and Jesus.

From Bethlehem it is possible to visit the *Sabas Monastery* (Mar Saba, see entry) to the W and the *Herodion* (see Herodeion), fort and burial place of Herod the Great, to the SE.

Model of ancient Jerusalem

From Jerusalem to Beersheba via Hebron (52 miles/83 km). – 5 miles/8 km along the road leading SE out of Jerusalem there is a fork. 2½ miles/4 km towards Hebron on the left is "Solomon's Pool", three open cisterns which provided water from Roman times until quite recently. After 13 miles/21 km is **Hebron** (3,042 ft/927 m above sea level) (see entry), burial place of the patriarchs of the Bible. The road continues to **Beersheba** (see entry; 31 miles/50 km) on the edge of the Negev desert. 8 miles/13 km before Beersheba a road goes off left to *Arad* (see entry; 20 miles/32 km), from where it is 15 miles/24 km to *Neve Zohar* on the Dead Sea and 12 miles/20 km to *Massada* (see entry).

From Jerusalem to Qiryat Gat (50 miles/81 km). – Jaffa Street soon becomes the broad road to Tel Aviv. Just N of the motorway is the Arab mountain village of *Abu Gosh* (see entry; 8 miles/13 km) with a Crusader church. 9 miles/15 km further on is the Trappist Monastery of *Latrun* (see entry) near the village of Amwas, which is probably the Emmaus of the Bible.

6 miles/10 km W of Abu Gosh a road goes off left to *Beth Shemesh* (see entry; 5 miles/8 km), founded in 1950 as a new town for recent immigrants and today an industrial town of 11,600 inhabitants. Excavations have proved that on a hill to the W the Hyksos and Canaanites (18th c. B.C.) had a town. – 2½ miles/4 km S of this town a road goes off left to *Bet Gamal* (1 mile/2 km) which has a Salesian orphanage containing a cloister with Byzantine fragments. Legend has it that Gamaliel, a member of the Sanhedrin, buried the Christian protomartyr Stephen here.

Further S (2½ miles/4 km) behind the Moshav *Kefar Zekharya* on the right is the Tell of the Azekah of the Bible; the tomb of the prophet Zachariah is supposed to have been to the N. Now comes the kibbutz of *Bet Guvrin* (see entry; 11 miles/17 km) on the site of an Arab village which was abandoned after 1948. – 1 mile/2 km S is where the Biblical town of *Mareshah* (see entry) was found, and 4 miles/6 km SW J. L. Starkey excavated the *Lakhish* (see entry) of the Bible near the present-day Moshav of the same name between 1932 and 1938. – 5 miles/8 km from Bet Guvrin is **Qiryat Gat** (24,000 inhabitants), founded in 1954, a town with industries based on agriculture, not far from the Tel Aviv–Beersheba road. It is named after the Tell to the N on which it is thought that Gath, one of the five towns of the Philistines (1 Samuel 6, 17), was sited.

From Jerusalem to Afula via Nablus (78 miles/125 km). – The road to Nablus runs N from the Damascus Gate. After 6 miles/9 km a road goes off to the left to the village of *El Qubeiba* which many people since the time of the Crusades have thought was the Emmaus of the Bible where the risen Christ appeared to two disciples (Luke 24, 13; cf. Latrun); in 1901 Franciscans built a church on the site of a Crusader church.

Past Jerusalem airport is *Ramallah* (see entry; 3 miles/5 km), then comes Ain Sinya and the fertile "Valley of the Thieves" (Wadi el Haramiye). The route leads up into the hills near Sinyil and down again to *Luban*, the Lebona of the Bible (Judges 21, 19). A little to the E lay *Silo* where the Ark of the Covenant was kept before Solomon's Temple was built.

Just before *Sichem*, Shekhem in Hebrew (see Nablus; 31 miles/50 km), a road turns off sharp right to Jacob's Well (Bir Yakub in Arabic), which according

to the tradition was dug by Jacob (Genesis 33, 18) and near which Jesus met the woman of Samaria (John 4, 5). 1 mile/2 km past Sichem, **Nablus** (see entry), the principal town on the West Bank, is reached. S of the town on Mount Gerizim is the shrine of the small Jewish community of the Samaritans. 7 miles/11 km NW of Nablus on the right of the road is the large ruined site of **Samaria** (see entry; Sebastiya in Arabic, Shomron in Hebrew) with imposing remains from the Israelite, Herodian, Roman and early Christian periods.

The road continues N through the hilly countryside of Samaria, past several Arab villages, drops down into the Dothan Valley where Joseph was sold by his brothers to an Ismaeli camel-train (Genesis 37, 17–28), to the Arab town of *Jenin* (20 miles/32 km) which has a monument to German pilots who died in the First World War as allies of the Turks. Beyond the village of Jalama the road leaves the West Bank and reaches **Afula** (see entry; 11 miles/18 km), the center of the Jezreel Plain.

From Jerusalem to Qumran (2G miles/11 km). To the E of Jerusalem the road passes the village of *El Azariye/Bethany* (see entry; 4 miles/6 km) where Jesus raised Lazarus (John 11, 1), stayed with his sisters Mary and Martha and was anointed by Martha (John 11, 2).

Near Ma'aleh Adummin (10 miles/16 km) a road goes off to the left on a right-hand bend into the *Wadi Qilt* (see entry) along which a Roman road led to Jericho. From the top, where there is a splendid view, the road leads down into the wadi and to the Greek Orthodox Monastery of St George. Beyond Ma'aleh Adummin on the right is the ruined caravanserai of Khan el Haturi near which the parable of the Good Samaritan (Luke 12, 30–34) was set. Above are the remains of the Crusader castle of Maldoim. 3 miles/5 km further on to the right is a short road to *Nebi Musa* (see entry), a ruined caravanserai near which, according to Islamic tradition, Moses was buried.

2 miles/3 km further on the road branching off to the left goes to the oasis of *Jericho* (see entry) with finds from prehistoric times and the Omayyad period. Continuing S along the shores of the Dead Sea on the right can be seen the site of **Qumran** (see entry; 7 miles/11 km) made famous by the scrolls discovered there in 1947. – Further along the shore is *En Gedi* (see entry; 22 miles/35 km) and the Herodian mountain fortress of *Massada* (see entry; 11 miles/18 km).

Jezreel Plain/ Emeq Yizre'el/ HaEmeq

District: North, Haifa.
ⓘ **Government Tourist Office,**
18 Herzl Street,
Haifa;
tel. (04) 66 65 21.

The large fertile valley of the Jezreel plain, frequently called "HaEmeq" ("the valley") for short, extends from the bay N of Haifa SE to the

Jordan valley and separates the hills of Samaria and Galilee. The Arabs call it "Marge Ibn Amer", and the Bible refers to it as "the Esdrelon Plain".

The Jezreel plain is the largest valley in Israel and one of its most fertile regions. In the SW the Iron Valley forms a crossing to the Plain of Sharon (see entry). Megiddo (see entry) in the Iron pass was of great military importance from ancient times right up until this century because of its strategic position. The Jezreel plain has frequently been contested not only as a passage for troops but also because of its fertility, as, for instance, in the time of Deborah (Judges 5, 19) and Gideon (Judges 7, 5).

Nowadays the capital and hub of communications for the Jezreel plain is the town of **Afula** (see entry). In 1938 on the road between Afula and Jenin, which more or less follows the watershed between the E and W sides of the plain, the kibbutz of Yizre'el was founded. It is one of the many Jewish settlements which grew up after the Jewish National Fund had begun in 1910 to buy up the area that since 1870 had been in the private ownership of Lebanese.

The kibbutz of Yizre'el is on the spot where the palace of King Ahab of Israel stood. Ahab had seized the vineyard of Naboth the Jezreelite and built his palace here (1 Kings 21). It was here that his wife Jezebel and his grandson Joram were killed by his successor Jehu (2 Kings 9, 27 and 33). Ahab's palace was destroyed by the Assyrians. On the Tell near the kibbutz are the remains of the *Crusader castle* of *Le petit Gerin* and its church (view.)

The Emeq Yizre'el is only fertile if there is enough rainfall and if the land is well enough drained not to become swampy. Many of the fields in the valley, which is bordered on the W by Mount Carmel, are laid out like the squares on a chess-board.

Jordan/Yarden

The *Jordan, Yarden in Hebrew, is **157 miles/252 km long and therefore the longest river in the country and the one with the greatest flow of water. It has three headwaters,** flows through the Sea of Galilee and after some meandering flows into the Dead Sea, bringing it fresh water.

Of the three headwaters of the Jordan the *Hazbani* rises in Lebanon, the *Dan* in the Dan national park and the *Banyas* near Banyas. These rivers unite in the Hula basin to form the Jordan, which then flows through a narrow valley to reach the Sea of Galilee after 37 miles/60 km. After it leaves the Sea of Galilee the *Yarmuk* flows into it from the E. The Yarmuk forms the border between Jordan and the Israeli-occupied Golan Heights.

After 1967 Israeli archaeologists began to excavate the important ancient spa of Hamad Gader (see entry) on the N bank. The Yarmuk was the scene of a dramatic historic event: on August 20, 636 during a fierce sandstorm the Arabs who had fought their way up from the S annihilated the army of the Byzantine emperor Heraklelos; thus Palestine and Syria were lost to the Byzantine Empire and the rule of Islam began.

One of the sources of the Jordan near Banyas

The flood plain between the Sea of Galilee and where the Yarmuk joins the Jordan is broad and fertile. In the S the W bank narrows but widens out again near Bet Shean. It is in this area that the *Nahal Harod* flows into the Jordan from the W. Further S the *Nahal Tirza* (from the W) and the *Nahal Yaboq* (from the E) flow into the Jordan. The E bank, from Naharayim to Damiya, is irrigated by the Jordanian government with the help of the U.S.A.; over 100,000 farmers have settled there since the sixties.

S of Damiya the W bank of the river widens out into the Jordan plain with the oasis of *Jericho* (see entry). Since 1967 numerous villages have sprung up and the inhabitants are able to harvest highly-valued agricultural produce out of season.

S of the Sea of Galilee on its way to the Dead Sea the Jordan takes a very tortuous course. This section of the river is crossed by the Adam, Allenby and Abdullah bridges. Between these last two bridges is the spot where Jesus is said to have been baptised (5 miles/8 km E of Jericho).

The Jordan trough is part of the Great Rift Valley which runs from Syria to Africa. The Dead Sea (−1,306 ft/−398 m at the surface, to 2,727 ft/831 m below sea level on the bed of the inland sea) is its lowest point and also the lowest place on the earth's surface. The fault continues through the Arava rift valley and the Gulf of Aqaba to East Africa.

Though the Jordan is neither especially deep nor wide, it is one of the best-known rivers in the world because of its significance for the Christian religion.

Judea/Yehuda

Districts: South, Central, Tel Aviv, Jerusalem, **West Bank.**
(i) **Government Tourist Office,**
24 King George Street,
Jerusalem;
tel. (02) 24 12 81/2.

Judea stretches from the Mediterranean to the Jordan and the Dead Sea, from the River Yarkon which reaches the sea near Tel Aviv to Gaza and En Gedi. It is divided into the Shefela Plain in the W, the central mountainous region (Har Yehuda) and the Wilderness of Judea (Midbar Yehuda) which stretches to the Dead Sea. It rises to 3,348 ft/1,020 m in the S near Hebron and to 3,335 ft/ 1,016 m in the N in the Betel Mountains. – Since 1967 the section of it on the W Bank has been occupied by Israel.

After Galilee and Samaria, Judea is the most southerly of the three provinces of the Bible W of the Jordan. In the S, where in Jesus' time it was bordered by Idumea, today it has the Negev (see entry).

HISTORY. – In ancient times the Philistines settled on the coastal plain about 1200 B.C. and in the mountains were the tribes of Judah and Benjamin which David united to form the Kingdom of Judah after the death

of the first king Saul, before he was recognised as king of all twelve tribes. After the death of his son Solomon the ten northern tribes formed the Kingdom of Israel and the two southern tribes formed the Kingdom of Judah, which came to an end in 586 B.C. with the Babylonian captivity.

Under Roman rule (from 63 B.C.) Judea, together with Galilee and Samaria, belonged to the area ruled over by Hyrkanos II and Herod, then came under Roman governors. After the Babylonian captivity (586–535 B.C.) had already led to the beginnings of the Diaspora, the dispersion of the Jews began in earnest with the destruction of Jerusalem. Although later in the 4th c. the country largely went over to Christianity and, from the 7th c., Islam, small pockets of Jews still remained in Jerusalem (see entry), Hebron (see entry) and the surrounding area.

During the War of Independence of 1948/49 the W part of Judea fell to the newly-founded State of Israel, and the E part, including Hebron, to Jordan which also got most of Samaria. These areas and E Jerusalem were occupied by Israeli troops in 1967.

The N part of the coastal plain of Judea is the most densely populated part of the country. In the S, where the plain has been widened by sand brought down by the Nile, grow citrus fruits and, further inland, wheat and vegetables. The mountains, rising up to over 3,000 ft/1,000 m, fall away steeply to the Dead Sea and form a rain barrier, so that their E slopes have become a desert which can be used for grazing only. The exceptions are oases such as that of *En Gedi* on the Dead Sea and *Jericho*. The oases are below sea level and have a hot climate so that many different varieties of plant can flourish.

Kefar Nahum
see Capernaum

Lakhish

District: South.
(i) **Government Tourist Office,**
Merkas Mis'hari (shopping center),
Afridar,
Ashqelon;
tel. (0 51) 2 74 12.

The Moshav Lakhish, 6 miles/10 km SE of Qiryat Gat, S of the road linking Ashqelon, Bet Guvrin, Bet Shemesh and Jerusalem, was founded in 1955 on the site of ancient Lakhish and was named after it. Together with the settlements of Bet Guvrin (see entry) and Tell Maresha (see entry) a few miles

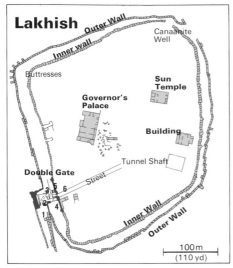

Lakhish

1 Ramp   4 Tower where the Lakhish letters were discovered
2 Outer Gate   5 Ancient Brick Building
3 Culvert   6 Inner Gate

a strong *gateway* with a tower (on the right behind the outer gate) where the Lakhish letters – clay tablets with Ancient Hebrew ink writing – were found. The remains of a **palace**, the governor's residence and, in the SE, of a well tunnel have also been unearthed. In the NE is a **Sun Temple** (*c.* 1480 B.C.), considered by Kathleen Kenyon to be the temple of a Canaanite trinity. Other finds here included a three-pronged iron fork and a vessel for sacrificial flesh (9th C. B.C.), evidence that the Canaanite cult survived even at this late period.

to the NE Lakhish is one of the most interesting archaeological sites in this region W of the Judean hills.

HISTORY. – Already settled in the 3rd millennium, Lakhish was a *Canaanite* town in the 2nd millennium B.C. King Zimridu (1375–1340 B.C.) defended himself against accusations of disloyalty in letters to his overlord, the Egyptian Pharaoh Akhenaton, which have been found in Tell el Amarna. In the 13th C. B.C. Joshua took Jericho, Ai and Gibeon and captured and killed, in the cave of Makkedah, five allied Amorite kings, including Japhia of Lakhish, whose city he conquered, together with neighbouring Mareshah (Joshua 10). The palace was rebuilt by David or Solomon in the 10th C. B.C. About 920 B.C. Solomon's son Rehoboam fortified the town, which covered an area of 89,700 sq. yd/75,000 sq. m (2 Chronicles 11, 11). In the 8th C. B.C. King Amaziah of Judah was slain here after fleeing from Jerusalem (2 Kings 14, 19).

Sennacherib, King of Assyria, took Lakhish in 701 B.C. (2 Kings 18, 13–17) and depicted this event in reliefs in his palace in Nineveh. During Starkey's excavations here a pit was found containing 1,500 skeletons of people who perished at that time. The Babylonian King Nebuchadnezzar then conquered the city in 588 B.C. (two years before Jerusalem). The period immediately before this catastrophe is documented in the 21 "Lakhish letters" (now in the British Museum in London, and the Rockefeller Museum, Jerusalem). Settled again after the return from the Babylonian captivity, Lakhish became the site of a Persian fortress. In the 2nd C.B.C. it dwindled away to a small village.

The old city, Tell Lakhish, has been excavated by John L. Starkey (1932–36) and Yohanan Aharoni (1967–68). Starkey found nine layers of settlement from the 3rd millennium to the 3rd C. B.C.

SIGHTS. – The remains of a **city wall**, consisting of an outer and an inner wall, have been exposed. This double wall has

Latrun

West Bank.
ⓘ **Government Tourist Office,**
24 King George Street,
Jerusalem;
tel. (02) 24 12 81.

The monastery of Latrun was built in 1927 by French Trappists on the E side of the Ayalon Valley. With its broad façade visible from a long way off, it is situated between the old road and the new Tel Aviv–Jerusalem highway shortly before the two roads merge (17 miles/28 km W of Jerusalem on the Israeli-occupied West Bank).

SIGHTS. – In the *monastery garden* is a collection of late-Classical and early Christian capitals and reliefs, and in the **monastery** itself the *church* is open to visitors. The wine made by the monks of Latrun is well-known (sales behind the entrance on the right).

On the hill behind the monastery (view!) are the ruins of the *Crusader castle of Toron des Chevaliers* (12th C.), hence the Arab name of El Torun/Latrun which led

Monastery of Latrun

Christian pilgrims in the late Middle Ages to believe that this was the home of the good thief who was crucified with Jesus (Latin latro=thief).

On a hill in front of the monastery is a ruined police fort dating from the time of the British Mandate. In 1948 the British gave the building to the Arab Legion who blocked off the road to Jerusalem. It was not opened again until 1967.

SURROUNDINGS. – ½ mile/1 km N, near the high-way, are the ruins of the Arab village of *Amwas*, a name derived from *Emmaus*. This was the Greek name for several places in Palestine. The Emmaus where the risen Christ appeared to two men (Luke 24, 13) lay 60 furlongs (=7 miles/11·5 km) from Jerusalem which would make it near present-day Qubeiba (see Ramallah), NW of Jerusalem. Another tradition has it that it lay 160 furlongs (=19 miles/30 km) from Jerusalem which would locate it at Anwas. Buildings here included a Roman villa with mosaic pavements (2nd c.), a synagogue with inscriptions in Greek and Hebrew (3rd c.) and two Byzantine churches dating from the 4th and 6th c. A Crusader church was destroyed by Ibrahim Pasha in 1834.

Lod (Lydda)

District: Central.
Population: 38,000.
Telephone code: 0 54.
(i) **Government Tourist Office,**
7 Mendele Street,
Tel Aviv;
tel. (03) 22 32 66/7.

Lod (Lydda), 14 miles/22 km SE of Tel Aviv and 2 miles/3 km NE of Ramla is nowadays known for its international airport, but its history and myths reach far back into the past.

HISTORY. – The town was founded in the period when the country was taken over by the Israelites from the tribe of Benjamin (1 Chronicles 8, 12), destroyed in the 8th c. B.C. by the Assyrians, rebuilt in the 5th c. B.C. and settled from the 4th c. B.C. onwards by *Greeks* who called it *Lydda*. In 143 B.C. it was conquered by the Hashmoneans (1 Macchabees 11, 34). There was already a Christian community at the time of the first Christians. Peter came to these believers and healed a man who had been bedridden for eight years (Acts 9, 32–34) before going on to Joppa (Jaffa, see Tel Aviv–Jaffa) and Caesarea (see entry). The *Romans* took the town during their advance on Jerusalem in 67 and later called it *Diospolis* (city of Zeus), which was the name it was still given on the map of Madaba (6th c.).

After the destruction of Jerusalem in A.D. 70 several Jewish schools were started in the town, but the rabbis left it in the 2nd c. because of its heathen nature. In Constantine's time (4th c.) Lod was predominantly Christian. It gained special importance as the town of St George.

According to tradition George was born here, served as a tribune in the Roman army and suffered martyrdom in 303 under Diocletian. His bones were brought back to his home town of Lod where his tomb has been shown to visitors since the 5th c. The portrayal of the saint as the slayer of the dragon seems to hark back to the more ancient myth of the dragon vanquished by the Greek hero Perseus when he freed Andromeda at nearby Jaffa (Th. F. Meysels) – and it would appear that behind the dragon of the Perseus myth lurks the Philistine god Dagon.

St George, first martyr of the Orthodox Church, also became the Islamic saint of El Chodr who will

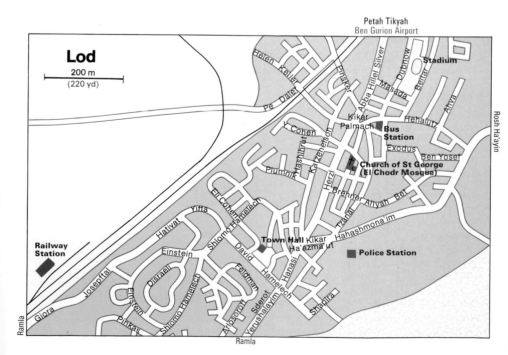

overcome the demon Dadjal before the gates of Lod on Judgement Day.

In the Byzantine period a basilica was built to commemorate this warrior-saint. This was lost when the Omayyad Abd el Malik destroyed Lod but was rebuilt by the *Crusaders* under the English king, Richard the Lion-Heart, and St George subsequently became the patron saint of England.

In the 13th c. the Mamelukes used some of the building material from the church for their El Chodr Mosque which was dedicated to the same George. The place subsequently sank into insignificance. In 1870 the Greek Orthodox Church took over what was left of the old church and incorporated it into a new church.

Most of the Arab inhabitants left the town in 1948 to be replaced by new Jewish immigrants. Today its inhabitants include 4,000 Arab Israelis as well as 34,000 Jews.

During the British Mandate an airport was built a few miles N of Lod. In November 1948, soon after the founding of the State of Israel, it was opened for civil aviation. The Israeli airline El Al was started in the following year and Lod became an international airport which, from 1975, was named after Israel's first prime minister, Ben Gurion.

SIGHTS. – The collapse of the minaret of the El Chodr Mosque in 1927 signalled the building of the white *minaret*, the feature that draws the eye to the Christian-Islamic *double shrine of St George. The two buildings cover the site of the 6th c. Byzantine church of St George and the 12th c. Crusader church which superseded it. Columns and apses from the preceding buildings have been retained in the present complex. The entrances to the church and the mosque are on either side of shops on the W front.

On the left of the shops is the Greek Orthodox **Church of St George**, rebuilt in 1870 with a relief of the saint as slayer of the dragon above the entrance. The church consists of the N sections of the nave and the left aisle of the Crusader church. The church's two apses, which contrary to the general rule face N rather than E, and two columns also date from this period. The paintings impinge upon the feeling of spaciousness. Between the two columns in front of the iconostasis are twin staircases down into the *crypt*. This is where the sarcophagus of the saint is kept. St George is depicted on the cover which, according to the inscription, was restored under the patriarch Kyrillos in 1871.

The S part of the site is taken up by the **El Chodr Mosque**. Past the purification well (left), which forms part of the Islamic cult, is the prayer room. An apse of the

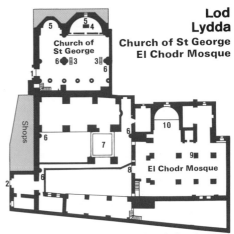

Lod
Lydda
Church of St George
El Chodr Mosque

1 Church Entrance
2 Entrance to the Mosque
3 Stairs to the Crypt
4 Altar
5 Crusader Apse
6 Pillars from the Crusader Church
7 Purification Well
8 Door to the Mosque
9 Column with Inscription
10 Byzantine Apse

Byzantine church is incorporated into the N section, and a column with an inscription of dedication in Greek also comes from the Byzantine church.

SURROUNDINGS. – 2 miles/3 km to the S is the town of *Ramla* (see entry) with Islamic and Christian monuments.

On the road N from Lod is a stone *bridge with pointed arches*; between two lions, which make the bridge very similar to the Lion or St Stephen's Gate in Jerusalem, is an inscription in Arabic which says that the Mameluke sultan Daibars had the bridge built in 1273.

Further N on this road, past *Ben Gurion Airport* and 6 miles/9 km from Lod, is a side road off to the E. Another 3 miles/5 km further on is a left turn to Rosh Ha'ayin, and 2½ miles/4 km further is the *Tomb of Mazor* named after the village of Mazor which is a short distance to the W. This Roman (or Nabataean) sepulchral temple was built of freestone blocks in the 2nd–3rd c. in the middle of an older necropolis. On the entrance side two Corinthian columns between powerful buttresses support the entablature. A staircase leads up to the roof. – From here it is another 3 miles/5 km to *Rosh Ha'ayin* (see entry) with its ancient and medieval monuments.

Lydda
see Lod

Maccabean Tombs
see under Modiim

Maktesh Hagadol

District: South.
(i) **Government Tourist Office,**
Bet Tnuat Hamoschavim,
Beersheba;
tel. (0 57) 3 60 01.

**Maktesh Hagadol ("Large Mortar")
is the middle one of the three depressions in the Negev caused by
erosion. Smaller than the Maktesh
Ramon, it is situated, like the Small
Mortar (Maktesh Haqatan), N of the
Zin Desert.**

The NW edge of the Mortar is 4 miles/7
km SE of the new town of **Yeroham** (20
miles/32 km SE of Beersheba) which was
founded in 1951 and now has 6,300
inhabitants. Many of its people work in
the *Oron* phosphate works which are
about 3 miles/5 km SW of the gorge on
the SE edge. A road runs N from the gorge
and after 7 miles/12 km, near Mount
Rotem, not far from the ruins of *Mampsis*
(see entry), joins the road from Beersheba
to the Dead Sea via Dimona.

In a Landrover it is also possible to leave
the Oron–Rotem road 2 miles/3 km
beyond the exit from the Hagadol Mortar
and to take a narrow road off to the right
leading SE to the *Hazeva* kibbutz in the
Arava valley (20 miles/32 km).

After the first 6 miles/10 km we are in the
region of the **Small Mortar** (*Maktesh
Haqatan*, left) which can be reached on
foot in half an hour. There is a gorge on the
SE side leading to the Zin Desert. 2½ miles/
4 km further on is the *Scorpion Staircase*
(Ma'ale Aqrabim). Moses was told that it
would be the southern border of the area
settled by the Jews: "And your border
shall turn from the south to the ascent of
Akrabbim, and pass on to Zin: and the
going forth thereof shall be from the south
to Kadesh-barnea" (Numbers 34, 4). The
"staircase", reconstructed by the British,
leads down steeply 1,477 ft/450 m into
the *Zin Desert* and then across to *Hazeva*
which is 450 ft/137 m below sea level.
The Eilat–Dead Sea road passes through
here.

Maktesh Ramon

District: South.
(i) **Government Tourist Office,**
Bet Tnuat Hamoschavim,
Beersheba;
tel. (0 57) 3 60 01.

YOUTH HOSTEL in Mizpe Ramon.

**Three elliptical depressions
("craters" or "mortars") are among
the characteristic landscape features of the Negev. The largest,
Maktesh Ramon, measures 19 by 5
miles/30 by 8 km and lies between
the Zin Desert and the Paran Wadi,
53 miles/86 km S of Beersheba.**

The route from Beersheba arrives at the
small town of *Mizpe Ramon* (Ramon
lookout point) which was founded in
1953. There is an impressive view SW into
the Mortar which, at its deepest, is 1,640
ft/500 m below. Enormous fossils have
been found here, remains of saurians 150
million years old. On the W rim towers the
Har Ramon (3,397 ft/1,035 m) with the
Har Ored (3,069 ft/935 m) in the S. In the
E are the remains of forts, including *Mezad
Mishhor*, built by the Nabataeans in the
1st centuries B.C. and A.D. to protect the
caravan route from their capital of Petra to
Avdat (see entry) and through Shubeita
(see Shivta) to Nizzana.

The road winds down the Ma'ale
Ha'azmaut (Independence Staircase) to
the gigantic Mortar 1,640 ft/500 m below,
crosses the desert and climbs out up the
smaller SE slope in the direction of Eilat.

Mamshit (Mampsis)

District: South.
(i) **Government Tourist Office,**
Bet Tnuat Hamoschavim,
Beersheba;
tel. (0 57) 3 60 01.

**The remarkable ruins of *Mampsis
(Mamshit in Hebrew, Kurnub in
Arabic), the most northerly town of
the Nabataeans in the Negev, are on
a hill 26 miles/42 km SE of Beersheba
and 4 miles/6 km SE of Dimona and
can be seen from a long way off.**

Mamshit – general view

HISTORY. – During his excavations (1966 onwards) Abraham Negev uncovered a settlement with a Nabataean lay out that had been so little altered in the Byzantine period that its original features are more clearly apparent than is the case at Avdat (see entry), Nizzana or Subeita (see Shivta).

The town was founded during the period when the Nabataeans were colonising the Negev from their capital Petra. Mampsis flourished in the 1st c. B.C. as a trading town with a caravanserai, stabling, houses and administrative buildings. After the fall of Nabatene in 106 the Romans built barracks here. During the Byzantine period, when Mampsis appeared on the map of Madaba, the Nabataean system of irrigation was extended, as at Avdat; two churches were also built. The onslaught by the Islamic Arabs also brought about the downfall of Mampsis.

SIGHTS. – The entrance to the town is through the *North Gate* in the town wall and the route continues between blocks of housing along ancient streets to two large neighbouring *administrative buildings*. Here there can still be seen, as in many of the houses, the ends of the stone arches which supported the ceilings. There is little decoration. A climb to the top of one of the buildings, which still has its stone arches, affords a fine view over the whole town. Further on in the same direction is the **West Church** against the town wall, a basilica divided by columns into a nave and two aisles, built by St Nilus of Sinai (*c.* 400) who is mentioned in an inscription in the mosaic floor of the nave: "Lord, help your servant Nilus who built this church. Amen." As well as this mosaic and the columns, the church has also retained its E apse and parts of the marble parclose that separated the chancel from the congregation.

Further E, directly in front of the remains of a police station dating from the time of the British Mandate, is the **East Church**, dedicated to the holy martyrs. Broad steps lead up to it from a square which was used as the market place from Nabataean until Byzantine times. This is also a basilica separated by columns into a nave and two side-aisles. There is a large cistern in the atrium. The nave of the church still has its mosaic pavement and there is a martyr's tomb in the right-hand side apse.

Elsewhere in the town there are informative signs indicating interesting buildings such as the large stables, a portico with Nabataean horn-shaped capitals and a building with very well-preserved wall-paintings.

Before leaving Mampsis one should turn W again to look at the **dams** far below in the wadi. Recently restored, they show how the Nabataeans and Byzantines stored the water which fell in the short

Original wooden threshold in the administrative building

West Church in Mampsis

Steps up to the East Church in Mampsis

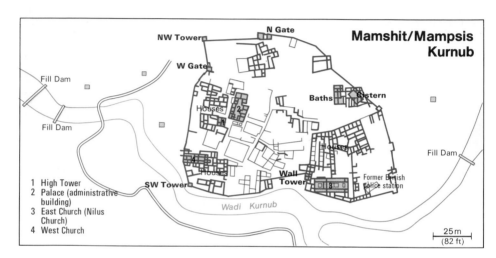

Mamshit/Mampsis Kurnub

NW Tower

N Gate

W Gate

Fill Dam

Fill Dam

Houses 2

Baths

Cistern

Fill Dam

Houses

Houses

4

SW Tower

Wall Tower

Former British police station

Wadi Kurnub

1 High Tower
2 Palace (administrative building)
3 East Church (Nilus Church)
4 West Church

25 m
(82 ft)

rainy season for use during the dry summer months.

The route back to the car park through the entrance to the excavations passes a sign on the right pointing to a *cemetery* NE of the town where many burial chambers have been unearthed.

Mareshah

District: South.

(i) **Government Tourist Office,**
Merkas Mis'hari (shopping center),
Afridar,
Ashqelon;
tel. (0 51) 2 74 12.

The ancient town of *Mareshah, with its impressive caves and excavations, is in Judea, on the Ashqelon–Qiryat Gate–Bet Shemesh–Jerusalem road, 10 miles/ 16 km E of Qiryat Gat and 1 mile/2 km S of Bet Guvrin. The Arabs called the hill on which the settlement is situated "Tell Sandahanna" after a church dedicated to St Anne.**

HISTORY. – According to the Book of Joshua (Joshua 15, 44) Mareshah belonged to the tribe of Judah. The town is an irregular quadrilateral of some 525 by 492 ft/160 by 150 m; its area of 28,704 sq. yd/ 24,000 sq. m was only a third of that of neighbouring Lakhish (see entry). Solomon's son Rehoboam, King of Judah, fortified Mareshah about 920 B.C. together with Lakhish and 14 other places – "which are in Judah and in Benjamin fenced cities" (2 Chronicles 8–10). Destroyed by Babylonians in 587 B.C., the town was not resettled by Jews after the Babylonian exile. As elsewhere in southern Judea and the Negev this area was settled by the Edomites who made Mareshah their capital. In the 4th c. B.C. the Phoenicians founded a colony here which ran counter to their usual practice of establishing coastal colonies. In the 3rd c. the town was Hellenised under the name of *Marissa* and was the capital of the province of Idumea. About 160 B.C. Judas Maccabeus took it on his march from Hebron to Asdod (1 Maccabees 5, 66); under the Hashmonean ruler, John Hyrkanos I, about 115 B.C. the town, together with the rest of Idumea, was forcibly Judaised. It was finally destroyed in 40 B.C.

It was identified as the Mareshah of the Bible in 1838 by the American E. Robinson, and the Palestine Exploration Fund carried out excavations in 1900.

SIGHTS. – On the W slope of the Tell is a 2nd c. B.C. **burial cave**, 105 ft/32 m long and 7½ ft/2·3 m wide. The walls contain no fewer than 1,906 urn recesses which is why the cave, like similar Roman cemeteries, is known as the "columbarium" (dove-cot). In the valley E of the Tell two 2nd c. *burial chambers* have been discovered, one of which is painted and has urns and eagles on the front. The interior is similar to tombs in Palmyra in that its ground plan is in the shape of an upside-down T. It contains 44 burial recesses with inscriptions in Greek. From the inscription of a girl to her boyfriend it is assumed that the burial cave was a meeting place for lovers.

A special feature of Mareshah are the many *caves, of which there are about 60. It is advisable to take a local guide when visiting this labyrinth. The caves are bell-shaped, a "weird subterranean chalk town" with "enormous cathedral-like caverns" (Hans Kühner) where light filters in through holes in the roofs. Mystery shrouds their significance and their reason for existence. It is assumed that the Phoenicians settled in Mareshah in the 4th c. B.C. because they found building materials here for the port of Askalon and that they forced their way into the depths through holes in the hard surface of the rock and then exploited the underground quarries.

Crosses scratched into the rock lead one to suppose that these caves were inhabited in the Christian period. The Church of St Anne, E of the Mareshah–Bet Guvrin road, dates from the later Christian period; it was built by Crusaders in the 12th c. (the central apse is well preserved).

Mar Saba/ Monastery of St Sabas

West Bank.

(i) Government Tourist Office,
Manger Square,
Bethlehem;
tel. (02) 94 25 91.

The Greek Orthodox * Monastery of St Sabas (Mar Saba), steeped in tradition and only 11 miles/18 km from Bethlehem, lies in the heart of the Judean mountains which over-look the Dead Sea, on the Israeli-occupied West Bank.

This region is inhabited by Bedouin of the tribe of Ubeidiya. Ubeidiya or Ibn Abeid means "son of the servant"; these Bedouin are said to be the descendants of the guards and servants who came here from Byzantium to protect the Monastery of Theodosius and the Monastery of Sabas.

HISTORY. – In the almost vertical rock walls of the Kidron gorge W of the Monastery of Sabas there are many caves which were inhabited by hermits in the early centuries of Christianity. Sabas, who, like the founder of the Monastery of Theodosius, was born in Cappadocia (439), decided as a young man to become one of these troglodytes. After entering a monastery in Jerusalem in 457, he opted in 478 for the solitude of the Kidron Valley. A community of anchorites grew up here, and in 492 Sabas founded the monastery named after him on the slope of the gorge opposite his first cave. Sabas was highly

regarded not only in Palestine but also in Constantinople, the capital of the empire. At the ripe old age of 90 he made the journey to visit Emperor Justinian and induced him to rebuild the Church of the Holy Nativity in Bethlehem (see entry). When he died in 532 at the age of 92 his tomb became a place of pilgrimage. His monastery was the source of many filial foundations.

Persians (614) and Arabs (636) destroyed the monastery and killed the monks. The monastery lived on, however, and in 712 it was to receive within its walls a man whose impact on the world of Orthodox Christianity equalled that of its founder, Sabas. That man was John of Damascus.

Born about 650, the son of a noble Christian Arab family, John attained high honour at the magnificent court of the Omayyads in Damascus and was the representative of the Christian subjects of the Caliph. At the age of 60, though, he decided he preferred "the mortification of Christ to the treasures of Arabia", left Damascus and became a monk in Mar Saba. When in 726 a decree of the emperor Leo II unleashed the violent iconoclasm which, at the cost of countless icons, was to rage on until 843, John of Damascus became the best-known advocate of the veneration of holy pictures which he substantiated on theological grounds in three famous speeches against the iconoclasts. It was here also that he composed his writings against Islam and against deviations from Christian orthodoxy (Nestorians and Monophysites). His main theological work, the "Source of Know-ledge", was also written in this monastery. When John of Damascus died about 750 at the truly venerable age of 104, according to tradition, he was held to be the greatest theologian of his time.

The two most important men in the history of the monastery, Sabas and John, were not to remain undisturbed even in death. The Crusaders carried the bones of St Sabas to Venice in the 12th c. and when the Russians rebuilt the monastery in 1838, after it had been destroyed in the early 19th c., they took the mortal remains of John of Damascus back to Moscow. – In the course of his policy of reconciliation between Rome and the Orthodox Church, Pope Paul VI returned the relics of St Sabas to the monastery in 1965.

A narrow but well-surfaced road leads NE from Bethlehem and Bet Sahur and after 7 miles/12 km reaches the walled square of the Monastery of Theodosius. Founded in 476 by St Theodosius of Cappadocia (Asia Minor), it housed in its heyday as many as 400 monks. In 614 the Persians, attacking Byzantium, destroyed this monastery as well as Mar Saba and the Monastery of St George in the Wadi Qilt, but they spared the Church of the Holy Nativity in Bethlehem. About 1900 it was rebuilt by Greek Orthodox monks.

The road crosses the Kidron Valley N to Abu Dis and enters Jerusalem near the Mount of Olives. Just beyond the Monas-tery of Theodosius (7 miles/12 km from Bethlehem) a road branches off right to the *Monastery of Mar Saba (4 miles/ 6 km) the watch-tower of which can be seen from far off amid the barren mountains of Judea. The road finally drops down right to the monastery gate.

SIGHTS. – Only men may enter the monastery of Mar Saba. Women may climb a hill on the right to a *tower*. Women visitors used to be put up here, and one stay here on June 7, 1842 is vividly described by Ida Pfeiffer in her book "Journey of a Viennese Lady to the Holy Land". From this tower, which contains a chapel and a dormitory, there is a good view of the monastery with its domes, courtyards and buildings ranged one above the other on the slope of the mountain.

Men visitors enter the **monastery** through a small portal and descend on a narrow stepped path into a courtyard. In the middle is the small domed building which housed the body of the founder of the monastery, Sabas, from 532 until the Crusades. After he was returned in 1965 he was laid to rest in the **main church** (catholicon). One of the resident Greek monks acts as a guide to the labyrinthine monastery, including this richly-painted cruciform domed church and its icons, and will also show visitors the relatively well-preserved remains of the saint. Visitors are also taken into a *chapel*, built on to the cave of St Sabas, where, as in the Monastery of St George in the Wadi Qilt (see entry), the skulls are stored of the monks murdered by the Persians in 614. These victims of a long-past war, and even more Sabas, the "Star of the Desert", his life, his abduction to Venice and his return, are very much things of the present for the monks. Finally visitors can look down from a balcony to the dry bed (in summer), 590 ft/180 m below, of the *Kidron Valley*. "The most delightful rock terraces," wrote Ida Pfeiffer in 1842, "shaped so beautifully and evenly by Nature that one is astounded at first sight of them, hem one in on each side like galleries."

Massada/Masada/ Mezada

District: South.
Population: 300.
ⓘ **Government Tourist Office,**
Bet Tnuat Hamoschavim,
Beersheba;
tel. (0 57) 3 60 01.

The massive rocky outcrop of ****Massada (Masada, Mezada), rising to 1,424 ft/434 m above the level of the Dead Sea, was an ideal site for the Jewish rulers to build a fortress. Yet Massada was a place of historical importance for a mere 100 years: as an impregnable refuge for King Herod the Great and as the place where the Zealots managed to**

Massada
Masada
Mezada

N palace

W palace

100 m
(110 yd)

1 East Gate (Snake Path Gate)
2 Casemate Wall
3 Buildings
4 Quarry
5 Storehouse
6 Storehouse
7 Upper Terrace of North Palace
8 Middle Terrace of North Palace
9 Lower Terrace of North Palace
10 Baths
11 Administrative Buildings
12 North Gate (Water Gate)
13 Tower
14 Synagogue
15 Casemate Wall
16 Tower
17 Byzantine Building
18 Church dating from when Byzantine monks lived here (5th c)
19 West Gate
20 Tower
21 Administrative Section of North Palace
22 Storerooms in West Palace
23 Royal Apartments in West Palace
24 Small Palace
25 Ritual Bath
26 Small Palace
27 Cistern
28 South Bastion
29 Underground Cistern
30 South Gate (cistern gate)
31 Ritual Bath
32 Columbarium
33 Small Palace
34 Byzantine Living Quarters
35 Zealots' Living Quarters
36 Cistern
37 Byzantine House
38 Tower
39 Zealots' Living Quarters

hold out against the Romans for three years after the fall of Jerusalem, i.e. until A.D. 73.

HISTORY. – The Jewish historian Flavius Josephus ascribes the first constructions on this hill to the high priest Jonathan. However, this was certainly not the brother of Judas Maccabeus but his great-nephew,

Massada – Roman ramp

Massada – seen from the E

Alexander Jannaois (103–76 B.C.), who was also known as Jonathan. Herod enlarged what was originally a small fort into a complex where royal magnificence combined with strong fortification to make Massada to all intents and purposes a fortress and a stronghold (metsuda).

During the unrest in 40 B.C., when the Parthians chose the Hashmonean Antigonos as their leader, Herod brought his family here for safety, together with his betrothed, Mariamne. He did the same in 31 B.C. when, after Antony and Cleopatra had been defeated by Octavian at Actium, he had to travel to Rhodes to swear allegiance to the new ruler of Rome; this time, however, his family at Massada did not include Mariamne and her mother Alexandra who were conducted separately to the fort of Alexandreia in Samaria.

Between 37 and 31 Herod had turned Massada into a massive fortress. A 1,422 yd/1,300 m long casemate wall, reinforced by 38 towers each 33 ft/10 m high, enclosed the 219 by 656 yd/200 by 600 m plateau at the summit with its palaces, administrative buildings, storehouses, barracks and cisterns. Herod had had twelve such cisterns built, each holding 5,232 cu. yd/ 4,000 cu. m; these and the stores of food were to keep the castle supplied even during a long siege.

Mosaic in Massada

This occurred a few decades later when the Jews rose up against Rome. In A.D. 66, before the beginning of the uprising, a group of Zealots, led by Menachem ben Judah, settled in Massada. They were members of the radical party who had left Jerusalem as a result of the internecine conflicts among the Jews. These quarrels soon led to Menachem being assassinated in Jerusalem. When the uprising finally came it was his nephew, Eleazar ben Yair, who assumed command at Massada. The Romans captured the castle of Herodeion (see entry) and the insurgents holding the fort of Machaerus on the East Bank of the Jordan surrendered and were allowed to go free; their garrison joined those living at Massada to make a final total of 967 men, women and children. They still refused to surrender after the fall of Jerusalem A.D. 70), so the Romans decided in A.D. 72 to break this last stand by a siege. Their commander Flavius Silvus surrounded Massada with a 4,923 yd/4,500 m long wall and set up eight camps on the other side, including his main camp, laid out on rhombic lines, on the W side. From here a ramp was built so that battering rams and other siege engines could be brought up to the wall. After eight months the Romans broke through the W wall and set fire to the Zealots' wooden defences. In this hopeless position Eleazar called on his comrades-in-arms in a speech reported by Flavius Josephus ("History of the Jewish War", VII, 8, 6–8) "to die rather than submit to slavery". They burnt all their possessions except their stocks of food (there since Herod's time) to show the Romans that they "voluntarily chose to die". Then, since the Jewish law forbids suicide, ten men were chosen by lot to put the rest to the sword, then one of the ten was chosen to end the lives of his nine companions before impaling himself on his sword. When the Romans began their attack the next morning they stumbled upon 960 bodies.

Two women who had crawled away into a water pipe with five children told them what had happened. "However, when they discovered the numbers of the slain they did not rejoice at the enemy's downfall but admired the noble decision and the unwavering defiance of death of so many people." (VII, 9, 2.) Because of this ultimately irrational heroism Massada has come to symbolise, for the Israel of today, Jewish assertion of will even in a hopeless situation. The oath of allegiance sworn by Israeli recruits on this spot is "Massada must not fall again".

Since Robinson identified the site in 1838 it has been investigated by the Americans, English and Germans

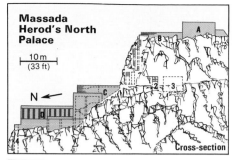

Massada
Herod's North
Palace

10 m
(33 ft)

N ←

Cross-section

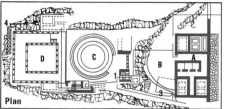

Plan

A Living Quarters
B Semicircular Terrace
C Middle Terrace
D Bottom Terrace, Peristyle

1 Spiral Staircases
2 Bathing Pool
3 Palace Cistern
4 Supporting Wall

but it has been the work of Yigael Yadin and Shemaria Gutmann in particular that has made Massada the important excavation site that it is today.

SIGHTS. – There are two ways into Massada. The road from Arad (12 miles/19 km) leads to the foot of the Roman ramp and it is then possible to climb 110 yd/100 m up to the West Gate. The approach from the Dead Sea is, however, much more impressive. The climb up the old snake path (2 miles/3 km) which was reinstated in 1954 starts near the kibbutz (restaurant, refreshments, car park), 2

Terraces of the North Palace

miles/3 km from the shore, or visitors can cover the 438 yd/400 m by taking the cable-cars which take them as far as the East Gate.

The path from the *East Gate* goes off to the right past a watch-tower and then leads to several buildings, followed by the large magazines and the narrow storerooms with their dividing walls that have been partially rebuilt in the wake of an earthquake. The most monumental building is on the summit of the rock. This is Herod's *North Palace, an extraordinarily bold three-storey construction. The top section with its living quarters ends in a semicircle from which one looks down on to the two lower terraces. They can be reached from the W side by a modern staircase. Water reservoirs can be seen in the rock on the way down. The middle terrace (66 ft/20 m below), thought by Yadin to have been the king's summer house, consists of two concentric circular walls. Another 46 ft/14 m lower down is the square bottom terrace, a peristyle (inner courtyard surrounded by columns) with fluted Corinthian columns on a base consisting of a wall covered in coloured plaster.

S of this palace were *baths* and next to them a building thought to have contained Herod's work-rooms; during their stay here from 66 to 73 the Zealots added a *ritual bath* (mikwe). Against the defensive wall W of this building is a *synagogue*, also built by the Zealots. Some scrolls were found here which today are kept in the Israel Museum in Jerusalem.

SE of the synagogue there is a much larger group of buildings and a **church** dating from the time when Byzantine monks had settled here in the 5th c. S of one of the towers is the *West Gate* (opposite the Roman ramp) and the extensive **West Palace**. As can be clearly seen, the Zealots restructured the rooms to provide themselves with accommodation and added another mikwe a little to the SE.

At the S extremity of this huge site are two large open *cisterns* and the *south bastion*. Along the E wall is a third ritual bath (near the S gate), another cistern and Byzantine (left) and Zealot (against the wall) living quarters, and then the E Gate. This path constantly affords magnificent *views of the Dead Sea landscape and the kaleidoscope of colour on the facing mountains.

Megiddo

District: North.
ⓘ **Government Tourist Office,**
18 Herzl Street,
Haifa;
tel. (04) 66 65 21.

*Megiddo, 7 miles/12 km W of Afula
and 20 miles/32 km SE of Haifa, was
an important fortress in ancient
times and, because of its strategic
position, continued to play a military
role right up into the 20th c. In order
to circumvent Cape Carmel, the old
road from Egypt to Syria leaves the
coast near Caesarea and turns NE
through the Iron Valley to reach the
Jezreel Plain. Megiddo controlled
this important line of communication where it left the valley to fork W
to Tyre and Sidon and E to Damascus
and Mesopotamia. Thanks to extremely thorough excavation and
the way it has been laid out by the
National Parks Authority, the Tell of
Megiddo is a very informative site
from the historical point of view.

HISTORY. – Excavation of the Tell of Megiddo began
in 1903–5 with the work of the German Palestine
Society, when Schumacher dug the deep wide ditch
named after him on the E side. In 1925–39 the Chicago
Oriental Institute carried out systematic investigations

and in 1960 Yigael Yadin began the work that settled
the question of the chronological order which can be
█████████ ███ ██ ████████ █████ ██ ██ ██████ ████
beginnings a Canaanite settlement grew up in the 4th
millennium B.C. and lasted until the Israelite invasion.
A chalcolithic shrine dates from this era as well as
another one nearby with a large round altar. After the
battle of 1479 when Tutmosis III took the pass on his
advance to the Euphrates, the town came under
Egyptian influence. Letters from the Egyptian
governor Biridja requesting military reinforcements
against the Chabiru (=Hebrews?) have been found in
the Amarna archives (14th c. B.C.). In the 13th c. B.C.,
after his triumph over the king of Hazor, Joshua also
defeated the king of Megiddo (Joshua 12, 21), but the
Israelites' hold on his capital was shortlived, for in the
12th c. the Philistines, advancing inland from the
coast, took Megiddo and the whole of the Jezreel
Plain as far as Bet Shean.

A new development began about 1000 B.C. when
David defeated the Philistines. In the 10th c. Solomon
made Megiddo the capital of his fifth administrative
area which, under the governorship of Baana, son of
Ahilud, extended as far as Bet Shean (1 Kings 4, 12).
From this period Yadin has unearthed E of the main
gate a North Palace for ceremonial occasions,
probably the royal residence, and next to it a casemate
wall typical of those built by Solomon and like those
also found in Hazor (see entry) and Gezer (see Ramla,
Surroundings), as well as a formidable gateway. In the
S section was the palace of the governor Baana and
another administrative building. "We are no longer
looking at a simple fort but a metropolis with imposing
buildings for ceremonial purposes." (Yadin.) Solomon's town was destroyed in 923 B.C. by Pharaoh
Sheshonk, the Sisak of the Bible, which meant that in
the 9th c. B.C. King Ahab had to undertake its
reconstruction. Solomon's North and South Palaces
were built over with Ahab's stables for 450 horses (for

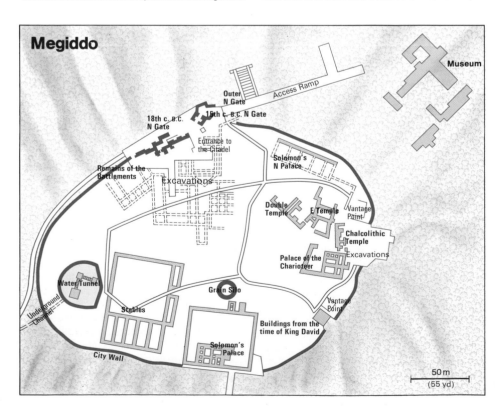

Megiddo – Canaanite shrine

a long time wrongly called "Solomon's Stables"). Ahab, for whom Megiddo must have been particularly important because of its position on the road to the Phoenician homeland of his wife, also rebuilt Solomon's gateway, erected a strong new protective wall and laid the large water tunnel. This was to be Megiddo's heyday which came to an end in 733 B.C. with its capture by the Assyrians under Tiglatpilesar III. In 609 B.C. Megiddo was the place where King Josiah of Judah fell in the battle against another foe, the Pharaoh Necho. Megiddo was abandoned during the Persian period (after 538 B.C.), but when the Romans ruled, their 6th Legion had a camp 1 mile/2 km S of the Tell – hence the name "Lajun" for the Arab village (now the kibbutz of Megiddo).

More recently Napoleon (in 1799) and General Allenby (in 1917) won victories over Turkish armies near Megiddo; in 1948 it was here that the Israelis halted the Arab push toward Haifa.

SIGHTS. Near the car park is a building which, besides a refreshment stall, also houses the *museum* which, with its charts and a large model of ancient Megiddo, serves as an introduction to the Tell. A footpath leads from here to the entrance in the N SECTION OF THE TELL. Passing a 15th c. B.C. doorway (right) the visitor arrives at *Solomon's Gate* on a bend in the path.

Here the three chambers on each side of the gateway are clearly visible. The site adjoining it to the S contains extensive remains of buildings in which some 13th c. B.C. ivory carvings have been discovered. The path turns left (E) and leads past the ruined stables or chariot-sheds that Ahab built over Solomon's North Palace (left), to a vantage point which affords a view to the N over the fertile Jezreel Plain to the Galilean hills around Nazareth. The other side of the platform

looks down into the "Schumacher ditch" where a *Canaanite Shrine* has been laid bare. Especially noticeable is a large round altar ("High Place") which dates from an earlier period but was renewed about 1900 B.C. when the neighbouring **East Temple** (level XV) was built. As is usual in Semitic temples this East Temple consists of porch, main chamber and the holy of holies. The rear wall of the holy of holies backs on to the area of the round altar. Side steps lead to a rectangular altar built against the inside of the wall. More buildings of worship adjoin it on the W at an angle, presumably a double temple for a pair of gods. On the valley side are the traces of the wall of an older temple dating from the Chalcolithic Age, the 4th millennium B.C. (level XIX).

Retracing one's steps and then turning left one comes to the S section of the Tell. This is where the large round *grain silo* dating from the reign of King Jereboam II (8th c. B.C.) is sunk into the ground. Inside are two sets of steps so that people could go up one side and down the other at the same time. Behind are two large groups of buildings built by Ahab over Solomon's palace buildings. On the right is a yard with the famous **stables** where the stalls, feeding troughs and pillars with holes bored in them for tethering the animals can still be seen. Megiddo had room for 450 horses, their chariots and charioteers.

The path now leads down to the huge **water tunnel** which guaranteed the water supply. Previously dated as 13th c.

(Canaanite) or 11th c. (Philistine) B.C., Yadin's investigations have conclusively put it at the time of the Israelites, i.e. 9th c. B.C. (Ahab). The source of Megiddo's water is a cave spring outside the confines of the fortress. During Solomon's reign a "gallery" 6 ft/2 m high and about 3 ft/1 m broad was cut that led outside the city to the SW slope of the Tell and hence to the spring. Ahab, who was also responsible for Hazor's water system, decided to construct a system which would connect the inner precincts of the fortress to the spring and which would be inaccessible to the enemy in the event of a siege. To achieve this he first drove a vertical 197 ft/ 60 m shaft through the layers of earlier settlements and the living rock and then had a horizontal 394 ft/120 m channel cut through the rock to reach the spring, thus sealing off previous access to it from outside.

To give the visitor an impression of one of the greatest feats of engineering of ancient times, steps and walkways have been built to enable him to negotiate this monumental system and emerge through the cave entrance that had been blocked up since Ahab's time.

Meron

District: North.
Population: 300.
(i) Government Tourist Office,
Safed;
tel. (0 67) 3 06 33.

The village of Meron in Upper Galilee, founded in 1949 N of the ancient Meron, is 6 miles/9 km W of Safed where the road forks to Nahariyya in one direction and Acre in the other on the E slope of Mount Meron which, at 3,965 ft/1,208 m, is the highest point in Galilee.

HISTORY. – Joshua was victorious over several kings here (Joshua 11, 7). Rabbi Simon Bar Jochai, one of the leaders of the last Jewish revolt in the 2nd c., hid from the Romans for a long time with his son Eleazar in a cave which is said to be near Peki'in in the valley of the same name on the W slope of Mount Meron.

The *tombs* of Simon Bar Jochai and Eleazar are still in Meron and their domes can be seen from a great way off. The name of Simon, to whom Jewish tradition ascribes the cabbalistic book "Zohar" (brightness), which, however, did not appear until 1270 in Spain, is also connected with the imposing ruined synagogue that can be seen on a hill. The Rashbi Hilula, a celebration in song and dance in honour of Simon, is held in Meron every May.

There are other tombs not far from Simon's mausoleum, including the rock tomb of Rabbi Hillel and his pupils, while on the other side of the valley there is the tomb ascribed to Rabbi Shammai. Both men founded Mishnah schools in the 1st c. Hillel represented liberal doctrines and Shammai taught along strictly orthodox lines.

The road to **Mount Meron** (*Hare Meron*) leaves the village of Meron in a N direction and then turns W to *Sassa* (6 miles/9 km) and 2 miles/3 km later turns left. The area around the summit is a **nature reserve**.

Mezada

see Massada

Modiim

District: Central.
(i) Government Tourist Office,
7 Mendele Street,
Tel Aviv;
tel: (03) 22 36 66/7.

Modiim, the home of the Maccabeans, is 7 miles/12 km E of Lod and SW of the Arab village of Midya in an area near the Herzl Forest accessible only by side roads.

HISTORY. – In 167 B.C. royal envoys came to Modiim to carry out the Hellenisation policy of Antiochos IV Epiphanes who at that time ruled Syria. When they demanded heathen sacrifices the priest Mattathias refused to comply. When another Jew expressed his willingness to carry out these sacrifices Mattathias and his five sons slew him and the envoys and fled into the mountains. That was the beginning of the Macchabean revolt which, under the leadership of Mattathias' five sons, particularly Judas Maccabaeus, led to the founding of the Macchabean or Hashmonean state which lasted until its destruction by Herod I in 37 B.C. (1 Macchabees 2, 15–30).

The "high monument visible from afar" that the high priest Simon, the last of the five sons, had erected over the tomb of his father and his brothers (1 Macchabees 13,

27) no longer exists, but the *rock tombs* of Judas Maccabaeus and his brothers with their huge tombstones survive. It is at these tombs that every year on the first night of the festival of Chanukkah, which commemorates the purification of the Temple by Judas Maccabaeus, a torch is lit and brought to Jerusalem to be used by the President to light the Chanukkah candles.

Montfort

District: North.
ⓘ Government Tourist Office,
Town Hall,
Weizmann Street,
Acre;
tel. (04) 91 02 51.

The castle of *Montfort, NE of Acre and 9 miles/14 km E of Nahariyya, is the largest ruin in West Galilee.

The ruined fortress of Montfort

HISTORY. – In the 12th c. the French Count Joscelin de Courtenay built this fortress to protect Acre, but it was destroyed by Sultan Saladin in 1187. In 1220 Hermann von Salza, Grand Master of the German Order, obtained the ruin and the suzerainty that went with it; his intention was to turn it into a residence fit for a Grand Master. In 1271 the Knights surrendered to the Mamelukes under Baibars after he had promised them safe conduct and allowed them to take the archives and treasures of the Order away with them. Since then the fortress, known to the Arabs as Qalat Quren, has been abandoned. In 1926 investigations were undertaken by the New York Metropolitan Museum; the items discovered (capitals, a sculpted head) are in the Rockefeller Museum in Jerusalem. Its isolated position has prevented the fortress from being used as a quarry, so there are still plenty of imposing remains.

Montfort can be reached only on foot. There are two paths. One starts 2 miles/3 km from the fortress at the village of *Elon* (on the road E from Rosh Hanikra near the Lebanese border) and descends the 427 ft/130 m to the fortress. The other starts at the Christian Arab village of *Mi'ilya* on the Nahariyya–Safed road. From Mi'ilya it is possible to drive 2 miles/3 km to the N to a car park and then walk for half an hour down a stony path and finally through a wood (820 ft/250 m descent). The **fortress** can then be seen on a high spur of rock above the deep cleft of the Quren wadi. The entrance is on the SE side of the castle ruins which ascend the hill from W to E. From the *tower* there is an impressive *view of the wooded landscape crossed

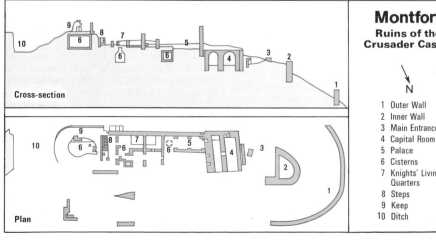

Montfort
Ruins of the
Crusader Castle

Cross-section

Plan

N

1 Outer Wall
2 Inner Wall
3 Main Entrance
4 Capital Room
5 Palace
6 Cisterns
7 Knights' Living
   Quarters
8 Steps
9 Keep
10 Ditch

by the rushing stream of the Quren. In the
bed of the stream there are the remains of
a dam and on one bank stand the ruins of
one of the Knights' mills.

Mount of the Beatitudes

Northern District.
(i) **Government Tourist Office,**
8 Elhadef Street,
Tiberias;
tel. (0 67) 2 09 92.

ACCOMMODATION. – *Ospizio Monte di Beatitudine*
(Tiberias, PO Box 87).

**On the N shores of the Sea of Galilee,
the *Mount of the Beatitudes, traditionally the place where Christ
delivered the Sermon on the Mount,
rises up above the ruins of Tabgha
and Capernaum.**

View over the Sea of Galilee

The route from the Sea of Galilee to the
Mount of the Beatitudes leaves Tiberias
and goes towards Rosh Pinna, leaving the
main road to the right after passing
through Capernaum. The domed chapel
can be seen in a commanding position on
the right, and a car track leads up to it.

From early times this hill has been seen as
the place where Jesus delivered the
Sermon on the Mount, the basis of his
teaching (Matthew 5–7). Originally there
was a church built lower down to
commemorate this event, immediately N
of the road to Capernaum near Tabgha
(see entry). The new church was built in
1937. It stands in a shady garden with the
Ospizio Monte di Beatitudine next to it.

SIGHTS. – The **Church of the Beatitudes** is constructed of local basalt. For
the arches white stone from Nazareth was
used, and Roman travertine for the pillars.
From the arcaded ambulatory around the
octagonal building there is a magnificent
*view of the Sea of Galilee. The eight sides
of the church are, as the Latin inscriptions
on the inside indicate, each dedicated to
one of the Beatitudes which Jesus pronounced at the beginning of the Sermon
(Matthew 5, 3–10), about the poor in
spirit, they that mourn, the meek, they that
do hunger and thirst after righteousness,
the merciful, the pure in heart, the
peacemakers and they which are perse-

cuted for righteousness' sake. The dome,
however, symbolises the ninth beatitude
(Matthew 5, 11–12), in which Jesus
addressed himself directly to those who
were persecuted for his sake "for great is
your reward in heaven".

Mount Gilboa/ Har Gilboa

Northern District.
Altitude: 1,631 ft/497 m.
(i) **Government Tourist Office,**
Casanova Street,
Nazareth;
tel. (0 65) 7 05 55.

**Gilboa is a mountain ridge that rises
to 1,667 ft/508 m above sea level.
Thus it is 2,061 ft/628 m above the
town of Bet Shean which lies 394 ft/
120 m below sea level. Mount Gilboa
is a spur of the Samarian highlands,
and is bordered by the Jezreel Plain
to the SE.**

HISTORY. – Mount Gilboa witnessed a tragic episode
in Jewish history. When King Saul, after being
abandoned by Samuel, had gathered his army here to
do battle with the Philistines who were encamped
near Shunem, he went to consult the Witch of Endor
(Shunem and En Dor: see Afula, Surroundings). As
the oracle foretold, the Israelites were defeated by the
Philistines. Saul's sons – Jonathan, Abinadab and

Malchishua – all fell in battle. In despair King Saul fell on his sword, and the Philistines hanged his corpse on the walls of Bet Shean (1 Samuel 31, 1–12). In his lament over this disaster (the Song of the Bow), David sang as follows: "Ye mountains of Gilboa, let there be no dew, neither let there be rain upon you . . . for there the shield of the mighty is vilely cast away" (2 Samuel 1, 21).

The present-day Afula–Bet Shean road climbs to the heights in zig-zags. The summit is a military restricted zone and is not open to the public. There are, however, fine views to be enjoyed along the way.

At the foot of Mount Gilboa on the N side, between Bet Shean and Bet Alfa, lies **Gan HaShelosha** *National Park* (restaurant and picnic area) with pools and natural waterfalls. The waterfalls used to provide power to drive a mill. Nowadays there is swimming in the larger pool, upstream from the falls.

There is a second National Park (**Ma'ayan Harod** – "Harod Spring", with a youth hostel and camp site) 6 miles/10 km further NW towards Afula, on the wooded N slopes of the chain of mountains.

The Harod Spring is supposed to be the one at which Gideon, one of the Judges, selected the fighters who defeated the Midianites (Judges 7, 5). Another battle was fought here, in the Middle Ages. It was at the Harod Spring that the Mameluke general Baibars gained a decisive battle against the Mongols who had already advanced as far as Gaza. He subsequently drove them away in to N Syria. After this victory Baibars became Sultan of Egypt and Syria.

Mount Tabor/ Har Tavor

Northern District.
Altitude: 1,938 ft/588 m.
ⓘ **Government Tourist Office,**
Casanova Street,
Nazareth;
tel. (0 67) 6 74 89.

ACCOMMODATION. – *Convento Francescano della Transfigurazione* (tel. (0 65) 3 72 19).

Mount *Tabor rises 1,938 ft/588 m above the Plain of Jezreel 13 miles/ 21 km NE of Afula. Mentioned several times in the Old Testament, it is also supposed to be the site of Christ's Transfiguration.

HISTORY and SCRIPTURE TRADITION. – In the 2nd millennium B.C. there was on Mount Tabor a Canaanite shrine, a High Place as on other mountain tops, such as Mount Carmel (see entry) and Mount Hermon. Here they worshipped Baal, whose name derives from the name of the place. It was in the 2nd millennium, too, that, as a result of trading links, the cult spread to Rhodes where Baal was revered under the name of Zeus Atabyrios on the 3,988 ft/1,215 m high mount Atabyrion. Atabyrion was the Greek name for Tabor.

In the period of the Judges (12th c. B.C.) the prophetess Deborah and Barak, the general, gathered their forces on the mountain to go forward and defeat Sisera, the general of Hazor, "with all his chariots and all his host" (Judges 4, 12–16).

The significance of the mountain in the history of Christianity begins in the 4th c. From this time on, the Transfiguration of Jesus was connected with this locality (Matthew 17; Mark 9, 2–13; Luke 9, 28–36). Jesus went up into a high mountain with his disciples Peter, James and John. "And he was transfigured before them, and his face did shine as the sun, and his raiment was as white as the light. And, behold, there

Mount Tabor

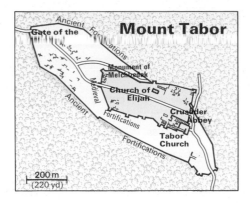

Mount Tabor

appeared unto them Moses and Elias." Thus Jesus appeared to the disciples in god-like form, as Christ and as God's dearly beloved Son. Together with his resurrection this concept became one of the central themes in the theology and iconography of the Eastern Church. The appearance of the transfigured Christ in a nimbus of light also exerted a decisive effect on the development of mysticism in monasticism in the Eastern Church. Its influence may be discerned even at the present day in the current of mysticism found on the sacred mountain at Athos where the hope is to attain, through asceticism, the "uncreated light" of Mount Tabor and thus to come to mystic union with the divinity.

The first churches on Mount Tabor must be dated as before 422. From 553 Tabor became a bishopric; the great mosaic depicting the Transfiguration in the church of St Catherine on Sinai (see Sinai Peninsula) is also of this date. The Crusaders restored and completed the castle, which was both a fortification and a base for pilgrimages. It was able to withstand Sultan Saladin in 1191, but was destroyed by Baibars in 1263. In 1631 the Druse Emir Fakhr ed Din ceded the summit to the Franciscans. Their settlement there survives to the present day. In 1911 the Greek Orthodox Christians erected a church dedicated to Elija on the N part of the plateau at the summit which was their property. Antonio Barluzzi was the architect of the great church of the Catholic monastery belonging to the Franciscans.

SIGHTS. – The *Daverat* kibbutz, named after the prophetess Deborah and founded in 1948, is 4 miles/7 km NE of Afula on the road to Tiberias. From its semicircular self-service restaurant by the roadside there is a very fine view of Mount Tabor. 3 miles/5 km further along a road forks off to the left towards the Arab village of *Dabburiya*. From it a zig-zag track – unsuitable for buses – leads to the summit which rises 1,477 ft/450 m above the plain. On the summit the road forks, leading, to the left, to the Greek Orthodox precinct where the **Church of Elijah** has stood on the site of a Crusader building since 1911. The courtyard, in which a deep open cistern may be seen, has ranges of cells on its N and E sides. The monastery is at present inhabited by three monks; it is a daughter house of the

Monastery of the Holy Sepulchre in Jerusalem.

Entry to the property of the Catholic Franciscans is on the right. Passing first through a walled cloister and then between the remains of an older church (on left) and the monastery garden with a memorial to Barluzzi, the architect of the church, and a tablet commemorating the visit of Pope Paul VI in 1964 (on right), a path leads to the *Tabor church. Constructed out of light-hued limestone, it adopts the style of ecclesiastical architecture which developed in Syria in the 4th to 6th c. This style did not only leave its mark on the appearance of the inner parts but also gave the exterior a certain monumentality for the first time. The façade, for instance, has two jutting towers between which an arch surmounted by a gable gives access to the main entrance. It belongs to the Syrian tradition, as exemplified particularly by Qalb Loze near Aleppo; so do the windows with their convoluted framing. – Inside, again following Syrian tradition, the central nave is divided off from the side aisles by great arches. The exposed roof beams are supported on small pillars in the clerestory.

The **church on Mount Tabor** comprises the three grottoes which Jonas Korte described in 1751 as "three chapels with a small altar; they are called

The church on Mount Tabor

tabernacles and are supposed to be the three tabernacles which Peter wanted to build, one for his Master, the other two for Moses and Elijah." *Christ's grotto* is at the E end of the church. A few steps lead down to a lower level where there is an altar sanctuary. Around it are the walls of a Crusader church, and over it is a barrel vault of modern construction. The apsidal vault in the upper part of the church contains a golden mosaic pavement representing the Transfiguration of Christ.

Two other chapels are constructed in the two towers on the façade. On the right (S) is the *chapel of Elijah*. On the left (N) is the *chapel of Moses*, and crosses are portrayed in its mosaic pavement. This indicates that it must have belonged to a chapel built before 422, for in that year the Emperor Theodosius II prohibited the use of the symbol of the cross in pavement mosaics in order to prevent the cross from being trodden underfoot.

N and S of the church stand walls from old buildings. From up here there is a view of the major part of the elliptical plateau on the summit, with the remains of ancient buildings nestling in verdant gardens. The main attraction, however, is a view far out over the mountains around Nazareth to the W, the Plain of Jezreel and the mountains of Samaria rising in the S, the Jordan rift valley and the mountains to the E, as well as the green land of Galilee with the characteristic "Horns of Hittim" in the N.

Nabi Musa

see Nebi Musa

Nabi Samuel

see Nebi Samvil

Nablus

West Bank.
Altitude: 1,805 ft/550 m.
Population: 44,200.
ⓘ **Government Tourist Office,**
7 Mendele Street,
Tel Aviv;
tel. (03) 22 32 66/7.

The town of Nablus is 26 miles/42 km NE of Tel Aviv and 37 miles/60 km N of Jerusalem in the mountainous countryside of Samaria. It is the hub of Arab nationalism in the N part of the Israeli-occupied West Bank. Nablus has a community of Samaritans.

HISTORY. – In A.D. 72, two years after the destruction of Jerusalem, Titus founded a settlement 1 mile/2 km NW of Sichem which had fallen into decay. The settlement, called *Flavia Neapolis*, soon began to thrive and in 244 was given the status of "colonia". At first mainly settled by heathen veterans as well as Samaritans, the town soon acquired a Christian community which produced the philosopher and martyr Justinus (c. 100–165). In 521 the Samaritans killed the bishop and razed the churches, whereupon Emperor Justinian had those rebels who had not fled or converted to Christianity executed or sold into slavery. In 636 the Arabs took Neapolis, which they called *Nablus*. At the time of the Crusades Queen Melisande, widow of King Fulko, fortified the town against her son Baldwin III, who shut her off from political life in 1152 but allowed her to retire to Nablus where she founded several churches. Christianity here was only short-lived, however, and as early as 1187 Nablus became Islamic again and has remained so to this day.

In the 16th c. Nablus was one of the four Ottoman administrative centers – the others were Gaza, Jerusalem and Safed. In 1915 it was linked to Afula by rail. From 1918 to 1948 it was part of the area covered by the British Mandate and in 1936 was the seat of an Arab uprising against the British. In 1948 Nablus became part of Jordan but in 1967 it was taken by Israelis. In 1972 it was damaged by earthquake.

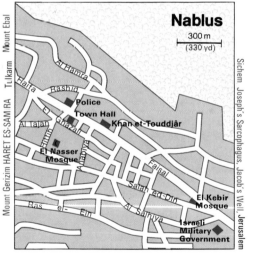

SIGHTS. – In the middle of Nablus, where soap-making is an important industry, are the two large *mosques* Kebir and Nasser. In the W is HARET ES-SAMIRA, the quarter where some 250 *Samaritans* live. The only other place where Samaritans are still to be found is in Holon near Tel Aviv, where there is a small colony of them.

The Samaritans resulted from inter-marriage between the Jews who were not deported after the fall of the Northern Kingdom of Israel in 721 B.C. and the "people of Babylon and Cuthah" who were settled here (2 Kings 17, 24). They therefore ceased to be recognised by official Jewry and began to evolve their own special religion. Their Torah scroll, probably dating from the 2nd c., contains only the five books of Moses which are their only holy writings. Their shrine is on Mount **Gerizim**. *Har Gerizim* (2,891 ft/ 881 m) and Mount *Ebal* (Har Eval; 3,085 ft/940 m) are on either side of the town.

Moses had ordered a blessing to be placed on Gerizim and a curse to be put on Ebal (Deuteronomy 11, 29). When Joshua conquered the land he erected a sacrificial altar on Ebal (Joshua 8, 30). The Samaritans' shrine on Gerizim has been there since 350 B.C. In 168 B.C. the Seleucid Antiochos IV converted it into a shrine to Zeus as part of his policy of Hellenisation. In 128 B.C. it was destroyed by the Hashmonean John Hyrkanos I who wanted to incorporate the Samaritans into his kingdom. The Samaritans were also persecuted under Pontius Pilate (26–36), Vespasian and the Roman and Byzantine emperors from Hadrian to Justinian II. Emperor Zeno had their temple on Mount Gerizim destroyed once again in 486 and replaced by a Christian church.

Yet despite all this persecution the Samaritans have survived to this day, albeit in very small numbers. Every year they celebrate the Passover on the summit of Mount Gerizim by slaughtering seven lambs over a channel, thus observing Moses' instructions (Exodus 12, 5–11).

SURROUNDINGS. – 1 mile/2 km SE of Nablus is the old village of **Sichem** (Shekhem in Hebrew) in the col between Mounts Gerizim and Ebal. Many incidents in the Old Testament are connected with Sichem, an important town even in the time of the Canaanites because of its position on the crossroads of the main routes E–W and N–S.

Abraham camped here on his trek from Mesopotamia to Canaan and built the first altar (Genesis 12, 7). His grandson Jacob also stopped outside the town after his return from Mesopotamia, purchased land for 100 gold pieces and built an altar (Genesis 33, 18–20). His sons Simeon and Levi, after seemingly successful parleys, killed and robbed all the men of Sichem in order to avenge the defiled honour of their sister Dinah (Genesis 34, 1–29).

In the 17th c. B.C. the Hyksos built a fortress. In the 13th c. B.C. Joshua, who had previously built a new altar on Mount Ebal (Joshua 8, 30), had the bones of Joseph brought from Egypt and buried in the field purchased by his father Jacob (Joshua 24, 32). After Joshua's death the Israelites forsook the "God of their fathers" and "served Baal and Astarte" (Judges 2, 12–13). At the end of the 12th c. B.C. Abimelech, a son of the first judge Gideon, was made king for three years at the shrine of Baal (Judges 9, 6). In 928 B.C. the ten northern tribes called upon Jeroboam to be king of Israel "from Bethel to Dan" (1 Kings 12, 2). When Omri founded the new capital of Samaria (see entry) Sichem lost its importance and became a village until the Samaritans made it their capital in 350 B.C. The history of the town ended in 128 B.C. with its capture by John Hyrkanos I.

On the E slope of Mount Gerizim, in a small chapel, is **Jacob's Well** (118 ft/36 m deep) where Jesus met

the woman of Samaria (John 4, 5–9). Nearby is a Greek Orthodox monastery with a church begun in 1860 over the remains of a Crusader church but left unfinished. *Joseph's sarcophagus* is shown to visitors in a domed building near the monastery.

Excavations by German archaeologists, starting in 1913 with E. Sellin, have unearthed the remains of the Sichem of the Bible on *Tell Balata*: Hyksos fortifications (17th c. B.C.), foundations of a large Canaanite temple and a temple to Baal (Baal Beelit) dating from the 13th/12th c. B.C. which was probably where Abimelech was made king.

From Nablus to Silo (26 miles/42 km). – 22 miles/ 36 km S of Nablus is the village of *Sinjil*, named after the Crusader Count St Gilles. A rather poor road leads E from here through the village of Turmus-Aya to **Silo** (*Khirbet Seilun* in Arabic, *Shillo* in Hebrew; 4 miles/6 km). Silo was an important shrine in the early years of Israelite settlement, since for about 100 years from 1175 B.C. the Tabernacle and the Ark of the Covenant were kept here (Joshua 18, 1). It was in Silo that Samuel was called to be a prophet (1 Samuel 3). Then the Ark of the Covenant was lost near Eben-Ezer during fighting with the Philistines (1 Samuel 4, 11), and Silo was destroyed by the Philistines. In the 10th c. the prophet Ahijah lived here; he it was who prophesied to Jeroboam that he would be the first king of the Northern Kingdom of Israel after Solomon's death (1 Kings 11, 29–37).

Danish archaeologists, excavating here from 1926 onwards, discovered a Canaanite temple and the mosaic pavement of a Byzantine church (6th c.). Nearby is the Mosque of the Sixty (Djami Sittin).

From Nablus to Mount Sartaba (25 miles/41 km). – The Tubas road NE out of Nablus leads after 9 miles/ 15 km to the *Tell Tirza* (Tell Faria in Arabic). Excavation work carried out here between 1946 and 1960 indicated that as early as the 4th millennium B.C. there was a settlement here which was abandoned about 2500 B.C. About 1700 B.C. a new Canaanite town grew up which was taken by Joshua in the 13th c. B.C. (Joshua 12, 24). In the 10th c. B.C. Jeroboam, who had lived first in Sichem and then on the East Bank of the Jordan in Pnuel, made Tirza the capital of the kingdom of Israel (1 Kings 14, 17). It lost its importance about 880 B.C. when Omri moved the capital to Samaria (see entry). In 772 B.C. the Assyrians destroyed Tirza. The layers above the ruins contained traces of Assyrian, Hellenistic and Roman settlements.

The two springs near the Tell feed the *Nahal Tirza*. 15 miles/24 km SE of the Tirza valley (4 miles/7 km before the Adams Bridge over the Jordan) the road to Jericho goes off to the right. 4 miles/6 km further along this road on the right is **Mount Sartaba** (1,237 ft/377 m) rising to about 2,297 ft/700 m above the Jordan valley. This is where the Hashmonean king Alexander Jannaios built the fortress of Alexandreia in the 1st c. B.C. It was rebuilt by Herod after it had been destroyed by the Romans and in 31 B.C. served as a prison for Queen Mariamne.

The remains of the fortress, destroyed in A.D. 70 by the Romans, can be seen after a difficult climb which, by way of compensation, affords a view as far as the Mount of Olives in Jerusalem (25 miles/40 km) in the SW and the Mount of Belvoir (see entry; 34 miles/55 km) in the NE. At the time of the Second Temple Sarbata, between these two points, was a beacon for transmitting signals from Jerusalem, indicating the beginning of the months and the religious festivals, to the outermost reaches of the Jewish world.

From Nablus to Netanya (27 miles/44 km). – 6 miles/10 km W of Nablus is *Deir Sharaf*; about 2½ miles/4 km N of here are the ruins of the ancient town of *Samaria* (see entry). From Deir Sharaf it is 12 miles/19 km to the border of the West Bank at the town of *Tulkarm*. From there the road runs over the fertile Plain of Sharon to reach the Mediterranean at **Netanya** (see entry; 9 miles/15 km).

Nahariya/ Nahariyya

District: North.
Altitude: 0–33 ft/0–10 m.
Population: 30,000.
Telephone code: 04.
ⓘ **Government Tourist Office,**
Haga'aton Street;
tel. 92 21 26.

Street scene in Nahariyya

HOTELS. – *Carlton* (k), 23 Gaaton Boulevard, I, 198 r., tennis; *Pallas Athene* (k), 28 Hamaapilim Street, II, 53 r., sauna; *Frank* (k), 4 Haaliya Street, II, 52 r.; *Eden* (k), Meyasdim Street, II, 50 r.; *Astar* (k), 27 Gaaton Boulevard, II, 26 r.; *Panorama* (k), 6 Hamaapilim Street, II, 25 r.; *Rosenblatt* (k), 59 Weizman Street, III, 35 r.; *Karl Laufer* (k), 31 Hameyasdim Street, III, 28 r.; *Kalman* (k), 27 Jabotinsky Street, III, 20 r.; *Gan Hashosanim* (k), 43 Weizman Street, IV, 15 r.; *Erna House*, 29 Jabotinsky Street, IV, 11 r. – YOUTH HOSTEL near Gesher Haziw (N of Nahariyya; tel. 04 92 13 43).

CAMP SITES. – Near Akhziv (4 miles/6 km N of the town and 110 yd/100 m from the beach; tel. 04 92 17 92) and Lehman (about 6½ miles/10 km N of Nahariya; tel. 04 92 62 06).

SPORT and LEISURE. – Bathing (the central beach of Galei Galil is protected by a breakwater; other beaches S and N), diving (Rosh Haniqra kibbutz), sailing, riding (Bacall's Riding School; tel. 92 05 34).

COMMUNICATIONS. – Nahariyya is linked by rail to Haifa and Tel Aviv. Coaches to all parts of Galilee from Egged Coach Station, Sderot Haga'aton (tel. 92 53 20). Buses to Acre and Haifa (every 15 minutes) and to Tel Aviv. Galil Taxis, 71 Rehov Herzl (tel. 92 55 55), has regular trips to Acre and Haifa. Buses to the suburbs of Amidar and Trumpeldor.

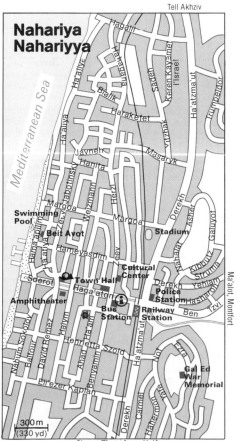

Shave Zion, Acre, Haifa

*Nahariyya, 19 miles/30 km NE of Haifa on a delightful stretch of the Mediterranean coast, founded in 1934 by Jews from Germany on the banks of the Ga'aton as an agricultural settlement, is a popular seaside resort set in countryside which is both picturesque and of historic interest.

SIGHTS. – Nahariyya is on the mouth of the River (i.e. Nahar, hence Nahariyya) Ga'aton which flows, before it enters the sea, between the two carriageways of the eucalyptus-lined main street of **Sderot Haga'aton**. Here the characteristic horse-drawn cabs, their bells jingling, ply their trade. On the N side of this street, which also has many cafés and restaurants, is the **town hall** (including

Ruined castle of Judin inland from Nahariyya

perfectly preserved mosaic pavement of an early Christian church. 4 miles/7 km S of here is the old port ꞏꞏ ꞏꞏꞏ ꞏꞏꞏ ꞏꞏꞏꞏ ꞏ ꞏꞏ ꞏꞏ ꞏꞏꞏꞏ ꞏꞏꞏꞏꞏꞏ buildings.

7 miles/10 km SE of Nahariyya is the international Christian settlement of **Nes Amim** ("Banner for the Nations"; Nes Ammim Center, 48 r.) which serves the cause of Christian and Jewish cooperation. It was founded in 1963 by young Christians, most of whom were Dutch. It is reached by driving S from Nahariyya to where the road turns off to Shave Zion, turning left, driving through Regba and then following the road which turns S. In Nes Amim there are guided tours around the farm (rose-growing) and lectures (by arrangement; tel. 92 25 66).

Driving inland from Nahariyya via *Mi'ilya* it is possible to visit the ruins of the Crusader castle of **Montfort** (see entry; 9 miles/14 km) and driving S via *Yehi'am* kibbutz (7 miles/11 km) the castle of *Judin*.

Nathanya

see Netanya

municipal museum; 5th floor: modern painting; 6th floor: archaeology); on the S side the *station*.

At the W end of the Sderot Haga'aton Hamaapilim Street leads off to the right to the quay and the open-air swimming pool by the beach. The *quay* is a reminder that in the uncertain times before Israel became independent in 1948 Nahariyya was cut off for months at a time from its hinterland and could be reached only by boat from Haifa. The Phoenicians had a harbour here which lasted until the Byzantine or early Islamic period. On a hill on the beach are the remains of a 15th c. B.C. **temple** to the Canaanite fertility goddess Astarte.

SURROUNDINGS. – 4 miles/6 km N, where the River *Keziv* flows into the Mediterranean, is the ruin-covered **Tell Akhziv** (Club Méditerrannée holiday village, 250 r.; camp site). The *Achzib* of the Old Testament had a mixed population, for "the Asherites dwelt among the Canaanites, the inhabitants of the land" (Judges 1, 31–32). The Phoenicians obtained their purple dye from shellfish here. A cemetery has been found where burials took place from the 8th to the 6th c. B.C. The Crusaders called the place "Castel Imbert". More recently Arab fishermen lived here (until 1948). Today the site of the ruins is a national park with a small private museum, a beach and a holiday camp. Nearby is the *Gesher Haziv* (Bridge of Fame) kibbutz with a youth hostel and picnic area.

½ mile/1 km S of Nahariyya is the *Evron* kibbutz, founded in 1945 and named after a town in the land of Asher (Joshua 19, 28). Excavations in 1951 brought to light Palaeolithic finds and the mosaic floor of a 5th c. Byzantine church. 1 mile/2 km further S is the village of **Shave Zion**, a seaside resort which has the

Nazareth/Nazerat

District: North.
Population: 39,000 (58,000 with Nazerat Illit).
Telephone code: 0 65.
ⓘ **Government Tourist Office,**
Casanova Street;
tel. 7 05 55.

HOTELS. – *Grand New*, St Joseph Street, II, 92 r.; *Hagalil*, Paul VI Street, II, 90 r.; *Nazareth* (tel. 7 20 45), II, 87 r.

PILGRIMS HOSTELS. – *Monastery of the Order of the Sacred Heart* (Roman Catholic, French, for groups only; tel. 5 42 16); *St Charles Borromeus* (Roman Catholic, German; tel. 5 44 35); *Sisters of Nazareth* (Roman Catholic, French, for priests and tourists; tel. 5 43 04); *Casa Nova* (for pilgrims and tourists), Casanova Street (tel. 7 13 67); *Franciscan Convent* (Roman Catholic, Italian, for women only; tel. 5 40 71).

COMMUNICATIONS. – The central long-distance coach station is in Garage Road below the Church of the Annunciation, and the companies concerned are Egged (tel. 5 42 03) and the Nazareth–Haifa Omnibus Company (tel. 5 41 20). Buses leave the Well of the Virgin Mary regularly for Kafr Kana (Galilee Bus and Transport Company, tel. 5 48 79). Taxis: Nazareth Taxis (tel. 5 40 27), 45 Taxis (tel. 5 47 45), Sherut Taxis (tel. 5 44 12).

Nazareth (Nazerat in Hebrew, En-Nasra in Arabic), the largest town in the Arab part of Israel, is above the Jezreel Plain on the S edge of the hills of Galilee. Its inhabitants are mostly Christian. As the site of the Annunciation and the place where Jesus spent most of his life, it has

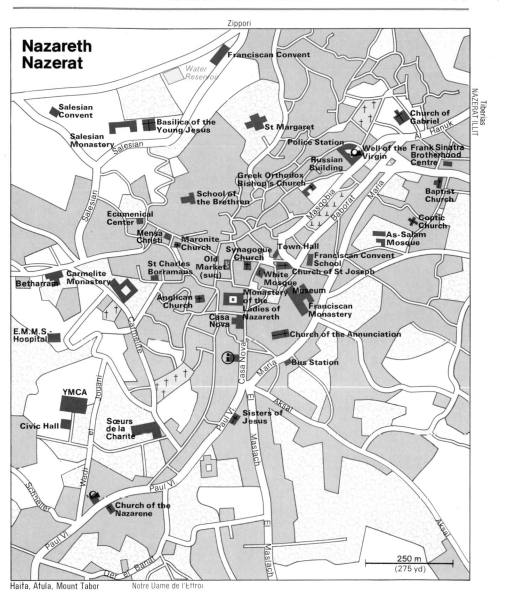

Nazareth
Nazerat

Zippori

Franciscan Convent

Water Reservoir

Salesian Convent

Basilica of the Young Jesus

Salesian Monastery

St Margaret

Church of Gabriel

Police Station

Russian Building

Well of the Virgin

Frank Sinatra Brotherhood Centre

Greek Orthodox Bishop's Church

School of the Brethren

Ecumenical Center

Baptist Church

Mensa Christi

Maronite Church

Synagogue Church

Town Hall

Coptic Church

As-Salam Mosque

Old Market (suq)

Franciscan Convent School

St Charles Borramaus

White Church of St Joseph

Carmelite Monastery

Betharran

Mosque

Anglican Church

Monastery of the Ladies of Nazareth

Museum

Franciscan Monastery

Casa Nova

E.M.M.S. Hospital

Church of the Annunciation

Bus Station

YMCA

Civic Hall

Sœurs de la Charité

Sisters of Jesus

Church of the Nazarene

250 m
(275 yd)

Haifa, Afula, Mount Tabor   Notre Dame de l'Effroi

Tiberias
NAZERAT ILLIT

attracted Christian pilgrims for the last 1,500 years. The town's main feature is its many churches and the Church of the Annunciation in particular.

HISTORY. – Nazareth is not mentioned in the Old Testament and was probably an insignificant village in the pre-Christian period. Yet excavations carried out since 1955 have shown that the hill of the Church of the Annunciation and the Church of St Joseph have been inhabited since the time of the patriarchs (2nd millennium B.C.). The village houses had been built on top of tombs of the 2nd millennium B.C. and underground rooms carved out of the tufa had been used for storage in the first half of the 1st millennium B.C.

The name of Nazareth is first mentioned in the New Testament in the description of the Annunciation (Luke 1, 26–33). Jesus lived here until he was baptised by John (Luke 3, 21), but after he began to

teach spent most of his time around Capernaum (see entry).

The grotto of the Annunciation subsequently became a place of worship, and the present church is the fifth on the site. An early site of Christian settlement, Nazareth was conquered in 614 by the Persians who, in conjunction with the Jews, destroyed the town. This led to a fall in the numbers of the Christian population. When the Byzantines took it back in 629 they took their revenge by destroying the Jewish houses in their turn. Reconstruction did not take place until the time of the Crusader Tancred who took Nazareth in 1099 and then ruled as prince of Galilee. Baibars and his Mamelukes caused more destruction in 1263. It was not for several centuries, when the Druse sovereign Fahreddin gave his permission in 1620, that Christians were allowed to live there again. The town developed in the 19th and 20th c. under Ottoman and then British rule. In 1948 Nazareth became part of Israel and since then the Jewish town of Upper Nazareth (Nazerat Illit), with its own administration, has grown up on the hills above.

Detail, main door, Church of the Annunciation

through the view into the older layers of building down below while the upper church shows the universality of the Church by means of pictures on which artists from all over the world cooperated.

His plan was based on the Crusader church, and he placed the modern outer walls on top of the stone layers that still remained from the side walls of that earlier church and incorporated its E apse, which was still extant, into the new building. Only on the W side, which contains the entrance, is the new building not as wide as the old. Like the 12th c. building, the modern church is a basilica with a nave and two side aisles but it is also the upper level of a second, central building. Through a large octagonal opening in the floor it is possible to look down on the lower level and the older building layers below: the Grotto of the Annunciation and what is left of the earliest church buildings on this site. Above this chamber is the dome.

The entrance gate on the W leads to the courtyard, the outer walls of which on the W and S sides are adjoined by a columned hall. The W façade of the church has friezes and a large relief of the Annunciation. The three *bronze doors* were designed by Roland Friederichsen of

SIGHTS. – The town is dominated by the ***Church of the Annunciation** with its 121 ft/37 m high dome.

Veneration of the Grotto of the Annunciation (Luke 1, 26–33) dates back, as archaeological investigations carried out since 1955 have proved, to the 3rd c. That was when the Judeo-Christians living in Nazareth built a modest first church on the pattern of the synagogue of the time ("Synagogue Church"). The *second church*, a small building with a round apse and an atrium in front, was built in the 4th c. by order of Empress Helena by the converted Jew Joseph of Tiberias. According to an inscription this building was extended by a "konon" from Jerusalem before 427. To the S was a small monastery. This complex was destroyed by the Persians in 614.

The *third church* was much bigger and was built in the early 12th c. by Tancred, the prince of Galilee. It was a basilica with a nave and two aisles, 98 ft/30 m wide, 246 ft/75 m long. Baibars destroyed it in 1263, sparing only the grotto.

It was not until 1730 that the Franciscans were able to build a new church, the *fourth*. Unlike the earlier ones it was not oriented E–W but N–S, so that the choir was over the grotto. The façade was not finished until 1877.

In 1955 the building was pulled down to make way for a new one, Israel's largest sacred building in recent decades. This *fifth church*, consecrated on March 23, 1969 by Cardinal Garrone, is the most important modern church building in Israel.

The Italian architect Giovanni Muzio based his design on two principles. Firstly, he wanted to show the history of the place from the very outset and he sought to depict the catholic nature of the Universal Church of Rome. By using modern methods he succeeded most convincingly in putting this concept into effect. The lower church illustrates the historical continuity

Church of the Annunciation   **Nazareth**

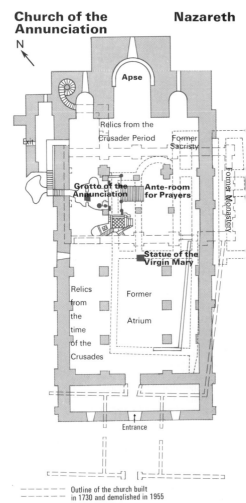

Grotto of the Annunciation   Nazareth

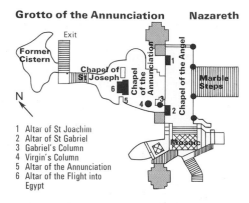

1 Altar of St Joachim
2 Altar of St Gabriel
3 Gabriel's Column
4 Virgin's Column
5 Altar of the Annunciation
6 Altar of the Flight into
   Egypt

Grotto of the Annunciation

Munich. On the middle door is, top left, the Birth of Christ; bottom left, the Flight into Egypt and Jesus as a Boy; bottom right, the Baptism in the Jordan; top right, the Sermon on the Mount and Crucifixion. To the right on the S side is the *S door*, decorated with scenes from the life of the Virgin Mary by Frederick Shrady (U.S.A.).

The W door of the Church of the Annunciation leads into the *lower church*. The pilastered wall of the Crusader church on which the new walls were built can still be seen on the N (left) long side. To the E is the octagon under the dome with its view down into the original level. In the N (left) can be seen the *Grotto of the Annunciation*; the altar bears the inscription "Verbum caro hic factum est" ("And the Word was made flesh"; John 1, 14). The copper baldachin over the grotto is of Belgian workmanship. Columns immediately in front of the grotto are ascribed to the 3rd c. synagogue church. In the center of the octagon is the modern altar and in the S section (right) is a nave wall with round apse of the second Church of the Annunciation (4th/5th c.).

Further E of the octagon are the three apses of the third (*Crusader*) church. Especially noteworthy here are several rich 12th c. capitals in the right-hand side apse.

Near the W side is a staircase to the *upper church*. This also has a nave and two side aisles and the octagonal opening in the floor through which it is possible to look down into the grotto. The dome above the octagon is an imitation of a lily, an old symbol for Virgin Mary.

The floor of the upper church is inlaid marble. It was designed by Adriano Alessandrini and depicts Mary and Marian councils. The E side is incorporated into the presbytery; on the wall behind the white altar is a mosaic depicting the church: Christ with Mary and Peter and saints. To the left is a chapel dedicated to the saints of the Franciscan order and to the right the chapel of the sacrament.

The walls of the upper church are covered with images of Mary from all over the world. Mosaics have been given by Australia, England, Japan, Ireland, Italy, Cameroun, Mexico, Czechoslovakia and Hungary; ceramics come from Canada, Poland and Portugal; Argentina gave a fresco, North America a work of steel and silver, Venezuela a wood-carving.

The N gate of the upper church leads into a courtyard where on the right is the *baptistry* designed by Bernd Hartmann and Ima Rochelle (W. Germany). Under this can be seen excavations of old Nazareth. Further N is the Church of St Joseph (right) and the exit (left). The **Church of St Joseph**, consecrated in 1914, is built over a cave which is said to have been Joseph's workshop; it contains the remains of a cistern and several storage pits that no doubt belong to the village of Jesus' time. Between the Church of the Annunciation and the Church of St Joseph is the *Franciscan Monastery* and *Museum*.

In the old parts of the town W of the Church of the Annunciation are the *Synagogue Church*, according to tradition the synagogue that Jesus attended, just S of it the *Monastery of the Ladies of Nazareth* and further W the Maronite Church, with next to it the *Franciscan Mensa Christi Church* on a spot where the risen Christ is supposed to have had a meal with his disciples. From here a zig-zag path leads up to the dominant site of the French Salesian monastery and the **Basilica of the Young Jesus**.

Well of the Virgin Mary

1 mile/1·5 km N of the Church of the Annunciation near the main road to Tiberias is the *Well of the Virgin Mary*. The orthodox tradition rests on an apocryphal gospel stating that the Archangel Gabriel first appeared to the Virgin Mary at the village well. The Well of the Virgin Mary is modern and is not on precisely the same spot as the old well, which was in fact under the altar of the Greek Orthodox **Church of Gabriel**, also worth a visit for its architecture and decoration.

The Church of Gabriel in Nazareth

SURROUNDINGS. – 4 miles/6 km NW is *Zippori* (see entry) with a ruined Crusader church. About the same distance away to the NE is *Kafr Kana*, where the Wedding at Cana took place (see entry).

On the far side of *Afula* (see entry; 7 miles/11 km) is **Bet Shean** (see entry; 15 miles/24 km SE of Afula) which has a Roman theatre and 6th c. mosaic pavements, and on the way back to Afula, on the left of the road, it is possible to visit **Bet Alfa** (see entry) with its mosaic pavement.

NE of Afula is **Mount Tabor** (see entry; about 19 miles/30 km), according to Christian tradition the place of Christ's Transfiguration.

Nebi Musa/ Nabi Musa

West Bank.
ⓘ **Government Tourist Office,**
24 King George Street,
Jerusalem;
tel. (02) 24 12 81.

The **Islamic shrine of Nebi Musa** (Nabi Musa – prophet Moses) is in the desert of Judah, part of the

Israeli-occupied West Bank, S of Jericho. It can be reached by driving from Jerusalem in the direction of the Dead Sea and turning off after 17 miles/28 km on to an asphalt road that after ½ mile/1 km arrives at the shrine.

HISTORY. – At the end of the long journey from Egypt through Sinai, the Zin and Paran deserts and the land of the Edomites, it was vouchsafed to Moses to see the Promised Land but not to enter it. From the 2,652 ft/ 808 m high Mount Nebo (SW of Amman) he looked down on the Dead Sea 3,938 ft/1,200 m below, the Jordan Valley and the oasis of Jericho, which was to be the first town W of the Jordan conquered by his people under the leadership of Joshua. Moses was "buried in a valley in the land of Moab, but no man knoweth of his sepulchre unto this day." (Deuteronomy 34, 1–6.) However, an old tradition, that probably dates back to Christian pilgrims in the Middle Ages and which was perpetuated by the Moslems, puts Moses' tomb W of the Jordan at Nebi Musa. Saladin (12th c.) knew this place, and the Mameluke Baibars (1260–77) built a mosque with the large cenotaph for Moses. In the 15th c. extensive accommodation was built for pilgrims.

SIGHTS. – The **mosque** with its outbuildings is in a dominant position on a hill. Also on its slopes is another Islamic *burial ground* for Moslems who wish to be near the prophet even in death.

The Easter- and Passovertide of Christians and Jews is also the time when Moslems make pilgrimages to Nebi Musa, a fact which meant that during the Ottoman period there were often riots against the Christians, while during the British Mandate hostility was frequently shown towards the Jews.

Nebi Musa – revered by the Moslems as the tomb of Moses

Nebi Samvil/
Nabi Samuel

West Bank.
ⓘ Government Tourist Office,
24 King George Street,
Jerusalem;
tel. (02) 24 12 81.

Nebi Samvil (Nabi Samuel), an Arab
village named after the prophet
Samuel where his tomb is venerated,
is 6 miles/9 km NW of Jerusalem on
the Israeli-occupied West Bank.

It can be reached by leaving Jerusalem by
the Ramallah road and turning left after
Shufat; or by taking the road out of
Jerusalem to the NW passing through the
suburbs of Mahanayim and Sanhedriya.

The 2,095 ft/885 m high mountain near
the village was called *Mons gaudii*
(Mountain of Joy) by the Crusaders
because it was here that they had their first
glimpse of Jerusalem. In the 12th c. they
erected a church here (as Emperor Justinian had done in the 6th c.) which the
Moslems later turned into a mosque. This
mosque, which is visible from far off,
contains the cenotaph of Samuel who
lived in nearby Zuph/Givat Shaul (see
Ramallah, Surroundings) and according
to tradition is buried here. Samuel was
also revered as a prophet by the Moslems,
and his tomb, like those of the patriarchs in
Hebron (see entry) is in a cave under the
mosque. It is possible to see a long way
from the roof of the massive mosque.

In 1948 Nabi Samvil was an Arab base
during the fighting between Arabs and
Jews; since 1967 Jewish pilgrims have
been able to visit it again.

Negev

District: South.
ⓘ Government Tourist Office,
Bet Tnuat Hamoschavim,
Beersheba;

Government Tourist Office,
Markas Mischari Rechter (shopping center),
Hatemarim Street,
Eilat;
tel. (0 59) 7 22 68.

The Negev ("desert", "dry land" in
Hebrew), the southernmost part of
Israel, is bordered in the W by the
Egyptian–Israeli border and the Gaza
Strip, in the E by the Arava valley and
in the N by what amounts to a line
running from Gaza to En Gedi. Geo-
graphically it merges with the Sinai
area in the SW. The largest town in
this huge triangle is Beersheba
(Be'er Sheva) on the border between
the Northern Negev, made fertile by
irrigation, and the arid Negev.

HISTORY. – The Negev probably became dry between
10000 and 7500 B.C. Abraham came from the N as far
as Beersheba. In the latter part of the 2nd millennium
B.C. three peoples lived in the Negev: in the N, around
Arad, there were *Canaanites* who had penetrated
furthest S; in the S the *Amalekites* whom David
exterminated about 1000 B.C.; in the E, around the
Arava rift valley, the *Edomites* who moved N in the 6th
c. B.C. and became known as the Idumeans after
settling between Beersheba and Hebron.

Desert scenery in the Negev

From the 1st c. B.C. onwards the *Nabataeans* sought to
settle and cultivate the Negev from their capital of
Petra. They succeeded in doing this by using
ingenious methods of irrigation; towns such as Avdat
(see entry), Subeita (see Shivta) and Mampsis (see
Mamshit) sprang up. The *Byzantines* took over in the
4th–6th c. and extended the area under cultivation.
After the *Arabs*, who had elsewhere improved
irrigation, invaded, the irrigation system broke down;
the Negev became dry for more than 1,000 years and
was inhabited only by Bedouin.

That changed when Jewish settlers arrived. The
decisive move to make the land fertile once more was
made by David Ben Gurion who belonged to the
kibbutz of Sede Boqer (see entry) and who created a
university there for investigating the Negev. The
scientific principles were worked out by the German
botanist Michael Even-Ari who had helped to start a
farm on the Nabataean pattern near Avdat and who
founded a plant research institute in Beersheba. Of
primary importance for resettlement was the laying of
a pipeline to bring water to the Negev from the N of
Israel.

Negev – Paran desert

The Negev can be divided into six sections: the NW coastal plain, the valley of Beersheba, the Negev Mountains, a plateau in the region of the Paran desert, the Arava rift valley and the Eilat Mountains in the S.

The NW coastal plain, a densely populated region, also includes the Gaza Strip. It has plenty of water and links the Judean coastal plain and the plain of El Arish in the N of Sinai.

The valley of Beersheba is divided by the *Nahal Be'er Sheva* which is dry for most of the year. In the E, between Arad and Dimona, this plain is narrow. It becomes wider near the sand dunes of Haluza. When irrigated this area can be used for agriculture.

Towards the S the land rises up into the **Negev Mountains**, the highest of which is *Har Ramon* at 3,397 ft/1,035 m. The jagged Negev Mountains dominate the central part of the area. Gorges and craters are characteristic features (see Maktesh Ramon and Maktesh Hagadol). Most of the rain which falls here collects in the *Nahal Zin* which flows to the Arava rift valley and from there into the Dead Sea.

To the SW is the **Paran desert** (Midbar Paran), part of a plateau which begins 1,969 ft/600 m above sea level in the Sinai and extends as far as the NE of the Arava rift valley. The *Nahal Paran* is usually dry but in the rainy season becomes a swollen torrent.

In the E the Negev drops down to the Arava rift valley which, like the Jordan and the Dead Sea, belongs to the Great Rift Valley which stretches from Syria to Africa.

Geologically the *Eilat Mountains* belong to the Sinai peninsula massif. They extend for about 19 miles/30 km N of Eilat and this mountainous region also includes the Timna copper-mine. These mountains are of soft sandstone – white, yellow and pink – and contain, inter alia, iron- and copper-ore.

The immigration of Jewish settlers, more extensive irrigation and the construction of tourist amenities on the Gulf of Aqaba have led to a huge increase in the population of the Negev in the last few decades. Whereas during the British Mandate some 12,000 people lived here (90% Bedouin and 10% settlers, most of them Jewish), today there are over 230,000 inhabitants, of whom 38,000 are Bedouin.

Using Beersheba, Arad or Eilat as a base it is possible to see the scenery and ancient sites of the Negev by means of the few good roads (see Surroundings of Beersheba and Eilat). There are also organised trips by cross-country vehicle.

Netanya/ Nethanya/ Nathanya

District: Central.
Altitude: 66 ft/20 m.
Population: 105,000.
Telephone code: 0 53.
(i) Government Tourist Office,
Ha'atmaut Square;
tel. 2 72 86.

HOTELS. – *Dan Netanya (k), Nice Boulevard, L, 129 r., SP, sauna, tennis; Blue Bay (k), 37 Hamelachim Street, I, 246 r., SP, tennis; Goldar (k), 1 Usishkin Street, I, 150 r., SP; King Solomon (k), 18 Hamaapilim Street, I, 99 r., SP, sauna; Park (k), 7 David Hamelech Street, I, 90 r., SP; Beit-Ami (k), 41 Shlomo Hamelech Street, I, 85 r., SP; Galil (k), Nice Boulevard, I, 84 r., SP; Metropol Grand (k), 17 Gad Makhnes Street, I, 64 r., SP; Yahalom (k), 15 Gad Makhnes Street, I, 48 r., SP; Princess (k), 28 Gad Makhnes Street, II, 147 r.; Residence (k), 18 Gad Makhnes Street, II, 96 r.; Maxim (k), 8 King David Street, II, 90 r., SP; Palace (k), 33 Gad Makhnes Street, II, 71 r.; Gali Zans (k), 6 Melahim Street, II, 65 r.; Topaz (k), 25 King David Street, II, 64 r.; Orly (k), 120 Hamaapilim Street, II, 54 r.; King David Palace (k), 4 King David Street, II, 48 r.; Yahalom (k), 11 Gad Makhnes Street, II, 48 r.; Gan Hamelech (k), 10 King David Street, II, 44 r., SP; Hof (k), 9 Haatzmaut Square, II, 34 r.; Feldman (k), 9 Hashiva Street, II, 27 r.; Grinstein (k), 47 Dizengoff Street, III, 37 r.; Margoa (k), 9 Makhnes Street, III, 34 r.; Ginot Yam (k), 9 David Hamelech Street, III, 32 r., Mizpe Yam (k), 4 Karlebach Street, III, 28 r.; Metropol (k), 18 Rishonle Zion Street, III, 27 r., SP; Reuben (k), 25 Usishkin Street, III, 27 r.; Gal Yam (k), 46 Dizengoff Stroot, III, 22 r.; Atzmauth (k), 2 Usishkin Street, III, 20 r.; Daphna, 29 Rishon le Zion Street, IV, 17 r.; Dror, 33 Dizengoff Street, IV, 13 r.; Galei Hasharon (k), 42 Usishkin Street, 24 r. – Green Beach holiday camp (k), PO Box 230 (tel. 4 41 66), 150 r., SP, sauna, tennis.

RESTAURANTS. – Burger Joe, 7a Ha'atzmaut Square (French and oriental cuisine); Capris Restaurant, 27 Herzl Street (European); Hasharon Restaurant, 4 Herzl Street (k); La Ruca, 25 Usishkin Street (S. American); Miami Restaurant, 2 Herzl Street (k, Moroccan); Tahiti, 7 Ha'atzmaut Square (oriental).

COMMUNICATIONS. – Long-distance coaches use the Central Bus Station, 3 Sderot Binyamin (tel. 2 29 55); bus 5 to Tel Aviv. Egged Tours: 7 Kikar Haatzmaut (tel. 3 72 96). – Netanya has rail links with Haifa and Tel Aviv (tel. 2 34 70. – Sherut taxis to Tel Aviv from 1 Schmuel Hantziv (Sharon Taxis, tel. 2 23 23).

*Netanya (Nethanya, Nathanya), 20 miles/32 km N of Tel Aviv and 39 miles/63 km S of Haifa on the Mediterranean, owes its popularity as a holiday and seaside resort to its pleasant climate and fine sandy beach.

HISTORY. – Netanya was founded in 1928 in the midst of the sand dunes of the Plain of Sharon. Its founders belonged to the organisation of Bene Binyamin, called after Baron Edmond (Binyamin) de Rothschild, and named their settlement after the American Jewish philanthropist Nathan Strauss. Until the Emeq Hefer (see entry) was drained after 1930 and roads were built, the settlement, at first only a village, could be reached only on foot or on horseback from the railway station at Tulkarm 11 miles/17 km to the E.

During the Second World War immigrants from Antwerp embarked upon diamond-polishing to help the war effort. Since 1945 they have mainly supplied the jewelry industry. Netanya has since developed into a flourishing town with a healthy infrastructure, an economically important industrial zone and well-developed tourist facilities.

SIGHTS. – The town's principal street, with its many public buildings and shops, is named after Theodor Herzl. It begins in the E at the main Tel Aviv–Haifa road and runs W past the main post office (on the corner of David Raziel), the main syna-gogue, the bus station (Binyamin Boulevard), the main taxi rank (Zion Square) and the Town Hall, before

Netanya – Mediterranean beach

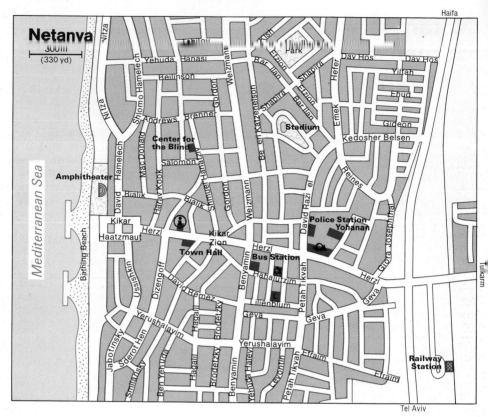

Haifa

Netanya

300m
(330 yd)

Mediterranean Sea

Tel Aviv

reaching *Ha'atzmaut Square* (Kikar Ha'atzmaut) with its lawns and fountains. On the side nearest the sea is the information office, and the W side adjoins the park above the long *bathing beach*. There are plenty of restaurants in Ha'atzmaut Square, but the hotels are to be found in the streets running N–S and almost all have a sea view.

A boulevard, known as *Binyamin Boulevard* S of Herzl Street and as *Weizmann Boulevard* N of it, forms the N–S axis of the town. W of the Weizmann Boulevard is the *Rehabilitation Center for the Blind*, built after the Second World War, which includes a library of braille books and a museum (art exhibitions). – Also worth visiting are the **diamond workshops** in the S of the town (Rehov Yahalom) with exhibition rooms (Sun.–Thurs. 8 a.m.–4 p.m., Fri. and days before public holidays 8 a.m.–noon).

SURROUNDINGS. – Netanya has good communications with the cities of **Tel Aviv** (see entry; 20 miles/ 32 km), **Jerusalem** (see entry; 59 miles/95 km) and **Haifa** (see entry; 39 miles/63 km). Between here and Haifa is the large ruined town of *Caesarea* (see entry; 16 miles/25 km). It is also worth making a trip inland: beyond *Tulkarm* on the border of the West Bank, occupied by Israel since 1967, are **Nablus** (see entry; 27 miles/44 km) and the ruined city of **Samaria/ Sebaste** (see entry; 24 miles/38 km).

Paran

District: South.

The River Paran, Nahal Paran in Hebrew, has the longest valley in the Negev. Initially flowing N, it then turns E where it is crossed by the Eilat–Gerofit–Avdat–Beersheba road and finally flows into the Arava rift valley S of the Dead Sea.

BIBLICAL HISTORY. – The Paran and the surrounding desert were an important stop on the Israelites' journey from Egypt into the Promised Land. They entered the Paran from Sinai (Numbers 10, 12). From here Moses sent out scouts to the land of the Canaanites as far as Hebron. They then journeyed further N to the Zin desert which stretches from the spring of Avdat (see En Avdat) to the Arava rift valley (Numbers 20, 1). The king of Edom would not allow them to pass through his land, so they turned E, crossed the Arava and came to Mount Hor on whose summit Aaron, the brother of Moses, perished and was buried (Numbers 20, 22–29); his tomb is venerated on Gebel Hor near Petra. Their way led then through Moab E of the Jordan and into the land of the Ammonites where Moses finally died, having been vouchsafed sight of the Promised Land (Deuteronomy 34). Even in his final blessing Moses named the Paran region: "The Lord came from Sinai; he shined forth from mount Paran." (Deuteronomy 33, 2.)

Paran Wadi – in the background the mountains around Petra (Jordan)

Dry almost all year, the Paran turns into a "raging torrent" ("wadi girafi" in Arabic) during the rainy season. Near the Eilat–Beersheba road the wadi is a wild eroded valley while the Eilat–Dead Sea road traverses its flat broad lower section. From the *Paran* Moshav founded in 1971 near this road there is a view to the E of the mountains of Edom with the characteristic outline of the 4,549 ft/1,386 m high Gebel Hor (Mount of Aaron) 37 miles/60 km away near the Nabataean capital of Petra in Jordan.

Qarne Hittim

see Horns of Hittim

Qumran

West Bank.

ⓘ **Government Tourist Office,**
24 King George Street,
Jerusalem;
tel. (02) 24 12 81.

***Qumran, 12 miles/20 km S of Jericho on the Israeli-occupied West Bank, became famous in 1947 when a Bedouin boy found the first Dead Sea Scrolls in a cave and when this was followed by the excavation of the monastery-like site of the Essenes where the scrolls originated.**

DISCOVERY OF THE SCROLLS. – The Bedouin of the Ta'amira tribe took their first finds to Bethlehem in 1947 and were then referred to Jerusalem. There Metropolitan Jeshue Samuel from the Syrian Monastery of St Mark realised that the texts were written in Hebrew and obtained five scrolls which he took with him to the U.S.A. when his monastery was damaged in the 1948 Arab–Israeli war. In America, after putting them on display several times, he found a buyer. This originally anonymous buyer was the Israeli general and archaeologist Yigael Yadin who bought the scrolls for 250,000 dollars and took them to Israel. There the "Shrine of the Book" was built for them in the Israel Museum. Yadin's father, E. L. Sukenik, was able to buy a further five scrolls in 1947 from a Jerusalem antique dealer, while two copper scrolls came into the possession of the Jordanian government and are now in the Amman Museum.

Altogether up to now over 500 Hebrew, Aramaic and occasionally also Greek manuscripts have been found in eleven caves in Qumran. Ten of these scrolls are almost perfectly preserved. Almost all the texts are written on parchment rolls which were kept in clay jars with lids. Dating from the 1st centuries B.C. and A.D., they are the oldest manuscripts of the Bible. They include all the books of the Old Testament except Esther, plus the Apocrypha and the Hebrew text of the book of Sirach, previously known only in translation, and writings of the community of Qumran, including the scroll over 10 ft/3 m long which contains the whole book of Isaiah in 54 columns and the 7 ft/2 m long scroll with the maxims of the Essenes of Qumran. There are also private documents in Hebrew, Aramaic, Greek and more rarely also in Nabataean and Latin, and letters, including some from Bar Kochba, found in the wadis S of Qumran.

The deciphering of the texts on the scrolls, whose discovery Albright already reckoned in 1948 to be the "greatest find of manuscripts in modern times", was revealing in three respects: first, when the texts were compared with later Biblical manuscripts it was obvious how extraordinarily reliable the textual tradition had been over the centuries; secondly, it brought greater knowledge of the Essene sect, previously known only from references in the literature of Jewish and Roman authors such as Philo, Flavius

Qumran – site of the finding of the famous scrolls

Josephus and Pliny; thirdly, the finds proved that Qumran was the center of this community.

HISTORY. – Along with the Sadducees and the Pharisees the Essenes were the third sect of the Jews to stem from the conflicts centered on the Temple and its services in Jerusalem around 150 B.C. The Essenes' protests were directed against the embodiment of the monarchy and the office of high priest in one person, against hidebound superficial Temple rites and against the influence of Hellenism. Rather than the apostate religious community of Jerusalem they saw themselves as the true Israel. The approximately 4,000 members scattered throughout the country made Qumran their center, as it was the home of some 200 Essenes.

This site came into being soon after 150 B.C. on what was left of a 9th–6th C. B.C. settlement. It was destroyed in 31 B.C. by an earthquake, rebuilt and finally destroyed in A.D. 68 by Roman troops during the Jewish War, but not until the inhabitants had hidden their library, archives and other treasures in the nearby caves where they were to survive. Qumran was inhabited again for a short time during the Bar Kochba revolt of 132–135.

During the 200 years or more that the Essenes lived here they lived as a strictly regulated community. Those who were accepted by baptism after several years as novices gave all their possessions to the community. After ritual purification the members gathered for the meals where there was ceremonial breaking of bread and offering up of wine. They devoted themselves to studying the Bible and praising God with hymns of thanksgiving. Their farming took place at nearby En Gedi (see entry). Their objectives were extreme abstinence, piety and above all purity (white clothing, diet, baths). Christoph Burchard looks upon this group as neither order nor sect but a "strictly Jewish, eschatologically-radicalised religious movement of sanctification allied to the Torah". At their head was the "teacher of justice", a priest descended from Zadok. The theology of Qumran was based on the coming of the Messiah and the dualistic doctrine of the ultimate struggle between the sons of Light and the sons of Darkness which is depicted on a scroll almost 10 ft/3 m long.

It is probable that John the Baptist belonged to the Essene community at least for a time and that the Qumran doctrine has an impact on the New Testament and the Jewish sect of the Karaites.

SIGHTS. – Near the entrance to the monastery-like Essene settlement are the remains of a tower. Behind it to the left is a courtyard adjoined on the tower side by the *kitchen* and on the other side by the

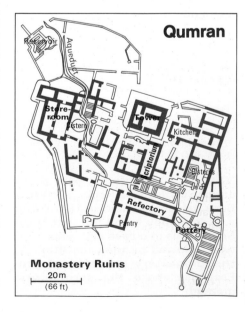

main building (123 by 123 ft/37·5 by 37·5 m). Its southern section is taken up by the 79 by 18 ft/24 by 4·5 m *assembly- and dining-hall*. On the upper floor was a room for scribes. In an adjoining room 1,700 clay jars were found as well as a clay jar with a lid like those used for storing the manuscripts in the caves. The pottery can be seen E of the main building, as can two cisterns damaged in the 31 B.C. earthquake. In the W of the precinct there was an aqueduct that fed the pools used for ritual bathing, as well as a cistern dating from the earlier Israelite period, a storeroom, kilns and ovens.

Out in the open on the other side of the buildings there is a wonderful view over a deep gorge to the mountains containing the caves where the first scrolls were found.

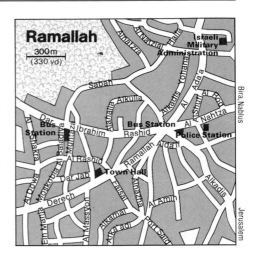

Ramallah

West Bank.
Altitude: 2,855 ft/870 m.
Population: 15,000 (24,000 incl. Bira).
Telephone code: 02.
Ⓘ **Government Information Center,**
Al Mughtaribin Square,
tel. 95 35 55.

Ramallah, a town with both Christian and Moslem inhabitants, 9 miles/15 km N of Jerusalem on the West Bank, which since 1967 has been occupied by Israel, is a holiday resort with many restaurants and cafés.

HISTORY. – Ramallah was founded in the 14th c. by Christians who had been driven out of Shobak (Jordan). In the 19th c. the Catholic Church formed a community and built schools.

Today Ramallah adjoins Bira, an Arab town; the population is partly Christian. Its proximity to Jerusalem has meant that it has developed considerably since the time of the British Mandate. Because of its position (2,855 ft/870 m) and its good climate Ramallah has become a high-altitude health resort.

NW of the town center on the road to En Qinya are the ruins of a *church* and a *monastery* dating from the Byzantine period.

SURROUNDINGS. – 2½ miles/4 km NE is the Arab village of **Beitin**, the *Betel* (house of God) of the Old Testament. E of this town Abraham, coming from the N, built an altar (Genesis 12, 8) as he had done in Sichem (see Nablus). After Joshua conquered the land Betel belonged to the tribe of Benjamin (Joshua 18, 13) and was later destroyed by the tribe of Ephraim (Judges 1, 22). After the kingdom was divided Jeroboam, king of the Northern Kingdom, built shrines to a golden calf in Dan (see entry) and in Betel. The shrine in Betel was removed by King Joshua in 621 B.C. In the Roman period the troops that captured Jerusalem in A.D. 70 were garrisoned here. In the 5th c. Betel was Christian. In 1892 Moslems built a mosque on the ruins of a Byzantine church. Excavation work has been carried out by Americans in the N and E of the village; there is a ruined Crusader castle in the SE.

9 miles/15 km SW of Ramallah is the village of **El Qubeiba** whose inhabitants are Christians and Moslems. Many Catholics believe it to be the site of Emmaus, which, according to Luke's Gospel (Luke 24, 13), was 60 furlongs (7 miles/11·5 km) from Jerusalem; another location puts it at Amwas, near Latrun (see entry). Qubeiba used to have a Byzantine church and the Crusaders built a new church over its ruins. – From the hill above the village there is a good view to the western coastal plain.

3 miles/5 km E of Qubeiba on a mediocre road is the Arab village of *Nebi Samvil* (see entry) which gets its name from the prophet Samuel whose tomb is venerated here.

Near the Jerusalem road (6 miles/10 km) S of Ramallah) is Mount **Givat Shaul** (2,754 ft/839 m) where Benjamin's Gibeath was situated (Joshua 18, 28). *Zuph* (today Shufat), ½ mile/1 km to the S, is where Samuel lived (1 Samuel 9, 5–6) and where he anointed Saul first king of the Jews in the second half of the 11th c. B.C. (1 Samuel 10, 1).

Ramla/Ramleh

District: Central.
Population: 40,000.
Telephone code: 0 54.

(i) Government Tourist Office,
7 Mendele Street,
Tel Aviv;
tel: (03) 22 32 66/7.

The town of Ramla (Ramleh in Arabic) is 12 miles/19 km SE of Tel Aviv on the Jerusalem road and on the N–S road between Haifa and Beersheba. The town has several buildings dating from the Islamic and Christian periods, including the White Tower and the Great Mosque which dates back to the Crusades.

HISTORY. – The town was founded in 716 by Caliph Suleiman, the second son of Abd el Malik who built the Dome of The Rock in Jerusalem (see entry), and named *Ramleh* (=sand) after the type of soil in the region. Palaces and mosques gave it the splendour of the Omayyad dynasty who had their capital in Damascus. In 750, when they were replaced by the Abbasids, orthodox Sufis left Baghdad, the new capital of the caliphs, for Ramleh where they were joined by Sunni and Shia Moslems, local and Diaspora Jews, and the Jewish Karaite sect. This sect came into existence in Babylon in the 8th c. They believe only in the written law of the Torah and not the Talmud. Even today their largest community is in Ramla, where 3,000 of their approximately 11,000 members live.

In the 11th c. (1025) the town was pillaged and in 1033 and 1067 it was struck by earthquakes; in 1099 came the Crusaders, who had three battles here with the Egyptian Fatimids; in 1101 and 1105 they won, but in 1102 they lost. They believed Ramleh to be the Arimathea of Joseph who gave up his tomb to Jesus.

In 1187, after the Battle of Hittim (see Horns of Hittim), Saladin also ended the era of the Crusades here. The Mameluke period, of which the White Tower is a reminder, began in 1267 with the conquest of the town by Baibars. In the 14th c. Christian monks lived here as well as Moslems and Jews. The town fell into decay in the 17th c. In 1799 Napoleon spent the night in Ramleh on his way to Acre. In 1917 General Allenby laid out a cemetery for 200 English soldiers who had fallen in the struggle against the Turkish rulers. In 1936 the Jews left the town during the Arab riots but it surrendered to the Israeli troops without a struggle on July 12, 1948. The Arab population of the town had fallen to 1,500 but it has now risen again to over 5,000.

SIGHTS. – In the E of the town, S of Herzl Street, is the *market* which has retained its oriental character. This is also where the *Great Mosque is to be found. Built by the Crusaders in the 12th c. as a basilica with a nave and two aisles, its bell-tower is now used as a minaret.

Ramla

White Tower Mosque

Further W along Herzl Street is the *Franciscan Church of St Joseph* (of Arimathea) and the *Nicodemus Hospice* with its clock tower. Between this group of buildings and the police station further W, a road leads S to the **White Tower** known by the Moslems as the "Tower of the 40 companions of the Prophet" and by the Christians as the "Tower of the 40 Martyrs".

This tower, completed by Baibars after 1267, is Gothic, has a square ground plan and is 27 m high; 128 steps lead up to its top platform. Anton Von Prokesh-Osten, who in his travel book published in 1831 described Ramleh as "a highly charming little town in rich surroundings with over 800 Greek and 200 Moslem inhabitants", also recounted how he waited up here "until the sun set, overlooking the beautiful land of the Philistines". In 1799 Napoleon climbed the tower and in 1917 General Allenby used it as an observation post.

Ramla

The White Tower stands on the N side of a broad unwalled courtyard which is a good 500 years older. On the S side of the courtyard are the substantial remains of the 98 by 13 yd/90 by 12 m **mosque** of Caliph Suleiman, dating from 716, and under the courtyard there are three large subterranean vaults which were probably storehouses for an old caravanserai or cisterns. In the 17th c. they were used as a lunatic asylum and in the 19th as accommodation for the Whirling Dervishes.

Another of the sights of Ramla, which in chronological terms comes between the mosque and the White Tower, is a huge **cistern** dating from about 800 located in a side street off the high street E of the police station. The Crusaders called it "Helena's pools" and ascribed it to the 4th c. empress who was responsible for a great deal of building, but in fact it dates from the time of the fifth Abbasid caliph, Haround al Rashid (766–809), famous for the Tales of the 1001 Nights and for his diplomatic relations with Charlemagne. The cistern, a good 600 sq. yd/500 sq. m in area and 30 ft/9 m deep, is covered by 24 groined vaults, each with a draw-hole at the top so that 24 camels could be watered at the same time. Steps lead down into this subterranean world, its water reflecting back from the arches and vaults.

SURROUNDINGS. – 2 miles/3 km to the N is **Lod** (see entry) with its Greek Orthodox Church of St George and El Chodr Mosque, and Ben Gurion airport.

4 miles/7 km SE of Ramla is the **Gezer** kibbutz, founded in 1945. It is S of the Tel Aviv–Jerusalem road in the Ayalon Valley, along which the route from the coast to Jerusalem has run since ancient times. SW of the village is the tell of ancient Gezer. The place is important because of its position which guaranteed its occupier control of the road. In fact excavations have proved that the Egyptians built fortifications here, and the Hyksos added a castle in the 18th c. B.C. Joshua besieged King Horam of Gezer who had hastened to the aid of the king of Lakhish (see entry) (Joshua 10, 33). Soon afterwards, in the 12th c. B.C., the town fell to the Philistines. About 1000 B.C. David marched out and "smote the host of the Philistines from Gibeon even to Gezer" (1 Chronicles 14, 16). Solomon fortified the strategically important town and, as at Hazor (see entry) and Megiddo (see entry), built casemate walls on the S side and a gateway which had three rooms on each side of its passageway. As in the other two towns here, the water was supplied by means of a tunnel leading to a concealed spring. Subsequently destroyed and rebuilt several times, in the 2nd c. B.C. Gezer was captured during the Macchabean uprising by the Macchabean Simon, cleansed of idols, and settled by orthodox Jews. During the Jewish revolts against Rome in the 1st and 2nd c. the settlement was destroyed; since then it has

remained virtually uninhabited. The tell of Gezer has been thoroughly investigated by British archaeologists (1902–09), American researchers (since 1964) and by Yigael Yadin, so it is well worth a visit by anyone with a special interest.

4 miles/7 km further SE of the kibbutz of Gezer is the monastery of **Latrun** (see entry).

Rehovot

District: Central.
Population: 58,000.
ⓘ **Government Tourist Office,**
7 Mendele Street,
Tel Aviv;
tel. (03) 22 32 66/7.

ACCOMMODATION. – In Rehovot: *Margoa* Hotel, 11 Moskowitz Street, IV, 17 r. In Givat Brenner: *Beit Yesha* kibbutz guest house, 63 r.

Rehovot, 13 miles/21 km SE of Tel Aviv on the coastal plain, is the center for orange cultivation and has pharmaceutical and glass industries. It has become particularly well known as the location of the Weizmann Institute of Sciences which was named after Israel's first president.

HISTORY. – Rehovot was founded in 1890 by Polish Jews as an agricultural settlement. They sank a well and called the settlement "Rehovot" after the place in the Negev where Isaac made a well which he called Rehoboth.

At first the immigrants produced wine, then at the turn of the century they started growing citrus fruit. Jews who came from the Yemen as part of the 2nd Alijah (surge of immigration) founded Shearaim, a suburb of Rehovot, in 1909.

When at the end of the First World War Rehovot was linked to the Lod–Gaza railway line, the rising town became the central point between the coastal plain and the Negev desert in the S. Its economy benefited as a result: exports of citrus fruits increased, the orange-processing industry expanded and the pharmaceutical industry started up.

Chaim Weizmann, who was born in Russia in 1874, had studied chemistry at several West European universities and had committed himself fully to the aims of the Zionist movement. He was attracted by the pleasant orange-scented region and settled in Rehovot in 1920. There he built an agricultural experimental station. When he celebrated his 70th birthday in 1944 his friends and admirers founded the Weizmann Institute of Sciences. Chaim Weizmann died in 1952 in Rehovot and was buried near the Institute.

The **Weizmann Institute of Sciences** covers a broad spectrum of research in the natural sciences. It has several departments – biology, physics and chemistry –

Tel Aviv

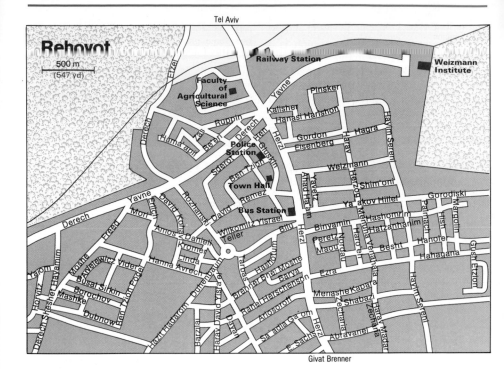

Givat Brenner

and sub-departments such as plant genetics and microbiology. Scientists from all over the world give lectures here. Over 1,000 people are employed at the Institute and during the 1978/79 academic year there were over 500 students.

The experimental station founded by Chaim Weizmann in 1920 became the *Agricultural Research Establishment* and comes under the jurisdiction of the Ministry of Agriculture. Some of the people who work there teach at the Faculty of Agriculture of the Hebrew University. This research establishment is mainly concerned with practical farming problems and the question of how agricultural products can be used for industrial production.

Weizmann's tomb is in a park (Yad Weizmann) surrounded by orange trees which can be reached from Herzl Street. The home of the great man is open to the public.

SURROUNDINGS. – 3 miles/5 km SE of Rehovot is the kibbutz of **Givat Brenner** (17,000 inhabitants) which was founded in 1928. It is named after the writer Joseph Chaim Brenner (Giv'a=hill, mountain) who was murdered by Arabs in Jaffa in 1921. Today it is one of Israel's largest kibbutzim and produces canned food and irrigation equipment; there is also a wood-processing industry. The sculptor Jacob Loutchansky, whose works, inspired by events from the history of Israel, decorate squares and gardens in

the kibbutz, lived in Givat Brenner. Yizhaq Sadeh (d. 1952), the writer and an officer in the Haganah, the Jewish terrorist organisation, is buried in the cemetery.

Rosh Ha'ayin

District: Central.
Population: 13,000.
ⓘ **Government Tourist Office,**
7 Mendele Stret,
Tel Aviv;
tel. (03) 22 32 66/7.

The town of Rosh Ha'ayin ("head of the spring", Ras el Ain in Arabic) is NE of Tel Aviv, 2½ miles/4 km beyond Petah Tiqwa directly E of the Lod–Hadera–Haifa railway line in the Plain of Sharon. Its importance, like that of old neighbouring settlements Tell Afeq and Migdal Afeq, stems from its position near the source of the Yarkon, which as one of Israel's few rivers supplies water all the year round.

HISTORY. – About 1080 B.C. the Philistines mustered their army near *Afeq* while the Israelites gathered at Eben-Ezer. During the battle the Philistines captured the Ark of the Covenant which had been brought from Silo (1 Samuel 4, 1–4) and first took it to Ashdod (see entry) and then later returned it to Bet Shemesh (see entry).

In the Hellenistic period Afeq was called "Pegai" because of the sources of the Yarkon; Pompey restored it after it had been destroyed by the Hashmoneans and called it Arethusa after the nymph of springs.

In 35 B.C. Herod built a rectangular fort and called it *Antipatris* after his father. The apostle Paul spent the night within its walls when he was being taken from Jerusalem to Caesarea in A.D. 60 (Acts 23, 31).

SE of Afeq/Antipatris is the hill of *Migdal Afeq* (Migdal Zedeq). Here, too, there were Roman and (according to an inscription in Greek) Byzantine fortifications to protect the sources of the Yarkon. It did not become important, however, until the time of the Crusades, when it became the site of Mirabel Castle that belonged to the Constable Manasses de Hierges. When King Baldwin III was contesting his right to the throne with his mother Melisande he captured her supporter and partisan Manasses in his castle of Mirabel in 1152. Manesses was sent into exile, the king appointed his friend de Toron as Constable, and Queen Melisande was allowed to retire to Nablus (see entry), which effectively cut her off from politics.

When the Crusades ended, Mamelukes and later Turks used Afeq/Antipatris as a fortress. Because of its water the place has also played a part in more recent times. During the Mandate the British laid a pipeline to carry some of the spring water to Jerusalem. To protect this they set up a military camp which developed into the town of *Rosh Ha'ayin* when many new immigrants, mainly from the Yemen, settled here after 1948. In 1955 the Israeli government laid a 62 mile/100 km long pipeline from the Yarkon springs to the Negev. In 1960 this was connected to the large pipeline which starts at the Jordan and crosses Israel.

SIGHTS. – On **Tell Afeq**, W of the town, are the huge square walls of a fortified *caravanserai* which was built in the Middle Ages over Herod's fortress of Antipatris.

Near the hill are the modern *waterworks of Rosh Ha'ayin.* On the hill of *Migdal Afeq* (2 miles/3 km SE) are the considerable but overgrown remains of *Mirabel Castle.*

Rosh Pinna

District: North.
Population: 1,000.
ⓘGovernment Tourist Office,
8 Elhadef Street,
Tiberias;
tel. (0 67) 2 09 92.

YOUTH HOSTEL. – *Nature Friends,* 100 b.

Rosh Pinna, 16 miles/26 km N of Tiberias and 6 miles/10 km E of Safed, was the first Jewish village in Upper Galilee and owes its present importance to its airport for domestic flights.

Immigrants from Rumania settled in this rocky region in 1882 and called it "Rosh Pinna" (=corner-stone) after Psalm 118, 22. Thanks to financial assistance from Baron Edmond de Rothschild (see Zikhron Yaakov) they were able to cultivate the land and develop the area.

SURROUNDINGS. – 1 mile/2 km N is the town of **Hazor HaGelilit** which was founded in 1953 and now has 5,500 inhabitants, more than Rosh Pinna. It is called after *Tell Hazor* (see Hazor; 5 miles/8 km) to the N.

A picturesque winding road leads W for 6 miles/10 km up to the town of **Safed** (see entry), once the center of the Cabbalists.

The road NE out of Rosh Pinna passes the kibbutz of *Mishmar Hayarden* (left) and at the bridge of *Benot Ya'aqov* (see entry) reaches the **Jordan** (5 miles/8 km) which, in its upper reaches, has been straightened and deepened in conjunction with the draining of the Hula Plain (see entry).

Sabas Monastery
see Mar Saba

Safed/Zefat

District: North.
Altitude: 2,462–2,739 ft/750–834 m.
Population: 17,000.
Telephone code: 0 67.
ⓘGovernment Tourist Office,
Town Hall;
tel. (0 67) 3 06 33.

HOTELS. – *Ron* (k; tel. 7 25 90), Hativat Yiftah Street, I, 50 r., SP; *Rimmon Inn* (k; tel. 3 06 65), Artists' Quarter, I, 36 r., SP; *Zefat* (k; tel. 3 09 14), Mt Canaan, I, 36 r.; *Rakefet* (k; tel. 7 22 04), Haari Street, II, 82 r.; *Pisgah* (k; tel. 3 01 05), Mt Canaan, II, 55 r.; *Central* (k; tel. 7 26 66), 37 Jerusalem Street, II, 54 r.; *David* (k; tel. 3 00 62), Mt Canaan, II, 42 r.; *Berinson House* (k; 7 25 55), II, 38 r.; *Nof Hagalil* (k; tel. 3 15 95), Mt Canaan, II, 34 r.; *Ruckenstein* (tel. 3 00 60), Mt Canaan, II, 26 r.; *Beit Yair* (k; tel. 3 02 45), 59 Jerusalem Street, III, 36 r.; *Hadar* (k; tel. 3 00 68), III, 20 r.; *Canaan Motel* (tel. 7 09 29), Mt Canaan B, 21 r.

RESTAURANT. – *Hanufgash*, 75 Yerushalayim.

COMMUNICATIONS. – Bus from Tiberias; buses to all surrounding areas.

The town of Safed (Zefat in Hebrew), a good 3,280 ft/1,000 m above the Jordan Valley in the Upper Galilean Mountains, 22 miles/36 km from Tiberias, 32 miles/51 km from Acre, has been a holy town for Jews since the 16th c. when it became a

center of cabbalistic mysticism.
Several synagogues in the N of the
Old town are reminders of this. The
quarter where Arabs lived until 1948
is now an artists' colony.

HISTORY. – In the 1st and 2nd c. several Mishnah and
Talmud scholars lived in the Safed region. In 1102 the
Crusaders built a castle which was restored in 1240 by
French Templars after it had been captured by Saladin
(1188) but in 1266 had to surrender to the Mameluke
sultan Baibars. The town became Jewish in the 16th
c. under Ottoman rule, under which it was a sanjak
(province) for a time. Jews from various parts of
Europe and N Africa settled here and in 1550
numbered over 10,000. These included Rabbi Jakob
Berab, who wanted to restore the Sanhedrin, Rabbi
Joseph Caro, author of the Schulchan Aruch, a
collection of maxims (c. 1560), and Rabbi Izhak Luria,
born in Jerusalem in 1531, known by the name of
Ha'ari (lion). 1578 saw the printing of the first Hebrew
book in Safed.

The population dwindled in the 18th c., although in
1778 Chassidic Jews came to Safed, as well as
Tiberias, from Poland. In 1834 the town was pillaged
by Druse and in 1837 it was destroyed by earthquake.
However, new settlement began during the latter part
of the 19th c. which brought the numbers up to 6,000
Arab and 6,000 Jewish families. By 1936, however,
the number of Jews had dropped to 1,800 following
Arab riots and at the time of Israel's independence
there were 12,000 Arabs and 1,700 Jews. In May
1948 a group of 120 Palmach terrorists attacked the
Arab positions and drove the Arabs out of the town,
which since then has been purely Jewish.

Although the war damage has been largely removed,
it is still possible to come across ruined houses in
several alleys in the old town. – Safed's altitude means
that it has a good climate, which attracts tourists.

Alley in Safed

These are catered for by the hotels that have been built
in the town and on nearby Mount Canaan (3,118 ft/
960 m).

SIGHTS. – After entering the town the
main street describes a long left-hand
curve around the castle hill (Hametsuda)
until it reaches some wide steps (right).
Down these on the left is the artists'

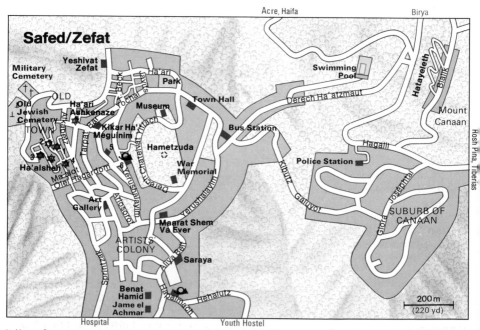

1 Abouav Synagogue
2 Joseph Bena'a Synagogue
3 Sephardic Ha'ari Synagogue
4 Joseph Caro Synagogue
5 Davidka
6 Council Offices

quarter where Arabs used to live; S of this is the *Red Mosque* (Jame el Achmar). Further down is the Jewish cemetery where Rabbi Ari (d. 1573) and Joseph Caro (d. 1575) are buried. Narrow streets off to the right lead to the *synagogues. First comes the *Joseph Caro Synagogue* and nearby is the *Alshech Synagogue*. A little further to the N are the *Hakel Tapunin Synagogue* and the *Ashkenazi Ha'ari Synagogue* which has a vault supported by old pillars. The *Sephardic Ha'ari Synagogue* is on the E outskirts of the town; visitors are shown a locked recess where the rabbi used to pray.

From the top of the steps the main street leads further S and SE to the *Cave of Shem and Eber*, on the left in the slope of the castle hill, where, according to Jewish tradition, Noah's son Shem and grandson Eber studied the Torah.

SURROUNDINGS. – 6 miles/9 km W of Safed is *Meron* (see entry) with its tomb monuments. The road continues NW to Sassa (6 miles/9 km), but a road turning off to the right before Sassa leads to the kibbutz of *Bar'am* which was founded in 1949 near the abandoned Christian (Maronite) village of Bir'am. The 2nd c. synagogue has been well restored and is worth visiting. According to legend this is the burial place of the prophet Obadiah and of Esther, wife of Xerxes, King of Persia.

Samaria

West Bank.

(i) **Government Tourist Office,**
Ha'atzmaut Square,
Netanya;
tel. (0 53) 2 72 86.

The extensive ruins of *Samaria (Shomron in Hebrew), the capital of the Kingdom of Israel from 880 to 721 B.C., are 1,411 ft/430 m above the Arab village of Sebastiya (7 miles/11 km NW of Nablus, 18 miles/29 km E of Netanya) in the green hills of the region also named Samaria after the town. The region of Samaria is bordered by the Plain of Sharon in the W, the Jezreel Plain in the N, the Jordan Valley in the E and Judea in the S. Since 1967 it has been occupied by Israel.

HISTORY. – When the kingdom was divided on Solomon's death in 928 B.C. the capital of the Northern Kingdom of Israel was at first Sichem (see Nablus), then Pneul E of the Jordan and finally Tirzah (see Nablus, Surroundings). Kings followed one another in quick succession until the fifth king of the Northern

Kingdom, Omri (882–871 B.C.), who founded the new capital "and called the name of the city after the name of Shemer, owner of the hill, Samaria" (1 Kings 16, 24). Omri and his son Ahab, who also proved to be a great builder in Hazor (see entry) and Megiddo (see entry), furnished it with palaces and temples within a circular fortified wall. This period also saw the advent in Israel of the cults of Baal and Astarte, along with the sophisticated culture of the Phoenicians, under the influence of Ahab's wife Jezebel who came from Sidon. The prophet Elijah bitterly opposed these developments and this led, inter alia, to his ordeal on Mount Carmel (see entry).

In 732 B.C. the Kingdom of Israel became dependent on Assyria. Under its last kings – Pekahiah, Pekah and Hoshea – it was limited to the capital and the area immediately around it. With the capture of Samaria by the Assyrian Salmanassar V (722 B.C.) and of the acropolis by Sargon II (721 B.C.) the kingdom ceased to exist. Many members of the upper classes were deported and in their place came Babylonians and Cuthahans (2 Kings 17, 24) who intermarried with the Jews who had remained behind and produced the Samaritans.

Subsequently Samaria was used as a military base by Assyrians, Babylonians and Persians. At the end of the 4th c. B.C. Macedonians settled there and Hellenised Samaria. When the Hashmonean Hyrkanos I captured the town in 107 B.C. he had all non-Jews put to death.

Herod brought new splendour to the town in which he had married the Hashmonean princess Mariamne in 30 B.C. He rebuilt it and called it **Sebaste** in honour of Augustus (=Sebastos in Greek). The ruins of his buildings are also a reminder that he had his wife Mariamne and her two sons put to death here. Sebaste flourished for only a short time. Jewish rebels set fire to the Temple of Augustus and shortly afterwards, in A.D. 68, Vespasian razed the fortress to the ground. When his son Titus founded Neapolis (Nablus, see entry) in A.D. 72 this set the seal on Sebaste's downfall.

Three of Jesus' disciples – Philip, Peter and John – who came to Samaria between A.D. 30 and 35 saw the town at the height of its splendour. They quarrelled with the sorcerer Simon who wanted to buy a share of the Holy Ghost (Acts 8, 4–24), hence the word "simony" for the corruptibility of holy orders.

Around A.D. 200 Emperor Septimius Severus tried to breathe new life into the town but did not succeed. Later there was a Christian community in Sebaste under a bishop; and since the 5th c. pilgrims have come here as a result of the discovery of relics of John the Baptist (though it was not here but in Machaerus, E of the Jordan, that he was executed). The cult of these relics has survived; they are still venerated in the mosque in the village of Sebastiya which continues the name of Herod's Sebaste.

SIGHTS. – There are two approaches to Samaria: it is either possible to take the turning at the white signpost and drive through the village of **Sebastiya** (cars only), or to turn a little further N near the yellow signpost pointing to the antiquities and then go uphill along the street lined with columns (also for buses).

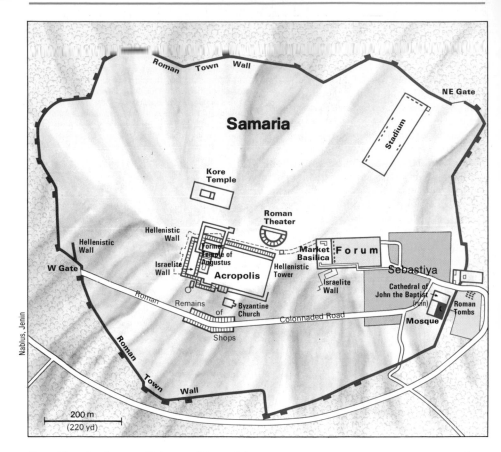

By taking the first road it is possible to visit the **mosque** in the village which covers only the E section of the ancient town. As can be seen from several pillars and parts of walls it was preceded by a Crusader church built in 1160, which in turn was preceded by a 4th c. Byzantine church. In a crypt under a dome are recesses where the tombs of the prophets Elishah and Obadiah and the burial place of the head of John the Baptist have been venerated since the 4th c. (since when the other relics of John the Baptist have been in the Omayyad mosque in Damascus).

Samaria – Roman theater

The narrow streets of the village lead up to the huge rectangle of the ancient *forum*. Both routes end here (car and coach park; restaurant where small antiques may be purchased). The long N side of the 420 by 236 ft/128 by 72 m square looks down into a hollow where the *stadium* used to be. At the W end of the square there was a **market basilica**, with a nave and two aisles, dating from the time of Septimius Severus (*c.* 200). Some of its columns are still standing and its foundation walls can be seen in the N. A footpath leads from the NW corner of the forum to the **acropolis**, which was partially excavated in 1908–11 and 1931–35. First comes an *Israelite wall* (9th–8th c. B.C.) on the slope, in front of which stands a Hellenistic reinforcing wall with a massive round *fortress tower* (3rd c.) and a Roman theater. Up on the left of the tower is a monumental flight of steps which used to front Herod's Temple of Augustus (*c.* 30 B.C.), of which no trace remains and which had been built on the site of what was then the ruined palace. Work on this palace had been started by King Omri (882–871) and it was magnificently extended by his son Ahab (871–852) and his Phoenician wife Jezebel. It also contained a cult figure of Astarte and a temple for Baal (1 Kings 16, 32–33). Among the finds made during excavation work were pieces of ivory, which confirm "Woe unto them that are at ease ... in the mountain of Samaria ... that lie upon beds of ivory" (Amos 6, 1–4); also 75 clay jars with tax rolls dating from the time of King Jeroboam II (787–747).

Walking anticlockwise around the group of buildings which are surrounded by a solid wall, one comes to the S side of the hill where there is a very well-preserved little *church* which was built in the Byzantine period on the spot where, according to tradition, John the Baptist's head was found. Returning through gardens to the car park in the forum, turn right at the end of the square.

This road does not lead to the village but, after passing between the columns of a Roman *colonnade with shops on either side* (*c.* 200), which can also be seen from up on the acropolis, arrives at the well-preserved W **town gate** which dates back to Omri but is more recent in its present form; the round Roman N tower stands on rectangular Hellenistic foundations.

Sea of Galilee

Sea of Galilee/ Yam Kinneret

District: North.

ⓘ **Government Tourist Office,**
8 Elhadef Street,
Tiberias;
tel. (0 67) 2 09 92.

ACCOMMODATION. – In *Tiberias* see Tiberias. – CAMP SITES at Kefar Hittim (W of Tiberias), Ma'agan (on the SE shore of the lake) and En Gev (on the E shore).

The *Sea of Galilee, Yam Kinneret in Hebrew, is in the Jordan Valley 689 ft/210 m below sea level. 7 miles/12 km wide and 13 miles/21 km long, it covers an area of 66 sq. miles/170 sq. km and has a depth of 151 ft/46 m at its deepest point. It serves as Israel's largest reservoir and its water is piped to various collection points and thence to the Negev.*

BIBLICAL HISTORY. – In the Old Testament the Sea of Chinnereth is mentioned when the Children of Israel arrive in Canaan and the future borders of the land and the areas to be inhabited by each tribe are mapped out (Numbers 34, 11; Joshua 13, 27). It is frequently mentioned in the New Testament because Jesus found his first disciples in Capernaum on the N shore where he spent most of his time after leaving Nazareth, and there is the famous story of Jesus and Peter caught in a storm on the lake (Matthew 14, 22–33; Mark 6, 45–56).

Today there are many places around the Sea of Galilee of historical and scriptural interest (see Capernaum, Tabgha, Tiberias). **Tiberias** (see entry), on the W shore of the Sea, is a popular holiday resort. Since ancient times its hot springs, about 1 mile/2 km S of the town center, have been used to treat various illnesses, especially rheumatism and respiratory diseases.

Another health resort known since ancient times is *Hamat Gader* (see entry) not far from the E shore in the lower Yarmuk Valley; Yizhak Hirschfeld is carrying out excavations here.

Tombs of David Ben Gurion and his wife

Sede Boqer

District: South.
Population: 600.
ⓘ **Government Tourist Office,**
Bet Tnuat Hamoschavim,
Beersheba;
tel. (0 57) 3 00 01.

The kibbutz of Sede Boqer (Farmers' Field) is 32 miles/51 km S of Beersheba. It was founded on May 15, 1952, the fourth anniversary of Israeli independence, by former soldiers in the Negev, at that time devoid of roads, not far from Wadi Zin.

The aim of its founders was to make the desert bloom. Today it is on the Beersheba–Eilat road, near the ruins of Avdat (see entry), and flourishes as an agricultural settlement.

HISTORY. – The kibbutz is closely linked with the name of David Ben Gurion. Ben Gurion, who was born David Grien in Poland in 1886 but who lived in Palestine from 1906, was co-founder of the Social Democratic Party, a trade union leader from 1921 to 1935 and president of the Jewish Agency from 1935 to 1948 and of the World Zionist Organisation in 1944. He it was who proclaimed the independent state of Israel on May 14, 1948 and became its first prime minister. When he left his post five years later, in 1953, he joined the new kibbutz of Sede Boqer in order to do "what really matters", i.e. to conquer the Negev. However, 14 months later he resumed political office, first as Minister of Defence and then again as Prime Minister. In 1963 at the age of 77 he finally returned to Sede Boqer which then became a hub of political life. In 1975 the indomitable patriarch died at the Biblical age of 89 and was buried here where he had found his homeland.

In his last book "Israel" – akin to a political testament – he conjured up his vision of a desert that had been made to bloom, the homeland for two million people. It was this bold idea that inspired him to found the Sede Boqer Midrashet, 2 miles/3 km S of the kibbutz. From its modest beginnings as a secondary school and teacher training college this institute for research into the development possibilities of arid regions has become a large organisation with over 400 students.

History, archaeology and sociology are taught here, as well as the natural sciences, but at all times with a view to the special conditions of the Negev. But Ben Gurion was also aware that, "Israel needs not only science and technology, though both are of great importance, but also the pioneering spirit." In this he saw the "moral treasure which is rooted in man's belief in his ability to overcome obstacles, even those which at first sight seem too great for an ordinary mortal." And he was convinced that: "As the Negev has hidden resources so has man, who will become fully aware of them once he is in the Negev and knows that he is called upon to use these powers creatively." Therefore, he declares the purpose of his Midrashet to be "a center of scientific research and work as a source of ethical inspiration."

SIGHTS. – 2 miles/3 km S of the kibbutz, 6 miles/10 km N of Avdat, a side-road leaves the main road for the **Negev Institute** (*Midrashet Sede Boqer*). The extensive site is dominated by the *library*, which contains not only a large collection of specialist books but also Ben Gurion's archives, with material of great importance for Jewish 20th c. history and the history of the state of Israel. On the far side of this building are the *tombs of David Ben Gurion and his wife*. The two simple stone tombs stand in a shady square of trees on the edge of the gorge of the Wadi Zin which starts at the gushing spring of Avdat (see En Avdat) and has towering walls of rock on all sides (impressive *view).

Library of the Negev Institute in Sede Boqer

Sepphoris

see Zippori

Plain of Sharon/ Emeq Sharon

District: Haifa, Central, Tel Aviv.
Government Tourist Office,
7 Mendele Street,
Tel Aviv;
tel. (03) 22 32 66/7.

The Plain of Sharon is the large coastal plain which stretches 37 miles/60 km from S of Mount Carmel to the River Yarkon (Tel Aviv) and from the Mediterranean to the hills of Samaria.

The Plain of Sharon owes its fertility to its abundant water supply, attributable mostly to rivers that never run dry, but the sand dunes on the coast have always impeded the flow of water into the sea, and this has led to the formation of malarial swamps in the absence of artificial drainage. The mouth of one of the drainage channels can still be seen at Herzliyya (see entry).

HISTORY. – The Plain of Sharon has been inhabited since the early Canaanite period. Tools dating from that time were found in 1962 in the Tell of Kefar Monash (6 miles/9 km NE of Netanya), a settlement founded in 1946. The old settlements were destroyed by the Assyrians and the Babylonians (7th–6th c.). Phoenicians settled there in the 5th c. B.C. and about 100 B.C. the Plain of Sharon became part of Judah. In 25 B.C. Herod founded the port of Caesarea (see entry) which was the capital of the country in the Roman and Byzantine periods. After the Mamelukes invaded in the 13th c. the drainage system broke down and the Plain of Sharon reverted to virtually uninhabited marshland.

A change took place when Jewish colonists settled in the region. In 1878 they founded *Petah Tiqwa* on the banks of the Yarkon in the S, and in 1890 *Hadera* (see entry) in the N. Drainage projects were subsequently embarked upon on a planned basis and this led to the founding of many settlements, including major towns such as *Herzliyya* (see entry) and *Netanya* (see entry).

Nowadays the Plain of Sharon is densely populated and subject to intensive agriculture (center of citrus cultivation).

Shivta (Subeita)

District: South.
Government Tourist Office,
Bet Tnuat Hamoschavim,
Beersheba;
tel. (0 57) 3 60 01.

The old town of Subeita, today called Shivta, is 34 miles/55 km SW of Beersheba, S of the road leading to the border between Egypt and Israel. Because of its military camp it is not always accessible.

HISTORY. – *Subeita* was built by Nabataeans in the 1st c. B.C. between Avdat (see entry) and Nizzana. It was an unfortified town which was captured by the Byzantines and underwent such thorough renovation that when the English were excavating in 1934 they found exclusively Byzantine remains and nothing Nabataean. It is worth visiting for the ruins, some of which are astonishingly well preserved, of a 5th–6th c. Byzantine town with its three monastery churches, dwellings, reservoirs and paved streets, which was still lived in during the Arab period.

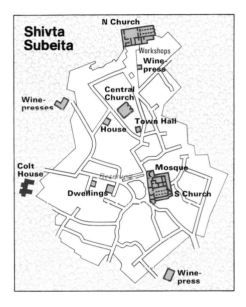

SIGHTS. – The ruins lie within a National Park. Near the entrance to the site is the **South Church**, a basilica divided by columns into a nave and two aisles, the apses of which are still standing. On the left of the porch is the baptistry with a cruciform font. In the 7th c. the Moslems built a mosque on to this church. To the N is the *Town Hall*, by a fork in the street. The left-hand street leads to the *Central Church*, which also had a nave and two aisles, of which only a few walls and the S apse are still standing. A baker's oven or potter's kiln and a wine-press can be found in the business quarter in front of the **North Church**, which has the rooms of a monastery built along its sides. This church also has a nave and two aisles, and next to it are the baptistry and a chapel, so that no fewer than five fully preserved apses stand side by side here. At the entrance is part of an entablature with the Chi-Rho monogram and the Greek letters alpha and omega.

SURROUNDINGS. – 11 miles/17 km to the SE is another Nabataean town, **Nizzana**, which survived the Byzantine and Islamic period into the 8th c. Excavation work in 1935 led to the discovery of churches and other buildings. One church still has its mosaic floor. In 1907 the Turks set up a border post near the Bedouin well of Auja el Hafir, and the British later built a prison camp. In 1948 the Egyptian army attacked Beersheba from Nizzana.

Sinai/
Sinai Peninsula

Egypt.
Altitude: sea level to 8,674 ft/2,642 m above sea level.

The *Sinai Peninsula, bounded in the N by the Mediterranean, in the W by the rift valley of the Gulf of Suez, in the S by the Red Sea and in the E and SE by the Jordan rift valley and its southern extension the Gulf of Aqaba, forms a link between Africa and Asia. It is an area which is for the most part steppe and desert, cultivable only in the N, on the coast and in some small oases, almost devoid of inhabitants. Yet the rugged Sinai massif with its lonely valleys, picturesque rocky landscape and magnificent views at every turn is an impressive region. – A major attraction is the Monastery of St Catherine with its very rich icon museum.

The peninsula is Egyptian territory. Under the terms of the September 1978 Agreement between Egypt and Israel the Israeli troops, that had occupied the Sinai since 1967, completed their gradual withdrawal by April 1982. Nowadays the border between Egypt and Israel runs N–S from Rafiah (Rafah) on the Mediterranean to Taba on the Gulf of Aqaba. – Since it continues to be possible to visit the Monastery of St Catherine from Israel the Sinai Peninsula is covered in this book.

Road to the airport near the Monastery of St Catherine

3,282 ft/1,000 m in height but the **Sinai Mountains** that cover the S of the peninsula rise to over 6,564 ft/2,000 m at *Gebel Serbâl* (6,794 ft/2,070 m), *Gebel Musa* (7,500 ft/2,285 m) and *Gebel Katerin* (8,610 ft/2,642 m).

The peninsula is Egyptian territory. In the September 1978 peace treaty between Egypt and Israel it was agreed that the Israeli troops that had occupied it since 1967 should gradually withdraw. The W half was handed back first and the temporary border ran N–S from El Arish to the Ras Mohammed Cape. The E half was returned to Egypt in April 1982. – As it is still possible to visit the Monastery of St Catherine from Israel the region will be covered in this book.

ACCESS from Israel to the Sinai Mountains. – For short trips from Israel to S Sinai and the Monastery of St Catherine an entry permit can be bought for a stay of up to seven days. – The Air Sinai airline flies from Tel Aviv and Eilat to Mount Sinai airport. The first part of the road from the airport to the Monastery of St Catherine, to a right fork into the Wadi Firan, is on an asphalt road and then a track goes off left to the Monastery. Buses to the Sinai region and the Monastery also operate out of Eilat. – Motorists can also visit the Sinai Peninsula in their own cars (7 days maximum) but are not allowed to use rented Israeli vehicles.

HISTORY AND SCRIPTURAL TRADITION. – The Sinai Peninsula has been a passage between N Africa and the Middle East since the dawn of history. The Egyptians were mining turquoise and copper here as early as the 3rd c. B.C., as is evidenced by inscriptions on the rocks and the remains of a temple to Hathor near Serâbit el Châdim in the W of the peninsula. The "Sinai inscriptions", discovered by Flinders Petrie in 1905, date back to the 2nd millennium B.C.: they are attributed to nomadic Western Semitic tribes who on reaching Egypt developed signs for consonants out of the pictograms of hieroglyphics, and this new alphabet was adopted by the Canaanites.

The Old Testament also tells of nomadic tribes that wandered between Palestine and Egypt. The Sinai ("Mount Horeb") is especially important because it was here that Moses received the divine revelation, with the result that he not only led the Jews out of Egypt but also became the founder of the religion named after him, the oldest of the world's three monotheistic religions. It was on Mount Horeb, where God had already appeared to him in the Burning Bush (Exodus 3, 1–2), that Moses received the Ten Commandments (Exodus 20) and other divine directions. – In the 9th c. B.C. it was to the holy Mount Horeb that Elijah fled from Ahab and Jezebel (1 Kings 20).

Sinai assumed fresh significance as a holy place during the Christian era. The first Christian church-historian Eusebius (c. 260–339), who came from Palestine, made the assumption that Sinai was the mountain where Moses received the Commandments. In his time monks and hermits lived in the Sinai. In

Monastery of St Catherine on the Sinai Peninsula

324, according to a reliable tradition, Helena, the mother of Emperor Constantine, founded a batos, i.e. a Monastery of the Bush, on the site of the Spring of Moses and the Burning Bush. After 548 Justinian, the Byzantine emperor who ruled over Sinai as well as Syria and Egypt, built the fortified monastery that we see today to afford the monks greater protection.

During his Egyptian expedition Napoleon granted the monastery his protection; in the 19th c. the Russian Tsars turned their attention to Sinai. In 1840 the area, which had belonged to the Ottoman Empire since 1517, became part of Egypt under its autonomous ruler Mehmed Ali. In 1903 the British drew a new border between Egypt, which they occupied, and Turkey. This border, which after the First World War became the international border, ran in a straight line from Rafiah on the Mediterranean to Eilat.

In the 20th c. a fresh, economic, aspect came to the fore. The presence of oil was confirmed on the W coast and of coal in other parts of the peninsula. This reinforced the Sinai's importance in the disputes between Israel and Egypt. Israel occupied part of Sinai in 1948 and took it over completely in 1956 and 1967. Under the Camp David Agreement of September 1978 the Israelis vacated Sinai by April 1982.

Monastery of St Catherine

The **Monastery of St Catherine**, at an altitude of 5,015 ft/1,528 m on a slope below the 7,500 ft/2,285 m high *Mount of Moses* (Gebel Musa), stands on the spot which since the 4th c. has been the traditional site of the Burning Bush and of the spring where Moses watered the animals of his father-in-law Jethro. Thus the Bedouin call the spot *Wadi Shueib*

("Shueib" is their name for Jethro), and it is also known as Wadi ed-Deir (Valley of the Monastery).

HISTORY. – The Franco-Spanish nun Etheria, who travelled to the Holy Land about A.D. 400, in her "Peregrinatio", the diary of her travels which was rediscovered in Arezzo in 1884, wrote of Sinai: "There were the cells of many holy men and a church on the spot where the Burning Bush stands ... In front of the church is a very pretty garden with plenty of good water and the Burning Bush stands in the garden." The church she mentions is the one said to have been founded by Empress Helena in A.D. 324.

On the site of this church Emperor Justinian built the present church within a fortified monastery. The building of the complex can be precisely dated as between 548 and 565: inscriptions on the original ceiling beams say that Justinian (d. 565) had it built by the master-builder Stephanos of Aila in memory of Empress Theodora who died in 548. According to Justinian's chronicler Prokop (De Aedificiis V, 8) the church was dedicated to the Mother of God.

In the 10th or 11th c. the church was dedicated to *St Catherine of Alexandria* who had been martyred under Emperor Maxentius (306–312). Legend has it that angels carried her bones to Sinai; they were found later on the Mount of St Catherine (Gebel Katerin) by monks who took them to their monastery. – Catherine had steadfastly defended her virginity and this must have contributed to the fact that the Burning Bush, formerly a symbol of the meeting of the young Moses with God, later became a symbol of the Immaculata.

Up to 400 monks lived in the monastery in its heyday and some of them were particularly outstanding. About 400 Neilos, who was later canonised but had hitherto been a high dignitary at the court of Emperor Arcadius in Constantinople, went to Sinai with his son. Over a thousand of his letters, written in Greek, plus a few tracts and maxims, are extant and are important as an account of the life of a monk at that time. – In the 7th c. Johannes Klimakos spent 40 years here as a hermit and then became abbot; his nickname ꞏꞏꞏꞏꞏ ꞏꞏ ꞏꞏꞏ ꞏꞏ ꞏꞏ "Kꞏꞏꞏꞏꞏ ꞏꞏ ꞏꞏꞏꞏꞏꞏꞏꞏꞏ" ("ꞏꞏꞏꞏꞏꞏ ꞏꞏ Paradise") which is of great importance for orthodox monasticism. – Reference should also be made to Simeon of Sinai, whom the Archbishop of Trier, Poppo, met when he visited Palestine. Simeon followed Poppo back to Trier where he had himself walled up in the Porta Nigra. After living as a strict ascetic he died in 1035 and was canonised only seven years later. Poppo turned the Porta Nigra into a double church to honour him and founded the nearby Monastery of St Simeon.

The number of monks started to decline when, in the 11th c., the harsh rule of the Seljuks meant fewer pilgrims to the Holy Land and consequently less funds for the monastery. Yet it has remained in existence to this day, although since the 7th c. it has been surrounded by Islam which it has allowed for by building a mosque within the monastery precincts.

The monastery maintains relations with Europe. In the 13th c. Roman Catholic monks built a chapel dedicated to St Catherine of the Franks. Monks from Sinai also journeyed to France, especially to Rouen, the capital of Normandy, to collect gifts of money and to sell relics, which is why Rouen Cathedral comes to have so many relics of St Catherine. European pilgrims came to Sinai in the 14th–16th c. as can be seen from their coats of arms in the Trapeza (refectory). Added Slavic influence began at a later date, firstly from the Moldavian principalities and then, beginning in the 17th c., from Russia. The monastery's material situation improved in the 19th c. when it was the recipient of rich gifts from the Russian Tsars.

It is a monastery of Greek Orthodox monks, mostly from Crete and Cyprus. In its heyday at the turn of the millennium they numbered btween 300 and 400 but today their numbers have declined to about 50. Only 20 of these live in the monastery itself; the rest are posted to filial foundations. The abbot ranks as an archbishop and since 1571 has exercised the right of autocephaly, i.e. is independent of any higher governing body. He is elected by the monks and enthroned by the Greek Orthodox patriarch of Jerusalem. He usually lives in one of the monastery's filial foundations in Cairo and is represented in the monastery by four archimandrites. Damianos has been archbishop and abbot since 1979.

The monks' main services are from 4.30 to 7.30 a.m. and from 2.30 to 4 p.m. Visiting times are 9 a.m. to noon. It is also possible by prior arrangement to stay overnight in the monastery.

SIGHTS. – The ground plan of the monastery is an irregular quadrilateral 279 by 246 ft/85 by 75 m. The *wall* around it is of blocks of granite and is 39 to 49 ft/12 to 15 m high. Despite being damaged in the 1312 earthquake, most of it (especially in the SW) dates back to the 6th c. When the original gate had to be walled up on grounds of security, for a long time the only access was via a rope winch on the N side. The gate now in use in the W wall was made in 1801 by a French expedition under Kléber which also restored major sections of the wall. Recently tourists have also been able to enter the monastery through a new gate on the N side.

The interior of the monastery is "a system of little alleys, poky staircases, passages, steps and a maze of interlocking buildings around the basilica" (E. Brunner-Traut). The tourist entrance leads through a room with a sales counter into a courtyard on the N side of the church. On the left is a bush behind the Chapel of the Burning Bush and on the right the Well of Moses.

It is possible to enter the narthex of the *Church of the Transfiguration** with its display of valuable icons and to go a little way into the nave of the basilica, but the E sections of the church and other parts of the monastery are generally not open to short-term visitors.

The church and the courtyard of the bush are situated at the lowest level in the monastery. The Justinian building, to which Tsar Alexander II had a *belfry* added in 1871, is a basilica with rows of columns separating the two side aisles from the nave. The portal leading to the narthex has carved statues of Mary and angels and dates from the time of the Fatimids (11th c.). The portal leading to the nave is 12 ft/3·63 m high and 8 ft/2·4 m wide; its four panels of cypress wood date from when it was built in the 6th c. The coolness of the *nave* is reinforced by the whitewashed walls and the fact that its two rows of six granite columns are

Entrance to the Monastery of St Catherine

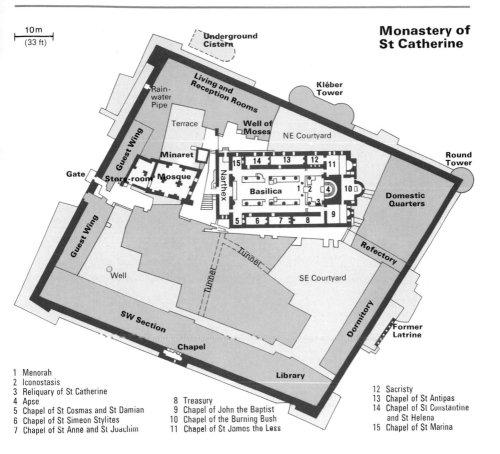

10 m
(33 ft)

Monastery of St Catherine

1 Menorah
2 Iconostasis
3 Reliquary of St Catherine
4 Apse
5 Chapel of St Cosmas and St Damian
6 Chapel of St Simeon Stylites
7 Chapel of St Anne and St Joachim

8 Treasury
9 Chapel of John the Baptist
10 Chapel of the Burning Bush
11 Chapel of St James the Less

12 Sacristy
13 Chapel of St Antipas
14 Chapel of St Constantine and St Helena
15 Chapel of St Marina

coated with plaster. The capitals are also granite. Each of the *side aisles* has three chapels opening off it: in the N (left) the *Chapel of St Marina*, the *Chapel of Constantine and Helena* and the *Antipas Chapel*; in the S (right) the *Chapel of Cosmas and Damian*, the *Chapel of Simeon Stylites* and the *Chapel of St Anne*.

The basilica is basically very much the same as it was when it was first built. The floor is of porphyry and marble and, like the flat wooden ceiling below the original open roof timbers, dates from the 18th c. There are huge candlesticks, given in 1799 by Matthäus Bleyel of Nuremberg, in front of the gilded *iconostasis*, the work of artists from Crete in 1612 when Laurentios was archbishop. This spot was originally occupied by a low stone barrier with columns, the templon, so that it was possible to see right into the sanctuary.

In the *sanctuary* just behind the iconostasis are two reliquaries given by the Tsars, and on the right another reliquary under a baldachin containing the relics of St Catherine. The original marble altar in the center was encased in wood in 1675 by Stamatios from Athens; this, like the contemporary altar baldachin, is richly inlaid with mother of pearl.

The *apse* of the sanctuary has a synthronon, semicircular benches for the priests, typical of the Justinian period. Nowadays a tabernacle stands on the abbot's throne in the center of the apse. Dominating the apse is an important 6th c. mosaic.

The *mosaic represents Christ's transfiguration on Mount Tabor, the "Metamorphosis". This theme is especially significant in the Orthodox church since Christ showed himself here to the disciples in his divine form. The scene shows Christ between the prophets Elijah and Moses, with the disciples John, Peter and James underneath. Below this main image is a row of medallions of 16 Old Testament prophets with King David in the center, above him apostles and saints, with the Cross in the middle. On the E wall above the apse are two scenes, with the double window in between, connected with Sinai: Moses in front of the Burning Bush and the handing down of the Commandments (in the form of a scroll). "The theme is first of all Christ's transfiguration, as depicted in the apse, and then Moses on Mount Sinai; top left is Moses being called by the Burning Bush, top right receiving the Tablets. Moses is the link, since he witnessed the Transfiguration and 'talked with Jesus'.

The prophet Elijah is also linked with Sinai; Elijah and Moses are shown in the mosaic in the apse on the left and right hand of Christ." (George H. Forsyth.)

In the spandrels Christ is shown again, this time as the Lamb of God, being handed a sceptre and a globe by two angels (this motif obviously comes from the victories on Roman triumphal arches). Below the angels are medallions of John the Baptist and Mary; these, together with the Lamb, form the earliest representation of a motif that was later to become very common – the deisis, John and Mary interceding with Christ.

The apse is flanked by two chapels, the Chapel of St James (left) and that of the Holy Fathers (or Chapel of John the Baptist; right).

From the N aisle a passage through the iconostasis leads into the *Chapel of St James* containing 15th c. wall-paintings. These show Christ and, below, Mary in the Burning Bush (motif of the Immaculata); at the sides are the Early Fathers John Chrysostomos (left) and St Basil (right) and at each edge a representative of the New and Old Testaments, St James the Great and Moses.

From here a passage leads behind the sanctuary to the most holy shrine in the monastery, the * **Chapel of the Burning Bush** (remove shoes before entering). Originally an open courtyard behind the apse of the church, it was made into a chapel in 1216.

That year the German pilgrim Thietmar visited the chapel and wrote: "The Burning Bush was removed and distributed as relics under the Christians." The chapel is covered in blue-green tiles and in the apse is a mosaic with a simple cross on a gold background; it marks the spot where God appeared to Moses and called him while he was tending the sheep of his father-in-law Jethro at a spring (the Well of Moses just N of the church). "And he looked, and, behold, the bush burned with fire, and the bush was not consumed . . . And when the Lord saw that he turned aside to see, God called unto him out of the midst of the bush, and said . . . Draw not nigh hither: put off thy shoes from off thy feet, for the place whereon thou standest is holy ground." (Exodus 3, 2–5.) It is therefore forbidden to wear shoes in the chapel. An eternal flame in a lamp under the altar marks the silver-plated spot where the Burning Bush grew. The rose and broom bush against the outside wall of the chapel is said to be a cutting from this bush.

In front of the church is the *mosque*, built in the 11th c. in a former guest house for the Moslem Bedouin of the region.

Past the end of the S side of the church is the long *refectory* (trapeza) containing a Cretan fresco of the Last Judgement (1573) and coats of arms and inscriptions

of Europeans who came here as pilgrims in the 14th–16th c.

The crypts under the Tryphon Chapel in the NW of the monastery contain the *ossuary* where the bones of thousands of monks are kept. At the entrance, ever vigilant, is the clothed body of Stephanos, a monk who in the 6th c. heard the confessions of pilgrims on their way up the Mount of Moses.

In the new guest quarters, built between 1932 and 1942 against the SW section of the 6th c. wall, with a tiny chapel in the middle, there is a museum and a library.

The **Museum** contains over 2,000 icons and is the most important collection of icons in the world in terms of quantity and quality. It is especially important because 5th and 6th c. icons survived in Sinai when they were being destroyed elsewhere, mostly at the urging of the iconoclasts (726–843) who were opposed to the veneration of holy images. Hence the presence here of three encaustic 6th c. icons (produced by fusing wax colours to the surface): Christ, Christus Pantokrator and Mary between the warrior saints Theodor and George.

There is also a considerable collection of liturgical objects, vestments, bishops' crowns and crosiers, etc., as well as magnificent gifts from the Tsars and a chalice presented by the French king Charles VI in 1411.

Of no less importance is the **Library** with its collection of approximately 3,500 manuscripts, in Greek (2,289), Arabic (580), Syrian (276), Georgian (98), Slavic (41), Ethiopian (6) and Armenian (1). There are also archives containing approximately 2,000 documents from the 12th to the 19th c. Only one manuscript in Latin survives, an indication that the monks systematically destroyed the "Frankish" writings. Important manuscripts include two commentaries on the gospels (967 and c. 1000), the Hiob book (11th c.), the writings of the Sinai monk and abbot John Klimakos (12th c.) and the 16 homilies of Gregor of Nazianz (c. 1150). – During his visits here in the mid-19th c. Konstantin von Tischendorf came across a 4th c. Greek Bible, the *Codex Sinaiticus*, and took 347 pages of it for himself. Some of them came into the possession of the library of Leipzig University, but most of them went to St Petersburg where the Tsar purchased them for 27,000 gold marks. In 1933 Stalin sold them to the British Museum for £100,000. In the monastery itself a facsimile of the Codex is on display. Several years ago some additional pages are said to have been discovered within the monastery in a cell that had previously been walled up. The facsimile, together with the other items – the genuine or alleged letter of safe-conduct from Mohammed and Napoleon's guarantee of protection – are in show cases at the entrance and in the salesroom.

Mount of Moses and Mount of St Catherine

There are two ways up the 7,500 ft/2,285 m high *Mount of Moses* (*Gebel Musa*)

Mount Moses in the Sinai Peninsula

– the climb takes at least three hours there and back. The best route to choose is the winding path rather than the steps. I his path, which starts E of the monastery, was laid out in the 19th c. as a "pasha path" which could also be negotiated by camel. After an hour a path goes off to the right to the *Hermitage of St Stephen* which has chapels dedicated to Moses and Elijah near a spring. The stepped path, with 734 steps up to the summit, begins on the left.

On the summit of Gebel Musa is a small *chapel* (built in 1930 on the site of the older one which had been destroyed) and a small *mosque* which is greatly venerated by the Arabs. At the NE corner of the rock with the chapel on it, visitors are shown the hollow in which Moses was standing when God appeared to him. The Moslems believe that Moses stayed, fasting, for forty days in a cistern-like hollow near the mosque while he committed the Commandments to two stone tablets.

The *view from the summit of Gebel Musa over the wild barren landscape is magnificent. In the SW it extends beyond the highest mountains in Sinai to the Red Sea and the Gulf of Aqaba and in the NW beyond the mountains to the low hills in the N of the peninsula.

By taking the other route of over 3,000 steps back down to the monastery 2,625 ft/800 m below, the visitor passes the *Gate of Faith* and the *Gate of St Stephanos* who heard the confessions of the pilgrims here and whose skeleton guards the monastery ossuary.

A well-signposted 5-hour route leads to the top of the 8,670 ft/2,642 m high **Mount of St Catherine** (*Gebel Katerin*), 4 miles/6 km S of the monastery. It is possible to drive past a chapel commemorating Aaron, Moses' brother, and a monastery garden to the rest house begun in the 19th c. as a seigneurial palace near the small *Monastery of the Apostles*. Further on is the *Monastery of the 40 Martyrs* from where the route climbs up to the summit. The *Summit Chapel* stands on the spot where monks, guided by a dream, found the bones of St Catherine of Alexandria, the saint who gave her name to the mountain and to the Monastery of St Catherine.

Subeita

see Shivta

Tabgha/En Sheva

District: North.
ⓘ **Government Tourist Office,**
8 Elhadef Street,
Tiberias;
tel. (0 67) 2 09 92.

According to tradition the "Place of the seven springs", Tabgha in Arabic, En Sheva in Hebrew, is the site of the miracle of the loaves and fishes (Mark 8, 1 0).

To get to Tabgha (7 miles/12 km from Tiberias) take the road N out of Tiberias and turn off right towards Capernaum after the kibbutz of *Ginnossar*.

HISTORY. – The first church here, a single-nave building 51 by 31 ft/15·5 by 9·5 m, was built in the 4th c. In the 5th c. it was replaced by a larger cruciform basilica with columns separating the two aisles from the nave. In 1932 Mader and Schneider found the mosaics of this second church, and in 1936 they were protected by the building of a new church. In 1956 a German Benedictine monastery was built beside this new church which has subsequently been removed and replaced by another, that built in 1980–82 for the "German Association in the Holy Land" (headquarters in Cologne). Tabgha's third church of the Miracle of the Loaves and Fishes was consecrated on May 23 1982.

SIGHTS. – The new **Church of the Miracle of the Loaves and Fishes** is in the Byzantine style. The architects were Anton Georgen and Fritz Baumann of Cologne. The *mosaics* in the nave and N aisle have simple geometric patterns. The mosaics representing various types of bird (geese, herons, etc.) in the five spaces between the columns are more figurative. The most interesting mosaics are in the arms of the transept. The pavement in the N transept has been preserved almost

Mosaic of the loaves and fishes

intact. The artist was obviously very familiar with the Nile Delta (and maybe even came from there) and here depicted the flora and fauna of that region: flamingoes, snakes, herons and ducks with lotus blossom, reeds, etc. The mosaics in the S transept have been only partly preserved and have the same motifs as those in the N transept plus a Nilometer for measuring the river's water level.

In the *presbytery* the altar is built on the stone on which Jesus is said to have stood when he performed the miracle of the loaves and fishes. In front of it is a mosaic showing the basket with the loaves and the two fishes.

Adjoining the site to the E is another shrine which is also part of Tabgha. From the entrance 220 yd/200 m further E a footpath leads down past a Byzantine enclosed spring to the shore of the Sea of Galilee and the remains of a small Crusader castle and the **Primacy Chapel** or *Church of St Peter*. Built in the 4th c. and destroyed in 1263, it was rebuilt in 1933 in black basalt by the Franciscans. The simple single nave commemorates the appearance of the risen Christ to the apostles here on the shore of the Sea of Galilee when Jesus transferred primacy over the Church to Peter with the three-fold instructions "Feed my lambs. Feed my sheep. Feed my sheep." (John 21, 15–17.) The rock in the E section of the chapel is supposed to be the table where Jesus dined with his disciples. The steps cut in the rock leading down into the lake in front of the S façade were described by the Spanish pilgrim Etheria about 400 as "those on which the Lord stood".

N of Tabgha is the *Mount of the Beatitudes* (see entry). Just N of the road between the entrance to the sites of the Church of the Miracle of the Loaves and Fishes and the Primacy Chapel are the ruins of the small **Monastery of the Sermon on the Mount** which was built in the 4th c. and is therefore almost contemporary with the first Church of the Miracle of the Loaves and Fishes and the original Primacy Chapel. In the S is the monastery and in the N the church whose apse, with seats for the priests inside, projects E over the exterior wall. The single-nave church measures only 24 by 15 ft/7·2 by 4·48 m. It used to have a mosaic pavement (remains in the garden of Capernaum) in the narthex and the

nave. The square sacristy on the N side is completely hewn out of the rock. The church, made of basalt with a white marble altar, existed until the beginning of the Islamic period (7th c.) and in 1938 was replaced by a new church further up the Mount of the Beatitudes.

SURROUNDINGS. – A short distance from Tabgha on the N shore of the Sea of Galilee is *Capernaum* (see entry) with Peter's Octagon and an old synagogue.

Tabor, Mount
see Mount Tabor

Tel Aviv-Jaffa (Yafo)

District: Tel Aviv.
Altitude: sea level.
Population: 330,000 (Greater Tel Aviv with Bat Yam, Bene Beraq, Giv'atayim, Holon and Ramat Gan: 1·18 million).
Telephone code: 03.
ⓘ **Government Tourist Office,**
7 Mendele Street;
tel. 22 32 66/7.
Ben Gurion Airport;
tel. 97 14 35

Municipal Information Bureau:
42 Frishman Street
(N of Dizengoff Square);
tel. 22 36 92.

EMBASSIES. – *British Embassy*, 192 Hayarkon Street, Tel Aviv, tel. 24 91 71; *USA*, 71 Hayarkon Street, tel. 25 43 38; *Canada*, 220 Hayarkon Street, tel. 22 81 22.

HOTELS. – In Tel Aviv: **Tel Aviv Hilton* (k), Independence Park, L, 617 r., SP, sauna, tennis; **Astoria* (k), 10 Kaufman Street, L, 504 r., SP, sauna; **Tel Aviv Sheraton* (k), with **Gold Carpet* Service, 115 Hayarkon Street, L, 470 r., SP, sauna; **Plaza Tel Aviv* (k), 155 Hayarkon Street, L, 350 r., SP; **Ramada Continental* (k), 121 Hayarkon Street, L, 340 r., SP; **Dan Tel Aviv* (k), 99 Hayarkon Street, L, 305 r., SP; **Diplomat*, 145 Hayarkon Street, L, 266 r., SP; *Carlton Penta Tel Aviv* (k), Hayarkon Street, I, 282 r., SP; *Mandarin* (k), on the seafront (N Tel Aviv); I, 225 r., SP, tennis, golf; *Sinai* (k), 11–15 Trumpeldor Street, I, 250 r., SP; *Grand Beach* (k), 250 Hayarkon Street, I, 208 r., SP, sauna; *Basle* (k), 156 Hayarkon Street, I, 138 r., SP; *Country Club*, Haifa Street, I, 138 r., SP, sauna, tennis; *Tal* (k), 287 Hayarkon Street, I, 126 r.; *Avia* (k), Savyon (Lod Airport), I, 118 r., SP, tennis; *Ramat Aviv* (k), 151 Haifa Street, I, 118 r., SP, tennis; *Park* (k), 75 Hayarkon Street, I, 99 r.; *Concorde* (k), 1 Trumpeldor Street, I, 92 r.; *Astor* (k), 105 Hayarkon Street, I, 68 r.; *Wishnitz* (k), 16 Damesek Street, II, 102 r.; *City* (k), 9 Mapu Street, II, 96 r.; *Moss* (k), 6 Nes Ziona Street, II, 70 r.; *Adiv* (k), 5 Mendele Street, II, 68 r.; *Ami* (k), Am Israel Hai Street, II, 64 r.; *Maxim* (k), 86 Hayarkon Street, II, 60 r.; *Ora* (k), 35 Ben Yehuda Street, II, 54 r.; *Commodore* (k), 2 Zamenhof Street, II,

Tel Aviv-Yafo

500 m
(550 yd)

Sede Dov
Airport

Port

Maccabia
Stadium

Shay 'Agnon

Sderot Israel Rokach

Mediterranean

Sea

Marina

Ussishkin

Yar

Bene   Da

Yehuda Hama

Sderot   Nordau

Gan
Ha'azma'ut

Ha-Yarqon

Dizengoff

Ben Yehuda

Sokolov

Gvirol

Ibn

Pinkas D

Jabotinsky

Bet
Ha-
More

Hame

Bet Ha-
Histadrut

Arlozorov

Arlozorov

Le

Sderot David Ben Gurion

Ben Yehuda

Zeo

Town Hall

TEL AVIV

Kikar
Malkhey
Yisra'el

Chief Rabbinate

Frischmann

David Ham.

Ichil
Hospi

Mendele

Kikar Zina
Dizengoff

Insurance
Agency

Art Gallery
(Tel Aviv Museum)

L

Old
Cemetery

Dizengoff

George

Sderot Sha-ul
Hamelech

Central
Municipal
Library

co

Opera House

Pinsker

Ben Tziyon

Helena-
Rubinstein-
Museum

Frederic-Mann-
Auditorium

Historical
Museum

Samuel

Hamelekh

Jabotinsky-
Museum

Hebimeh
Theater

HAQIRYA

Herbert

Sheinkin

Ha-Karmel

Allenby

Rothschild

Carlebach

Central
Market

Petah

Hassan Bek
Mosque

Nahalat Binyamin

Great
Synagogue

Sderot Yehuda

Derekh

Sa

Bet Ha-No'ar

Tel Aviv
Dolphinarium

Shalom
Tower

Hagana-Museum

Ohel Moed
Synagogue

Bet Dizengoff
(Bible Museum)

Post Office

Bus
Station

Levanda

Yafo

Ha-Mered

Elat

Herzl

Levinsky

Har Tsiyon

New
Bus
Station

Great
Mosque

Clock Tower

Derekh

Shalma

Greek
Orthodox
Monastery

St. Peter

Artists
Quarter

Archaeological
Museum

GIV'AT HERZL

Derekh

Siksik
Mosque

Church of the
Sacred Heart

Bloomfield
Stadium

SHEKUNAT
SHAPIRA

SHEKUN

Yefet

Yehuda Hayamit

Coptic
Church

Yerushalayim

Derekh Yizhaq Ben Zevi

Russian
Church

Kibuts Galuyot

Sohmb

YAFO

GIV'AT
'ALIYYA

S Station

Holon, Jerusalem

52 r.; *Florida* (k), 164 Hayarkon Street, II, 52 r.; *Ambassador* (k), 2 Allenby Street, II, 50 r.; *Shalom*, 216 Hayarkon Street, II, 42 r.; *Imperial*, 66 Hayarkon Street, III, 48 r.; *Excelsior*, 88A Hayarkon Street, III, 24 r.; *Armon Hayarkon* (k), 268 Hayarkon Street, III, 24 r.; *Wagshal* (k), *Bnei Brak*, III, 18 r.; *Riviera*, 52 Hayarkon Street, IV, 30 r.; *Monopol*, 4 Allenby Street, IV, 25 r.; *Bell*, 12 Allenby Street, IV, 23 r.; *Migdal David* (k), 8 Allenby Street, IV, 22 r.; *Nes Ziona*, 10 Nes Ziona Street, IV, 21 r.; *Nordau*, 27 Nachlat Benjamin Street, IV, 18 r.; *Europa*, 42 Allenby Street, IV, 16 r.; *Hagalil* (k), 54 Allenby Street, IV, 9 r.; *Tamar*, 8 Gnessin Street, IV, 9 r.; *Sandi*, 15 Allenby Street, 18 r.; *Habakook*, Exclusive Apartment Hotel, 7 Habakkuk Street, 18 suites; *Kfar Hamaccabiah* (k), holiday village, Ramat Gan, Barnstin Street, 103 r., SP, sauna, tennis. – YOUTH HOSTEL, 32 Bnei Dan Street, 200 b.

In Bat Yam: *Marina*, 279 r.; *Armon Yam*, 95 Ben Gurion Street, II, 66 r.; *Bat Yam* (k), 53 Ben Gurion Street, III, 20 r.; *Sarita*, 127 Ben Gurion Street, III, 10 r.

RESTAURANTS. – *Acropolis* (Balkan cuisine), 46 Hamasger Street; *Alhambra* (French), 30 Jerusalem Boulevard; *American House Restaurant* (European), 35 Shaul Hamelekh Boulevard; *Andromeda* (European), Jaffa; *Assa* (Balkan), 49 Bograshov Street; *Balkan Corner* (Balkan), Rokah Boulevard, Jakkabi Tzafon Tennis Courts; *Capriccio* (Italian), 288 Hayarkon Street; *Cartier* (Chinese), 2 Shaul Hamelekh Street; *Casbah* (European), 32 Yirmiyahu Street; *Dan* (Jewish), 147 Ben Yehuda Street; *Delphini* (Continental and seafood), 33 Yirmiyahu Street; *Désirée – la petite différence* (French), 95 Ben Yehuda Street; *Dolphin* (European), 16 Shalom Aleikhem Street; *El Cid* (Continental), 2 Mazal Teumin Street, Jaffa; *Gaby's* (Balkan), 17 Aluf Sadhe Street; *Harel* (European and Balkan), 95 Hahachmonaim Street; *Herbert Ron* (Italian and French), Samuel Esplanade; *Hong Kong* (Chinese), 0 Mendele Street; *La Barohotta* (European and seafood), 326 Dizengoff Street; *La Couronne* (French), 22 Pinsker Street; *Le Versailles* (French), 37 Gueulah Street; *Mandy's Drugstore* (European-American), 206 Dizengoff Street; *Me and Me Pizzeria* (Italian), 293 Dizengoff Street; *Olympia* (Balkan), 25 Qiryat Sefer Street; *Olympus* (Balkan), 12 Hakshon Street; *Pninat Hakerem* (Yemeni-Oriental), 38 Hakovshim Street; *Rimini* (Italian), 24 Ibn Givrol Street; *Rishon Cellar* (Central European), 11 Allenby Street; *Shaldag Inn* (seafood), 256 Ben Yehuda Street; *Shaul's Inn* (Yemeni and Oriental), 11 Elyashiv Street; *Singing Bamboo* (Chinese), 317 Hayarkon Street; *Taj Mahal* (Indian), Kikar Kedumin, Jaffa; *Tandu* (Continental), 199 Dizengoff Street; *The Patio* (Continental), 48 Sha'arey Nikanor Street, Jaffa; *Toutonne* (French), Simtat Mazal Dagim; *Triana* (Balkan), 12 Carlebach Street; *Tripoli* (N African), 27 Raziel Street; *Via Maris* (French and Italian), 6 Kikar Kedumin, Jaffa; *Yordei Hasira* (seafood), 1 Voridei Hasira Street; *Zion Exclusive* (Oriental and Yemeni), 28 Peduyim Street.

EVENTS. – *Concerts* (Israeli Philharmonic Orchestra, Frederic Mann Auditorium, 1 Rehov Huberman); *Opera* (National Opera, 1 Rehov Allenby); *Theater* (Habimah Theater, 6 Tarsal Boulevard; Little Theater, 1 Rehov Allenby); *Israeli folk dancing and singing*, Friday evenings in the ZOA building (Zionist Organisation of America; 1 Rehov Daniel Frisch).

SPORTS AND LEISURE. – Swimming (beaches: Bat Yam, Bograshov, Frishman, Givat Alijah, Gordon,

Tel Aviv – view from Jaffa

Sheraton; swimming pools: Galej Gil in Ramat Gan, Galit in Yad Eliyahu, etc.; regular buses to Herzliyya), sailing, tennis.

TRANSPORT in Tel Aviv-Jaffa (Yafo)

AIRLINES: The Ben Gurion airport in Lod is Israel's international airport. El Al terminal: Derekh Petah Tikva (near N station). Internal flights by Arkia to Eilat, Haifa, Jerusalem, Mizpe Ramon, Rosh Pinna and Sodom from Sede Dov airport in the N of the city.

RAILWAY: Trains to Haifa from N station, Rehov Arlosoroff; Jerusalem, Beersheba and Dimona from S station, Rehov Harakevet.

BUSES: Central bus station at the junction of Derekh Yafo Street and Derekh Petah Tikva Street and in Derekh Shalma Street leading E from Jaffa. Apart from the municipal buses there are also the Egged buses (main office 8 Rehov Mendele, tel. 24 22 71).

SHERUT TAXIS: Arje, 4 Mikve Israel, tel. 61 50 11 (to Haifa, Nahariyya, Safed and Jerusalem); Atid, 46 Rehov Lilienblum, tel. 61 38 36 (to Jerusalem); Aviv, 32 Rothschild Boulevard, tel. 62 28 88 (to Haifa, Jerusalem and Tiberias); Barclay, 25 Rehov Ahad Ha'am, tel. 61 10 55 (to Hadera, Afula); Hasharon, 4 Rehov Mikve Israel, tel. 61 21 32 (to Netanya); Kesher, 33 Rothschild Boulevard, tel. 61 14 88 (to Jerusalem); Ron, 1 Rehov Perez, tel. 62 15 60 (to Ashdod); Yael Daroma, 44 Rehov Javne, tel. 6 22 55 (to Ashqelon, Kiryat Gat, Beersheba, Eilat).

The two-fold city of *Tel Aviv-Jaffa (Yafo), some 40 miles/65 km NW of Jerusalem on the Mediterranean, is Israel's largest conurbation as well as the hub of the country's commerce. Whereas Jaffa's origins stretch back as far as prehistoric times, Tel Aviv ("Hill of Spring") is a modern city. In recent times Tel Aviv and Jaffa have increasingly tended to merge into each other and are **now surrounded by a common belt of new residential suburbs.**

MYTHOLOGY and LEGEND. – According to Jewish tradition Noah's son Japheth founded the town of Jaffa after the Flood, and according to Greek tradition it dates back to Joppa, one of the daughters of Aliolos, the god of the winds. The Greeks also thought that a rock in the sea outside the harbour was where Joppa's daughter Andromeda was chained up until Perseus the hero, son of Zeus and Danaë, freed her from the sea-monster. The story of the prophet Jonah dates back to the 8th c. B.C. It was here that, seeking to evade God's command to preach in Nineveh, he boarded a ship, was cast into the sea by the sailors during a mighty storm, was swallowed by a great fish and then disgorged on the shore (Jonah 1 and 2). The New Testament links Jaffa with the story of the raising of Tabitha by the apostle Peter, who then stayed at the house of Simon the tanner (Acts 9, 36–43).

HISTORY. – Building work in the N of Tel Aviv near the corner of Ibn Givrol/Nordau unearthed tombs from the Chalcolithic Age (the transitional period between the Stone Age and the Bronze Age – 4000–3150 B.C.) representing the earliest traces of settlement found to date.

Settlement of the area, which has continued without a break until the present day, first began on the 120 ft/ 37 m high hill above the natural harbour of Jaffa. Excavations in the past few decades have revealed a wall dating from the time of the Hyksos (18th–16th c. B.C.). In 1468 B.C. Tutmosis III, pharaoh of Egypt, captured Jaffa; a 13th c. B.C. stone door has been found bearing the name of Ramses II. About 1200 B.C. Philistines settled in Jaffa and on Tell Qasila (N of the River Yarkon). About 1000 B.C. David captured the city. His son Solomon imported cedars from the Lebanon for the construction of the Temple in Jerusalem through the port of Jaffa or the port at Tell Qasila (2 Chronicles 2, 15). During the following centuries, however, the population of Jaffa was predominantly Phoenician, and from the 3rd c. B.C. onwards it was Greek or Hellenist. In the 2nd c. B.C. there were conflicts between the latter and the Maccabeans who set fire to Jaffa in 142 B.C. (2 Maccabeans 12, 3–8) and settled more Jews there. In the 1st c. B.C. the port of Jaffa was overtaken in importance by the newly founded Caesarea.

Jaffa's Christian era begins with the stay of the apostle Peter (Acts 9, 36–43), and in the 4th c. Jaffa was a Christian bishopric. In 636 it was captured by *Arabs* and enjoyed a period of prosperity under the Omayyad and Abbasid caliphs. The *Crusaders* destroyed the settlement in 1099, then provided it with new walls; Jaffa became the port of disembarkation for pilgrims bound for Jerusalem. Louis IX (Saint Louis) of France reinforced the walls in 1251. The Crusader period ended in 1267 with the capture of the town by the *Mamelukes* under Sultan Baibars and after this Jaffa was virtually a ghost town for centuries.

In 1650 the Franciscans received permission from the Ottoman authorities, who had ruled in Palestine since 1520, to build a church and a hostel for pilgrims. In 1799 Napoleon stopped in Jaffa on his way from Egypt to Acre. In 1807 Mahmut, who because of his strength earned the nickname of Abu Nebut (father of the club), became pasha of Gaza and made Jaffa his capital. The harem (today a museum), the nearby Hamman, the mosque named after him and the Abu Nebut well all date from his reign. In 1818 Jaffa had 6,000 inhabitants. In 1834 the Egyptians under Ibrahim Pasha took the town and founded the suburb of Abu Kabir a little inland.

New development under European auspices began in the mid-19th c. In 1852 American Adventists set up a farm on the "Mountain of Hope" near the River Ayalon but in 1857 this was pillaged and surrendered (the Shevah technical college now stands on the site in Hamasger Street).

After the surrender agreement concluded with Turkey had ensured great influence for the European powers in Palestine, the French built hospitals and extended monasteries and churches. The Russians built a church dedicated to St Peter at the "Tomb of Tabitha" near Abu Kabir hill. In 1866 members of the American Church of the Messiah started up a colony which foundered because of Arab hostility and the unfavourable climate. In 1869 the German Templars took over the abandoned site and turned it into the agricultural settlement of Jaffa-Valhalla. In 1871 they also founded Sarona NE of Jaffa. 1877 and 1890 saw the advent of Jewish settlements, Newe Zedek and Newe Shalom, further to the N. In 1892 the French built the railway line to Jerusalem. Then in 1909 Russian immigrants founded the purely Jewish suburb of Ahusat Bayit with the Herzl grammar school (on the site of the present Shalom Tower); this marked the beginning of the modern city which was named *Tel Aviv* in 1910, and, following Arab riots in 1921, became independent shortly after the end of Turkish rule. During the British Mandate (1920–48), for easier enforcement of the administration wide streets were made through the maze of alleys in Jaffa. By 1924 Tel Aviv already had a population of 35,000. A power station was built and it was the first place in the country to have electricity. Renewed tension between Jews and Arabs in 1929 caused many Jews to leave Jaffa for Tel Aviv. In 1936 the port of Jaffa was closed down and Tel Aviv got its own port near Tell Qasila.

In 1947 under the United Nations Partition Plan Jaffa (which had 100,000 inhabitants, 30,000 of them Jews) was to remain Arab and Tel Aviv (230,000 inhabitants) was to become Israeli. In 1948 the Israelis occupied the town of Jaffa. On May 14, 1948 David Ben Gurion proclaimed the state of Israel in the former house of the first mayor of Tel Aviv, Meir Dizengoff. In 1950 the old town of Jaffa was combined with the new Jewish city under the name of *Tel Aviv-Yafo*.

Places of interest

Archaeological Museum,
in Jaffa;
Sun. to Tues., Thurs. 9 a.m.–4 p.m., Fri. and the day before a public holiday. 9 a.m.–1 p.m., Sat. 10 a.m.–2 p.m.

Ben Gurion House,
Ben Gurion Boulevard.

Bible Museum (*Bet Tanach*),
see Dizengoff House.

Dolphinarium,
Herbert Samuel Street (Charles Clore Park); Every day 9 a.m.–10 p.m.

Diaspora Museum (*Bet Ha Tefoutsoth*),
in the quarter of Ramat Aviv;
Sun., Mon., Thurs. 10 a.m.–5 p.m.; Tues., Wed. 3–10 p.m.

Dizengoff House (*Bet Dizengoff*),
16 Rothschild Boulevard;
Sun. to Thurs. 9 a.m.–4 p.m., Fri. 9 a.m.–1 p.m.
Jewish art and Biblical manuscripts (Bible Museum).

Bialik House (*Bet Bialik*),
Bialik Street;
Sun. to Thurs. 9 a.m.–7 p.m., Fri. 9 a.m.–1 p.m.
Manuscripts and translations of the writer Chaim Nachman Bialik (1873–1934).

Great Synagogue (*Bet HaKnesset HaGadol*),
Corner of Allenby Street and Ahad Ha'am Street;
Sun. to Thurs. 9 a.m.–2 p.m.

Ha'aretz Museum,
Entrance in University Street;
Sun. to Thurs. 9 a.m.–4 p.m., Fri. and days before public holidays 9 or 10 a.m.–1 p.m., Sat. 10 a.m.–2 p.m. Closed on religious festivals.

Haganah Museum,
23 Rothschild Boulevard;
Sun. to Thurs. 10 a.m.–3 p.m., Fri. 10 a.m.–1 p.m.

Hayarkon Park,
in the N of the city;
Sun. to Thurs. 8 a.m.–5 p.m., Fri. 8 a.m.–4 p.m., Sat. closed.
Fine view of Ramat Gan from Tel El Yerish.

Helena Rubinstein Museum,
Habimah Square;
Sun. to Thurs. 10 a.m.–5 p.m., Fri. 10 a.m.–2 p.m., Sat. from sunset to 10 p.m.

Historical Museum,
27 Bialik Street;
Sun. to Thurs. 9 a.m.–4 p.m., Fri. and the day before a public holiday 10 a.m.–1 p.m.

Israeli National Museum,
see Ha'aretz Museum.

Jabotinsky Museum,
King George Street;
Sun., Tues., Thurs. 8 a.m.–3 p.m., Mon. and Wed. 8 a.m.–1 p.m. and 6–8 p.m., Fri. and the day before a public holiday 8 a.m.–1 p.m.
Testaments to the resistance to the British Mandate authorities.

Carmel Market,
Corner of Allenby Street and Hakarmel Street;
every day until sunset, except Fri., Sat. and public holidays.

Art Gallery,
see Tel Aviv Museum.

Shalom Tower (*Migdal Shalom*),
N end of Herzl Street;
Sun. to Thurs. 9 a.m.–10 p.m.; closed 3 p.m. Fri. to 5 p.m. Sat.

Tel Aviv Museum,
King Saul Street;
Sun., Mon., Wed., Thurs. 10 a.m.–5 p.m. Tues. 9 a.m.–1 p.m. and 4–10 p.m., Fri. 10 a.m.–2 p.m., Sat. and public holidays 7–11 p.m.
Guided tours in English every day at 10 a.m., not Sat.

Tell Qasila,
N of the Yarkon;
Sun. to Thurs. 8 a.m.–3 p.m., Sat. 8 a.m.–1 p.m.
Archaeological excavations.

Zoo,
Milkhey Yizra'el Square;
Sun. to Thurs. 8 a.m.–5 p.m., Fri. 8 a.m.–4 p.m.

Sightseeing in Tel Aviv-Jaffa

Center

The best place to begin a tour of **TEL AVIV** is **Dizengoff Square**, named after Meir Dizengoff who became the first mayor of Tel Aviv after its separation from Jaffa in 1921. From this square, with its well and its palm trees, Dizengoff Street leads SE over King George Street (Hamelekh George) to Habimah Square, the cultural center of the city. In this square are the **Habimah Theater**, Israel's national theater built in 1935, N of which are the **Helena Rubinstein Museum** of modern art and the *Frederic Mann Auditorium* (Heikhal Hatarbut), the concert hall of the Israeli Philharmonic Orchestra.

Dizengoff Street continues on the far side of Ibn Givrol Street as Kaplan Street. Near the end of this street is the HAQIRYA quarter which was the location of the settlement of Sarona, founded by German Templars in 1871 and in existence until 1948 (the Templars were expelled under the British Mandate during the Second World War).

Leading off Ibn Givrol to the right is Rehov Daniel Frisch. No. 1 is the home of the Zionistic Organisation of America (ZOA) where visitors can attend sabbath celebrations on Friday evenings. Leading off to the right is King Saul Street (Sha'ul Hamelekh). On the left are the *Shaarey Zion Library*, the **Tel Aviv Art Gallery** with works of 20th c. Jewish masters and European and American pictures of the last 300 years, and the *Law-Courts*. The route turns left at the back of the building into Weizmann Street and then left again into King David Street (David Hamelekh), arriving at the *Chief Rabbinate* and the Malkhey Yisra'el Square where the **Town Hall** and the *Zoo* are situated.

Oldest quarters

Walking SW from Dizengoff Street along Pinsker Street and then turning right into Trumpeldor Street, the visitor arrives at Tel Aviv's *Old Cemetery* containing the com-

Tel Aviv – a sea of houses

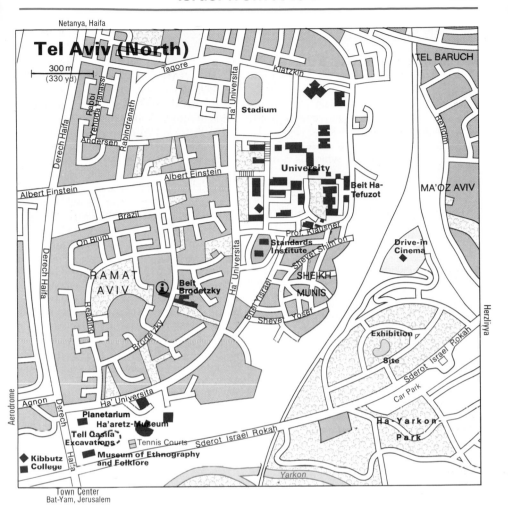

Netanya, Haifa

Tel Aviv (North)

300 m
(330 yd)

TEL BARUCH

Tagore

Klatzkin

Derech Haifa

Rabbi Tehuda Hanassi

Rabindranath

Andersen

Ha' Universita

Stadium

Albert Einstein

University

Albert Einstein

Beit Ha-Tefuzot

MA'OZ AVIV

Brazil

On Blum

Prof. Klausner

Standards Institute

Shever Shimon

Sheva Israel

Drive-in Cinema

Derech Haifa

Ha' Universita

RAMAT AVIV

Beit Brodetzky

Bnei Yisrael

SHEIKH
MUNIS

Reading

Brodetzky

Shevet Yosef

Exhibition

Site

Sderot Israel Rokah

Car Park

Herzliya

Aerodrome

Agnon

Derech Haifa

Ha' Universita

Planetarium
Ha'aretz-Museum

Tell Qasila
Excavations

Tennis Courts

Sderot Israel Rokah

Ha-Yarkon
Park

◆ Kibbutz
■ College

Museum of Ethnography
and Folklore

Yarkon

Town Center
Bat-Yam, Jerusalem

munal grave of victims of the unrest in 1921, the tombs of leading Zionists such as Chaim Arlosoroff, Meir Dizengoff and Max Nordau and of the poets Chaim Nahman Bialik and Shaul Chernikovsky. SE of this cemetery in Bialik Street is the old town hall which now houses the **Historical Museum** (documents on the history of the city of Tel Aviv, 27 Rehov Bialik). The street is named after the poet Chaim Nahman Bialik who lived in the house next door (memorabilia).

Further along Bialik Street is Allenby Street, one of the city's main roads. It leads to the **Great Synagogue** (on the corner of Rehov Ahad Ha'am) and to the *Haganah Museum* in the house of the commander of the Haganah Eliahu Golomb where there is a display of weapons used by the Jewish underground terrorists during the British Mandate (23 Rothschild Boulevard). Nearby (16 Rothschild Boulevard) is the former home of Mayor Dizengoff, **Bet**

Dizengoff. This is where the state of Israel was proclaimed on May 14, 1948. The house is also called Bet Tanach, House of the Bible, and houses a *Bible Museum*.

The next street is Herzl Street, the first street in the newly founded Tel Aviv of 1909. At its N end the Hebrew grammar school named after Theodor Herzl was built in 1909. It was demolished in 1958 to make way for Tel Aviv's first multi-storey building, the **Migdal Shalom** (Peace Tower). From the 433 ft/132 m high platform there is a panoramic view (observatory). Between here and the sea is the *Carmel Market* (SW of the corner of Rehov Allenby and Rehov Hakarmel) with its colourful bustling activity. Herbert Samuel Street follows the coast and leads to Allenby Street where the **Opera House** is located. – Situated at the S end of Herbert Samuel Street is the *Tel Aviv Dolphinarium* (dolphin shows; aquarium).

North

1 mile/1·5 km along Dizengoff Street N off Dizengoff Square is Nordau Street on the left. Near this crossroads building work uncovered the earliest settlement in what is now Tel Aviv, dating from the Chalcolithic Age (4000–3150 B.C.). Nordau Street leads to *Independence Park* (Gan Ha'azma'ut) which is not far from the **harbour**.

Past the *Maccabia Stadium* and over the *Yarkon* is the **Qasila Tell** in Rokah Street, a hill on the far side of Haifa Street.

In ancient times the Yarkon (yarok=green) was the border between the tribes of Ephraim (N) and Dan (S). The Tell of Qasila has been investigated by the archaeologist B. Mazar. Twelve layers of settlement have been found, going back as far as the 12th c. B.C. Finds include a brick building from that period (XII), and a stout wall and two copper-smelting furnaces from the 11th c. (level XI). Both these strata are ascribed to the Philistines. Level X, on the other hand, dates from the 10th c. B.C. when the kings of the Israelites had a port here after David had conquered the region. Recently some experts have advanced the view that the cedars of Lebanon which Solomon used to build his Temple were unloaded here, at the mouth of the Yarkon, rather than in the port of Jaffa. The discovery of store-rooms and containers have shown that at that time Tell Qasila was used as a port trans-shipping the agricultural produce of the region.

After destruction by Egyptian troops the kings of Israel rebuilt the site in the 9th c. B.C. Destroyed once more in 732 B.C. by Assyrians, the place was again being used as a harbour in the 5th c. B.C. when it took delivery of the cedars of Lebanon for the Second Temple (Ezra 3, 7). Later layers show that people were still living on Tell Qasila in Hellenistic, Roman, Byzantine and Islamic times before its abandonment in favour of Jaffa.

Today Tell Qasila is in the extensive grounds of the *Israeli National Museum (Ha'aretz Museum)* which has its entrance in University Street (Ha'universita). By the car park is the *Numismatic Museum*; apart from this the National Museum also encompasses the collections of the *Museums of Ceramics, Glass, the History of Writing* (Alphabet), *the History of Science, Ethnology and Folklore* and a department called "Man and his Work", each dealing with its own particular theme and its history from earliest times to the present; the Museum also contains a *Planetarium*. The Tell with its excavations is in the E section of the grounds (entrance and small museum between the car park and the Museum of Ethnography). – From Tell Qasila Ha'universita Street leads to Tel Aviv **University**. – Opposite Hayarkon Park is the new Trade Fair Conventions Center.

East

E of the center is the hilly suburb of RAMAT GAN (Garden Hill) built in 1920, an industrial area with large gardens. *Napoleon's Hill* (Tell el Gerish) on the W edge of Ramat Gan recalls a military camp he had here in 1799; the hill was inhabited as early as the 18th c. B.C. Further inland is the suburb of BENE BERAQ, founded by Polish orthodox Jews whose religious outlook is maintained in several Talmud schools (Yeshivot). The Derekh Hanassi Harishon leads S to the grounds of the *Bar Ilan University*, founded in 1955 and named after an orthodox Jewish leader. In all its faculties great emphasis is placed on the study of the Jewish religion (2 miles/3 km).

E of Bene Beraq is **Petah Tikva** (Gate of Hope). Founded in 1878 as the first Jewish agricultural settlement, after a difficult start on marshy land it has grown into a flourishing town of 122,000 inhabitants. The ground in the center is called **Gan Hameyasdim** ("Founders' Garden") and is a tribute to the early days of the settlement. Alongside stand the settlement's first synagogue and the new town hall. On the Bene Beraq side of the town is a stone arch commemorating Baron Edmond de Rothschild and the financial assistance he gave the founders. – 2½ miles/4 km NE of Petah Tikva, near the source of the Yarkon, is the town of *Rosh Ha'ayin* (see entry) with the remains of Afeq/Antipatris and Mirabel.

South

On the left of Jaffa Street (Derekh Yafo) at the S end of Allenby Street is a church tower. It belonged to the Jaffa colony of the German Templars which came into existence in 1869 on the site of an American mission society. In 1888 the site adjoining it to the NE was purchased and Jaffa-Valhalla came into being after Sarona (today Haqirya in Tel Aviv) had already been founded in 1.871. Finally in 1902 the settlement of Wilhelmina was founded near the present-day Lod airport.

The road continues to *JAFFA (**Yafo** in Hebrew), the Jappho or Joppa of the Bible (if arriving by bus get out at the clock tower).

Jaffa has undergone considerable change in the 20th c. During the British Mandate, the authorities carved wide streets out of the maze of alleys to maintain better order at the time of the 1921 riots. After the mass exodus of the Arab population following the founding of the state of Israel in 1948 extensive redevelopment was called for. Part of the bazaar remains, but the streets were widened, damaged houses pulled down and other buildings restored. Many are used today as

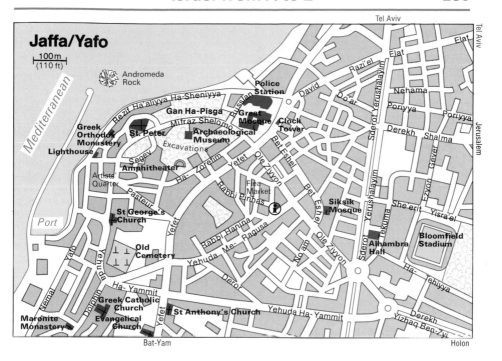

bars, restaurants and artists' quarters. What has remained are the monuments on the acropolis which had been the oldest site of settlement. Recently the historical fabric of the old town has been well restored.

The **clock tower** in the center of Jaffa was built in 1906 to celebrate the fiftieth jubilee of the Ottoman sultan Abd ül Hamit II. On it is a plaque commemorating the Israelis who fell in 1948 fighting for the city. – Next to it is the **Mahmudiye Mosque** which was built in 1810 by the Ottoman governor Mahmud Pasha, nick-named Abu Nebut ("Father of the Club"), using Classical columns from Ashqelon and Caesarea but mistakenly placing them upside down with the capitals on the ground.

SW of here is the acropolis (120 ft/37 m). The **Franciscan Monastery of St Peter** was built here in 1654 on the site of a 13th c. Crusader castle. Its name commemorates the visit of the apostle Peter to Jaffa (Acts 9, 36–43; visitors are shown the tomb of the risen Tabitha in the Russian Monastery). Steps lead down from the monastery courtyard to the still intact vaults of the Crusader castle.

In the square in front of the monastery (Gan Ha-Pisga) excavations have now brought to light earlier layers of settlement, including a massive wall 20 ft/6 m across dating from the time of the Hyksos (18th–16th c. B.C.), a town gate bearing

the name of Ramses II (1290–1224 B.C.), remains of the Canaanite town and a 4th c. B.C. Jewish settlement. There have also been finds of objects dating from Maccabean and Roman times. The square affords a fine view of the **harbour**. Its importance dates from the 2nd millennium B.C. but it was subsequently superseded by the modern ports of Haifa and Ashdod and is now a fishing port. The

Franciscan Church of St Peter in Jaffa

many rocks around the harbour include the Andromeda rock. According to the Greek legend, Andromeda, the daughter of Joppa, the mythical founder of the town, was chained to this rock until she was freed by Perseus, the Greek hero from Argos.

A little further inland in the old Turkish harem is Jaffa's **Archaeological Museum**. Its collection of local finds is well worth seeing.

S of here, towards the lighthouse, through the alleys dotted with picturesque houses, is a small *mosque* dating from 1730; it is said to be on the site of the house of Simon the tanner where Peter stayed after raising Tabitha from the dead.

From here Yehuda Hayamit Street leads E. Where it crosses Yaphet Street (which leads back left to the clock tower) is the *Church of St Anthony*. Further on (1 mile/ 1·5 km) in Ben Zvi Street, which is a continuation of Yaphet Street, is the vaulted *well* of Mahmud Abu Nebut who built the Mahmudiye Mosque. A little further on, on the far side of Herzl Street, is the slender tower of the palm-fringed *Russian Monastery* on the left. In 1860 Russia bought the hill of Abu Kabir and built a monastery dedicated to St Peter to provide lodging for pilgrims. Under the monastery courtyard is a burial cave with numerous sepulchral recesses which was part of a 1st–4th c. Jewish cemetery and, according to Christian tradition, contained the tomb of Tabitha whom Peter raised from the dead.

A little to the S of Jaffa is the coastal town of **Bat Yam** (Daughter of the Sea) which was founded in 1925 and has a $2\frac{1}{2}$ mile/4 km long sandy beach, Adam's Rock near the shore and major industrial plants.

SURROUNDINGS. – **From Tel Aviv to Gaza** (47 miles/76 km). – Just S of the city is *Rishon Le Zyyon* (9 miles/14 km; 95,000 inhabitants) which was founded in 1882 and was therefore one of the first Jewish agricultural settlements. Then comes **Rehovot** (see entry; 3 miles/5 km). It was founded in 1890 and is the home of the Institute of Natural Sciences established by Chaim Weizmann who was later to become the first president of the state of Israel. The Institute is named after him and today its work covers fields ranging from biology to atomic research. Weizmann's tomb is in the grounds of the Institute.

4 miles/7 km SE of Rehovot is *Yavne* (see entry), formerly Jamnia; the port is 5 miles/8 km to the NW near the kibbutz of Palmahim. 4 miles/6 km further on the road forks off to the right to the port of Ashdod (see

entry) which was enlarged in 1957 to take international shipping. The road now follows the Holot Aŋhdud and dldŋtu Tull Aŋhdud (on the right, 6 miles/ 10 km) to **Yad Mordechai** (18 miles/29 km) which in 1948 was held against Egyptian troops by members of the kibbutz founded in 1943 and named after the leader of the Warsaw uprising. The battle area has been faithfully reproduced and a memorial hall commemorates the fighters in the Warsaw ghetto. 9 miles/15 km further on is **Gaza**, an ancient port, today the main port in the Gaza Strip (130,000 inhabitants).

From Tel Aviv to Jerusalem (40 miles/65 km). – The arterial road leaves Tel Aviv and passes *Ramla* (see entry; 12 miles/19 km) and Lod Airport (left) to reach the Ayalon Valley and the village of *Gezer* (3 miles/5 km). Further to the SE is the monastery of *Latrun* (see entry; 8 miles/13 km) beyond which the old highway joins the new motorway to Jerusalem. 9 miles/15 km further on is the village of *Abu Gosh* (see entry) and 8 miles/13 km beyond that is **Jerusalem** (see entry).

From Tel Aviv to Haifa (61 miles/98 km). – 9 miles/ 15 km from Tel Aviv, on the far side of the Yarkon, is *Herzliyya* (see entry) from where the coast road leads to *Netanya* (see entry; 11 miles/17 km) and *Hadera* (see entry; 11 miles/18 km). From here there is a choice of two routes: one route goes via *Caesarea* (see entry; 6 miles/10 km), *Dor* (see entry; 9 miles/14 km) and *Atlit* (see entry; 9 miles/14 km), with ancient and medieval monuments, while the other route is a little further inland via *Binyamina* (9 miles/15 km), *Zikhron Ya'akov* (see entry; 6 miles/9 km) and the artists' village of *En Hod* (9 miles/14 km). The two routes merge at Cape Carmel (6 miles/10 km) just before **Haifa** (see entry).

Tell Arad
see Arad

Tell Dan
see Dan

Tiberias/Teverya

District: North.
Altitude: 696 ft/212 m below sea-level.
Population: 27,000.
Telephone code: 0 67.
ⓘ **Government Tourist Office,**
8 Elhadef Street;
tel. 2 09 92.

HOTELS. – **Jordan River Hotel*, L. 400 r., marina and watersports center (opening mid-1984); **Tiberias Plaza* (k), PO Box 375, L, 272 r. SP; **Galei Kinnereth* (k), Kaplan Street, L, 125 r., SP; *Ganei Hamat* (k), Habanim Street, near hot springs, I, 190 r., tennis; *Golan* (k), 14 Achad Ha'am Street, I, 72 r., SP; *Hartman* (k), 3 Achad Ha'am Street, I, 69 r., SP, sauna; *Washington* (k), 13 Zeidel Street, I, 68 r.; *Eden*, 4 Nazareth Street, Qiryat Shmuel, II, 82 r.; *Galilee* (k), Nazareth Street, II, 82 r.; *Quiet Beach* (k), Gdud Barak

Tiberias on the Sea of Galilee

Street, II, 76 r., SP; *Chen*, 17 Ohel Ya'acov Street, II, 75 r., sauna; *Daphne* (k), PO Box 502, II, 73 r.; *Yaalon* (k), Plus 200, II, 72 r.; *Peer* (k), 2 Ohel Ya'acov Street, II, 70 r.; *Ariston* (k), 19 Herzl Boulevard, II, 62 r.; *Astoria* (k), 13 Ohel Ya'acov Street, II, 57 r.; *Menora Gardens* (k), III, 58 r.; *Arnon* (k), 28 Hashomer Street, III, 20 r.; *Heler* (k), 10 Yehuda Hanassi Street, III, 15 r.; *Polonia* (k), Hagalil Street, IV, 25 r.; *Florida*, 4 Herzl Boulevard, IV, 11 r. – YOUTH HOSTELS: *Yosef Meyouhas*, 240 b.; *Taiber*, 6¼ miles/10 km S in Poria, 40 b.

HOSPICES. – *Scottish Hospice, Terra Sancta*.

RESTAURANTS. – *The House*, Lido on the lakeside (Chinese); *Mizpe Hagolan*, Upper Tiberias Road (Oriental-Lebanese); *Pizzeria Rimini*, Nazareth Street. – *En Gev*, in the kibbutz of En Gev on the eastern shore of the lake (fish); *Vered Hagalil* (9 miles/15 km to the N).

BOAT TRIPS on the Sea of Galilee. – Operator: Kinneret Sailing Ltd (tel. 2 18 31).

TRANSPORT. – There are bus services from Tiberias to all the surrounding towns (Egged Tours, tel. 2 04 74).

*Tiberias (Teverya in Hebrew) is a popular holiday resort in the cooler season. 44 miles/70 km from Haifa, it lies on the W shore of the Sea of Galilee and the newer parts of the town are gradually spreading up the hillsides overlooking the lake. Its medicinal hot springs have been known since ancient times but treatment nowadays takes place in a modern setting. One of the four holy cities of the Jews, together with Jerusalem, Hebron and Safed, Tiberias is rich in historical and religious interest, as are the places on the shore of the lake and in the surrounding area.

HISTORY. – Herod Antipas, a son of Herod I and ruler at the time of Jesus, founded Tiberias in A.D. 17 and named it after the Roman emperor Tiberius. The new town lay between Hammat and Raqqat, mentioned in the Old Testament as fenced cities in the area of the tribe of Naphtali (Joshua 19, 35). Since it was built on the site of the cemetery of Hammat the pious Jews considered it to be unclean and so at first only heathens settled here. Even Jesus, who taught mostly in this area, apparently never came here.

After the death of Herod Antipas, Tiberias was ruled by Agrippa II who provided it with paved streets, a palace and baths. At the end of the Jewish War in A.D. 70 he moved his residence to Sepphoris (Zippori, see entry). After Rabbi Simon Bar Jochai, who is buried in Meron (see entry) had declared Tiberias to be a clean city at the end of the 2nd c. it became the seat of the Sanhedrin. As the Nassi (prince), its head became the Jews' highest spiritual authority until Theodosius II abolished the office in 429. – From the 3rd c. onwards Tiberias became the religious center of the Jews. Its name was changed to *Teverya*; the Jews derived this not from Tiberias but from the Hebrew word "tabur" ("navel") and looked upon the city as the navel of the world. This is where the Mishnah (*c.* 200) and the Jerusalem Talmud (*c.* 400) were completed and where the vowel signs of the Hebrew alphabet were invented. Now, as then, it contains the tombs of many famous rabbis.

In the 4th c. the converted Jew Joseph of Tiberias provided his native city, and other places, with Christian churches; there is known to have been a Christian bishop in the 6th c. After the Persian (614) and the Arab (636) conquests Jewish scholars joined the community in Babylon or went to Jerusalem. From 1099 to 1187 Tiberias belonged to the area governed by the Crusader prince Tancred and the Kings of Jerusalem. In 1247 the city was destroyed by Baibars and was not occupied again until the beginning of the Ottoman rule (1517).

In 1561 Sultan Suleiman the Magnificent handed the city over to Don Joseph Hanassi, the Jewish refugee from Spain whom he had already made duke of the Greek island of Naxos, and to his aunt Gracia Mendes, and they set up in Galilee a Jewish state under

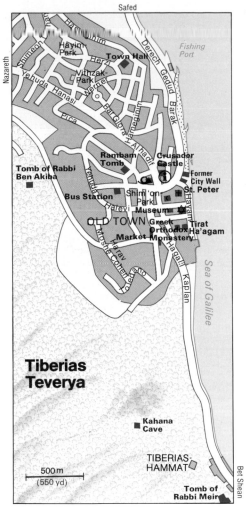

Tiberias
Teverya

The side streets lead to the shore of the lake and the *Municipal Museum* (in one of the former mosques) which contains items found in Tiberias and the surrounding area, and nearby the **Monastery of St Peter**, a Franciscan monastery with a fine cloister; the apse of the church projects like the bows of a ship.

About 274 yd/250 m NW of the post office in Rehov Hatanaim are some old *tombs*, including that of the philosopher and doctor Maimonides (Rabbi Mose ben Maimon, also known as Rambam after the intials of his name).

Maimonides was born in Córdoba in 1135. He left Spain because of religious persecution, was Saladin's personal physician in Cairo while also a rabbi and later became the spiritual leader of the Jews in Egypt. This scholar's commentaries on the Mishnah were influential and his philosophical work "Dalalat al Hairin" (Guide for the Perplexed) was held in high esteem by Albertus Magnus and Thomas Aquinas. When he died in Cairo in 1204 his body was brought to Tiberias.

Nearby is the tomb of Johanan Ben Zakkai who founded a Jewish school in Yavne (see entry; 17 miles/28 km S of Tel Aviv) after the destruction of Jerusalem in A.D. 70 and also moved the seat of the Sanhedrin there. – The tomb of Rabbi Akiba, who had looked upon Bar Kochba as the Messiah and was put to death by the Romans after the 135 uprising, is above these tombs on the next hill in the center of the new residential area. It is reached via a path leading S off the main street near the police station in Qiryat Shmuel.

Ottoman sovereignty. This did not last long, however. In the 17th c. Tiberias again fell into decay and was not reoccupied until the 18th c. when the Druse prince Taher el Umar rebuilt the city and its citadel in 1738 and settled Jews in it. Soon afterwards, in 1765, a first group of Jewish immigrants from Poland settled here. Many of the inhabitants lost their lives during the 1837 earthquake but Tiberias was rebuilt once again. About 1940 the city had 12,000 inhabitants, half of them Arabs and half Jews; since 1948 it has been purely Jewish.

SIGHTS. – Tiberias consists of the Old Town, the large new quarter of *Qiryat Shmuel* adjoining it to the N, and *Hammat* with its hot springs in the S.

The main street in the OLD TOWN is *Hagalil Street* which runs around the outside of the city wall. Some parts of this wall, last restored by Taher el Umar in 1738 with the local black basalt, can still be seen, especially on the side near the lake. W of Hagalil Street is a park (and next to it the post office).

The coast road leads S out of the Old Town past a Jewish cemetery to TIBERIAS-HAMMAT with its hot springs (1 mile/2 km; "Tiberias Hot Springs", car park). There is the entrance to a very well laid out **park** here; the top of the park is dominated by the *domed tomb* of Rabbi Meir (2nd c.) who is surrounded by legend. It consists of a Sephardic and an Ashkenazi section.

The chief attraction of the area is the **synagogue** which has been excavated here. The first synagogue was built in the 3rd/4th c. and a new one was built at a higher level on its ruins in the 6th/7th c. Both had a nave and two aisles. In the S part of the older one is a rectangular recess for the Torah shrine, while the more recent building has a semicircular apse. Especially important is the **mosaic pavement* in the older synagogue, noted for its pictorial

Synagogue mosaic pavement (Tiberias-Hammat)

the kibbutz of *Deganya* (1 mile/2 km) where the Jordan flows out of the Sea of Galilee (parking just on the other side of the bridge).

On the far side of the river the road forks. The road straight ahead continues to *En Gev* on the E bank or (right 2 miles/3 km further on) via Sha'at Hagolan to the excavation site of *Hamat Gader* (see entry). The other road turns S to follow the Jordan Valley. 6 miles/9 km beyond **Tell Shaharit** (2 miles/3 km, right) a side road on the left leads to the *Naharayim* hydroelectric power station. It was here, where the Yarmuk flows into the Jordan, that in 636 the Byzantines were decisively beaten by the Arab army of Caliph Omar. 2 miles/3 km further on the road crosses the *Tavor Valley* and the Crusader castle of **Belvoir** (see entry) can be seen on the hill on the right. After another 9 miles/14 km comes **Bet Shean** (see entry) with its Roman theater opposite the tell where the Canaanites built their temples.

From Bet Shean a road leads W through the **Gan Hashelosha National Park** at the foot of Mount Gilboa and *Bet Alfa* (see entry; 6 miles/10 km) to *Afula* (see entry; 9 miles/15 km). From here it is possible to return to Tiberias past *Mount Tabor* (see entry; 27 miles/43 km), or via *Nazareth* (see entry) and *Kafr Kanna* (25 miles/40 km).

The road continues S of Bet Shean through the Jordan Valley to *Jericho* (see entry; 53 miles/85 km) and from there to **Jerusalem** (see entry; 24 miles/38 km).

From Tiberias to Nazareth and back (49 miles/79 km). – Take the road W out of Tiberias. When the road reaches the top of the hill the *Horns of Hittim* (see entry), the volcano where Sultan Saladin annihilated the Crusader army in 1187, can soon be seen on the right; the top can be reached on foot in under half an hour. 12 miles/20 km from Tiberias on the left is *Kafr Kanna* (see Cana) where, at the wedding of Cana, Jesus performed his first miracle in Galilee (John 2,

representation, which has been preserved intact. The aisles are decorated simply, but the rich mosaic in the nave is in three parts. At the entrance is the dedication that mentions one Severus, son of the head of the Sanhedrin; this Roman name testifies to the influence of Graeco-Roman culture even on pious Jews of that time, and the same is true of the use of Greek script as well as Hebrew, and the figurative aspect of the main mosaic.

The main mosaic has the head and shoulders of the sun god Helios in the center, surrounded by the twelve signs of the Zodiac, and the four seasons in the corners. In the S section the Torah shrine is depicted between two seven-branched candlesticks, with incense-scoops and Shofar horns. The subjects correspond in the main to those of Bet Alfa (see entry) but the Hammat mosaics are of a much higher artistic level.

SURROUNDINGS. – **From Tiberias to Bet Shean and back** (*c.* 62 miles/100 km). – Leaving the city by the S and passing through Hammat with its excavations the route follows the shore of the lake to the kibbutz of *Kinneret* (4 miles/6 km), founded in 1908 as the first Zionist agricultural settlement. Here is the agricultural college of Bet Yerah on a site which has been occupied since the 4th millennium B.C. Two stone circles, each 23 ft/7 m in diameter, connected with moon-worship, remain from the early Canaanite period (Bet Yerah=House of the Moon). Later epochs are recalled by a ruined synagogue, Roman baths and a Byzantine church. In 1909 Russian émigrés founded

Rabbi Meir's tomb (Tiberias-Hammat)

1–11). The event is commemorated there by a Greek Orthodox and a Catholic church. **Nazareth** (see entry) is 4 miles/6 km further on. From here it is possible to return to Tiberias via *Afula* (see entry; 6 miles/10 km S) and past *Mount Tabor* (27 miles/43 km). Other routes lead to Nazareth to **Haifa** (see entry; 24 miles/39 km) and NW via *Zippori* (see entry), *Shefar'am* and *Ahihud* to the old port of **Acre** (Akko) (see entry; 25 miles/41 km).

A short trip from Tiberias into the region N of the Horns of Hittim is also worthwhile. Follow the Nazareth road but before leaving the town take a road off to the right after a long left-hand bend to the *Arbel Valley* where there is a kibbutz of the same name on the right. From the hill overlooking the kibbutz there is an impressive view down into the Wadi al Hammam with its precipitous walls. 6 miles/10 km from Tiberias the road comes to an end at *Nabi Shueib* at the N foot of the "Horns of Hittim". It is a shrine of great importance for the Druse, who venerate the tomb in a domed building here of Jethro, Moses' father-in-law. Every April they observe a commemorative festival for Jethro whom they regard as the first of their seven prophets. The last of these was Caliph El Hakim (11th c.), a contemporary of Darazi who formulated the secret religion of the Druse. Their belief is that Jethro, whom they call Nabi Shueib, was brought here from the land of the Midianites when his descendants moved to Kedesh S of the Sea of Galilee (Judges 4, 11).

The canyon-like valley at the N foot of Mount Arbel, the *Wadi al Hammam*, is reached from *Migdal* (4 miles/7 km N of Tiberias). Migdal was the native town of Mary Magdalene (=Mary from Magdala) an early follower of Jesus. According to Flavius Josephus its people fought Herod I and the Romans, finally seeking refuge in the innumerable caves in the Wadi al Hammam. An important town when the Crusaders built a church here in the 12th c., it subsequently fell into utter decay. The present agricultural settlement was founded in 1910.

From Tiberias to Israel's N border via Capernaum (*c.* 44 miles/70 km). – The road N out of Tiberias passes *Migdal* (4 miles/7 km) and the kibbutz of *Ginnosar* (3 miles/5 km), founded in 1937, with its smart inn on the shore of the lake. In 1925 the skull of *Homo galilensis*, who lived 100,000 years ago, was found in a cave in the valley of the *Amud* which reaches the lake here. To the right of the road is the Kinneret pumping station which pumps water out of the lake into a canal and thence to the Negev. A path near the pumping station leads towards the lake to the ruined palace of *Minya* (½ mile/1 km) which was built by the Omayyad caliph Al Walid (705–715) who also built the Omayyad Mosque in Damascus and the El Aqsa Mosque in Jerusalem.

Just N of here are several places of importance in the history of the Christian religion: *Tabgha* (see entry), the place where the Five Thousand were fed, with the Church of the Miracle of the Loaves and Fishes (5th c. mosaic pavement); nearby the Church of St Peter with the "Mensa Christi", and *Capernaum* (see entry; 2½ miles/4 km) with a partly restored synagogue and other excavations.

Near Tabgha the road leaves the lake-shore and climbs N into the hills where the church on the Mount of the Beatitudes (see entry) can be seen on the right; 3 miles/5 km further on there is a path on the right to the ruined synagogue of *Chorazin* (see entry).

Further N, in *Rosh Pinna* (see entry; 4 miles/7 km), the winding road leading up to **Safed** (see entry; 6 miles/10 km) branches off to the left. The road straight ahead, however, leads to the tell of *Hazor* (see entry; 4 miles/6 km) on the left where 23 layers of settlement have been excavated, and immediately afterwards on the right is the kibbutz of *Aiyelet Hashahar* with an inn and a museum containing objects found at Hazor. The road now continues through the former swamp of the *Hula Basin*, now under cultivation. At **Qiryat Shemona** (15,500 inhabitants; 15 miles/24 km), which was founded in 1949, a right turn takes the route through *Dan* (see entry) after which comes the fork leading to *Banyas* (see entry; 8 miles/13 km) and the source of one of the three headstreams of the Jordan. From here it is possible to drive through the *Golan Heights* (see Golan) before returning to Tiberias.

Timna

District: South.
ⓘ **Government Tourist Office,**
New Shopping Centre,
Eilat;
tel. (0 59) 7 22 68.

N of Eilat is *Timna, the area of the ancient copper-mines that were in operation right up until the 20th c.

16 miles/25 km N of Eilat a road turns off W from the main N–S road, and the flat Arava landscape is replaced by the hills of Timna. The road follows a wadi between

Timna – "Solomon's Pillars"

Ancient Egyptian temple to Hathor

the rock can now be reached by steps and paths. On the S side of the huge formation are the remains, surrounded by railings, of a *temple dedicated to the goddess Hathor* which serve as a reminder of the presence of the Egyptians here over 3,000 years ago.

Wadi Qilt

West Bank

The *Wadi Qilt on the Israeli-occupied West Bank leads E through the hills of Judea down into the plain of Jericho. Its aqueduct, which was built by Herod the Great and restored by the British during their Mandate, supplies water all the year round.

HISTORY. – The Romans built a road to carry the traffic from Jerusalem to Jericho that took the old route through the wadi, and traces of this road can still be distinguished. – In the early Christian period the caves in the harsh mountain landscape were inhabited by hermits and this led to the founding, inter alia, in the Byzantine period (5th–6th c.) of the Monastery of St George.

strangely shaped rocks. After a long left-hand curve the asphalt road ends at the foot of a wall of sandstone towering 164 ft/50 m above the floor of the wadi. Over thousands of years erosion has shaped it into the form of columns to which the archaeologist Nelson Glueck gave the name *Solomon's Pillars*. This was an apt description but historically inaccurate.

This marks the start of the *copper-mining* area which has its center some distance further S.

Benno Rothenberg from Jerusalem University excavated here between 1932 and 1934 and was consequently able to correct N. Glueck's dating and to establish that copper was already being mined here about 3000 B.C. He ascertained that, as inscriptions have proved, the Egyptians were maintaining a particularly high level of output in the 14th and 13th c. B.C., i.e. during their 18th and 19th dynasties. He found smelting ovens, cisterns and workshops dating from long before Solomon. In 1955 copper-mining was resumed by the Israelis which is why there are new slag heaps alongside the old ones but they called a halt in 1976 when the operation ceased to be profitable.

The big sandstone columns, which glow red in the sun, and the natural archway in

The road from Jerusalem to Jericho leads after 14 miles/22 km to *Ma'aleh Adummim* where a left turn (signposted) leads to a car park on the left of the road. The visitor gets his first glimpse of the Qilt gorge from its slightly more elevated N rim. From the car park a rough road suitable only for cross-country vehicles leads further NE to a hill with a cross ($1\frac{1}{4}$ hours on foot) from which the visitor has his first view of the Greek Orthodox **Monastery of St George** and far to the left a rivulet flowing down the slope of the hill from a spring; this water is channelled to the monastery. The stony path continues and in about another 30 minutes one arrives at the entrance to the monastery which with its cave church clings most impressively to the N face of the gorge. Shaded by the rock face from early afternoon onwards, it is "one of the most accessible desert monasteries" (A. Levensohn). The monks live on the produce from a garden by the stream. They show the visitors a cave containing the remains of the monks who perished during the Persian march against Byzantine Jerusalem in 614.

The road continues to **Jericho** which lies just S of the road bridge over the Qilt. On the way there, at the start of the plain, the excavated remains of the *Winter Palace* can be seen on the opposite bank. Built by Herod, this is where he died in 4 B.C. (see Jericho).

Yafo

see Tel Aviv-Jaffa

Yam Hamelach

see Dead Sea

Yam Kinneret

see Sea of Galilee

Yarden

see Jordan

Yavne

District: Central.
Population: 11,200.
(i) **Government Tourist Office,**
7 Mendele Street,
Tel Aviv;
tel. (03) 22 32 66/7.

Yavne is 17 miles/28 km S of Tel Aviv on the Ashqelon road. Founded in 1946 on the site of the abandoned Arab village of Yibnah, it has since grown into a town of 11,200 inhabitants.

HISTORY. – Already mentioned in the early Canaanite period (3000 B.C.), Yavne was captured by Joshua in the 13th c., by the Philistines in the 12th c. B.C. and then became part of the Kingdom of Judah. During the Persian period Phoenicians and Greeks settled here and called it *Jamnia*. This town was destroyed by the Maccabeans but in 147 B.C. they rebuilt it, together with the harbour, and settled it with a Jewish population. When the future emperor Vespasian captured Yavne in A.D. 68 he gave Rabbi Johanan ben Zakkai permission to set up a Jewish school where a start was made on the Mishnah which was to be completed in Tiberias about the year 200.

After the destruction of Jerusalem in A.D. 70 Yavne became the seat of the Sanhedrin. The rabbis Gamliel II and Ben Akiba worked in the school alongside

Johanan. In 135 the Romans put down the Bar Kochba rebellion and also destroyed the school at Yavne since it had supported Bar Kochba. The Sanhedrin were moved to Usha (½ mile/1 km E of Qiryat Ata on the bay of Acre, today a kibbutz) and then to Tiberias (see entry).

SIGHTS. – A *church* dating from the Crusades (12th c.) which later became a mosque stands on a hill E of the main road. A *tomb* W of the road is thought by the Jews to be that of Rabbi Gamliel and by the Moslems to be that of Mohammed's friend Hureira.

After 1948 the dunes W of Yavne became the site of the *nuclear research center* with the first Israeli atomic reactor. Industry has been established in the area around the center.

The old *port of Yavne Yam*, where a fort with stone and brick walls has been found, is approximately 4 miles/7 km NW, just S of the Palmahim kibbutz.

Yehuda

see Judea

Yeriho

see Jericho

Yerushalayim

see Jerusalem

Yodefat

District: North.
(i) **Government Tourist Office,**
Town Hall,
Acre;
tel. (04) 91 02 51.

The Galilean village of Yodefat (Jotapata in ancient times) lies 12 miles/20 km SE of Acre at the N foot of Mount Azmon (1,799 ft/548 m).

From Acre take the road to *Ahihud* (5 miles/8 km), then turn right after *Yavor* (2 miles/3 km) and take the narrow road E to *Segev* (6 miles/9 km). Yodefat is a short distance further on, on the right.

Wadi Qilt – Monastery of St George

HISTORY. – The town played a role in the Jewish uprising of A.D. 66–70. An eyewitness account is ⁙⁙⁙⁙ ⁙⁙ ⁙⁙⁙⁙⁙ ⁙⁙⁙⁙⁙⁙ ⁙⁙⁙ ⁙⁙⁙ ⁙ ⁙⁙ ⁙⁙⁙ ⁙⁙ the affair, in two chapters of his "History of the Jewish War" (III, 7–8). According to his description the town is "almost entirely built on a steep cliff falling away into such deep gorges that anyone looking down into them feels dizzy before his gaze reaches the very depths; the town can be reached only from the N where it stands astride the mountain ridge which is less steep at this point." Its situation therefore made it a suitable place for a fortress.

In 67 many Jewish rebels made this their stronghold; they were led by Joseph ben Matthias, a young priest from Jerusalem. He was so successful in defending Jotapata against the Romans that their commander Vespasian hastened here himself and surrounded the town with a double row of troops. As happened six years later at Massada (see entry), the Romans built a ramp on the N side where access was easiest and the beleaguered rebels raised up the wall to oppose it. The rebels' situation became critical. They ran out of food and had soon used up the water in the cisterns (the town had no other water supply). Many of their number had been killed on sorties and by catapults. On the 47th day of the siege the Romans managed to make a breach in the wall with a battering ram and took the town. They "knew neither mercy nor compassion". Many of the Jews were killed and 1,200 were taken prisoner.

Josephus, the commander, had hidden in a cistern but he came out and gave himself up a few days later. He was spared because he prophesied that Vespasian would become emperor (as in fact he soon did). In A.D. 70 Josephus – then in the service of the Roman conqueror, Titus – witnessed the capture of Jerusalem. Later, in Rome, under the more familiar name of Flavius Josephus, he was to write his "History of the Jewish War" and "Antiquities of the Jews", thus providing us with the main source of information on the events of this period.

The present-day village of Yodefat was founded in 1926 as a reafforestation centre. Some of the *ruins* of the old town are close by and can be seen from an observation tower. There is a panoramic view from the summit of Mount *Azmon* (1,799 ft/548 m) in the S.

Zefat
see Safed

Zikhron Ya'akov

District: Haifa.
Altitude: 164 ft/50 m.
Population: 5,000.
ⓘ **Government Tourist Office,**
18 Herzl Street,
Haifa;
tel. (04) 66 65 21.

Zikhron Ya'akov, founded in 1882 by Rumanian immigrants on the S slopes of Mount Carmel, 21 miles/33 km S of Haifa, is today one of Israel's most important wine-producing towns.

SIGHTS. – In 1885 the de Rothschild family presented the settlement with a synagogue, the *Beit Ya'akov* ("House of Jacob") which stands in the middle of the town. In 1887 de Rothschild had vineyards and almond orchards planted; 6 miles/9 km to the W, in Nahsholim, a bottle factory was built. To show their gratitude the settlers called the town and the synagogue after Edmond de Rothschild's father Jacob (James).

In the main street is *Bet Aaronsohn*, the house of Aharon Aaronsohn, who made a name for himself as a botanist and during the First World War founded an underground organisation to fight the Turkish rulers. The house contains his comprehensive collection of plants. The district, once riddled with malaria, has become a holiday area with a pleasant climate.

Mausoleum of Edmond de Rothschild

SURROUNDINGS. – On the S edge of the town a road branches off right to *Ramat Hanadiv* (Benefactor's Hill). Baron Edmond wanted to be buried here. In 1954 it was possible to bring his remains and those of his wife Ada from France to Israel on an Israeli warship and give them a state burial here. The entrance to the lush, well-kept park containing the **Rothschild Mausoleum** is in the S. In the W of the park is a map in stone showing all the settlements Edmond de Rothschild founded in Israel. In the centre is a rectangular walled courtyard with a passage leading down into the burial chamber, an impressive room, monumental but simple.

The settlement of **Binyamina**, 3 miles/5 km S of Zikhron Ya'akov, was also founded by Baron Edmond (Benjamin) de Rothschild in 1922.

1 mile/2 km W of Binyamina the Moshav of *Bet Hananya* was founded in 1950. It has two Roman

aqueducts which used to supply Caesarea with water. Excavations in *Tell Meborakh* N of the village have shown that the Hyksos (18th–16th c. B.C.) had a fortress here. A mausoleum has also been found on the E slope dating from the much later Roman period. This probably belonged to a family from Caesarea. Two sarcophagi from the vicinity are now in the Rockefeller Museum in Jerusalem.

The coast road W of Bet Hananya leads N across the *Crocodile River* (Nahal Hataninim). Crocodiles lived in the river until about 1900 and its estuary is a well-stocked *nature reserve*. The road then reaches **Ma'agan Mikhael**, a kibbutz founded in 1949 on a sandstone ridge. This is where Herod quarried the stone for the buildings of Caesarea (see entry). He was also responsible for the system of water ducting that was partly hewn out of the rock and partly carried by aqueducts.

Zippori (Sepphoris)

District: North.

(i) **Government Tourist Office,**
Casanova Street,
Nazareth;
tel. (0 65) 7 05 55.

The Moshav of Zippori, founded in 1949, is 4 miles/6 km NW of Nazareth in a region with many springs. The hill bearing the ruins of the ancient town of Zippori (=Sepphoris) lies ½ mile/1 km to the N.

HISTORY. – The town, which is not mentioned in the Old Testament, unlike nearby Yodefat (see entry) did not take part in the uprising in 66 and was therefore spared by the Romans. Near the castle American archaeologists have found Roman remains from the period when it was called *Diocaesarea*. The town became important in 135 when, after the second unsuccessful Jewish revolt against Rome, the High Council of Yavne (see entry) moved to Galilee and settled in Sepphoris as well as Bet Shearim (see entry), and Rabbi Juda Hanassi was its supreme spiritual authority. After his death the High Council moved to Tiberias (see entry) taking its school with it.

In the 4th c. the converted Jew Joseph built a church here, as he also did in his home town of Tiberias. The Crusaders came upon a Christian community and built a church dedicated to St Anne (the place is supposed to have been the home town of Anne, Mary's mother). On July 2, 1187 they assembled their army here before marching on to Hittim (see Horns of Hittim) where two days later they were annihilated by Saladin. Their castle was rebuilt by Taher al Umar in 1745.

SIGHTS. – Near the **fortress** are the remains of the Crusader castle with an ornate portal. Remnants of the walls of a Byzantine *church* and of a Roman *theater* (excavated in 1931) can also be seen. The *Church of St Anne*, which was rebuilt in 1860, contains part of the mosaic of its predecessor. There is a delightful panoramic view from the little *fort* built about 1745 on the hill. – In the W are the remains of the old water pipe and large *cisterns*, now known as the "Caverns of Hell".

Practical Information

Jerusalem – "Ship of the desert" on the Mount of Olives

When to go

Spring and autumn are particularly suitable seasons for visiting Israel. Since, however, many hotels have air-conditioning, a visit is also possible in the summer months when it can often be oppressively humid along the Mediterranean coast but is relatively dryer and cooler in the city of Jerusalem which is some 2,600 ft/800 m above sea level.

Although a small country, Israel has several climatic zones and tourists should bear this in mind when deciding where to go. The Red Sea coast near Eilat is very hot in summer but between autumn and spring it is excellent for a holiday. At the height of summer the air and water temperatures there climb to 104°F/40°C and 81°F/27°C respectively. The temperatures are similar around the Dead Sea but they are slightly lower for the Sea of Galilee and the Mediterranean.

Weather

The coastal region between Haifa and Gaza has a very pronounced Mediterranean climate with hot dry summers (April to October) and mild winters (November to March). In summer it is cooler in the mountains and these occasionally experience snowfalls in the winter.

The Negev Desert and the Jordan valley have a subtropical climate during the summer. The nights are often very cold in the desert.

For a more detailed account of the climate in Israel see page 15 to 18.

Time

Israel observes **Eastern European Time** (EET=GMT+2 hours). The introduction of Summer Time has been postponed for orthodox religious reasons.

Electricity

The power supply in Israel is 220 V AC with a frequency of 50 cycles per second.

Adapters, which are available throughout the country, have to be used for electrical equipment brought in from abroad.

Travel Documents

For a stay of less than 3 months nationals of the United States and Western countries require a **full passport**. This full passport must be valid for at least 9 more months. Children under 16 must either have their own full passport or be entered on the passport of one of their parents. American and Canadian citizens require a visitor's visa, which is issued free of charge at the port of entry. A permit must be obtained from the Israeli Ministry of the Interior for a stay of more than 3 months. It is also worth noting that almost all Arab countries will refuse entry to passport-holders with an Israeli stamp in their passport.

U.S. and Western **driving licences** and **car documents** are accepted and should be carried. Third party insurance is required and the *international insurance certificate* ("**green card**") is accepted provided that it is endorsed for Israel. If this is not the case then corresponding insurance cover must be taken out on entry; *short-term comprehensive vehicle insurance cover* is also highly recommended. All foreign cars visiting Israel must display an *international distinguishing sign* of the approved pattern and design.

Information: **Israel Insurance Association,**
Allenby Road 113,
Tel Aviv.

Tourists wishing to take *pets* (dogs, cats) to Israel must have an official veterinary health certificate as well as a certificate in duplicate of vaccination against rabies.

Vaccination Regulations

Vaccinations are not generally required but anyone who has been in an area where there is a possibility of infection in the two weeks before entering Israel must have a smallpox vaccination.

The Weather in Israel

Figures giving the air (A) and water (W) temperatures in Fahrenheit (F) and Centigrade (C), and the number of sunny days (S) in several locations during the tourist season

Location		January	February	March	April	September	October	November	December
Haifa	A	46–63°F	48–64°F	46–70°F	55–79°F	68–86°F	61–81°F	55–73°F	48–64°F
(Mediterranean)		8–17°C	9–18°C	8–21°C	13–26°C	20–30°C	16–27°C	13–23°C	9–18°C
	W	64°F/18°C	64°F/18°C	64°F/18°C	66°F/19°C	84°F/29°C	82°F/28°C	73°F/23°C	66°F/19°C
	S	16	16	22	25	29	27	22	19
Tel Aviv	A	48–64°F	48–66°F	50–68°F	54–72°F	68–88°F	59–84°F	54–77°F	48–66°F
(Mediterranean)		9–18°C	9–19°C	10–20°C	12–22°C	20–31°C	15–29°C	12–25°C	9–19°C
	W	64°F/18°C	64°F/18°C	64°F/18°C	66°F/19°C	84°F/29°C	81°F/27°C	73°F/23°C	66°F/19°C
	S	17	16	23	26	29	28	22	19
Tiberias	A	48–64°F	48–68°F	52–72°F	55–81°F	72–95°F	66–90°F	59–79°F	52–68°F
(Sea of Galilee)		9–18°C	9–20°C	11–22°C	13–27°C	22–35°C	19–32°C	15–26°C	11–20°C
	W	63°F/17°C	59°F/15°C	63°F/17°C	70°F/21°C	86°F/30°C	82°F/28°C	75°F/24°C	72°F/22°C
	S	19	18	25	27	30	30	25	23
Sodom	A	54–70°F	55–72°F	61–79°F	72–90°F	81–97°F	75–90°F	66–81°F	57–72°F
(Dead Sea)		12–21°C	13–22°C	16–26°C	22–32°C	27–36°C	24–32°C	19–27°C	14–22°C
	W	70°F/21°C	66°F/19°C	70°F/21°C	72°F/22°C	88°F/31°C	86°F/30°C	82°F/28°C	73°F/23°C
	S	30	26	31	30	30	31	30	29
Eilat	A	50–70°F	52–73°F	55–81°F	63–88°F	75–97°F	68–91°F	61–82°F	52–73°F
(Red Sea)		10–21°C	11–23°C	13–27°C	17–31°C	24–36°C	20–33°C	16–28°C	11–23°C
	W	72°F/22°C	68°F/20°C	70°F/21°C	72°F/22°C	81°F/27°C	79°F/26°C	77°F/25°C	75°F/24°C
	S	30	27	29	29	30	31	29	30
Jerusalem	A	43–52°F	45–57°F	46–61°F	54–70°F	64–82°F	61–79°F	54–66°F	45–59°F
(mountainous)		6–11°C	7–14°C	8–16°C	12–21°C	18–28°C	16–26°C	12–19°C	7–15°C
	S	19	19	23	27	30	29	23	22
Safed	A	39–50°F	41–52°F	43–55°F	48–66°F	63–81°F	59–75°F	54–61°F	41–48°F
(mountainous)		4–10°C	5–11°C	6–13°C	9–19°C	17–27°C	15–24°C	12–16°C	5–9°C
	S	18	13	26	27	20	21	20	19

Customs Regulations

The customs offices at Israel's international ports and airports are open 24 hours a day.

On entry. – Personal effects and tourist items may be temporarily imported free of duty. This includes 1 camera and 1 movie camera (up to 16 mm) with 10 rolls of film each, 1 portable typewriter, 1 tape-recorder with 700 m of tape, 1 record-player with records, 1 portable radio, a pair of binoculars, tools, musical instruments and sports equipment, 1 bicycle and camping equipment.

These items must be declared on entry. You will be asked to provide a guarantee for portable television sets, video equipment or diving equipment. No duty is charged on the following items for private consumption: 250 cigarettes or 250 g tobacco, 2 litres wine, 1 litre spirits, 0·25 litre of perfume, gifts and foodstuffs up to a value equivalent to 125 U.S. dollars. It is forbidden to import drugs, knives with fixed blades and claspknives with blades longer than 10 cm (4 in.), fresh meat and fruit, pornography and publications that have been published in Arab countries.

Cars, trailers and boats may also be imported duty free, and import permits valid for one year are issued at the border. Foreign visitors' cars remain free of duty for three months.

Warning

Film should be removed from all cameras before customs inspection. It is forbidden to photograph installations of military importance. This includes airfields, ports, bridges, buildings guarded by soldiers, border installations and railway stations.

The duty-free allowances are approximately one-third greater for goods bought in the ordinary shops in EEC countries but not for goods bought in a duty-free shop, on a ship or on an aircraft.

Currency

The unit of currency is the Israeli Shekel (*IS*) which is made up of 100 *Agorot*.

There are banknotes for 1, 5, 10, 50, 100 and 500 IS (1,000 and 2,000 notes are in the course of preparation) with coins in the denominations of 1, 5 and 10 Agorot and ½ shekel.

Exchange rates fluctuate and there is a very high rate of inflation.

Currency Regulations

There are no restrictions on importing Israeli or foreign currency but it is advisable to declare how much foreign currency you bring in with you. Foreign currency can be exported up to the amount declared on entry and up to 500 IS may be taken out of the country.

Only banks are allowed to change money and cash traveller's checks. It is advisable to keep your receipt in case you want to change your money back again.

Bills for hotels, travel agencies, domestic airlines and car rental firms paid in foreign currency are not subject to value added tax (currently 15%). The same applies to purchases from special shops which in this case mostly give an extra discount. It is advisable to take credit cards and traveller's checks.

Long-distance telephone calls are made from public telephone booths in the central telegraph offices which are open 24 hours a day. For long-distance and international calls you have to use telephone tokens (assimon) which are obtainable at post offices. Many countries can be dialled direct. Local calls can be made in many shops, restaurants and drugstores. Telephone directories are in English and Hebrew.

Travel to Israel

The airplane is the most important means of travel to Israel from Europe and North America. There are direct flights between the main European airports and Tel Aviv (Ben Gurion international airport at Lod) while charter flights also land at Eilat on the Red Sea.

It takes much longer to travel by road or rail to one of the Italian Adriatic ports or to the Greek Port of Piraeus and then embark on a ship for Haifa. Many Mediterranean cruise liners call at Haifa and Ashdod.

Information:

U.S.A.

World Dynamics Travel
New York
tel. 212 697 4224
(for sailings to and from Israel; also agents for major cruise lines)

Great Britain

Associated Oceanic Agencies
Eagle House
109–110 Jermyn Street
London SW1Y 6ES
tel. 01–930 9534/7449
(for sailings to and from Israel; also cruises)

Chandris Ltd
5 St Helen's Place
London EC3A 6BJ
tel. 01–588 5984
(cruises)

Cit-Costa Line
256 High Street
Croydon CR9 1LL
tel. 01 686 5533
(cruises)

Epirotiki Lines
Westmorland House
127–131 Regent Street
London W1R 7HA
tel. 01–734 0805
(cruises)

"K" Lines
50 Pall Mall
London SW1Y 5JQ
tel. 01–930 7610
(cruises)

Lauro Lines Ltd
85 Roseberry Avenue
London EC1R 4QS
tel. 01–837 2157
(cruises)

Norwegian American Cruises
11–12 Pall Mall
London SW1 5LH
tel. 01–930 1843
(cruises)

P & O Cruises
Beaufort House
St Botolph Street
London EC3A 7DX
tel. 01–283 8080
(cruises)

Royal Viking Union Lloyd
50 Curzon Street
London W1Y 7PN
tel. 01–409 0844
(cruises)

Sol Maritime
c/o Cyprus Travel London Ltd
42 Hampstead Road
London NW1
tel. 01–387 7854
(for sailings to and from Israel; also cruises)

Zenon Travel & Tours
15 Kentish Town Road
London NW1
tel. 01–267 0269/2657
(for sailings to and from Israel; also cruises)

Travel from Israel to Arab countries.
– Anyone wishing to travel to an Arab country after a stay in Israel should ask the border officials to stamp their visitor's form and not their passport since many Arab countries will refuse entry to anyone with an Israeli stamp or visa (even if it is out of date) in their passport. – An entry permit for a stay of up to 7 days can be purchased for short trips from Israel to the S tip of the Sinai and the Monastery of St Catherine at the Taba frontier-crossing (S of Eilat).

The Israeli-Egyptian border can be crossed in either direction. This requires a special permit and a carnet de passage as well as a valid International Driving Permit, International Certificate for Motor Vehicles and Nationality Plate which can only be obtained in the visitor's country of origin. It is not possible to drive to or from Israel from or into any other neighbouring country.

Travel in Israel

By Car

Israel has over 2,500 miles/4,000 km of asphalt roads. Most of the roads are in the northern part of the country around Tel Aviv; the Negev S of Beersheba is crossed by two major roads from N to S and by a road running westwards to Egypt and the Suez Canal.

There are *expressways* along the coast from Akko to Ashdod and in the vicinity of Tel Aviv, Jerusalem and Beersheba. Most of the other main roads are in good condition.

Driving in Israel. – Seat-belts must be worn outside built-up areas and motorcyclists must wear crash helmets. Driving under the influence of alcohol is forbidden. Caravans must not be wider than 7 ft/ 2·10 m or longer than 16 ft/5 m including towbar and they must not weigh over 1,650 lb/750 kg.

The present **speed limits** are **30 miles/ 50 km per hour** in built-up areas; elsewhere they are **50 miles/80 km per hour** for cars, **40 miles/70 km per hour** for motorbikes and **35 miles/60 km per hour** for vehicles with trailers.

Gasoline (petrol) prices vary, but are in general considerably higher than in the U.S.

By Air

Israel's main airport is Ben Gurion international airport at Lod near Tel Aviv, which has direct flights to all the major European and North American cities.

El Al, the *state airline*, flies the international routes while **Arkia**, *Israel Inland Airlines*, flies between Tel Aviv, Jerusalem, Haifa, Rosh Pinna, Eilat, En Yahav and Mizpe Ramon. – There are also *Air Sinai* flights from Tel Aviv and Eilat to the Monastery of St Catherine in Egypt on the Sinai Peninsula.

An airport charge of about $10 is levied at Israeli airports for flights outside the country. It takes at least two hours to check in. It is also possible to check in on the eve of departure at the El Al air terminals in Tel Aviv and Jerusalem (closed Friday evenings and public holidays) – this cuts down the time you need to spend at the airport to about an hour and a quarter.

Orthodox politicians are trying to further restrict public travel on the Sabbath, and a ban on flights on that day is now under discussion. In any case it is advisable to confirm bookings and the times of flights with El Al and Arkia at least 72 hours before take-off. Only one piece of luggage is permitted on domestic flights.

By Rail

Israeli railways (appr. 340 miles or 550 km of main lines) operate lines from Nahariya to Haifa and Tel Aviv and from Tel Aviv to Jerusalem. All trains have a buffet service; it is cheaper to travel by rail than by bus. There are no trains on the Sabbath and public holidays.

Communications
in Israel

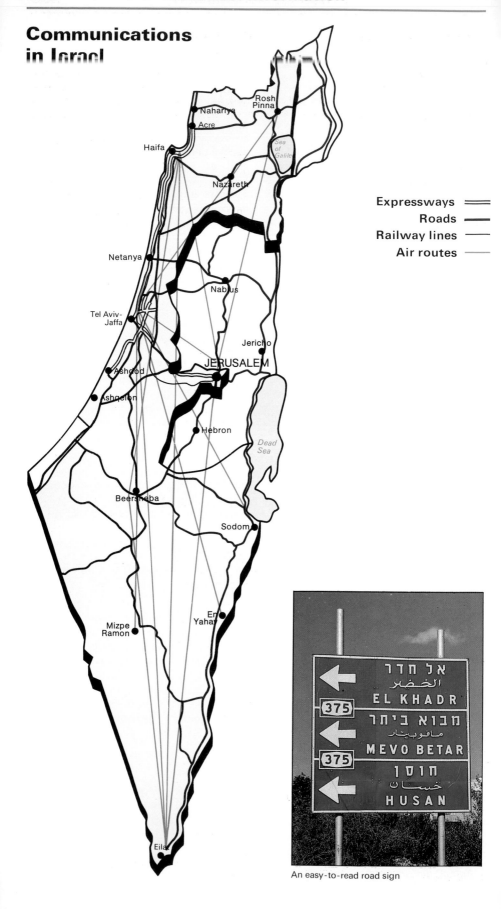

Expressways ═══
Roads ━━━
Railway lines ──
Air routes ──

Rosh
Pinna
Nahariya
Acre
Haifa
Sea
of
Galilee
Nazareth
Netanya
Nablus
Tel Aviv-
Jaffa
Jericho
JERUSALEM
Ashdod
Ashqelon
Hebron
Dead
Sea
Beersheba
Sodom
En
Yahav
Mizpe
Ramon
Eilat

אל חדר
الخضر
EL KHADR
מבוא ביתר
مافوبيتار
MEVO BETAR
חוסן
خسان
HUSAN
375
375

An easy-to-read road sign

By Bus and Taxi

Israel has an extensive network of urban and rural *bus routes*. It is sensible to book a seat for longer journeys. Bus services are severely restricted on the Sabbath and the Jewish public holidays. *Shared taxis* (sherut) ply in and between cities and larger towns. These take up to seven passengers with each passenger only having to pay for himself. – Ordinary *taxis* mainly operate within the city. If a taximeter has not yet been adjusted to the current fare scale, passengers can ask to be shown this scale.

Car Rental

Cars can be hired in Jerusalem, Tel Aviv, Eilat, Ashqelon, Haifa, Herzliya, Netanya, Rehovot, Safed and Beersheba where there are offices of the main international car-rental firms (Avis, Budget, Eurocar, Hertz).

You must have an international or national driving licence; national driving licences must be accompanied by a certificate of confirmation in Hebrew. Drivers must be over 21. Because of the Sabbath car-rental firms' offices are closed from Friday evening until Sunday morning.

Tour Operators Offering Trips to Israel

Most holiday-makers visiting Israel either want to see the historic sights or simply enjoy the beaches and sporting facilities. Young people are often interested in staying and working for a time in a kibbutz.

Some tour operators cater to groups such as the disabled, senior citizens or people suffering from ill-health; there are also special holidays for people with particular interests such as geology, archaeology or agriculture.

For those who prefer to explore the country themselves by car, a number of tour operators offer Fly/Drive holidays where you pick up your car at the airport. It is also possible to hire a camper.

In the following list of operators the initials at the end of each entry indicate the type of vacation they offer.

T   – Touring holiday
H   – Health resort/Spa
D   – Holiday for the disabled
P   – Pilgrimage
S   – Sporting holiday
K   – Kibbutz holiday
Sa – Safari
FD – Fly/Drive
ST – Study tour
SI – Special interest holiday
Cr – Cruise
E   – Combined with Egypt
J   – Combined with Jordan

Tour Operators in the U.S.A.

Arkia Israeli Airlines
350 Fifth Avenue
New York NY 10118
tel. 212 695 2998
T, S, E

Avantours
8500 Wilshire Blvd
Beverly Hills CA 90211
tel. 213 652 2160/651 0024
T, P, E

BibleLand Travel
1204 S. Third
Louisville KY 40203
tel. 502 636 9211
T, P

Canaan Tours Inc.
289 E. Main Street
Smithtown NY 11787
tel. 516 360 0250
ST

Catholic Travel Office
1019 19th NW, Suite 520
Washington DC 20036
tel. 202 293 2277
P

Club Universe
P.O. Box 57929
Los Angeles CA 90017
tel. 213 484 1671
T, E

Command Travel
6 E. 45th Street
New York NY 10017
tel. 212 490 1213; 800 221 4840
T (by chauffeured car), E

Concorde 55 Israel Ltd
56 W. 45th Street
New York NY 10036
tel. 212 391 8681; 800 223 7173
K, FD

The Cortell Group
3 E. 54th Street
New York NY 10022
tel. 212 751 3250; 800 223 6626/7
T, E, J

Cosmos
69–15 Austin Street. P.O. Box 862
Forest Hill NY 11375
tel. 212 268 8088; 516 354 0076; 800 221 0742
T, E

Council on International Education Exchange
205 E. 42nd Street
New York NY 10017
tel. 212 661 0311; 800 223 7402
Sa

Dona Ltd
181 E. 73rd Street. Suite 6E
New York NY 10021
tel. 212 988 4776
H

Foreign-Sharon Tours
461 Eighth Avenue
New York NY 10001
tel. 212 947 9595; 800 223 7500; 800 223 9100
T, P, Cr, E

Forum Travel International
2437 Durant Avenue
Berkeley CA 94704
tel. 415 843 8294
T, E, J

Four Winds Travel
175 Fifth Avenue
New York NY 10010
tel. 212 777 0260; 212 473 2588
T, E, J

General Tours
711 Third Avenue
New York NY 10017
tel. 212 687 7400; 800 221 2216
T, E

Gogo Tours
15 E. 40th Street
New York NY 10016
tel. 212 532 8484
T, E

Gray Line of Tel Aviv
c/o Kopel Tours
40 E. 49th Street
New York NY 10017
tel. 212 838 0500
T

International Theatre & Historical Productions
5855 Green Valley Circle, Suite 302
Culver City CA 90230
tel. 213 670 3048; 800 421 1510
T (including visits to Passion and Nativity plays)

Isis Tours
12 Station Road
Bellport NY 11713
tel. 516 286 2626; 800 645 1084
T, E

Isram Travel
630 Third Avenue
New York NY 10017
tel. 212 477 2352; 800 223 7460
T, E

Ivory Tours
P.O. Box 1234
Freeport NY 11520
tel. 615 882 1234; 800 251 9999
T, E, J

Kopel Tours Ltd
40 E. 49th Street
New York NY 10017
tel. 212 838 0500; 800 223 7408
T, P

Lama Tours International
Southeast Plaza, Suite 105
4528 S. Sheridan Road
Tulsa OK 74145
tel. 918 665 1065
T, E

Leisure Time Tours
310 Madison Avenue
New York NY 10017
tel. 212 599 2323; 800 223 2624
T, E

Maupintour
P.O. Box 807
Lawrence KS 66044
tel. 913 843 1211; 800 255 4266
T, Cr, E, J

Melia Travel International
168 Michigan Avenue
Chicago IL 60601
tel. 312 253 6815; 800 621 5318
T, E

Nawas International Travel
20 E. 46th Street
New York NY 10017
tel. 212 682 4088; 800 221 4984
T, P, E

Nyman & Schultz Tours
135 E. 55th Street
New York NY 10022
tel. 212 751 8664
SI

Olson-Travelworld
P.O. Box 92734
Los Angeles CA 90009
tel. 213 670 7100; 800 421 2255
T (including visits to Passion and Nativity plays), E

Peltours
70 W. 40th Street
New York NY 10018
tel. 212 354 6968; 800 223 6393
T, E

Persepolis Travel Ltd
667 Madison Avenue
New York NY 10021
tel. 212 838 8585; 515 222 0015; 800 221 1680
T, E

Professional Group Travel
3468 Lawson Blvd
Oceanside NY 11572
tel. 516 764 5100; 800 645 2222
T, ST

R Voyages Inc.
744 N. Glendale Avenue
Glendale CA 91206
tel. 213 246 9356; 800 423 2856
T, P

Wailing Wall and Dome of the Rock in Jerusalem

Red Sea Divers
580 Fifth Avenue, Suite 821
New York NY 10036
tel. 212 877 8240
S (scuba diving), E

Religious Group Tours
P.O. Box 6749
San Jose CA 95150
tel. 408 244 1191
P, E

Rich Worldwide Travel
1495 Weaver Street
Scarsdale NY 10583
tel. 914 723 4600
SI, student groups

Starship Tours
1000 Route 23
Hamburg NJ 07419
tel. 201 827 6201; 800 382 9224
T (groups only)

Sundowners Adventure Travel
3 E. 54th Street
New York NY 10022
tel. 212 980 9070
T (18–35-year-old tourists)

Tek Travel, Inc.
45 E. 17th Street
New York NY 1003
T, P

(Nazzal's) Terra Sancta
10 Woodchuck Lane
P.O. Box 231
Rowayton CT 06583
tel. 203 866 6003
T

Touring Express
7301 Sepulveda Blvd
Van Nuys CA 91405
tel. 213 787 2622
T, P, E

Tours of the Way
38 Brookhollow Drive
ⅠⅠⅠⅠⅠⅠⅠⅠ ⅠⅠⅠⅠⅠⅠ
tel. 714 957 8740
T, K

Tours Specialists
1400 Broadway
New York NY 10018
tel. 212 840 4356; 800 223 7552
T, E

Travcoa
4000 MacArthur Blvd
Newport Beach CA 92660
tel. 800 432 8373; 800 854 7204
T, Cr, E

Travel Bug
83 W. Main Street
Lake Zurich IL 60047
tel. 312 438 9292
T, SI, E

Travelink Tours International
9575 W. Higgins Road
Rosemont IL 60018
tel. 312 692 5790
T, Cr

Travel Plans International
1200 Harger Road
Oak Brook IL 60521
tel. 312 655 5678; 800 323 7600
T, ST, E

TWA Getaway Tour Center
28 S. Sixth Street
Philadelphia PA 19106
tel. 215 925 7885; 800 523 4828
T

Unitours Inc.
60 E. 42nd Street
New York NY 10165
tel. 212 949 9500; 800 223 1780
T, SI, E

Wilcox World Tours
1705 NW Bank Building
Asheville NC 28801
tel. 704 253 0453; 800 452 2803; 800 438 5828
T, E, J

Tour Operators in Great Britain

London Area

Albany Foremost Travel
3 Broadway
Victoria
London SW1H 0BA
tel. 01–222 0881
T, K, FD, E

Atlantis Holidays
43 The Market Place
Hampstead Garden Suburb
London NW11 6JT
tel. 01–458 9422
T, K, FD, E

Canon Tours
8 Canon Corner
Edgware
Middlesex
tel. 01–958 3144
T

Club Méditerranée
62 South Molton Street
London W1W ⅠⅠⅠⅠ
tel. 01–409 0644
T

Cosmos Air Holiday
Cosmos House, 1 Bromley Common
Bromley
Kent BR2 9LX
tel. 01–464 3311
T, E

Dalgety World Travel
63 Conduit Street
London W1R 4FD
tel. 01–734 5417
SI

E.R.O.S. Travel
117 Brighton Road
Coulsdon
Surrey CR3 2TD
tel. 01–668 0437
P, K, ST

Exodus Expeditions
All Saints' Passage
100 Wandsworth High Street
London SW18 4LE
tel. 01–870 0151
T

Farthings International
Plaza Hotel, 42 Princes Square
Bayswater
London W2
tel. 01–229 1377
T (young people/students)

Global of London
Glen House, 200 Tottenham Court Road
London W1P 0JP
tel. 01–637 4261
T, P

Golden Circle Holidays
Glen House, 200 Tottenham Court Road
London W1P 0JP
tel. 01–580 9872
Senior Citizen holidays

Goodmos Tours
9/13 St Andrew Street
Holborn Circus
London EC4A 3DH
tel. 01–353 8682
T, H, P, K, FD, E

Go Travel
87 Edgware Road
London W2 2HX
tel. 01–724 0841
T, H, P

Highway Holidays
45 High Street
Penge West
London SE20 7HW
tel. 01–778 1600
P, E, J

Ibesco Travel
42 Ealing Road
Wembley, Middlesex
tel. 01–903 3051
T, H, P, K, J

Herod's Gate in Jerusalem

Insight International Tours
6 Spring Gardens
Trafalgar Square
London SW1A 2BJ
tel. 01–930 6581
T, E

Inter-Church Travel
13–17 New Buckingham Place
London W1X 2LB
tel. 01–734 0942
T, P, FD, E, J

Libra Travel
15–16 Newman Street
London W1P 3HD
tel. 01–637 7701
T, P

Lionheart Tours
66 Stamford Hill
London N16 6XS
tel. 01–806 0991
T, H, P

Man Around
1 Kensington Mall
London W8 4EB
tel. 01–221 1140
T

Maof Four Seas Holidays
Godfrey House, 128–136 High Street
Edgware, Middlesex
tel. 01–951 1383
T, P, K, FD

Marvel Tours
25 New Cavendish Street
London W1
tel. 01–486 8615
T, P, E

Nawas Tourist Agency Ltd
19 Gt Portland Street
London W1N 5DB
tel. 01–580 6405/8
T

Nichols Travel
72 Ballards Lane
Finchley
London N3 2BW
tel. 01–349 2046
ST

Orientours
Kent House, 87 Regent Street
London W1R 8LS
tel. 01–434 1551
T, P, E, J

Peltours
Mappin House, 156/162 Oxford Street
London W1R 8LS
tel. 01–580 0372
T, H, P, K, FD, ST, SI, E

Project 67
36 Gt Russell Street
London WC1
tel. 01–636 1262
ST, SI

Pullman Holidays
79/80 Petty France
London SW1H 9HA
tel. 01–222 8731
P, K, E

Sabra Travel
9 Edgwarebury Lane
Edgware, Middlesex
tel. 01–958 3244
T, H, D, FD

Sarasten Ltd
13 The Broadway
Mill Hill
London NW7 3LN
tel. 01–906 0966
FD

Serennissima Travel Ltd
2 Lower Sloane Street
London SW1W 8BJ
tel. 01–730 9841
ST

Slade Travel
Slade House, 15 Vivian Avenue
London NW4 3UT
tel. 01–202 0111/0877
T

Sovereign Holidays
West London Terminal
Cromwell Road
London SW7 4ED
tel. 01–370 4545
T

Sunquest Holidays
43/44 New Bond Street
London W1Y 9HB
tel. 01–409 0103
T, P, K, FD

The Sundowners
8 Hogarth Place
London SW5 0QT
tel. 01–370 6231
T, E

Superstar Holidays
193 Regent Street
London W1R 8BS
tel. 01–734 1492
T, FD

Swan Hellenic
237–238 Tottenham Court Road
London W1P 0AL
tel. 01–636 8070
ST, J

Thompson Holidays
Greater London House
Hampstead Road
London NW1 7SP
tel. 01–387 9321
T

Trafalgar Travel
9–11 Bressenden Place
Victoria
London SW1E 5DF
tel. 01–828 4388
T, P

Travel Lore Ltd
150 Finchley Road
London NW3 5HS
tel. 01–794 1051
K

Travel the World
683–685 Finchley Road
London N2
tel. 01–278 8955
T, H, P, FD

Travel Young
8 Buckingham Palace Road
Victoria
London SW1W 0QP
tel. 01–630 5855
T, K, FD

Twickenham Travel
84 Hampton Road
Twickenham TW2 5QS
tel. 01–898 8351
T, K, FD, SI

Vexas (Discoveries) International
45 Brompton Road
Knightsbridge
London SW3 1DE
tel. 01–589 3315/0500
T, E

VIP Travel
42 North Audley Street
London W1A 4PY
tel. 01–499 4221
H

West End Travel
1 Maddox Street
London W1R 0PR
tel. 01–439 1605
T, H, P, FD

Worldwide Student Travel
37 Store Street
London WC1E 7BZ
tel. 01–580 7733
T, K, FD, E

YHA Travel
14 Southampton Street
London WC2E 7HY
tel. 01–836 8542
T (young people/students), FD

Outside London

Albany Travel
190 Deansgate
Manchester M3 3WD
tel. 061–833 0202
T, H, P, K, FD, E

Alfah Tours
23 Market Square
Bicester
Oxford OX6 7AD
tel. 08692 45763
P

Bales Tours Ltd
Bales House, Barrington Road
Dorking
Surrey RH4 3EJ
tel. 0306 885991
T, E, J

Countrywide Holidays Assn
Birch Heys, Cromwell Range
Manchester M14 6HU
tel. 061–225 1000
K, S, SI

Crusade for World Revival
Box 11
Walton on Thames
Surrey
tel. 093 22 44499
P

Cunard Crusader (Brocklebank Travel)
Friary House, 15 Colston Street
Bristol BS1 5AP
tel. 0272 24386
P, K, FD

Fellowship Tours
Answered Prayer
South Chard
Somerset TA20 2PR
tel. 0460 20540
P, K, ST, SI, E

Holiday Adventure Ltd
The White House, 45/51 Marlowes
Hemel Hempstead
Herts HP1 1LD
tel. 0442 40061/2 & 44703
T

Laker Holidays
Kent House
Sandgate
Folkestone
Kent
tel. 0303 57444
T

Mancunia Travel Ltd
30 Brown Street
Manchester M2 2JF
tel. 061–834 4030/0516
P, E

Page & Moy
136–138 London Road
Leicester LE2 1EN
tel. 0533 552521

Peltours Farber Ltd
27/29 Church Street
Manchester M4 1QA
tel. 061–834 3721/3
T, H, D, P, K, FD, ST, SI

Pilgrims Agency
Stone Court, Gillsmans Hill
St Leonards on Sea
Sussex
tel. 0424 430277
T, P

Raymond Cook Holidays
118 High Street
Dover
Kent CT16 1EG
tel. 0304 204404
T, J

Saga
119 Sandgate Road
Folkestone
Kent
tel. 0303 30000
ST (Senior Citizens)

The Best Of Israel
Rock House, Boughton
Monchelsea
Maidstone
Kent
tel. 0622 46678
H, P, K, FD

Threshold Travel
Wrendal House, 2 Whitworth Street West
Manchester M1 5WT
tel. 061–236 9763
D

Trans World Travel
19 High Street
Oxford OX1 4AH
tel. 0865 726875/6
T, P, K, FD

Venus Travel (Northern) Ltd
396 Harrogate Road
Leeds 17
tel. 0532 693117
H, K, FD

Language

In Israel you can usually find someone local that you can communicate with in English. In some of the remoter parts, however, it is useful to have at least a basic knowledge of Hebrew.

The official languages in Israel are **Ivrit** (*modern Hebrew*) and **Arabic**. Both belong to the Semitic group of languages and both are written from right to left but the characters are quite different.

Ivrit (*modern Hebrew*)

Ivrit (Iwrith, Iwrit) is based on the Hebrew of the Old Testament but differs considerably. The Hebrew alphabet has 22 letters. Since Hebrew words consist of a more or less fixed *framework of consonants* while vowels can vary, written Hebrew was originally confined to the consonants that gave a word its meaning. *Vowels* came to be added at a later stage and were written under the consonant that they followed. Their phonetic quality varies considerably. Each letter has a *numerical value* (and is a number as well) and this played an important part in the numerical mysticism of the Cabbala.

The written and printed languages are similar. All the characters tend to fit into an imaginary square, and in calligraphy the first stroke of each character is always begun at the top left-hand corner.

Arabic

Modern Arabic evolved from the northern Arabic of antiquity and accompanied the spread of Islam throughout large parts of the southern and eastern Mediterranean. The spoken language came to have many dialects; the Arabic in this Guide is the Egyptian version.

Hebrew Alphabet

Letter	Name	Pronunciation (Ivrit)	Numerical Value
א	Alef	Silent (denotes inclusion of vowel)	1
ב	Beth	B or V	2
ג	Gimel	hard G	3
ד	Daleth	D	4
ה	Hay	H	5
ו	Vav	V	6
ז	Zayin	Z	7
ח	Heth	As in German *ch*	8
ט	Teth	T	9
י	Yod	Y (as consonant)	10
כ	Kaf	K	20
ל	Lamed	L	30
מ	Mem	M	40
נ	Nun	N	50
ס	Sameth	hard S	60
ע	Ayin	Gutteral	70
פ	Pay	P or F	80
צ	Sade	Z, Tz, Ts	90
ק	Kuf	K, Q	100
ר	Resh	R	200
ש	Sin	S	300
ש	Shin	Sh	300
ת	Tav	T or Th	400

Stress. – The main stress in Hebrew is theoretically on the penultimate syllable but since short final vowels are often missed out it often tends to be on the last syllable.

Vowels. – Long vowels are denoted by the letters Alef, Vav and Ayin while short vowels are mostly omitted or represented by a system of dots and dashes placed over or under the letters. The pronunciation of the short vowels varies considerably according to what consonants are on either side of them and the literacy of the speaker.

Arabic Alphabet

Letter	Name	Pronunciation	Letter	Name	Pronunciation
١	Alif	(fixed vowel inclusion)	ظ	Za	Z, Tz, Ts (emphatic)
ب	Ba	B	ع	Ain	(gutteral sound)
ت	Ta	T	غ	Ghain	Gh (velar sound)
ث	Tha	Th (as in "thing")	ف	Fa	F
ج	Dschim	G	ق	Kaf	Q (velar)
ح	Ha	H (strongly aspirated)	ك	Kaf	K (palatal)
خ	Cha	Ch (as in Scottish "loch")	ل	Lam	L
د	Dal	D	م	Mim	M
ذ	Dhal	Dh (as in "the")	ن	Nun	N
ر	Ra	R (rolled r)	ه	Ha	H
ز	Saj	Z	و	Waw	W (as "w")
س	Sin	S (as in "boss")	ى	Ya	Y
ش	Scin	Sh			
ص	Sad	S (soft s; emphatic)			
ض	Dad	D (emphatic as in "day")			
ط	Ta	T (emphatic as in "tn")			

Most letters in the Arabic alphabet can assume *four forms* depending on whether they are on their own, are joined only to the preceding or the following letter or are between two letters.

Vocabulary

English	Hebrew	Arabic
Good morning!	Bóker tow!	Sabach el-cher!
Good day, Hello!	Shalóm!	Es-salamu 'alekum!
Good evening!	Érew tow!	Misa el-cher!
Good night!	Láila tow!	Leltak saida!
Good bye!	Lehitraót	'allalah! Ma'as-salama!
I do not understand	Ejnéni mewín (mewiná) otcha (otách)	A'na mish fahmak
Excuse me	Slach (silchi) li	A'sif
Yes	Ken	Aiwa
No	Lo	La
Please	Bewakashá	Min fadlak
Thank you	Todá	Shukran
Yesterday	Etmól	Embarich
Today	Hajóm	En-nahar-da
Tomorrow	Machar	Bukra
What time is it?	Ma hasha'á?	Es-sa'a kam?
When is (are) . . . open?	Matái potchim . . . ?	I'mta jiftach (tiftach) . . . ?
When is (are) . . . shut?	Matái sogrim . . . ?	I'mta jiqifil (tiqifil) . . . ?

Numbers

Hebrew	Arabic
(masculine first, feminine after comma)	

	Hebrew	Arabic
0	–	sifr
1	echád, achát	vachid, vachda
2	shnáyim, shtáyim	itnen
3	shloshá, shalósh	talata
4	arba'á, arbá	arba'a
5	chamishá, chamésh	chamsa
6	shishá, shesh	sitta
7	shivá, shéva	sab'a
8	shmoná, shmoné	tamanya
9	tishá, tésha	tis'a
10	asará, éser	ashara
11	achád asár, achát esré	hadashar
12	shneym asár, shteym esré	itnashar
13	shloshá asár, shlosh esré	talatashar
14	arba'á asár, arbá esré	arbachtashar
15	chamishá asár, chamésh esré	chamastashar
16	shishá asár, shesh esré	sittashar
17	shivá' asár, shva esré	sabachtashar
18	shmoná asár, shmoné esré	tamantashar
19	tish'á asár, tsha esré	tis'atashar
20	esrím, esrím	'ishrin
21	esrím veechád, esrím veachát	vachid u ishrin
22	esrím ushanyim, esrím ushtáyim	itnen u'ishrin
30	shloshím	talatin
40	arbaím	arba'in
50	chamishím	chamsin
60	shishím	sittin
70	shivim	sab'in
80	shmoním	tamanin
90	tishím	tis'in
100	meá	miya, mit
200	matáim (shtey meót)	miten
300	shlosh meót	tultemiya
1000	élef	alf
10 000	aserét alafím	ashart alaf
100 000	meá élef	mit alf

Fractions

	Hebrew	Arabic
$\frac{1}{2}$	hachézi	nuss
$\frac{1}{3}$	shlish	tult
$\frac{1}{4}$	réva	rub
$\frac{1}{10}$	asirít	'oshr

Arabic Numbers

•	١	٢	٣	٤	٥	٦	٧	٨	٩	١٠
0	1	2	3	4	5	6	7	8	9	10

Arabic numbers are written *from left to right*, Hebrew numbers *from right to left*!

English	Hebrew	Arabic
Single room	Chéder bishvíl ben adám echád	Ghurfa bisirir vachid
Double room	Chéder kafúl	Ghurfa bisiriren
How much is bed and breakfast?	Kamá olé chéder im aruchat bóker?	Qadd-e bitsawi el-oda bil-a'kl?
What time is breakfast?	Matái magishim et aruchát habóker?	I'mte chaikun el-fitar?
Druggist	Beit merkáchad	Agsacha'ne
Doctor	Rofé klali	Tabib
Dentist	Rofé shináyim	Tabib asna'n

Rail and Air Travel

Airplane	Avirón	Tayya'ra
Airport	Sde teufá	Mata'r
Arrival	Biá, haga'á	Vusul
Baggage, luggage	Mitán	Shu'nat
Baggage check	Shovér chafazim	Vasl el-afsh
Bus	Otobús	Otobis
Cabin	Ta	Kabina
Compartment	Machleká	Divan
Conductor	Mevakér kartisim	Kumsa'ri
Connection	Késher	Muvasia
Departure	Jeziá, haṭlagà	Safar
Dining car	Kerón misnón	Arabiyyit a'kl
Exchange bureau	Chilúf ksafim	Taghyir el-fulus
Hotel	Malón	Funduq
Information	–	Istialama't
Passport	Darkón	Basbort
Platform	Razif	Rasif
Porter	Sabál	Shayyal
Ship	Óniyá	Bachira
Sightseeing tour	Siyúr ir	Richle lisiya'rit el-ba'lad
Sleeping car	Kerón shená	Arabiyyit nom
Station	Iachanát harakévet	Macha'tta
Stop	Shehiyá	Vukuf
Taxi	Monit, táksi	Taxi
Ticket	Kartisnesiá	Taska'ra
Timetable	Lúach sman im	Mavaid el-qitar
Toilet	Beit kise	Mir'chad
Train	Rakéwet	Qatr
Travel agency	Misrád nésiot	Maktab es-siyyacha
Waiting room	Ulam hamtana	Salit intisar
Window seat	Makóm leyád hachalón	Maka'n biga'nib esh-shibbak

At the Post Office

English	Hebrew	Arabic
Address	Któvet	Unvan
Airmail	Bedóar awir	Beri'd ga'wi
Counter	Eshnáv	Shibbak
Express mail	Mesirá meyuchédet exprés	Gavab musta'agil
Letter	Michtáv	Gavab
Letter-box, Mail-box	Tevát michtavim	Sanduq gavabat
Long-distance call	Sicha beinironit	Muha'dse charigi'yye
Packet	Chavilá ktaná	Tard sigha'yyar
Parcel	Chavilá	Tard
Postage	Ta'arif mishlóach	U'grit beri'd
Postcard	Gluyá	Taska'ra
Post office	Beit dóar	Ma'ktab beri'd
Poste restante	Michtavim shmurim	Machfu's
Stamp	Bulim	Wara'qit posta
Telegram	Mivrák	Taligraf
Telephone	Telefón	Telefon
Telephone booth	Ta hatelefón	Kabina telefon
Telephone directory	Madrich telefón	Da'ftar telefon
Telephone number	Mispár hatelefón	Ni'mrit telefon

Motoring Terms

English	Hebrew	Arabic
Accelerator	Davshát délek	Davasit bensin
Air pump	Mashevát avír	Tulu'mbit el-hawa
Axle	Zir	Aks
Brakes	Hablamím	Farma'la
Bumper, Fender	Meamém	Eksda'm
Car	Mechonít; óto	Sayya'ra
Carburetor	Meajéd	Karborate'r
Clutch	Mazméd	Debria'sh
Cylinder	Galíl	Sili'ndr
Engine	Manóa	Motor
Exhaust	Zinór plitá	Il-adim
Garage	Beit melachá	Wa'rshit arabiyya't
Gasoline (petrol)	Bensín, gasolín	Bensin
Gasoline (petrol) tank	Meychal	Tank
Gasoline (petrol) station, filling station	Tachanát délek	Macha'ttit bensin
Gearlever, gearshift	Chilúf mahalachim	En-naql
Headlights	Sarkór	Kashafa't
Horn	Zofár	Kala'ks
Indicator	Chezitút	Ishara
Inner tube (tire)	Zinór	Chartu'm
Jack	Dshek	Kore'k
Lights	Panasím	La'mba
Motor-bike	Ofanóa	Motosi'kl
Oil	Shémen	Set
Radiator	Mezanén-máyim	Radiate'r
Repair	Tikún	Tasli'ch
Screw	Bóreg	Qalawu's
Screwdriver	Maftéach beragím	Samu'la
Spare can	Pach resérvi	Safi'cha ichtia'ti
Spare tire	Galgál chilúf	A'gala stepn
Spark plugs	Hamazatím	Sha'ma
Speedometer	Madmehirút	Ada'd es-sura
Starter	Matnéa	Marsch
Steering	Higúi	Suwa'qa
Steering wheel	Hége	Fola'n
Tires (Tyres)	Zamíg	Kawi'tsh
Valve	Shastóm	Sima'm

Road Signs

Crossing	Hitzalvút	Ma'fraq et-tu'rug
One-way street	Rehov ben kivún echád	Tariq fi ittiga'h vachid
Parking	Mekóm haniyá	Macha'l vuqu'f es-sayyara't

Glossary of Hebrew Words

Agam	Lake	Horva(t)	Ruin
Ain	Spring	Ir	Town, city
Atar	Archaeological site	Iriya	Municipality
		Kefar	Village
Bayit, Beit	House	Kerem	Vineyard
Beer	Well	Kever	Tomb
Bereicha(t)	Pool	Kevish	Trunk road
Bik'a(t)	Valley	Kibbutz	Commune, collective settlement
Derech	Street		
Emeq	Valley, plain	Kikar	Square
Erez	Country	Kirya(t)	District
Gan	Garden	Ma'abara	Transit immigrants camp
Gay	Gorge	Ma'ale	Pass, climb
Gesher	Bridge	Ma'ayan	Spring
Gevul	Border	Mathaf	Hotel
Giv'a	Hill, mountain	Metsuda(t)	Castle, fortress
Hakirya (+city)	Seat of government	Mifrats	Gulf, bay
Har	Mountain	Migdal	Tower
Hava	Farm	Mis'ada	Restaurant
Hof	Coast	Mishtara	Police

Mo'etsa	Council meeting	Rov'a	Town quarter
Moshav	Co-operative settlement	Sderot	Boulevard
		Sha'ar	Entrance gate
Moshava	Village	Shalom	Peace (used as greeting)
Mughara	Cave	Sharav	Desert wind
Nahal	Brook, stream	Shechuna	Town quarter
Nahar	River	Shikun	Settlement
Nave	Oasis, home	Simta	Alley
Pardess	Citrus grove	Tel	Hill (in name of town)
Rama	Height, plateau	Ya'ar	Wood
Rehov	Street	Yam	Sea

Glossary of Arabic Words

Abu	Father	Mai	Water
Ain	Spring	Mar	Saint
Bab	Gate, door	Masdschid	Small mosque
Bahr	Sea	Mauristan	Hospital
Bakshisch	Tip	Medina	Town
Balad	Town, village	Medresse	Koran school
Beit, Bet	House	Mihrab	Prayer niche
Beit Mirkahat	Druggist	Mina	Port, harbour
Bilad	Country	Minbar	Mosque pulpit
Bir	Well	Nahr	River
Birke(t)	Pool	Naqb	Mountain pass
Bury	Tower, fortress	Nebi	Prophet
Dahr	Mountain pass	Qalaat	Fortress
Darb	Path	Qantara	Bridge
Deir	Monastery, cloister	Qasr	Castle, fortress
		Qubba	Dome, tomb
Djami	Mosque	Quneitra	Small bridge
Djebel	Hill, mountains	Ras	Head, cape, peak
Djissr	Bridge	Sahel	Plain
Djubb	Cistern	Salam	Peace (be with you – greeting)
Ein	Spring		
Funduk	Hotel	Sahra	Desert
Ghab	Wood	Shari(a)	Street
Hamsin	Desert wind	Sheik	Sheik, old man
Haram	Shrine	Sherif	Nobleman
Kaber	Tomb	Serail	Palace, city hall
Kafer	Village, village floor	Suk	Market, market alley
		Tell	Hill (in name of town)
Karem	Vineyard	Wadi	Dry watercourse
Khan	Caravanserai	Wali	Holy man, holy monument
Khirbe(t)	Ruin		
Madni	Minaret	Zeitun	Olive tree

Customs and Traditions

There are a number of customs that should be observed when visiting holy places in particular. Do not wear shorts or sleeveless clothing in churches, synagogues or mosques and do not visit these during services. Devout Jews cover their heads in the synagogue and visitors should do the same. Footwear must be removed on entering mosques.

One should also observe the national customs on the Sabbath (Saturday) and on important festivals. Try not to smoke in public. It is also forbidden to take pictures of the Wailing Wall in Jerusalem which is one of Judaism's holiest places. Most public transport comes to a stop and it will be seen as a mark of respect if visitors also refrain from using their cars on the Sabbath.

Ramadan (9th month of the lunar year) is Islam's month of fasting when Moslems are forbidden to eat, drink or smoke between sunrise and sunset and non-believers are only allowed into mosques at certain times. For Moslems Friday is their day of rest and Arab shops are closed on Fridays.

If invited to an Israeli home it is the custom to take a small present (e.q. flowers or candy). If you are invited for the evening you should arrive about 8.30 and leave towards midnight. There is no visiting as a rule on the Sabbath.

Clothing. – For the nine months of the summer weather it is best to wear light clothing. Synthetic fabrics do not "breathe" and are therefore less suitable. The intensity of the sun's rays makes it necessary to shade your head and wear sunglasses, particularly on the coast and in the S of the country. Inland a light coat may be useful for the evening. In the winter you should take warmer clothing and a raincoat. As a rule there is no need to dress up in the evening.

Accommodation

Hotels

In Israel there are approximately 300 **hotels** which are approved by the Ministry of Industry, Trade and Tourism. Accommodation ranges from luxury hotels to simple houses as well as guest houses or private homes. The hotels are listed in "Israel Tourist Hotels" which is a brochure obtainable from the Israel Government Tourist Office.

The Israel Hotel Association has its headquarters in Tel Aviv and branch offices in Jerusalem, Eilat, Haifa and Netanya.

Ariel Hotel in Jerusalem

Information: **Israel Hotel Association,**
29 Hamered Street,
Tel Aviv;
tel. (03) 65 01 31.

Israeli hotels are classified in five categories – one, two, three and four stars and luxury.

Category			
Official	In this guide	Tariff for one night (in shekels)	
		1 Person Single room	2 Persons Double room
****L	L	7200–9200	8500–11000
****	I	3700–5200	5900–6500
***	II	3300–3700	4900–5300
**	III	2200–2600	2700–4100
*	IV	1900–2300	2600–3300
Hotels add on a service charge of 15%.			

Holiday Villages

On the country's coastline and its inland seas there are a number of **holiday villages** which provide all kinds of sporting facilities on water and dry land, as well as sightseeing programs and evening entertainment. These villages are particularly recommended for younger holiday-makers.

Kibbutz Guest Houses

Many of the approximately 250 agricultural communes or "kibbutzim" have modern **guest houses**, often with their own swimming pools or beach. Some offer excursions into the surrounding countryside and there are also cultural events and talks on life in a kibbutz. More detailed information can be found in the brochure entitled "Kibbutz Inns".

Information: **Central Office of the Kibbutz Guest Houses,**
Allenby Street 100,
Tel Aviv;
tel. (03) 61 48 79.

Youth Hostels

There are 31 **youth hostels** in the Israel Youth Hostel Association. These can be used by holders of valid youth hostelling permits from their own country or from the Israel Youth Hostels Association. Israeli youth hostels have no upper age limit. It is necessary to book in advance.

● Kibbutz Guest Houses

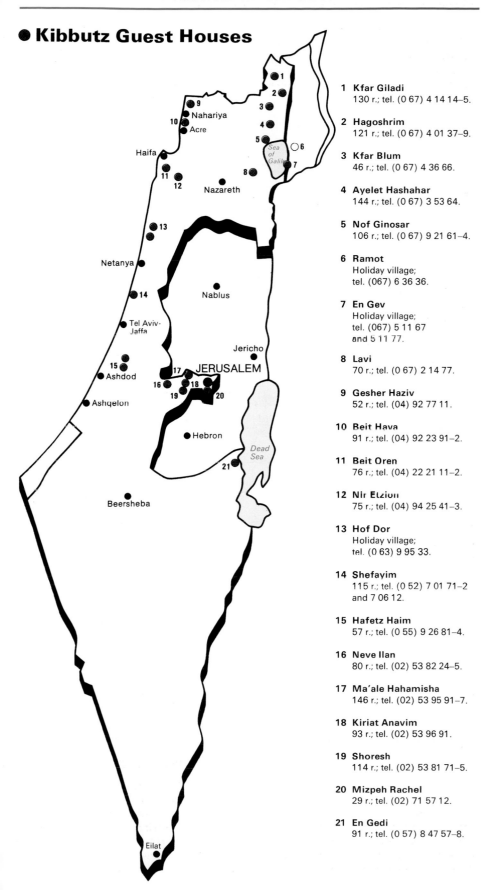

1 **Kfar Giladi**
   130 r.; tel. (0 67) 4 14 14–5.

2 **Hagoshrim**
   121 r.; tel. (0 67) 4 01 37–9.

3 **Kfar Blum**
   46 r.; tel. (0 67) 4 36 66.

4 **Ayelet Hashahar**
   144 r.; tel. (0 67) 3 53 64.

5 **Nof Ginosar**
   106 r.; tel. (0 67) 9 21 61–4.

6 **Ramot**
   Holiday village;
   tel. (067) 6 36 36.

7 **En Gev**
   Holiday village;
   tel. (067) 5 11 67
   and 5 11 77.

8 **Lavi**
   70 r.; tel. (0 67) 2 14 77.

9 **Gesher Haziv**
   52 r.; tel. (04) 92 77 11.

10 **Beit Hava**
   91 r.; tel. (04) 92 23 91–2.

11 **Beit Oren**
   76 r.; tel. (04) 22 21 11–2.

12 **Nir Etzion**
   75 r.; tel. (04) 94 25 41–3.

13 **Hof Dor**
   Holiday village;
   tel. (0 63) 9 95 33.

14 **Shefayim**
   115 r.; tel. (0 52) 7 01 71–2
   and 7 06 12.

15 **Hafetz Haim**
   57 r.; tel. (0 55) 9 26 81–4.

16 **Neve Ilan**
   80 r.; tel. (02) 53 82 24–5.

17 **Ma'ale Hahamisha**
   146 r.; tel. (02) 53 95 91–7.

18 **Kiriat Anavim**
   93 r.; tel. (02) 53 96 91.

19 **Shoresh**
   114 r.; tel. (02) 53 81 71–5.

20 **Mizpeh Rachel**
   29 r.; tel. (02) 71 57 12.

21 **En Gedi**
   91 r.; tel. (0 57) 8 47 57–8.

● Camp Sites

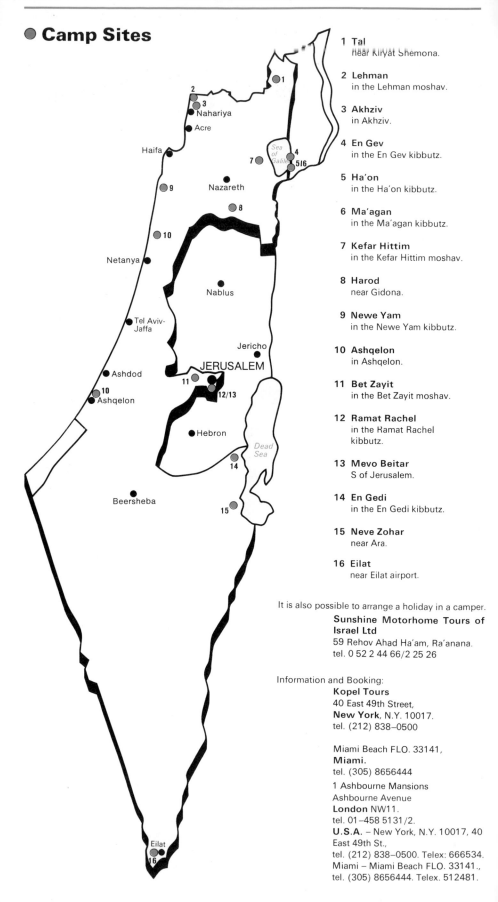

1 **Tal**
near Kiryat Shemona.

2 **Lehman**
in the Lehman moshav.

3 **Akhziv**
in Akhziv.

4 **En Gev**
in the En Gev kibbutz.

5 **Ha'on**
in the Ha'on kibbutz.

6 **Ma'agan**
in the Ma'agan kibbutz.

7 **Kefar Hittim**
in the Kefar Hittim moshav.

8 **Harod**
near Gidona.

9 **Newe Yam**
in the Newe Yam kibbutz.

10 **Ashqelon**
in Ashqelon.

11 **Bet Zayit**
in the Bet Zayit moshav.

12 **Ramat Rachel**
in the Ramat Rachel
kibbutz.

13 **Mevo Beitar**
S of Jerusalem.

14 **En Gedi**
in the En Gedi kibbutz.

15 **Neve Zohar**
near Ara.

16 **Eilat**
near Eilat airport.

It is also possible to arrange a holiday in a camper.
**Sunshine Motorhome Tours of
Israel Ltd**
59 Rehov Ahad Ha'am, Ra'anana.
tel. 0 52 2 44 66/2 25 26

Information and Booking:
Kopel Tours
40 East 49th Street,
New York, N.Y. 10017.
tel. (212) 838–0500

Miami Beach FLO. 33141,
Miami.
tel. (305) 8656444

1 Ashbourne Mansions
Ashbourne Avenue
London NW11.
tel. 01–458 5131/2.
U.S.A. – New York, N.Y. 10017, 40
East 49th St.,
tel. (212) 838–0500. Telex: 666534.
Miami – Miami Beach FLO. 33141,
tel. (305) 8656444. Telex. 512481.

Menu outside a restaurant in Jerusalem

The hostels are generally closed between 9 a.m. and 5 p.m. with reception between 5 and 7 p.m. Stays are limited to three nights but can be extended with the warden's permission. The price for accommodation includes the hire of a sleeping bag since the use of one's own sleeping bag is not permitted.

A youth-hostelling permit also entitles the holder to reduced rates for visits to national parks, nature reserves and museums and for boat trips on the Sea of Galilee.

Information: **Israel Youth Hostel Association,**
Rehov Dorot Rishonim 3,
P.O. Box 1075,
Jerusalem;
tel. (02) 22 20 73 and 22 20 76.

Christian Hospices

The different Christian denominations maintain **hospices** as inexpensive accommodation for pilgrims. A list can be obtained from the Israeli Government Tourist Office.

Information: **Israel Pilgrimage Committee,**
P.O. Box 1018,
Jerusalem.
Israel Ministry of Tourism
(Pilgrimage division),
23 Rehov Hillel,
Jerusalem.
tel. (02) 24 01 41.

Camping and Caravanning

There are camp sites on the shores of the Mediterranean and the Red Sea as well as near the Dead Sea and the Sea of Galilee. They usually have every facility and are easy to reach. There are also chalets for hire on some sites.

Information: **Israel Camping Union,**
P.O. Box 53,
Nahariya;
tel. (04) 92 33 66.

Food and Drink

Israel does not have a true cuisine of its own. The Jews who emigrated there from many different countries brought their own traditional dishes with them and these are subject to eastern, central and western European and Arabic influences.

In Jewish restaurants the food is mostly **kosher** ("pure") which means that it has been prepared in accordance with the Jewish dietary laws. (In this Guide kosher hotels and restaurants are indicated by "(k)" after their names.) Ingredients or dishes which run counter to these laws are termed *trefe* ("impure"). Pork, game, some types of poultry and certain parts of animals as well as the flesh of invertebrates (e.g. crayfish, shellfish, snails) come into this category, while meat and dairy products must not be served during the same meal. Certain restrictions apply on the Sabbath and on Jewish fast-days (unleavened bread, called "Matzos", no beer, etc.) and one should not smoke in public on these days.

In Arab restaurants and some others you can get dishes which are not "kosher" but the Koran also forbids the eating of pork.

Israelis usually have a big breakfast. Their main meal is lunch and they usually only have a light meal in the evening. Hotels often provide a large buffet for breakfast with plenty of choice.

Drinks. – Beer, fruit juice and Coca Cola are popular. Israeli wines (mostly red) are like those found in Europe – vine growing was promoted by Baron Edmond de Rothschild. There are also local brandies and liqueurs but generally speaking alcohol is not popular in Israel.

Beaches

There are many seaside resorts on the Mediterranean and most of the beaches are supervised during the season. Many hotels have freshwater swimming pools, some of which are not used in the winter. You can swim in the Red Sea near Eilat (Gulf of Eilat/Aqaba). There are also beaches on the Dead Sea where the salt content is so high that it is impossible to sink but it is also necessary to shower with fresh water after a swim in order to prevent skin damage.

There is freshwater bathing in the Sea of Galilee near Tiberias where you usually have to pay to use the beaches.

● **Beaches**   Map p. 273

1 **Rosh Haniqra**
Supervised, picnic site.

2 **Akhziv**
Supervised, picnic site, diving area, holiday village, youth hostel.

3 **Nahariya**
Supervised, picnic site, holiday village, youth hostel.

4 **Shave Ziyon**
Supervised, holiday village.

5 **Akko**
Supervised, picnic site, holiday village.

6 **Haifa**
Supervised, picnic site.

7 **Atlit-Newe Yam**
Supervised, picnic site, holiday village, youth hostel.

8 **Dor**
Supervised, diving area, holiday village.

9 **Caesarea**
Supervised, diving area, holiday village.

10 **Mikhmoret**
Supervised, picnic site, diving area, holiday village, youth hostel.

11 **Netanya**
Supervised, picnic site, holiday village.

12 **Shefayim**
Supervised, holiday village.

13 **Herzliya**
Supervised, holiday village.

14 **Tel Baruch**
Supervised.

15 **Tel Aviv-Yafo**
Supervised, diving area.

16 **Bat Yam**
Supervised.

17 **Palmahim**
Supervised.

Seaside Resorts and Spas

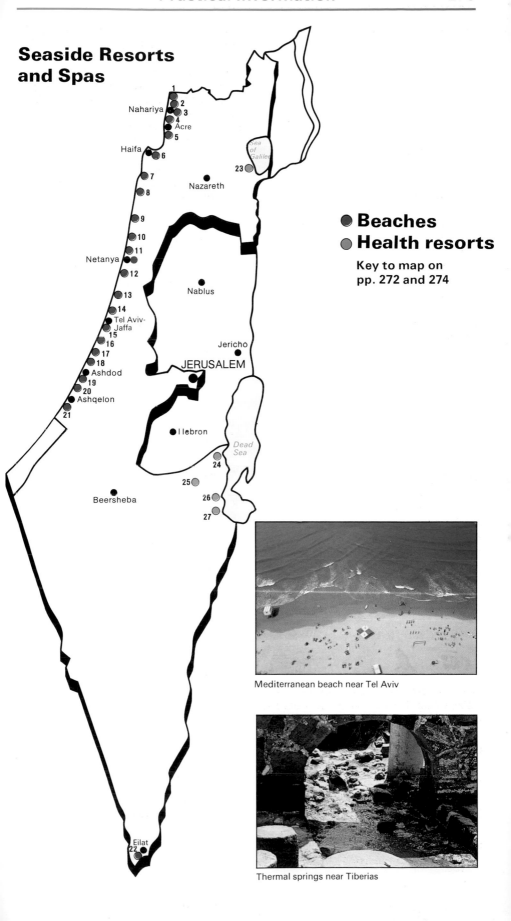

Nahariya

1
2
3
4
Acre
5

Haifa
6

7
Nazareth
8

9

10

11
Netanya
12

13
Nablus

14
Tel Aviv-
Jaffa
15
16
Jericho
17
18
JERUSALEM
Ashdod
19
20
Ashqelon
21

Hebron
Dead
Sea
24
25
26
Beersheba
27

Sea of Galilee
23

● Beaches
◐ Health resorts

Key to map on
pp. 272 and 274

Eilat
22

Mediterranean beach near Tel Aviv

Thermal springs near Tiberias

18 Yavne
Supervised.

19 Ashdod
Supervised.

20 Nizzanim
Supervised.

21 Ashqelon
Supervised, picnic site, holiday village, youth hostel.

22 Eilat
Supervised, diving area, underwater observatory, holiday village, youth hostel.

Spas

Most Israeli spas were already being visited in ancient times. They are mainly located around the Sea of Galilee and the Dead Sea.

● **Health Resorts** Map p. 273

23 Hamme Teverya
Rheumatism, bones and joints, sinusitis, recovery from injuries.

24 Hamme Yesha
Rheumatism, bones and joints.

25 Arad
Asthma, allergies.

26 En Boqeq
Psoriasis.

27 Hamme Zohar
Rheumatism, bones and joints, allergies, skin diseases, recovery from injuries.

Information: **Health Resort Authority,**
Rehov Shalom Aleichem 4,
Jerusalem.

Water Sports

There are facilities for sailing, rowing, water skiing, wind surfing, piloting motor-boats, etc. on the Mediterranean coastline, also known as the "sun coast", and on the Red Sea. Sailing boats can be hired from Tel Aviv Marina and fishing tackle can be hired in a number of places (although fishing in parts of the Red Sea is forbidden).

Scuba Diving

Snorkellers and scuba divers can have a wonderful time on the Mediterranean coast, and the Red Sea, with its rich underwater flora and fauna and wealth of coral reefs, tropical fish and invertebrates, has also become a favourite spot for scuba divers. In some places you can hire the appropriate gear or join a diving course (in Eilat). If you bring your own aqualung you will need an adapter for the different type of pressurised air cylinders.

Watch out for the fact that tropical waters have many more poisonous creatures than temperate zones. Sea anemones and jellyfish (including the Portuguese Man-o'-War, *Physalia physalis*, and the Mediterranean Sea-wasp, *Charybdea marsupialis*) can inflict painful stings; Philippi and other Sea Urchins have poisonous spines which break off easily and can turn septic; Weevers, Scorpionfish and Stargazers have venomous spines on their fins, while Moray Eels, Rays, Barracudas and Sharks can also be dangerous. It is therefore sensible to seek advice before diving in unknown waters. The regulations governing underwater hunting should also be observed.

Snorkellers in particular can easily forget that salt water and exposure to intense sunlight can quickly lead to severe sunburn, so it is advisable to wear a pale cotton shirt or T-shirt when out snorkelling. Be careful about touching unknown (and possibly poisonous) creatures – strong rubber gloves afford a certain amount of protection – and think twice before poking about inside coral caves.

There is a decompression chamber in the hospital at Eilat.

Information: **Israel Diving Federation,**
Hanatsiv Street 16,
Tel Aviv;
tel. (03) 3 08 41.

Ami & Suellyn Ben-Zvi,
c/o Lucky Divers Eilat Scuba Center,
Eilat;
tel. (0 59) 7 31 04
and 7 57 49.

Tel Aviv Office,
Namir Square 432,
Tel Aviv;
tel. (03) 28 39 82.

Golf, Tennis, Riding

Caesarea has an 18-hole *golf course.* – Many hotels have *tennis courts*; the tennis center for the country is at Ramat Ha-Sharon, N of Tel Aviv. – *Riding clubs* include those at Beersheba, Caesarea, Netanya and Eilat.

● National Parks

See p. 276
for the rest
of the key

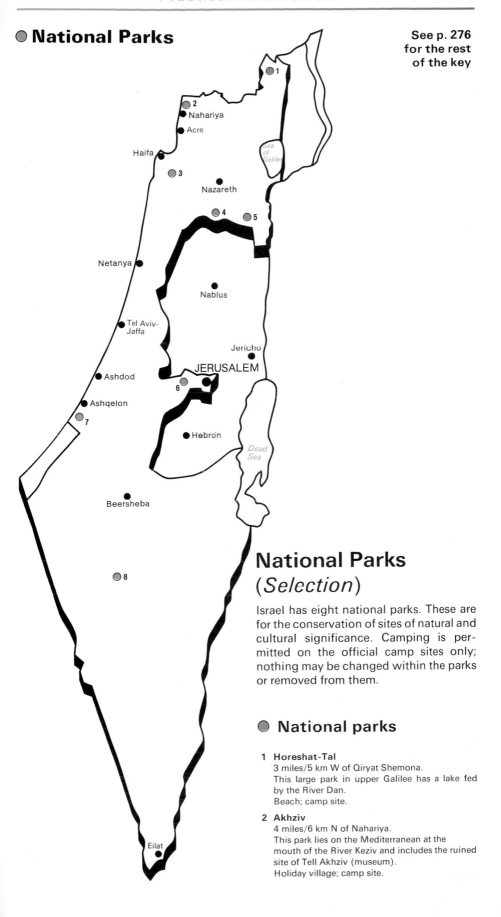

National Parks
(*Selection*)

Israel has eight national parks. These are for the conservation of sites of natural and cultural significance. Camping is permitted on the official camp sites only; nothing may be changed within the parks or removed from them.

● National parks

1 Horeshat-Tal
3 miles/5 km W of Qiryat Shemona.
This large park in upper Galilee has a lake fed by the River Dan.
Beach; camp site.

2 Akhziv
4 miles/6 km N of Nahariya.
This park lies on the Mediterranean at the mouth of the River Keziv and includes the ruined site of Tell Akhziv (museum).
Holiday village; camp site.

3 Carmel Park
SE of Haifa.
The park extends over Mount Carmel
several camp sites.

4 Ma'ayan Harod
6 miles/10 km S of Afula.
This park at the foot of Hare Gilboa contains a
spring surrounded by eucalyptus trees.
Camp site; youth hostel.

5 Gan Hashelosha
Between Bet Shean and Bet Alfa.
This park is named "park of the three" after three
settlers who died here when the area was seized
in 1938. Impressive waterfalls.
Swimming; picnic site.

6 Aqua Bella
6 miles/10 km W of Jerusalem.
The park is named after a spring and contains
the ruins of a nunnery.
Picnic site; camp site.

7 Ashqelon
S of Ashqelon.
The park is bordered by a semicircular city wall
dating from the time of the Crusaders, and
contains the ruins of the ancient city of Askalon.
Camp site.

8 En Avdat
35 miles/55 km S of Jerusalem.
The park includes the spring of En Avdat and its
surroundings; the River Nahal Zin which rises
here contrasts sharply with the surrounding
desert landscape.

Cultural Events

Concerts. – The country's best known
orchestra, the Israeli Philharmonic, gives
150 concerts a year and often plays under
the baton of internationally famous con-
ductors. Its permanent seat is the Frederic
R. Mann auditorium in Tel Aviv. During
the winter season Radio Israel's
Jerusalem symphony orchestra, which
mainly performs works by national com-
posers, plays once a week in the
Jerusalem Theatre. Concerts are also
given by the orchestras of Haifa, Ramat
Gan, Beersheba and by the Israeli Chamber Ensemble as well as by various Trios
and Quartets. Famous soloists also make
guest appearances in Israel.

Theater. – The country's best known
theaters are the Habimah, the national
theater (Tel Aviv), the Cameri, Tel Aviv's
own theater, the civic theaters in Haifa and
Beersheba and the Khan theater in
Jerusalem. The Habimah (Hebrew for
"stage") was founded at the end of the
twenties by actors who had emigrated to
Palestine after establishing a theater of the
same name in Moscow in 1916. Acting
companies based on the theaters in the
larger cities go on tour throughout the
country. While many classical and contemporary plays are performed in Hebrew,
smaller theater groups mostly perform in
English, Yiddish or other languages.

Ballet. – The Inbal ballet company which
was founded in 1949 performs Jewish
folk dances from the Yemen and other
parts of the Middle East. The Batsheba
and Bat-Dar dance companies present
contemporary and classical works. These
companies give guest performances in the
towns and in some of the kibbutzim.

Tourist Programs

In addition to its concerts, theater and
ballet, Israel also offers other events
whereby visitors can get to know the
country and its people. These include
folklore evenings which are regularly
staged in Jerusalem, Tel Aviv, Haifa and
Tiberias as well as at Ashqelon, Netanya,
Eilat and the Dead Sea.

Hotels in Jerusalem and Tel Aviv organise sessions
entitled "**You put the questions**", when Israelis
can be questioned on all manner of topics.

"**Get to know Israel**" is another widespread
scheme whereby local tourist offices arrange meetings
with local people in their homes so that visitors can
chat freely with their hosts and find out more about
everyday life in Israel.

Calendar

Israel uses the Jewish, Moslem and Christian calendars, all three of which differ considerably from one another.

Jewish chronology begins with the creation of the world which is put at 3761 B.C. The **Hebrew calendar** is based on the fixed lunar year and has 353, 354 or 355 days. Since this makes the lunar year shorter than the solar year every 19-year cycle contains seven *leap-years*. These have a 13th month of 30 days, thus bringing the calendar into line with the solar year.

The 12 months of the Hebrew calendar are as follows:
1. *Thishri* (September/October)
2. *Heshvan* (October/November)
3. *Kislev* (November/December)
4. *Tevet* (December/January)
5. *Shevat* (January/February)
6. *Adar* (February/March)
7. *Nissan* (March/April)
8. *Iyar* (April/May)
9. *Sivan* (May/June)
10. *Tamuz* (June/July)
11. *Av* (July/August)
12. *Elul* (August/September)

The days of the week in the Hebrew calendar are:

Monday	*Yom sheni*
Tuesday	*Yom shlishi*
Wednesday	*Yom rewii*
Thursday	*Yom chamishi*
Friday	*Yom shishi*
Saturday	*Shabát*
Sunday	*Yom rishón*

The **Moslem calendar** begins with the flight of the prophet Mohammed from Mecca to Medina (July 15th, 622). It is based on a pure lunar year and the months have 30 or 29 days. There are 354 days in a normal year and 355 in a leap year.

Public Holidays and Festivals

Jewish holidays. – In Israel the **Sabbath** (pronounce "shabbat"), which falls on our Saturday, is the Jewish weekly public holiday and day of rest. Days of rest begin at sunset the day before and finish at sunset of the day of rest itself. There is no public transport. Jewish shops, offices and public places of entertainment are closed. Since the Hebrew calendar is

---

Jewish Holidays

1st–2nd Tishri (Sept./Oct.)	*Rosh Hashana* (New Year)
10th Tishri (Sept./Oct.)	*Yom Kippur* (Day of Atonement) commemorating the Israelites' sojourn in the wilderness
15th–21st Tishri (Sept./Oct.)	*Sukkoth* (Tabernacles) commemorating the Israelites' sojourn in the wilderness
23rd Tishri (Sept./Oct.)	*Simhath Torah* (Rejoicing over the Law, i.e. Torah)
25th–2nd Tevet (Dec.)	*Hanukkah* (Festival of Lights, Feast of Dedication) commemorating the rededication of the Temple by Judas Maccabaeus
15th Shevat (Jan./Feb.)	*Tu Be Shevat*
14th Adar (Feb./March)	*Purim* (Festival of Queen Esther) commemorating deliverance of the Jews from the massacre planned by Hamam in 6th c. B.C.
14th/15th–22nd Nisan (March/April)	*Pesach* (Passover) commemorating the Exodus from Egypt
5th Iyar (April/May)	*Independence Day* proclamation of the State of Israel in 1948
18th Iyar (April/May)	*Lag Ba'Omer* (literally 33rd day of the Omer)
28th Iyar (May/June)	*Jerusalem Day*
6th/7th Sivan (May/June)	*Shabnoth* (Feast of Weeks, Pentecost) commemorating the revelation of the Law and the giving of the Ten Commandments to Moses
9th Av (July/Aug.)	*Tisha B'av* commemorating the destruction of the Temples in Jerusalem

Official days of rest are the Rosh Hashana, Yom Kippur, Sukkoth (1st day), Simhath Torah, Pesach (1st and 7th day), Independence Day and Shabnoth.

based on the moon, the Jewish public holidays fall on a different date each year from the point of view of the Gregorian calendar.

Christian holidays. – Different denominations celebrate these public holidays on different days. They are the same for Protestants and Catholics but different for members of the Greek Orthodox and Armenian churches who observe the Julian calendar.

The most important are: *New Year, Epiphany, Palm Sunday, Good Friday, Easter, Ascension Day, Whitsun and Christmas.*

Moslem holidays. – Friday is the holy day for Moslems. From the Gregorian point of view Moslem holidays occur on different dates every year (lunar calendar). The most important are: *Id el-Adha* (4 days of sacrificial celebrations), *New Year, Mohammed's birthday, Ramadan* (month of fasting), *Id el-Fitr* (end of Ramadan, 3 days).

Druze holidays. – *Id el-Adha* (sacrificial celebrations), *Nabi Shu'eb, Nabi Sablan.*

Shopping and Souvenirs

In Israel visitors can buy a whole range of items at different prices. There is an important diamond and jewelry industry the products of which are on sale in special shops or at the workshops. Oriental rugs, furs or leather goods are available in excellent quality and variety. Embroidery and other handicrafts, pictures, ceramics and objets d'art make good souvenirs and mementos. Items with a more middle-eastern flavour are to be found in the Arab town of Akko (Acre), Bethlehem, Hebron, Nazareth and the Druze villages on Mount Carmel. Bethlehem's manger figures carved out of olivewood are typical of Israel, while blown glass can be found in Hebron, and small genuine antiques in Samaria.

The Ministry publishes a shopping guide listing shops and restaurants for the cities of Jerusalem, Tel Aviv and Haifa and for the southern region (Beersheba, Eilat, Ashdod, Ashqelon and the Dead Sea).

Many shops display a **vignette** showing two customers carrying a large bunch of grapes. This is awarded by the Ministry for Industry, Trade and Tourism for outstanding service and can be regarded more or less as a **seal of approval.**

Opening Times

Most shops are open from 8 a.m. to 1 p.m. and from 4 to 7 p.m. They close at 2 p.m. on Fridays and on the eve of Jewish holidays. Jewish shops are closed on public holidays and on the Sabbath, Christian shops do not open on Sundays and Arab shops are usually shut on Fridays.

Banks are open from 8.30 a.m. to 12.30 p.m. on Sunday to Thursday, and on Fridays and the eve of public holidays from 8.30 a.m. to noon. They also open on Sunday, Monday, Tuesday and Thursday from 4 to 5.30 p.m. Branch offices in the leading hotels also provide a service outside these opening times.

Information

Israel Government Tourist Office (*IGTO*),
Rehov Hamelekh George 24,
Jerusalem;
tel. (02) 23 73 11.

Israel Government Tourist Office,
18 Great Marlborough Street,
London W1V 1AF;
tel. (01) 434 3651.

Israel Government Tourist Office,
350 Fifth Avenue,
New York,
New York 10118;
tel. (212) 560 0650.

5 South Wabash Avenue,
Chicago Illinois 60603;
tel. (312) 782 4306.

6380 Wilshire Boulevard,
Los Angeles,
California 90048;
tel. (213) 658 7462.

4151 Southwest Freeway,
Houston,
Texas 77027,
tel. (713) 850 9341.

Israel Government Tourist Office,
102 Bloor Street West,
Toronto,
Ontario M5S 1M(8);
tel. (416) 964 3784.

Within Israel tourist information is supplied through the IGTO offices, often in conjunction with local branches. Information can be found in Akko, Arad, Ashqelon, Bat Yam, Beersheba, Bethlehem, Eilat, Haifa, Jerusalem, Nahariya, Nazareth, Netanya, Safed and Tel Aviv-Yafo (as well as at Ben Gurion Airport).

Israel Automobile and Touring Club (*MEMSI*)

Head office:
Petah, 19 Tkvah Road,
Tel Aviv;
tel. (03) 62 29 61–2.

Branch offices:
163 Hanesi'im Street,
Beersheba;
tel. (0 57) 3 81 57.

Shopping center (c/o Ya'alat),
Eilat;
tel. (0 59) 7 21 66.

1 Palmer's Gate,
Haifa;
tel. (04) 66 18 79.

31 King George Street,
Jerusalem;
tel. (02) 24 48 28.

6 Shmuel Hanatziv Street,
Netanya;
tel. (0 53) 3 13 43–4.

Yochanan Ben Zakai Street,
Tiberias;
tel. (0 67) 9 07 15.

Diplomatic and Consular Offices in Israel

American Embassy,
71 Hayarkon Street,
Tel Aviv;
tel. (03) 25 43 38.

British Embassy,
192 Hayarkon Street,
Tel Aviv;
tel. (03) 24 91 71.

Canadian Embassy,
220 Hayarkon Street,
Tel Aviv;
tel. (03) 22 81 22.

Diplomatic and Consular Offices in the U.K., U.S.A., Canada

3514 International Drive,
Washing DC 20008;
tel. (202) 364 5500.

Embassy of Israel,
2 Palace Green,
London W8;
tel. (01) 937 8050.

Suite 601,
410 Laurier Avenue West,
Ottowa,
Ontario K1R 7T3;
tel. (613) 237 6450.

Airlines

El Al *Israel Airlines*
Head Office:
Ben Gurion International Airport,
Tel Aviv;
tel. (03) 97 61 11.

185 Regent Street,
London W1;
tel. (01) 437 9277.
For reservations (01) 437 9255 (Freephone 2003 available only from outside London area).

500 Royal Exchange,
Manchester;
tel. (061) 832 4208 (Freephone 646).

607 Boylston Street,
Boston;
tel. (617) 267 9220
   (800) 223 9733 (Reservations).

174 North Michigan Avenue,
Chicago;
tel. (312) 236 7264
   (800) 223 6280 (Reservations).

Suite 715,
1 Greenway Plaza East,
Houston;
tel. (713) 871 9595
   (800) 223 6700 (Reservations).

Suite 1250,
6404 Wilshire Boulevard,
I●● ●●●●●●●
tel. (213) 852 1252
   (800) 223 6700 (Reservations).

1602 Washington Avenue,
Miami Beach;
tel. (305) 532 5441
   (800) 223 6700 (Reservations).

Rockefeller Center,
610 Fifth Avenue,
New York;
tel. (212) 940 0750
   (212) 486 2600 (Reservations).

1845 Walnut Street,
Philadelphia;
tel. (215) 563 8011
   (800) 223 9733 (Reservations).

Suite 1502,
7777 Bonhomme Avenue,
St Louis;
tel. (314) 862 2100
   (800) 223 6700 (Reservations).

555 Dorchester Boulevard West,
Montreal;
tel. (514) 875 8900
   (514) 875 8900 (Reservations).

102 Bloor Street West,
Toronto;
tel. (416) 967 4222
   (416) 864 9779 (Reservations).

British Airways,
113 Hayarkon Street,
Tel Aviv;
tel. (03) 97 14 56.

Pan Am: General Sales Agent,
Andal Aviation Ltd,
9 Frishman Street,
Tel Aviv;
tel. (03) 24 72 72.

TWA,
74–76 Hayarkon Street,
Tel Aviv;
tel. (03) 65 42 66.

Canadian Pacific Airlines,
P.O. Box 4001,
Yehudi Street,
Tel Aviv;
tel. (03) 65 21 63.

International Telephone Dialling Codes

From the United States to Israel	011 972
From the United Kingdom to Israel	010 972
From Canada to Israel	011 972
From Israel to the United States	00 1
From Israel to the United Kingdom	00 44
From Israel to Canada	00 1

When dialling from Israel the zero prefixed to the local dialling code should be omitted.

There are *patrol cars* from the Israel Automobile and Touring Club (MEMSI) in operation round the clock throughout the country.

In the event of a *breakdown* the Automobile Club in Tel Aviv can be contacted at any time by ringing (03) 62 29 61. Assistance after 5 p.m. is subject to a charge.

Emergency numbers for Haifa, Jerusalem and Tel Aviv

Police	100
Emergency service	101
Fire brigade	102

101 is the emergency service operated by "Magan David Adom", the Red Star of David, which is an organisation that corresponds to the Red Cross. The daily papers list the hospitals that are taking emergencies as well as druggists that are open in the evening, on public holidays and at weekends.